MW00531701

BROKEN SOUTHS

Broken Souths

Latina/o Poetic Responses to Neoliberalism and Globalization

MICHAEL DOWDY

THE UNIVERSITY OF
ARIZONA PRESS
Tucson

The University of Arizona Press
© 2013 The Arizona Board of Regents
All rights reserved

www.uapress.arizona.edu

Library of Congress Cataloging-in-Publication Data
Dowdy, Michael.
Broken souths : Latina/o poetic responses to neoliberalism and globalization /
Michael Dowdy.
    pages cm
  Includes bibliographical references and index.
   ISBN 978-0-8165-3029-8 (pbk. : acid-free paper)
   1. American poetry—Hispanic American authors—History and criticism.
   2. Hispanic Americans in literature. I. Title.
   PS153.H56D69 2013
   811.009'868—dc23
                                    2013011196

"Sonnet for Ambiguous Captivity" is reprinted from *Sonnets from the Puerto Rican* © 1996
by Jack Agüeros, by permission of Hanging Loose Press.
"Not Here" is reprinted from *The Republic of Poetry* © 2006 by Martín Espada, by
permission of the author.
"June Journals 6-1-88" is reprinted from *Notebooks of a Chile Verde Smuggler* © 2002 by
Juan Felipe Herrera, by permission of the University of Arizona Press.
"1968," D.R. © Pacheco, José Emilio, *No me preguntes cómo pasa el tiempo*, Ediciones
Era, México, 2010, is reprinted and translated by permission of Ediciones Era.

Publication of this book is made possible in part by a subvention from the Presidential
Fund for Faculty Advancement at Hunter College of the City University of New York.

Manufactured in the United States of America on acid-free, archival quality paper
containing a minimum of 30% post-consumer waste and processed chlorine free.

18   17   16   15   14   13   6 5 4 3 2 1

Contents

Preface

Juan loosened his shirt collar, peered to the south. He took Maga's hand in his. "They are looking this way too," he said. "From the edges of every border, they look back—mud and cardboard kingdoms, from a busted makeshift hotel they pace; huddled, caught by surprise, by their own hunger and history; a broken hotel, made of smoke, revolution, and the strange intersections of global invasions [. . .] Outside, the future lurks and stalks."
—Juan Felipe Herrera, "One Year Before the Zapatista
Rebellion" (*187 Reasons* 182–183)

Asymmetrical dialogue, equivocal silence, structural inequality, mistrust, and fascination have long defined relations between North and South in the Americas. The Chicano writer Juan Felipe Herrera's fictionalized persona, Juan, portrays these conditions in a dramatized conversation with his partner, Maga, through the provocative figure of mutually uneven gazes. While addressing the difficulty of writing about Mexico and Latin America from the United States, Juan adjusts his collar uncomfortably and looks south, reminding both Maga and himself, in addition to his readers in the United States, that they, and we, are also the objects of plural, fragmented gazes. This figurative gesture proceeds according to a logic of multiple "broken" souths that confront the North's best intentions, even when these intentions come from a presumably sympathetic subject—the Latino writer with deep, enduring roots in Latin America. As an iteration of an emergent Latina/o poetics, Herrera's lyric essay seeks clarity on inter-American relations by acknowledging the "smoke," ideological and material, that frequently obscures them. This poetics operates by multiplying "the border," the most pliable, falsely singular figure mediating US–Mexican and US–Latin American relations, into "every border," each of which has its *own* borders ("edges"). Rather than a Janus figure with two visages facing opposite directions, these multiple figures looking north and south simultaneously evoke the urgency of finding spaces for Latino and Latin American gazes to meet.

Herrera's meditation on the dimensions of this challenge underscores the discourses of globalism, mobility, transience, dispossession, upheaval, and inequality underlying literary and theoretical examinations of inter-American relations in recent decades. Images and tropes of liminality ("borders"), impermanence ("makeshift"), material and psychological deprivation ("hunger"), and individual and communal fragmentation ("broken") appear repeatedly in Latino writing, particularly in the poetry, and in influential cultural theories. Yet Herrera also emphasizes the idea of "revolution," which is discussed with relative frequency in Latin American studies but now rarely in Latino studies. He searches for an expressive register to rethink revolution as a concept, living historical possibility, and widely discarded relic of the late 1960s. "We are now told, with the force of considerable authority," Román de la Campa writes, "that revolutions belong to modernism and realism, a failed legacy best left behind by a postmodern aesthetic" (*Latin Americanism* 36). As revolutions rise in the Middle East, do "mud and cardboard kingdoms" offer sufficient reason for the dispossessed of the Americas to remain quiescent through insistent claims that there is no viable alternative to the status quo? Are the markedly individual and grim consolations of hollow "kingdoms" adequate foreclosure against the collective potential of revolt? How do Latino writers challenge this "considerable authority," often through a version of the "postmodern aesthetic" complicit in reinforcing such authority?

Broken Souths explores how Latino poets imagine, negotiate, resist, struggle against, and often acquiesce to the ideals, impacts, constraints, and occasional pleasures comprising the era of neoliberal globalization, many of which Juan depicts in his conversation with Maga. To map Latino literary responses to these conditions within Latin and North America, this book establishes another critical focus common in Latin American studies but largely absent from Latino and US literary studies. That the term "neoliberalism" frequently garners blank stares from even intellectuals in the United States testifies to its hegemony and obfuscation, while silence about "revolution" persists as a sign of the neoliberal counter-revolution's tentative yet trenchant victory over other ways to structure economies and societies, including socialism and communism but also other forms of capitalism. For quite some time, however, Latino poets have been grappling with neoliberalism's core concepts and material consequences. The neoliberal project, this book shows, necessitates new configurations of Latino studies. Neoliberalism is a theory of political economy emphasizing the free market as the best way to organize social and economic life. Whereas the theory rejects nearly all state interventions in the economy and promotes privatization, deregulation, free trade, and other similar arrangements, in practice neoliberalism has often eschewed principle for plunder, abject violence, and corporate welfare. In short, profit has trumped ideals and plunder has been exposed as the ideal.

The recent rise of the Tea Party, which is animated by a version of neoliberal orthodoxy and agitates for outcomes already largely won by its ultra-rich benefactors, signifies the endurance of free-market ideology against overwhelming empirical evidence that neoliberal "reforms" have largely failed to produce economic growth. They have, however, been highly successful in concentrating extreme wealth at the top, producing dramatic inequality and unevenness, and crushing the power of labor. As the critical geographer David Harvey and others argue, these strategies and outcomes demand that neoliberalism be understood as a global political project to restore capitalist class power by any means necessary, including state, paramilitary, and extraterritorial violence. By developing a Latino literary geography of these contradictions and ultimately of the ongoing neoliberal era they define, from its roots in response to the iconic urban, student, and leftist movements of 1968 to the present economic crisis, *Broken Souths* foregrounds relations between Latino poetics, the mechanisms of literary production, and the neoliberal norms and constraints reshaping both. But it also participates in a sustained critique of this recent iteration of capitalism, its most radical in theory and most Machiavellian in practice. "You can tell that the capitalist system is in trouble," Terry Eagleton writes, "when people start talking about capitalism. It indicates that the system has ceased to be as natural as the air we breathe, and can be seen as the historically rather recent phenomenon that it is" (xi). *Broken Souths* extends this conversation by showing how Latino poets see the violence and paradoxes of the neoliberal era, including the transformations of everyday practices and grand narratives and the emancipatory possibilities emerging from their intersections.

In addition to the contentions that literary studies neglects to critique neoliberal ideals, goals, and outcomes at its detriment and that understanding Latino literary cultures, in particular, requires a thorough engagement with these conditions, *Broken Souths* uses other interrelated approaches to the growing archive of Latino texts. Given that an abiding "inquiry into the nature of place," as Victor Hernández Cruz remarks, underlies "the writings of many Latinos in the United States" (*Panoramas* 119), the book examines how Latino poems imagine place and space. I am especially interested in how Latino poetics reframes debates in cultural studies and critical geography on the relation between place, space, and nature and how struggles over the ways in which they are produced are key points of contestation between neoliberal capitalism and those who would challenge it. This approach offers a counterpart to Mary Pat Brady's *Extinct Lands, Temporal Geographies: Chicana Literature and the Urgency of Space*, which examines Chicana literature's "alternative cartographies" and "alternative methods of conceptualizing space" (6). While her study theorizes how Chicana narrativity sees space in the geographic context of the Southwest borderlands, *Broken Souths* focuses on poetry by Latino writers from multiple groups in the contexts of neoliberalism and inter-American relations.

Given this focus on Latino poetics as it bridges national groups and locations, I attend to commonalities and differences across Latino groups, often along North-South and East-West (i.e., New York–Los Angeles) axes. Although this approach is common in Latino studies, it remains mostly marginal to studies of Latino poetry. This study thus fleshes out the poet-critic Urayoán Noel's expansive, if admittedly skeletal, map of "the far-flung coordinates" of "postmillennial Latino poetries" as they "span a heretofore unseen variety of geographies and styles" (854, 856–857). My goal—taken on with humility and in view of its difficulties and exclusions—is the first book-length study of Latino poetry as a dynamic field spanning from the late 1960s to the present. My reading of Latino poetics in relation to Latin American poetry, moreover, has warrant in Latino poets' recurrent turns to the south in search of forms, models, traditions, and literary histories for their own poetry. As in the case of neoliberalism and literary studies, scholars have just begun reading Latino and Latin American poetry concurrently, perhaps due to the fact that, as Herrera implies, intellectual commerce between Latino norths and Latin American souths has been more important to the former. Even a quick perusal of the cover jackets of Latino poetry published in recent decades reveals literary-marketing tropes promoting Latino writers through proximate Latin American icons. "The literary market sells Latin American literature as part of their Latino market," Frances R. Aparicio writes, and "this conflation has less to do with the mutual influences or literary continuities between these two canons than with the economic benefit" ("[Re]constructing Latinidad" 43). While Latino self-fashioning also undergirds this dynamic, a profit motive that flattens differences and further confuses North American conceptions of Latinos and Latin America counteracts this agency.

As a literary-historical compass to a map of "Broken Souths," my introductory chapter offers an extended presentation of the guiding tropes, figures, and images comprising Latino poetics under the neoliberal order. This chapter sets up the locations of subsequent chapters, each of which focuses on a "Broken South" in Latin America (the global South) or the US South. These places—from Santiago, Chile, to Birmingham,

Alabama, to the book's critical locus, New York City, where migrants from "Broken Souths" frequently converge—ground Latino poems in particular spaces and times. In Herrera's terms, these places are produced by "strange intersections of global invasions," a phrase suggestively linking the global designs of the neoliberal project to local, national, regional, and hemispheric scales, where modes of resistance, critique, and accommodation arise. When read through the lens of Latino poetics, these "strange intersections" shed light on neoliberalism's injustices and provide glimpses of potential otherwises and alternative values. In combining referential concerns, which are often understood narrowly in US literary studies as "political" and identity-based, and those of language, which are frequently understood through the frame of "postmodern aesthetics," this inter-American poetics occupies a unique position among recent literatures: Latino poetry is simultaneously innovative, even vanguard, socially engaged, and often surprisingly accessible to a broad range of readers.

Figure 1 locates my initial textual "intersection" in Bogotá, where I took the photograph in September 2010 and where *Broken Souths* returns in chapter 4. This handbill was posted to walls in La Candelaria, a gentrifying neighborhood in central Bogotá characterized by a bohemian Left and university students known for political agitation. The simple but provocative message, "MIGRATION . . . IS NOT A CRIME," comes in a neat package that ironically belies its complex contexts. The dissonance between a child's sad-faced teddy bear carrying her few possessions and putative criminality, along with the English-language message and Spanish-language locational direction, registers immediately through defiantly bold capital letters. Closer inspection reveals further dissonance between handmade flyer and the mass-produced, clean aesthetic of the "Banana Republic" brand, which signifies its prestige in part by concealing and effacing the history of corporate exploitation and dispossession. Yet this is a knock-off, mock "Banana Republic"—no franchise exists in Colombia. "BANANA REPUBLIC GRAFFITI T-SHIRT" thus suggests an inverse relation between subversive, artistic criminality (graffiti) and a commodified, popular US form, the T-shirt, even as it reproduces a version of that very form.

Such reversals, reinscriptions, and critiques of commodification and consumer identities across North-South geographies structure the Latino poetics of *Broken Souths*. Because migration underlies so many Latino experiences and texts and remains a key element of neoliberal logic and outcomes, it serves as a primary content and context throughout the book. Hyper-urbanization; labor "flexibility"; the dissolution of rural, peasant, and indigenous forms of life; scores of recent and future persons displaced by global climate change; exiles from the Southern Cone's "Dirty Wars"

Figure 1

and US anticommunist (and pro-neoliberal) interventions in Central America; and the North American Free Trade Agreement's (NAFTA) untold number of dispossessed migrants in the cities of Mexico and the fields, factories, and kitchens of the North comprise some of these multiple migratory trajectories. At the same time, "the Latino Threat Narrative," as Leo R. Chavez calls the ensemble of tropes of crime and punishment guiding popular discourse about (im)migrants in the United States, continues to roil the state legislatures of Arizona and the US South, most notably in Alabama. Under neoliberalism, capital is free to transgress any and all borders. Migrants, on the other hand, and labor in general, are criminalized, banished to "busted makeshift hotel[s]" and constant struggles for survival. "It is never easy," Harvey writes, "to construct a critical assessment of a condition that is overwhelmingly present" (*Condition of Postmodernity* 336). Those of us who find this condition unjust and intolerable must join Juan in loosening our collars and getting to the difficult work of imagining and building alternatives to the neoliberal order. *Broken Souths* proceeds in this spirit.

Acknowledgments

My belief in the cooperative dimensions of intellectual work and the necessity of collectivist solutions to the problems of our current historical moment often clash with my preference for working in solitude. I say with certainty, however, that the ideas in this book are valuable only insofar as they have emerged from, and inspire, conversation. I may claim the initial plans and final forms of the ideas in *Broken Souths*, but the bricks and mortar holding them together would have been impossible without the helping hands of other scholars, mentors, and colleagues. As a fellow at the National Endowment for the Humanities' summer seminar "Toward a Hemispheric American Literature" at Columbia University, my early thinking on the project especially benefitted from the insights of Rachel Adams, Caroline Levander, Marissa López, and Justin Read. My year as a faculty fellow at the Center for Place, Culture, and Politics at the CUNY Graduate Center fundamentally shaped the project's modes of critique. Weekly conversations with David Harvey and Peter Hitchcock and other seminarians sharpened my ideas about neoliberalism and culture. Feedback from Amy Chazkel and Karen Miller, in particular, refined my thinking about the poetics of Mexico City.

Three mentors have continued to provide essential support. I will always be thankful for the incomparable Linda Wagner-Martin. María De-Guzmán jump-started my thinking on Ciudad Juárez and offered superb feedback on the organization of the chapters. And John McGowan's generosity and practical advice have been invaluable; I admire him greatly and hope to emulate his intellectual and mentorship model. Many conference panels and presentations also advanced my thinking on this project. Audience comments at my talk in September 2010 in the Latina/o Cultures Speakers Series at the Institute for the Arts and Humanities of the University of North Carolina at Chapel Hill were essential in puzzling out the connotations of the "broken" in *Broken Souths*.

I am proud to teach at Hunter College, where my students consistently inspire and challenge me. Their insightful, engaged readings of Juan Felipe Herrera and of femicide texts were especially helpful during the latter stages of this project. I have many terrific colleagues at Hunter; Jeff Allred and Cristina Alfar have been particularly supportive, while Thom Taylor and the English Department administrative staff have been indispensable. Our union, the PSC-CUNY, has been a bulwark against the neoliberalization of public higher education. I am especially grateful to Hunter's president Jennifer Raab and the President's Fund for Faculty Advancement, which provided essential funding to complete this project. I also want to thank the research librarians at the Archives and Special Collections at Amherst College and at the New York Public Library at Bryant Park for their assistance.

Some of the discussion in *Broken Souths* first appeared elsewhere in dramatically different forms. An article on Puerto Rican poetry appeared in a special issue of *MELUS* on multiethnic poetics coedited by Keith Leonard and Meta Jones; their questions probing the poetic dimensions of my argument there remained valuable in composing this book. An article in *College Literature* featured an early version of part of the argument in chapter 1, an article in *Appalachian Journal* the core of chapter 4, and an article in *Hispanic Review* part of chapter 6. I want to give special thanks to Francisco Aragón, Sandy Ballard at *Appalachian Journal*, Edward Carvalho, Martín Espada, and Maurice Kilwein Guevara for their generosity and support.

The University of Arizona Press has made an outstanding home for this project. Two anonymous reviewers offered excellent comments for improving the manuscript, especially in regard to the conceptual and theoretical framework. My editor at the University of Arizona Press, Kristen Buckles, has been insightful, supportive, and enthusiastic, and I am extremely grateful for her professional stewardship of the process.

In addition to its visionary social dimensions, poetry is, as José Emilio Pacheco writes, "a form of love that exists only in silence." A scholar who invests years in a book relies on many such forms of love that often go unacknowledged. My parents, brother, parents-in-law, and de facto sisters offer widely divergent but durable forms of love; each sustained me over the course of this project. Finally, my partner, Shelley Welton, steadied me when I wobbled and pushed me when I wanted a nudge. *Broken Souths* is for her and for our daughter, Alice.

BROKEN SOUTHS

Contesting the Counter-Revolution

A Latina/o Literary Geography of the Neoliberal Era

Maps have been of no use because I always forget that they are metaphors and not the territory; the compass has never made any sense—it always spins in crazy circles.

—Guillermo Verdecchia,
Fronteras Americanas/American Borders (20)

"To break" has surely been turned into a verb without yesteryear's magic. Deferred to the past and to the future, it is also deprived of the present.
—Martín Hopenhayn, *No Apocalypse, No Integration* (53)

Among literary representations of relations between Latin and North America, and the Latinos negotiating the upheavals and inequalities defining them, Guillermo Verdecchia's *Fronteras Americanas/American Borders* stands out for its virtuosity. The play tracks the ascendancy of neoliberalism, the deeply contradictory political project and economic theory that has been the underlying narrative guiding North-South relations over the past four decades. The Latino-Canadian Verdecchia first performed his one-man play in Toronto in January 1993, but as he explains in the published version's preface, *Fronteras Americanas* "began as a long letter to a close friend" on a 1989 visit to his native Argentina (13). Early in Act 1, the character Verdecchia enters the stage and addresses the audience warmly: "Here we are." Even as he stutters to express his excitement, repeating "Here we are," it becomes apparent that the simple deictic, *here*, and the following pronoun, *we*, are unclear. Questioning where "here" is and who "we" are, he informs the audience that he has in mind not only

1

the Tarragon Theater but also "America," a term he reconstructs for them: "And when I say AMERICA I don't mean the country, I mean the continent. Somos todos Americanos. We are all Americans" (19–20). After disorienting the Canadian audience's understanding of the term and, undoubtedly, teasing its tendency to oscillate between inferior and superior relations to the empire to the south, he confesses that he is "lost," which he attributes to his proximity to "the border," "a tricky place" rendering maps and compasses inoperable. Yet Verdecchia also supposes the audience "ended up here, tonight" because they, too, are lost (20). This collective condition of inter-American dislocation necessitates a trip into the territory of North American misconceptions about Latinos, Latin America, and the Americas *within* Canada and the United States.

For this trip to "the border," Verdecchia hires a "translator" to guide and teach the audience. Also played by Verdecchia, the self-proclaimed Wideload McKennah, whose given name is Facundo Morales Segundo, enters the stage to simulated gunshots (21–23). As a pan-Latino tour guide, trickster, and minstrel, Wideload probes what he calls the audience's "estereotypes" (56) by enacting images and languages associated with Latina/o cultures, including the pachuco, his controlling type. Because the border is a "minefield of cultural misunderstanding," as Coco Fusco and Guillermo Gómez-Peña describe it, Wideload uses it as a pedagogical tool. Yet whereas Gómez-Peña suggests that proximity to the border equates to greater Latino "control over the possibilities of cultural misunderstanding" ("Bilingualism" 149), Wideload teaches by spinning misunderstandings out of control. Wideload challenges stereotypes and corporate appropriations of Latino and Latin American cultures by parodying them. He uses the audience as a control group to test the idea of "a third-world theme park" in Canada (24). He calls the white audience the "Saxonian community" to transpose the typology "Latino," which effaces cultural, political, and class differences between diverse Latino groups. And he provokes. On the theme park, Wideload declares, "You people"—the Saxonians, laughing uneasily—"love dat kinda *shit*" (40, 25).[1]

As the brash, hyper-masculine Wideload teaches the audience about Latino cultures by inverting class, ethnic, and epistemological hierarchies, his alter ego, the brooding, melancholic Verdecchia, a struggling actor, sets out for the Southern Cone, visiting Argentina and Chile in 1990. But he leaves the audience with a caveat: "I myself will walk backwards so that it looks like I'm heading north" (21). This image alludes to Walter Benjamin's "Angel of History" backing into the future as wreckage piles up at her feet and to Juan Felipe Herrera's figure of uneven North-South gazes.

By disorienting relations between North and Latin America, it mocks narratives of "progress" and "backwardness" that have structured North-South epistemologies. Under these conditions, Verdecchia's compass will "always spin in crazy circles." When it appears he's heading north, he's actually heading south, and the attraction of magnetic North no longer holds. Rather, the North must be explained by reading the South and the South by encountering the North, while minding that either way the compass spins between poles, no matter the direction Latino Canadian and pan-Latino alter ego face. For Verdecchia, as for many cultural critics, conventional North-South divides have crumbled through hemispheric migratory pressures, technological innovations, capital flows, and transnational consumption patterns, even as certain manifestations of them—stereotypes, borders, and inequalities—have retrenched.

"The 'Latinization' of the US and the simultaneous 'North Americanization' of Latin America," Tomás Ybarra-Frausto argues, "calls for a deeper and franker dialogue" between scholars and writers in the North and the South (294).[2] Verdecchia's split-subject searches for such a dialogic language to replace the maps and compasses that fail to navigate "the territory" undergoing these processes. As "metaphors," maps shape perceptions of "the territory"; it is appropriate that Latino texts use broken ("spinning") compasses to navigate the Americas, a "territory" Herrera says is "made of smoke." In this sense, *Fronteras Americanas* is an attenuated historical geography of neoliberalism, the ideological "compass" that reshaped "the territory" with euphemistic, obfuscating metaphors of "free trade all de way from Méjico to Chile," as Wideload says (77). The neoliberal era spans Verdecchia's first day in Canadian grade school after leaving Argentina, at the end of the 1960s; the play's origin at the end of the Cold War (the 1989 letter), along with, as the neoliberal story has it, the end of "history" and "ideology";[3] his trips to the Southern Cone in 1990 following the Dirty War and the Pinochet dictatorship, both of which promoted neoliberal policies; and the play's debut in January 1993, weeks after NAFTA was signed (December 17, 1992) and a year before it went into effect on January 1, 1994. These dates mark the origins and ascendancy of neoliberalism subtending the play's representation of Latin America from a Latino perspective. The play thus performs an uncertain Latino identity at the interstices of North and South by projecting images of multiple souths to a hermetic northern audience. The Latino subject split between a desire to acquiesce to (as in Verdecchia) and a desire to provoke (as in Wideload) the dominant culture dramatizes the deterritorializations of neoliberal globalization, the fragmentations of the self underlying postmodern thought, the psychological turmoil of exile and immigration, and the North's complicity in southern upheavals.

The broken compass, moreover, measures the presence of multiple Latino souths within the North that Verdecchia and Wideload sort through to find the derivation of, and cure for, the former's confusion. The play's allusions to marketing slogans, corporate icons, debased popular cultures, and abstract, deific figures of "Money and Markets" (77) produce what W. B. Worthen calls the play's "commodified imaginary" (284). This imaginary draws the map on which the Latino subject split between north and south finds himself. Verdecchia's inability to locate himself in a hyper-capitalist consumer geography undermines the neoliberal maxim that the immutable economic laws of free markets always and everywhere give individuals a plethora of noncoercive consumer choices. At the same time, the play shows discourses of difference and commodified multicultural identities—the "third-world theme park," the "Latin Lover," the pachuco as Cheech and Chong, and the Taco Bell Chihuahua as a sly, animalistic Mexican—proliferating under neoliberal cultural-economic arrangements. These, *Fronteras Americanas* suggests, are the choices Latino subjects negotiate in the North American marketplace. The play thus shifts "the border" from United States–Mexico to multiple North-South borders (United States–Canada, Canada–Mexico, and North America–Latin America) that individual Latinos internalize *in* and *through* the putatively "free market."

In these ways, *Fronteras Americanas* introduces the objectives of *Broken Souths*.[4] This study charts a Latino poetic geography of the neoliberal era, from its latent cultural origins in 1968 in reaction to the Student Movement in Mexico City and the outset of the Chicano movement in East Los Angeles, by reading poets' responses to free-market fundamentalism and transformations of subjectivity, citizenship, language, and perceptions of space and time. The place-based poetics identified, mapped, and analyzed in *Broken Souths* targets neoliberalism's ideological tenets and material transformations, offers insight into the era's upheavals, and creates visions of "elsewheres" or "otherwises" against the neoliberal maxim that "there is no alternative" to its logic and organization of social and economic life.[5] Because Verdecchia's broken compass accurately measures the uneven geographic development of the Americas, *Broken Souths* often returns to the play to take critical bearings. "Uneven geographic development" refers to capitalism's structural logic of inequality, which is, Neil Smith argues, neither random nor accidental but "determinate" and "unique to capitalism." "Development at one pole and underdevelopment at the other," he writes, "takes place at a number of spatial scales" (*Uneven Development* xiii, xv), including between North and Latin America and within cities and nations north and south. Neoliberalism's emphasis on radical individualism in the form of *homo economicus* (economic man) augments this unevenness and uncertainty by placing the onus of navigating structural constraints totally on the individual, regardless of her access to resources. The Latino poems critiquing the conditions created by the global project to push radical free-market reforms and to consolidate corporate power therefore require critical approaches focusing on the uneven production of space and the deficiency of consumer-based identities. To this end, I now introduce a model for reading Latino poetry from North to South.

The Broken/To Break Relation and the Latino Imaginary

My goal of reading Latino poetry in relationship to neoliberalism did not begin as such a broad undertaking. It began in exploring connections between Latino and Latin American poetry published since the late 1960s. In searching for a way to read Latino poets alongside their Latin American counterparts, I discovered in Victor Hernández Cruz's poem "The Lower East Side of Manhattan" a spatial figure echoing Herrera's "broken" border "hotel" that pinpoints the outcomes of neoliberalism. "Broken Souths" appears across enjambed lines to depict the plural migratory routes those "in exile from broken / Souths" take into New York City (*Panoramas* 32). These geographically displaced, plural "Souths" include places in the Caribbean and Latin America (the global South) and in the US South. Cruz's enjambed figure maps the heterogeneity and multitemporality of migrant and immigrant cultures within New York, as well as neoliberal-era Latino migrations and the emergence of Latino souths in the North. It is an apt framework for reading a place-based poetics that has arisen concurrently with, and often in direct response to, neoliberal upheavals. "Broken" registers in four key ways in this study, by (1) configuring neoliberal capitalism's conquest of time, space, and borders; (2) allegorizing environmental devastation produced by neoliberalism's near-total subjection of nature to capitalist valuation; (3) personifying those excluded from neoliberal plenty; and (4) stressing the urgency of conceptualizing Latino place(s) *through* displacement(s).[6] "Souths," moreover, has a positive pluralism that obviates attempts to lump diverse Latinos into an undifferentiated whole. Latino poets are well positioned for imagining these fragmented pluralities. Their transnational poetic forms, inter-American conceptions of belonging, and patterns of exile, settlement, and return offer critical and creative refractions of neoliberal-era subjectivity.

The figure also integrates a critique of the dormant verb "to break," which the Chilean cultural critic Martín Hopenhayn laments as a word stripped of its previous power. Hopenhayn has in mind the leftist critique of capitalism in the movements of 1968, in Paris and Mexico City, in particular, in which "to break" conjured hope for a radically different social order apart from the alienations and oppressions of capitalist property, class, and gender relations. Hopenhayn's elegy for this verb also challenges postmodernist discourses celebrating fragmentation, uncertainty, and hybridity. He laments "broken[ness]" and its consequences, positive and negative: the supposed deaths of metanarratives, the unified self, territorial boundaries, and possibilities for organizing social-economic life differently. Put another way, the loss of the verb "to break" accompanies the loss of hope in transformative structural change itself.[7] In Cruz's figure and Verdecchia's split subject, the active infinitive "to break" guiding future possibilities becomes a passive, adjectival figure of the "broken" exile, displaced and "lost." Yet neither Cruz nor Verdecchia forfeit the noticeably plural potentialities within the neoliberal order and, counterintuitively, the place-based subjectivities set in motion and magnified by migratory upheavals.

In incorporating migration, exile, fragmentation, split subjectivities, and diaspora in its figurative logic, "Broken Souths" recuperates a historical dialectic in which each era holds possibilities for transformation despite increased and intensified forms of oppression. The texts discussed here search for alternatives held tentatively between "broken" and "to break," not as binaries but as imaginative axes between the actual and the possible. The infinitive that galvanized 1960s movements remains dormant in "broken" migrants, laborers, and cultural workers. Recuperating "to break" is possible when neoliberalism is seen as a counter-revolution that took as its earliest targets the cultural modes and collectivist ideals of these movements. Yet this recuperation departs from the hierarchical models of the late 1960s, including the masculinist, centralized cultural nationalism of the Chicano and Nuyorican movements, in order to examine how poets imagine plural, transnational identities emerging in specific places. Latino studies, María Josefina Saldaña-Portillo writes, has "often evolved [. . .] to round-out the 'American' student's liberal education" by becoming the "guardian" of national ethnic literatures. This trajectory erases the "deeply *internationalist*" perspective of "the radical student movements that led to the founding of these departments" (505). Pairing "broken" and "to break" locates the roots of the current era's extreme inequalities in the neoliberal counter-revolution, which has "broken" the earlier era's collectivist ideals, in part by promoting a facile multicultural ethos of market-based inclusion. Examining how poetic visions of "to break" emerge from "broken" subjectivities ensures that "liberal" and "radical," which Saldaña-Portillo wisely opposes, are not lumped into an undifferentiated "Left." Further, reading Latino and Latin American poems together emphasizes the outward-looking dimension of Latino studies by attempting to elucidate their points of divergence and convergence.

Broken Souths critiques postmodernist celebrations of fragmentation through reimagined, plural souths and the enduring possibility of other possibilities. The poems tell a story of hope, even as my use of "Broken Souths" cuts to the ugly quick of neoliberalism.[8] This titular choice is not neutral, as Diana Taylor says of her use of "hemispheric" as a field designation. "All projects bear the mark of their inception," she writes, "and *hemispheric* seemed less practiced, less violent and overdetermined, than *America* or *Americas*" (1424). "The mark" of my study's "inception" is the tension between the largely negative "broken" and the potentially positive pluralism of Souths, which meet at the "break" between enjambed lines. In this slight pause, an inter-American imaginary troubles assumptions about global-local and North-South power relations. With multiple, contingent spaces for contestation, this "Broken Souths" poetics ultimately surfaces from "bajo el signo neoliberal" (under the neoliberal sign), in John Beverley's terms ("Dos caminos"; my translation). His phrase suggests neoliberalism's ubiquitous but often nebulous influence on daily life, mental conceptions, political-economic structures, and language, from literary to marketing. The libratory forms latent within a harsh neoliberal order are particularly prominent in Latino poetics. Poems, as the poet-critic Joshua Clover notes, can deploy global capitalism's strategies in resistance to it. Imagery, metonymy, synecdoche, parataxis, disjunction, and indirection are central symbolic devices to each. Like financial capital movements in their compressed immediacy and self-referential, even obscure textualities, moreover, poems can function largely unfettered by the unity of time, place, and action structuring prose forms. The Nicaraguan poet and priest Ernesto Cardenal surely had these shared features in mind when meditating on the blinking corporate logos on a Managua street in 1965, on the cusp of the neoliberal era: "I don't defend the cruelty behind these lights / And if I have to give a testimony about my times / it's this: They were primitive and barbaric / but poetic" (*Pluriverse* 77). In this poetic dialectic between cruelty and beauty, utopian thinking, which is cynically "deferred to the past," as Hopenhayn says, can carve out potential alternatives. Such tensions between the current order and imagined exits inform many texts discussed in this book.

Herrera's meditation, Verdecchia's compass, and Cruz's figure measure "Broken Souths" as the "cultural dominant" of neoliberalism through which alternative visions confront its deprivations. Resuscitating Fredric Jameson's phrase "cultural dominant" redirects conversations about "globalization" to capitalism, neoliberalism in particular. Tim Libretti writes that economic imperialism is "euphemistically referred to as 'globalization'" (138), and Gérard Duménil and Dominique Lévy explain that the related terms "globalization" and "neoliberalism" are "two distinct sets of mechanisms" (9). The first refers to "the internationalization of the world economy," which Marx identified as the logic of capitalist expansion; the latter "refers to new rules of functioning of capitalism." And there's the rub: neoliberalism "is *its own* globalization" (10). In *Broken Souths*, I explore how Latino poetry configures and critiques these new globalizing processes. This approach attends to relations between literary production and neoliberal forces, literary representations and neoliberal ideology, and figurative language and neoliberal rationality. Neoliberalism remains undertheorized in US literary studies and, in particular, in Latino literary studies. It is usually subsumed under discourses of "globalization," the "free market," and "free enterprise" and lost in equations of "liberalism" with a set of social values rather than an economic ideology. Given the growth of Latino populations and literatures, the work of mapping antagonistic relations between the dominant ideology of our time and Latino literature is urgent and necessary. Even within hemispheric American studies paradigms, after all, it is rare to encounter the word "neoliberalism," let alone engagement with the theory that has transformed citizenship, subjectivity, and legal, government, and educational institutions across the Americas.

As such, some definitions are in order.[9] As a theory of political economy developed by Milton Friedman and Austrian economists currently worshipped by the Tea Party, neoliberalism's keywords are "freedom" and "radical individualism."[10] When the market is left to its own devices, the theory goes, individual and societal well-being follow. Free-trade agreements, privatization, deregulation, financialization, and prohibitions against organized labor, among other arrangements, create efficient, "free" societies. Jodi Dean defines neoliberalism as "a philosophy viewing market exchange as a guide for all human action. Redefining social and ethical life in accordance with economic criteria and expectations, neoliberalism holds that human freedom is best achieved through the operation of markets" (51). *Broken Souths* grapples with competing conceptions of freedom emergent during the neoliberal ascendancy. On one hand, neoliberal theory aims to maximize freedom by reducing citizenship to a rational choice model of atomized, possessive individualism. This conception ties all valences of freedom to the market, dismantles collective forms of organization and ownership, converts states into servants to capital, guts social safety nets and the public sphere, and relentlessly commodifies culture, including modes of resistance. On the other hand, a range of creative pushback has emerged in response to the rigid ideology and often violent implementation of neoliberal policies. The cultural modes and historical geographies of this pushback are varied, but Latino poets' plural figurations of collective freedoms constituted across Latino groups and between Latin and North America are among the most lucid and powerful. They model freedom as a relational concept rooted in diachronic place-based cultural practices and constituted interpersonally rather than held individually. This notion is often expressed in recurrent figures of "between"—languages, geographies, and cultures—in Latino writing that entangle split subjectivities with interpersonal relations and collective formations.[11]

In practice, neoliberalism has been a class-based global political project undertaken in response to student and leftist movements, the diminution of the economic elite's concentrated wealth by the end of the 1960s, and as a repudiation of Keynesianism and the welfare state. Its policies, moreover, have often been ensured by violence and have produced dramatic inequalities and uneven development. It has been very successful, not in creating higher growth rates or greater equality, but in concentrating wealth in fewer hands. Critically, this outcome is not an unintended consequence of capitalist competition but the logic of the neoliberal project. Contradictions between the theory and the practice of neoliberalization appear throughout *Broken Souths*, particularly when poets contest violence used to achieve neoliberal "reforms." The "main characteristics" of neoliberalism, Naomi Klein writes, are "huge transfers of public wealth to private hands" and "an ever-widening chasm between the dazzling rich and the disposable poor" (18). The blind spot in literary studies to the power and influence of neoliberal ideas is especially disturbing given these inequalities and their reproduction in education reforms driven by ideological tenets of "choice," "efficiency," instrumentality, and labor "flexibility," of which language and literature departments are acutely aware.

Because neoliberal ideology guides the academy's ongoing changes, we would do well to understand how our objects of study respond to, acquiesce to, and challenge its contradictions and effects.[12]

Jeff Derksen describes the silence about neoliberalism in cultural and literary studies in relation to other debates. "Unlike culture's centrality in the previous debates on modernism, postmodernism, and globalization," he writes, "the debate on neoliberalism lacks a cultural focus, or even a sustained speculation on what the role of the cultural might be within neoliberalism." Identifying and theorizing "the *cultural effects* of neoliberalism," he continues, demands that we "investigate how an economic philosophy has become transformed into an alleged common sense of the values of the market and free trade" (29). *Broken Souths* offers "sustained speculation" on how neoliberalism shapes Latino poetry. Reading poems against the theory and material impacts of neoliberalism is guided by questions raised by Derksen and theorists such as Wendy Brown. How do Latino poets imagine and resist neoliberal rationality, the idea that "there is no morality, no faith, no heroism, indeed no meaning outside the market?" (Brown 45). How do poems contest fundamentalism without deploying polemic? How do they respond to a counter-revolution that sees literary texts as mere exchange-values among others? How do they deploy figurative language within a "new social order" (Duménil and Lévy 9) that redefines freedom as solely a product of capitalist relations? How do Latino writers configure and challenge the "common sense" ideology that a purer capitalism produces ideal, stable national formations? If Theodor Adorno is right in saying that poems are "philosophical sundial[s] telling the time of history" (*Notes* 46), how do Latino poetic forms chart the era's changes, deprivations, and possible exits? In imperial national and hemispheric registers, "American" literary histories under neoliberalism remain untold.

This approach to Latino poetry offers a corollary to Kirsten Silva Gruesz's "new geography of [late nineteenth-century US] American literary history that emphasizes its formation within and around a culture of the Americas" (*Ambassadors* 6). Since the early 1970s, and with roots in 1968's upheavals, a "culture of the Americas" has been formulated through and in response to neoliberal ideology and material impacts. Unlike in the United States, debates about neoliberalism play key roles in Latin America, where the term has real currency—elections are decided with the word used as a metonym for social ills, while uprisings, such as the Zapatistas, explicitly name it as their target. Neoliberal ideology

and counter-revolutionary actions underwrite the era's definitive historical geographies, from the embryonic stages of 1968, when state violence
shook Mexico City and the Chicano and Nuyorican movements rose in
the United States, to the economic crisis of 2008 and ongoing violence
in northern Mexico. The US-backed coup in Chile on September 11,
1973, and subsequent economic shock treatments that modeled future
neoliberal reforms, New York City's fiscal crisis and response in the 1970s,
the Reagan revolution's anti-communist Central American interventions,
NAFTA and Clinton's "third way," ongoing "illegal" immigration, responses to "natural" disasters like Hurricane Katrina, and the Tea Party's
ascendancy are each part of the neoliberal narrative. As the key relational
axis between North and Latin America, it indelibly shapes the forms and
contents of Latino texts.

This metanarrative of upheaval and resistance delineates inter-
American contours for an alternative periodization of Latino poetry. As
Raphael Dalleo and Elena Machado Sáez note, periodization in Latino
studies is generally a function of degrees of political engagement. They
wisely dismantle the critical consensus dividing the "social justice" literature associated with the Chicano and Nuyorican movements in the
late 1960s from the supposedly apolitical writing of the 1990s (due to
Latino fiction's "remarkable market success") by exploring how the latter "rethink[s] the relationship" between literature, politics, and the market (3). In contesting the claim that contemporary writers "cease to carry
on the legacy" of 1960s-era politics, Dalleo and Machado Sáez write that
they try "to revitalize progressive politics by thinking *through* the market"
with individualist, consumer modes (7, 11). Neoliberal realities make this
important work. The Latino poet and critic Urayoán Noel, for instance,
foregrounds Dalleo and Machado Sáez's "post-sixties" construct to examine how the circulation and performance of Latino poetry create diverse
"modes of political engagement" and "nuanced conception[s] of identity that self-reflexively address the complexities of being and belonging
in a global, neoliberal society" (852, 855). Yet periodizing terms such as
"post-sixties" and "post–civil rights" (11) follow the neoliberal ideological
constructs of "the end" of history, ideology, and race that replace politically conscious collective ideals with individual, consumerist ones. *Broken
Souths* tacks differently, to ask: How do Latino poets think *against* and
beyond capitalism while acknowledging the influence of its ideals and outcomes? How might "Broken Souths" constitute an alternative, contestatory canon and inter-American periodization for Latino poetry? How do

poets recuperate and recast the emancipatory ideals, though usually not the forms and languages, of the late 1960s? How does specific attention to representations of place and space uncover Latino poetry's aesthetic critiques of neoliberalism?

The location from which I read Latino and Latin American poetry focuses these questions. Cruz's "broken / Souths" within New York make the epicenter of finance capital a site for "reading North by South," as Neil Larsen calls the relationship between US scholars and Latin American literatures. "In reading 'North by South,'" he writes, "the North, concurrently, rereads itself" (2). Similarly, *Broken Souths* uses a "Latina/o by Latin American" framework for reading Latino poetry, with Latino poets as guides to Latin America, in the necessarily partial ways of Juan and Wideload.[13] Latino poems, essays, correspondence, marketing materials, and ephemera serve as maps to inter-American relations and to Latin American poetic responses to neoliberal upheavals. These latter texts inform, in turn, Latino views of Latin America. This guidance reveals how relations between Latinos and Latin America have changed "under the neoliberal sign," and how they might reshift to contest its power.

I use the word "guide" here to foreground questions of place. The place-based poetics examined in *Broken Souths* attends closely, even romantically and defensively, to specific places in response to neoliberalism's maxim that all places are the same, or at least subject to identical economic laws. This approach expands Mary Pat Brady's work on Chicana literature's challenges to capitalist constructions of space and Caren Kaplan's deconstruction of theoretical metaphors of travel (such as "tourist" and "guide"). Whereas the narrative forms Brady examines are more direct "guides" to place, my focus on poetry reinforces her emphasis on "the relevance of aesthetics" to theories of space (6) while also stressing figurative, metaphoric, metonymic, and image-driven mappings of space. Viewing Latino poets as guides to places in Latin America ultimately maps emergent relations between Latino and Latin American literatures. "Are Latino texts produced in the US directly transferable to the study of Latin American literature?" de la Campa asks (*Latin Americanism* 6). "Some scholars from both sides of this growing nexus," he later adds, see this tact "as a dubious conflation of distinctly different phenomena" ("Latinas/os and Latin America" 464). Scholars such as Teresa Longo, who reads Latino poetry as part of a nascent pan-American canon ("Poet's Place"), are just beginning to map these relations. To map confluences and divergences carefully, *Broken Souths* uses two inter-American approaches drawn from Gustavo

Pérez Firmat's seminal *Do the Americas Have a Common Literature?* I put Latino and Latin American poems "side by side without postulating causal connections" and discuss texts that "embed an inter-American or comparative dimension" in form or content (4). This latter approach critiques neoliberalism on its own ground. Initiated as a hemispheric project between Chilean universities and Friedman's economics department at the University of Chicago, it was designed to erase specificities of places and to displace socialist as well as Keynesian versions of economy and society.

Along with Herrera, Cruz, and Verdecchia, my study's leading Latino guide to inter-American historical geographies "under the neoliberal sign" is Martín Espada. His poems set in Mexico, El Salvador, Nicaragua, Chile, and elsewhere in Latin America critique North-South relations, while those set in the United States draw from Latin American and Latino histories and poetic traditions. Their touchstone allusions include Operation Bootstrap in Puerto Rico, which prefigures the project (and logic) of neoliberal state formation; September 11, 1973, which produced the first neoliberal state; and NAFTA's aftermaths. When combined with his geographical range, hemispheric conceptions of subjectivity, critique of consumer identities, and generative locus in New York City, his embrace of "Latino" as a potentially empowering collective idea energizes Latino poetics through its multiple internal diversities. Espada "see[s] [him]self as a Latino poet, a Puerto Rican poet, [and] a poet coming out of the so-called 'Nuyorican' experience" (*Lover of a Subversive* 75). He embraces "Latino" because it is "descriptively accurate," in that both his "subject matter" and "perspective arise from that identity" ("Correspondence: Louis"). As de la Campa points out, "the idea of the Latino is quite fertile precisely because it is problematic" ("Latinos and the Crossover Aesthetic" xv). Conceptually, "Latino" has the potential to question regional, national, and ethnic groupings, along with the possibility of making common cause across human geographies. In this sense, Espada and other poets create what Juan Flores calls a "Latino imaginary." Unlike the "official, demographic version" of "Latino," this imaginary is "a unity fashioned creatively on the basis of shared memory and desire, congruent histories of misery and struggle, and intertwining utopias" (198). The figurative broken/to break relation constitutes a Latino poetic imaginary that has formed under neoliberal norms, emerged from new points of origin, and shifted to new geographic locations. This approach complements studies of Latino poetry that focus on a single group by taking seriously confluences across backgrounds and between Latino and Latin American poets.[14]

A Literary Geography of Latina/o Space-Times

The chapters of *Broken Souths* focus on poetic depictions of places by Latino poets primarily and poets in Latin America secondarily. I call these places "strange intersections," in Herrera's terms, but also "space-times," a critical geographic term combining the spatial and temporal coordinates that together produce "place" through human activities and natural-ecological forces.[15] Whereas Gruesz proposes an "alternative set of emblematic moments in nineteenth-century history" to map the inter-American origins of Latino writing (*Ambassadors* 11), *Broken Souths* charts poetic representations of "emblematic" places—those subject to neoliberal ruptures and conquests—to map the locations, migratory routes, and expressive range of Latino poems, including their relation to Latin American literary-historical formations. Saldaña-Portillo outlines the necessity of such transnational approaches to Latino literary studies by calling for "Marxist analyses of the active production of 'Latina/o' identities." This type of analysis "moves beyond the nation as a unit of analysis precisely because 'Latina/o' identities begin their formation not in the US but in Latin America, as an effect of US intervention and compulsory neoliberalism" (506). While many Latino identities arguably *begin* in the United States, as with Puerto Ricans and Chicanos, poets such as Espada, Cruz, and Herrera see Latin America as a troubled generative locus for Latino subjectivities. Many poems, moreover, depict Latin and North American space-times using shared images and tropes. I identify and examine these direct and indirect responses to neoliberalism from some of the hemisphere's most transformed places, weaving together a Latino "history of locations," Santa Arias's term for Espada's settings across the Americas (232). These interconnected places map a literary geography of the neoliberal era.[16]

The following chapters and coda are thus organized by hierarchical geographic scales to chart relational tensions between places across the hemisphere and the scales at which these tensions gain expression. In this geographic practice, scales of signification, or levels of representation, move from the widest scale, the global, to the hemispheric, nation-state, region, city, neighborhood, street, and apartment. Beginning with the hemispheric scale and moving through smaller ones, the chapters explore how texts imagine multiple scales in relation to the global project of neoliberalism, how neoliberal ideas and practices produce space, and how contestatory social movements and literary practices produce and envision space differently. Depictions of interchanges between local scales, like apartments and streets, and global forces, provide keen visions of subjectivity and resistance. This study's texts present figures of the forces reshaping places "from above," by global capital and states, and "from below," by a range of dispossessed and dissatisfied subjects who negate any notion of a pacified, monolithic working (or creative) class undone by informal markets and capital flight. As a shifting power relation rather than a static class formation, above/below stresses flexible modes of contestation and the creation of new economic elites, a hallmark of neoliberal privatization, deregulation, and financialization.

These tensions attain defining registers with figures of movement. In "Broken Souths" poetics, figures of transportation (cars, taxis, buses, trains, planes, boats, subways, horses, and pedestrian feet) are metaphors for the necessity and consequences of constant change in capitalism. Poetic tropes of movement correlate to Kaplan's identification of "the prevalence of metaphors of travel and displacement" (1) in postmodern theory. Whereas she interrogates how colonial discourses underlie theoretical ones, I focus on how poetic figures critique and reinforce neoliberal ideas. "Ever since the invention of trains," Tony Judt writes, "travel has been the symbol and symptom of modernity" and transportation modes "have been invoked in art and commerce as proof of a society's presence at the cutting edge" (212–213). In Latino poetics, however, transportation is a "symbol and symptom" of hard truths about migration, displacement, access to resources, and the relation between mobility and agency. The Chicano poet Javier O. Huerta's "Toward a Portrait of the Undocumented" distills these negative valences with sparse, declarative couplets echoed by parenthetical, interrogative refrains questioning a distant interlocutor, the speaker's nativist persecutor. It begins: "The economy is a puppeteer / manipulating my feet. // (Who's in control when you dance?) // Pregnant with illegals, the Camaro / labors up the road; soon, I will be born" (6). Like the dialectical broken/to break and above/below, vehicles register in empowering and enervating ways in Latino poems. Noel argues that Latino poetry "embod[ies] the possibility of a nomad Latinidad that, while profoundly grounded in a specific geography and sets of experiences, helps us see beyond the marked and marketable identities demanded by the state and corporate apparatus" (855). This combined mobility ("nomad") and place-consciousness ("grounded") underlies "Broken Souths" poetics, from Herrera's figures of "drifting" to Cruz's empowering migrations. Due to movement's positive ideals, it is easy to conflate movement with power. Yet, as Huerta's poem suggests, this ideologically inflected view of mobility also facilitates the flow of cheap, expendable labor while clouding the actual workings of neoliberal policies and augmenting their contradictions.[17]

To conclude this introduction, I discuss Cardenal's poem "Room 5600" to detail these figures of movement. Then the book unfolds as follows. Chapter 1, "Hemispheric Otherwises in the Shadow of '1968': Martín Espada's Zapatista Poems," reads "Sing Zapatista" and "Circle Your Name," which the poet wrote after visiting Mexico in March 2001, alongside documents in the Martín Espada Papers in the Latino Collection at Amherst College's Archives and Special Collections. E-mails with his translator, Camilo Pérez-Bustillo, a human-rights lawyer and scholar in Mexico City, show Espada working to sustain a collaborative hemispheric poetics. Whereas poetry is often viewed as a mode of private interiority in the United States,[18] Espada sees poetry as an empowering collective form. In viewing the Zapatistas as "otherwises" to neoliberalism, the poems critique neoliberal constructs of place, space, and nature that subject all forms of life to market rationality. The chapter ends by following Espada's e-mails with Pérez-Bustillo, who calls José Emilio Pacheco "THE BEST in the Mexican poetry world" ("Mexico–'Sing'") for Espada's edification. I theorize that Pacheco's "1968" maps the counter-revolution's origins and casts a long shadow on the present. First published in 1969 in response to the Mexican Student Movement and the Tlatelolco massacre, by 2000 Pacheco had whittled the poem's twenty-six lines to two. This version retains traces of 1960s optimism but through the lens of neoliberalism's logic of turning places into "blank pages" for capital accumulation. Although Alfredo Saad-Filho and Deborah Johnston argue that neoliberalism's "emergence cannot be dated precisely" (2), my discussion broadens narratives of 1968 to account for neoliberalism's targets, logic, and potential otherwises.[19]

Chapter 2, "Molotovs and Subtleties: Juan Felipe Herrera's Post-Movement *Norteamérica*," moves from Espada's hemispheric poetics and Pacheco's "1968" to Herrera's North American poetics. I argue that Herrera reconciles the Chicano movement's collective spirit to consumer-based individualism by reclaiming commodified images of revolution and resistance. His reassessments of the Chicano movement and travels to Mexico in 1970 and on the eve of the Zapatista uprising contextualize his restless search for languages to understand fraught terms such as "the Indian," "revolution," "Mexico," and "citizenship" (*187 Reasons* 182). Reading Herrera's experimental poetics emerging from a collective Chicano subjectivity expands Maria Antònia Oliver-Rotger's argument that he rethinks "the role of the Chicano writer" in light of the Zapatistas (172). Although

Herrera's fragmentary poetics contrasts Espada's apparently seamless but hard won lucidity, together they offer transnational Latino perspectives on "revolutionary textuality," de la Campa's term for self-reflexive, intertextual writing on revolution (*Latin Americanism* 42).

Chapter 3, "Against the Neoliberal State: Roberto Bolaño's 'Country' of Writing and Martín Espada's 'Republic' of Poetry," reads Bolaño's poetry and essays and Espada's *Republic of Poetry*, a collection based on his visit to Chile on the Neruda centennial in 2004, as critiques of the first neoliberal state. Their poetic figures of the coup and its aftermaths counter the totalitarian instrumental calculus of the neoliberal state. Pinochet's economists, called "Los Chicago Boys" for their training under Friedman, "considered [his] the ideal regime," claiming that "freedom can only be ensured through an authoritarian regime that exercises power by implementing equal rules for everyone" (30; cited in Valdés). Bolaño's and Espada's textual "countries" constitute September 11, 1973, as a disaster stuck in time that haunts the present. Maurice Blanchot's idea that "disaster," like "revolution," is partly a textual phenomenon that "de-scribes" experience (7) illuminates how the Chilean exile and Latino visitor struggle to write the past. While Bolaño deplores what he sees as a Chilean (and hemispheric American) proclivity for violence, his trope of the library-as-nation turns disaster to creation: "The refrain, repeated by Latin Americans and by writers from other poor and traumatized regions, insists on nostalgia, on the return to the native country, and to me this refrain has always sounded like a lie. The only country for a true writer is his library, a library that may be on bookshelves or in the memory" (*Entre paréntesis* 43).[20] This passage distills Bolaño's ideal of exilic Latin American literary citizenship based in a haunted romantic conception of poetry in contrast to Espada's conception of poetry as an emancipatory transnational "republic" of letters.

Chapter 4, "'Andando entre dos mundos': Maurice Kilwein Guevara's and Marcos McPeek Villatoro's Appalachian Latino Poetics," examines how two poets critique stereotypes of backwardness that define a world region (Latin America for North America) and a region within a state (Appalachia vis-à-vis the United States). Kilwein Guevara, a Colombian Pittsburgher, and Villatoro, a Salvadoran-Tennessean, create Appalachian Latino subjectivities that symbolize "the full spectrum of the Americas" *within* the United States (de la Campa, "Latin, Latino, American" 380). The emergence of Appalachian Latino literature expands Latino studies beyond the major groups (Cuban, Mexican, Puerto Rican, and, arguably, Dominican), showing the new locations and innovative new forms of Latino writing. "When the Chicano Movement emerged" in 1968, Carlos

Muñoz Jr. writes, "there were only three visible Latino/a groups in the nation, with Mexican Americans the overwhelming majority." "US intervention and economic domination throughout the Americas [. . .] brought about by neoliberal economic policies," he concludes, has created a more diverse population (7). These shifts come into focus in Appalachia and the US South, regions with expanding Latino populations and anti-immigrant legislatures, most infamously with Alabama's H.B. 56 (2011).

Chapter 5, "'MIGRATION . . . IS NOT A CRIME': Puerto Rican Status and 'T-shirt solidarity' in Judith Ortiz Cofer, Victor Hernández Cruz, and Jack Agüeros," reads Cofer's "Latin Deli," Cruz's ecopoetic essays, and Jack Agüeros's "Sonnets from the Puerto Rican" as critiques of Puerto Rico's colonial status and the neoliberal form par excellence: the citizen *as* consumer. In *Puerto Rico Is in the Heart*, a history of Espada's father, the documentary photographer Frank Espada, Edward J. Carvalho argues that Puerto Rico preceded Chile as the first neoliberal state experiment, beginning with the US occupation in 1898 and then formalized in 1948 with Operation Bootstrap's "proto-neoliberal" model (9). Rather than emphasize this model of foreign direct investment, export-led production, and labor exploitation, my parallel approach focuses on the ambiguous, mobile subjectivity instantiated in 1952, when Puerto Rico became an Estado Libre Asociado (ELA), or "commonwealth" of the United States. This strategy triangulates three critical views: Frances Negrón-Muntaner's claim that Puerto Rico's "cultural hybridity, citizenship multiplicity, and economic disjuncture" are common in the neoliberal era (10), Arcadio Díaz-Quiñones's and Flores's notion that Puerto Rican migration constitutes a particular type of "break," and Néstor García Canclini's idea that consumption is a critical citizenship mode. Consumer-based citizenship has transformative potential, but it often commodifies political struggle. Such "T-shirt solidarity," in Espada's words (*Alabanza* 179), can link likeminded (if not similarly positioned) actors across space, but it rarely contests the idea that creativity is the product of corporate, moneyed classes rather than of indigenous and working-class cultures.

Chapter 6 is set in the hemisphere's largest city. "Godzilla in Mexico City: Poetics of Infrastructure in José Emilio Pacheco and Roberto Bolaño" creates a model for reading urban imaginaries. I develop what Patricia Yaeger calls a "poetics of infrastructure" by reading figures of industrial agriculture, plumbing and water supplies, apartments, and pollution. Against the estimation that the city as a whole is an incomprehensible "non-place" under homogenizing neoliberal globalization, Pacheco and

Bolaño imagine Mexico City as a pulsating totality. Jill S. Kuhnheim, for instance, shows how poets see Latin American cities as "spectacle[s]," "no-place[s]" of "continued problems" and "unanticipated possibilities" (11). The play of "problems" and "possibilities" guides *Broken Souths*, but Pacheco and Bolaño see Mexico City as a distinctive place measured through pollution and uncertainty.

Chapters 5 and 6 consolidate my goal of combining ecopoetics and "metropoetics," Yaeger's name for infrastructural poetics. Metropoetics creates a taxonomy of "the urban imaginary" that includes "overurbanization," "decaying or absent infrastructures," "the unevenness of shelter," and "the importance of inventing counterpublics, or communal alternatives to the official, bureaucratized polis" (13). Yaeger's otherwise astute framework omits nature, thereby bracketing environmental degradation and a concomitant ecological awareness, key paired outcomes of neoliberal hyper-urbanization. "The social metabolic order of capitalism is inherently anti-ecological," John Bellamy Foster, Brett Clark, and Richard York write, "systematically subordinat[ing] nature in its pursuit of endless accumulation" (113, 74). Mapping Latino poetry's emergent locations and forms, many of which critique this "order," means linking border, rural, urban, and ecopoetic practices across Latino groups. That ecocriticism goes unmentioned by Yaeger, moreover, marks unexplored ground between urban, environmental, and Latino studies. While growing interest in ecocriticism in Latino studies focuses on fiction, *Broken Souths* shows how fractious relations between urban economic and ecological processes structure Latino poetics.[21]

The coda, "'Too much of it': Marjorie Agosín's and Valerie Martínez's Representations of Femicide in the *Maquila* Zone," returns to the border in Ciudad Juárez. If Chile was the neoliberal state's "laboratory," Juárez is the "laboratory of our future," as Charles Bowden writes, with NAFTA's legacy of violence and inequality. "Any discussion of Latino poetry," the poet, editor, and translator Francisco Aragón rightly claims, "would be incomplete without consideration of life on or around the US-Mexico border" (4). This is also true of any discussion of neoliberalism. I end in Juárez to critique neoliberalism's globalizing logic: open borders for capital and discipline for labor. This logic shapes the search for languages to express the horror of femicide in Agosín's and Martínez's book-length poems. Although scholarship on femicide texts focuses on fiction, poetry acutely renders the challenges of writing about violence and the need for a radical imagination to do so. As Clover boldly proffers, poetry is "the signal literary form of the [neoliberal] period" because it is the best "cognitive mode" for mapping the nonnarrative accumulation processes of the fictitious financial capital dominating the global economy (39, 49).[22]

The Inter-American Aesthetic Critique of Neoliberalism: An Illustration

"Room 5600," the twenty-third canticle of Cardenal's epic *Cosmic Canticle*, performs a foundational aesthetic critique of neoliberal conceptions of citizenship, subjectivity, and the common good that introduces the poetic figures of subsequent chapters.[23] When Espada himself introduced Cardenal at readings in Hartford, Connecticut (September 15, 1998), and in Northampton, Massachusetts (October 29, 2002), he presented himself first as a reader and second as a poet. In 1998, Espada explained when he "met" Cardenal: "I was twenty years old, a working class kid from Brooklyn [and] I had never *heard* of Nicaragua." In 2002, he added how: "I met him in the way all of you should meet him: in the pages of a book." Espada then linked his experience reading the book, Roberto Márquez's *Latin American Revolutionary Poetry*, to his own poetics: "Here was an artistry of dissent. Here poetics met history, craft met commitment. As a young poet, I had found the great table where I could sit. I had found a tradition, a teacher. Over the years, I paid my Cardenal books the highest honor I could bestow: I carried them around until they fell apart" ("Cardenal, Ernesto"). Espada insists here that Latino practices can emerge from Latin American "tradition[s]" and that "meeting" Cardenal through "revolutionary poetry" makes Latino poetry inter-American. These insights suggest how Latino poets turn south for models to ground their work against the political vacuity of, and frequent indifference to, poetry in the North. Yet it is also useful to recall Juan's turn south to find ruin and mistrust. In each, a "Latina/o by Latin American" reading underscores the North-South mobility of Latino poetic forms, as in Espada's figure of portability ("carrying"), and their grounded, stabilizing sustenance, as in Espada's "table" where writers "sit" in common cause.

"Room 5600" maps the North-South networks that have consolidated capitalist class power under a totalizing, coercive neoliberal rationality. Paradoxically, Brown argues, this rationality is not "primarily focused on the economy" but on *"extending and disseminating market values to all institutions and social action"* (39–40). In assessing hard-to-quantify impacts on social relations and relations to nature that result from this production of subjectivity and space "from above"—literally, from the Rockefeller office, Room 5600, on the Rockefeller Center's fifty-fifth and fifty-sixth floors in midtown Manhattan—the poem establishes figurative parameters for mapping poetic depictions of "Broken Souths" across the hemisphere. Its geography of the Rockefeller empire extends from "the banks of the Hudson / on a 3500-acre estate / with 11 mansions and 8 swimming pools / and 1500 servants" to "all the businesses in Latin America / (and its misery) / [that] are linked to that Room 5600" (184). This cartography of "misery" spans the hemisphere, yet the Rockefellers are incidental placeholders to the poem's overarching critique of the neoliberal project, just as the poem's images of the state-bound Sandinista revolution inadequately confront the placeless and borderless forces of neoliberalism and the avalanche of numerical quantities (5600, 3500, 11, 8, 1500, and so on) symbolizing the augmentation of capitalist class power.[24]

This idea requires an illustration. Direct references to Solentiname, Cardenal's commune on Lake Nicaragua and the symbolic center of his poetics, appears seventeen times between canticle 1 and canticle 23. That's 212 pages. In contrast, "Room 5600" appears twenty-four times in the four pages of canticle 23. This inequity suggests North-South, global-local (Room 5600–Solentiname), urban-rural, and economic-aesthetic inequalities. It also reveals how the *idea* of Latin America often fails to account for internal elites ("the businesses in Latin America") promoting and benefiting from them. Walter Mignolo describes how the "disguised" idea of Latin America as "a large mass of land with a wealth of natural resources and plenty of cheap labor" underlies development rhetoric (12). This view of "'Latin America' From Above," as a "Convenience Store" (96), and "as a resource to be consumed by the United States" (Longo, "Introduction" xx), exemplifies many cultural studies perspectives. Though largely accurate, the idea minimizes networks of money power between North and South, sources of exploitation in the South, and the South's internal unevenness. The "composition [and locations] of the capitalist class," Harvey writes (*Enigma of Capital* 98), continues to change through technological innovations and the sell-off of state enterprises. After all, the world's richest man, Mexico's Carlos Slim, was basically created by the privatization of the state's telecommunications industries.

"Room 5600" complicates such North-South dichotomies by depicting concentrations and dispersals of class power between the United States and Latin America. These North-South networks register in the individual consciousness and as external flows of knowledge and exchange emanating from Room 5600,

where hundreds and hundreds of foundations and corporations
are managed like
                    —what truly is—
          a single *fortune.*
Dependent on Room 5600 the millionaires in Venezuela
private enterprise in Brazil
          and you and I. (184)

By viewing connection through money power, which is notably cooperative and plural, and division by atomized individualism ("you and I")
imposed on those below, this passage "work[s] out the apparent contradictions of connection and division." This is how Sandhya Shukla and
Heidi Tinsman put the guiding directive of hemispheric American studies
paradigms (1), and it applies equally to transnational Latino studies. The
passage views social relations on a diminishing hierarchical scale, from
the "hundreds and hundreds" of corporations that are yet one fortune, to
measly millionaires, to unquantified "private enterprise," to "you and I,"
a frequent pairing in *Cosmic Canticle* converted here from wonderment
to subservience. Whether "the Americas" are "a fragmented or integrated
entity" merits flexibility, as Shukla and Tinsman argue (17), yet the poem
shows capitalism fragmenting and integrating the hemisphere by reproducing inequality.[25] Similarly, Rockefeller wealth is the metaphor ("like")
and the thing itself ("truly is"), the form of appearance and the material reality. Further, as this finance capital searches across scales for new spaces
for investment, forms of "monopoly" recur in the poem, reflecting their
dramatic increase through proliferating mergers, acquisitions, consoli-
dations, and privatizations. These capital forms mediate every "you and
I," as shifting pronominal relations, from the global scale to individual
consciousness.

"Room 5600" envisions the destruction of borders by capital and their
augmentation between rich and poor, "you and I," and millionaires and
the "hundreds and hundreds" of corporations who "truly" control the
means of production and ideological supports like the media. Nonetheless, "dependent" calls to mind outmoded dependency theories and over-
wrought North-South hierarchies, even as "millionaires" in the South
helps to "reverse the top-down view of imperialism as a one-way process
of North-South domination" (Shukla and Tinsman 16). Within these uneven North-South measures, the interpretive axis of "dependent" turns
on the relation between "globalization" and "neoliberalism." Whereas
the former is often understood in terms of interconnection, proximity,

interdependency, and leveling, as in Thomas L. Friedman's class-blind and technologically deterministic "flat" world hypothesis, the latter suggests the mechanisms reproducing unequal power relations and uneven access to resources the former neglects.[26] Put simply, globalization connotes integration, neoliberalism separation. Neoliberalism's *own* globalizing processes integrate corporate capital (in Brazil and New York, for example) to consolidate power over "you and I." These processes are defined by what Klein calls "the policy trinity": "the elimination of the public sphere, total liberation for corporations and skeletal social spending" (18). These goals serve the neoliberal ideology of economic growth as the sole measure of progress, which "Room 5600" satirizes with corporations "growing like a carcinoma" and "getting fat on malnutrition" (186). In this reckoning, uneven development is a globalizing process as well as its product, and deprivation is the sine qua non for corporate growth. What's more, a purportedly outmoded class struggle continues apace, but differently: capitalists wage it while insisting classes vanished at the "end of history." "Everywhere the Chicago School crusade has triumphed," Klein writes, "it has created a permanent underclass of between twenty-five and sixty percent of the population. It is always a form of war" (512).

This "form of war" operates in "Room 5600" through capitalism's contradictory formal logics of concentration and dispersal, monopolistic and decentralizing tendencies. Money power concentrates in Room 5600, while its influence spans the Americas, to cities, "the academies," "the presses," "the thoughts of a lady who runs a boardinghouse," and "the man walking some lonely beach." Further, Chase Manhattan Bank is "'tied to almost every important business in the world,'" a "whole huge and scattered fortune" that nonetheless "is only one fortune, there in one single Office" (185, 186). Monopoly, a fundamental contradiction of capitalism, is especially revealing "in a neoliberal world where competitive markets are supposedly dominant" (Harvey, "Art of Rent" 96). The poem thus undermines the justificatory apparatus that increased competition across all scales and all aspects of social life increases choice and quality of life. Alongside the poem's bemused tone, its repetition—unnecessary in terms of content—reinforces how capital accumulates, against neoliberal "common sense," in one room. This strategy underlies the poem's response to these contradictory dynamics *as* a poetics. Repetition portrays concentration, and the proliferation of locations, institutions, and quantities dispersal.

Although strategically repetitive, "Room 5600" is "radically polyvocal," as William Rowe writes of Cardenal's poetry (102). These techniques reject discrete contestations of empire per se—locatable in space-time, as in the United States—to confront neoliberalism, a ubiquitous foe dispersed across space, between New York, Washington, international banks, and "Broken Souths" across the globe. The poem's dozen unattributed quotes, such as "'tied to almost every important business in the world'" (186), enact a polyvocal discourse derived from business documents, news accounts, and shareholder reports, in both conversational and formal registers, that multiply the voice of neoliberal ideology in Room 5600.[27] The poem operates through centralization, with Room 5600 and the poet's lyric I, which appears in instances such as "ever since I was 25 years old" (187), and dispersal, with voices drawn from sources and registers often considered outside "poetry." This poetics mimics and parodies capital's mobility and constitution across space and between states and corporations. Against this moving target no direct contestation is possible, and lines such as "A silhouette of lovers kissing in the moonlight / (influenced more by Room 5600 than by the moon)" (185) suggest that cursing nature would be equally effective. And yet this power figuratively concentrated at the top cruelly taunts with the place itself. If the physical space, Room 5600, were to disappear, capital flows and processes of dispossession and control would continue apace.

This idea reminds us that capital is a process, not a thing, and that its continual circulation, between that room and the rest of the Americas, constitutes its increasing power and influence over everyone ("lovers," "you and I") and everything up to and including nature (the moon's rotation around the earth). This reveals the limits of the poem's revolution-as-solution and dramatizes Jameson's sense that "the more powerful the vision of some increasingly total system or logic, the more powerless the reader comes to feel" (5). Unlike other writers in *Broken Souths*, Cardenal fought a revolution per se. Thus the precipitous "That's why [. . .] Nicaragua's boys are fighting" (187) near the end sounds so resolute. Does "that" refer to every power structure preceding it? If so, Cardenal's declaration would insist on the *idea* of revolution as much as the outcome of the Sandinista revolt. But it also calls us, in the present, to the limits of local and national responses to neoliberalism's global project. Corporations, García Canclini writes, are globalization's "protagonists," producing space "on a global scale, [and] subordinating the social order to their own private interests" (*Consumers* 156). As such, citizenship and contestation strategies must also be formed across global-local interfaces. This task challenges place-based poetics, as coming chapters show.

It is no surprise, then, that "Room 5600" suggests that neoliberal rational choice theory, understood as the individual's ability to maximize advantages and minimize disadvantages in the market through instrumental decision making, is illusory. Structural inequalities, barriers to entry, and justificatory discourses promoted by the media constrict the choices of "you and I."[28] The media (Room 5600 "manufacture[s] *facts*" [186]) and state apparatus (news about and in Latin America "originat[es]" in Washington [185]) delink knowledge from place, which hinders individual negotiation of markets. Against the maxim stating otherwise, imperfect information actually works perfectly for capital, which shapes individual consciousness, agency, and taste to its benefit. Two verbless sentence fragments denote this condition: "Our perceptions conditioned by Room 5600" and "Our minds, our passions" (185). By disconnecting action (verbs) from affective and mental states ("perceptions," "minds," "passions") and language from agency ("Whether you say" *x* or *y* is "influence[d]" by Room 5600 [185]), the poem depicts radical individualism fragmenting language, social bonds, and collective identities. The verb-driven syntax of "Broken Souths" poetics implies that "to break" is impossible without verbs. Yet "conditioned" and "influence[d]" are not determinate, so opportunity remains for contestation. The poem suggests the challenge must be against "corporate public pedagogy," in Henry A. Giroux's terms. This media model severely limits knowledge and modes of freedom by deploying an "ensemble of ideological and institutional forces [. . .] to produce competitive, self-interested individuals vying for their own material and ideological gain" (113). The consolidation of class power symbolized by and located in Room 5600 asserts ideological control behind "our" backs, above "our" heads, and from the "silhouettes" to convert "you and I" into self-interested monads with waning interest in "our" collective conditions.

The poem sees this contradiction between market "freedom" and corporate control of "free" individuals as capital's constitutive failure of judgment. In neoliberal theory, the market is an impersonal, noncoercive force that aggregately organizes social and economic life by mitigating destructive behaviors and rewarding innovative ones. For Cardenal, this deeply personal force lacks discernment: "manufacturing chocolates or napalm, it's the same to them" (186). And: "Whether milk or poison / the product doesn't matter / bread or napalm / the product doesn't matter" (187). This is not to say that the Rockefellers, or capitalists, are evil. Instead, good capitalists follow the logic of capital wherein use-value is secondary— only exchange-value matters for making profit. This lack of discernment between poison and sustenance is, under capitalist logic, "rational." Alain Badiou writes that "for those who own and run this system, their only 'responsibility' is to make a profit. Profit is the measure of their 'rationality.' It is not just that they are predators; it is their duty to be predatory" (96). This "duty" also applies to language. As capitalists smash the power of labor and demean collectivist modes, the "hundreds and hundreds" of corporations appropriate iconic workers rights language, capture transnational governing bodies, and display class solidarity in board rooms and foundations and by bailing out massive financial institutions. The poem's heterogeneous, polyvocal form exposes these contradictions by mimicking capitalist logics of concentration and dispersal.

Ultimately, the poem critiques neoliberal conceptions of nature and place. Its fittingly prosaic (because commonplace) catalogue of environmental devastation—"carbon monoxide, mercury, lead" and "Ducks drenched with oil. / Poison wind over deserts and dead rivers" (185, 186)—*is* nature produced by capitalism. This vision emerges from a taxi approaching New York City, which "look[s] like a sacred mountain" with "seemingly heavenly skyscrapers": "At dusk you see from your car, above sulfurous bogs / the flickering fires of the oil refineries like Purgatory / and above them like a city in Oz / the glass skyscrapers lit up / Wall Street and Rockefeller Center / with its Room 5600" (186–187). Like many poems in *Broken Souths*, "Room 5600" uses planes, trains, and cars as revelatory figures for critique. "Your car" suggests the privilege of the poet's visit to New York, but it also disorders the hierarchy of "above" and "below." "Sacred mountain" and "heavenly skyscrapers" are not only symbols ("like" and "seemingly") of capitalist power but also the deific yet material repositories of capital, gods dwarfing the car. Yet the car also travels "above sulfurous bogs," as if navigating purgatory, between shifting images of above and below. Wall Street, capital's engine powering the neoliberal economy through destruction, generates "flickering fires" under the city.

Cardenal depicts the relation between city and nature through infrastructure connecting debased ecosystems ("bogs"), natural resources ("oil"), and industry ("refineries") to the built environment ("skyscrapers") and symbols of individualism (cars). This relation notably reverses the North-South gaze. Shawn William Miller writes that "Latin American nature has generated an unusually large share of first-world environmental anxiety" (194), evident in ecotourism and "save the rain forest" NGOs. He attributes this concern to the "Pristine Myth" in which Latin America is a paradise destroyed by its residents (195). The taxi, along with a reference to Lake Erie's pollution (186), creates a South-to-North gaze that undermines such myths, as if to say *the north imports the polluting ethos to the south.* To this end, "Room 5600" depicts the moon as an ideological construct and the sea as "fake" and "servile" (185). In this reckoning, nature is produced in the image of capital in order to serve its needs. New York is thus "like a city in Oz" that reduces nature to another commodity.[29] With references to the late 1970s (Jimmy Carter, Lake Erie, the Sandinistas) and allusions to "moral," "phony" bonds issued after New York's "bankruptcy" (187), the poem marks the city's neoliberal turn in the mid-1970s. This restructuring, Harvey notes, provided a model for Reagan, Thatcher, and the financialization of the post-Fordist global economy.[30]

"Room 5600" depicts the free market as the product of a counter-revolution that enforces capitalist values. Unlike classical political economists, neoliberals do not assume market laws will appear naturally when the state retreats and the "invisible hand" takes over. Instead, the neoliberal "constructivist project," in Brown's terms (40–41), creates legal and institutional frameworks to *produce* the world. "The neoliberal model does not purport so much to describe the world as it is," Simon Clarke writes, "but the world as it should be" (58), an "Oz" of gated communities for those who pulled themselves up by their bootstraps. And yet capitalism's justificatory logic remains largely unchanged. In 1989, Jameson posited the claim "the market is in human nature" as "the most crucial terrain of ideological struggle" (263–264). This claim, along with the dog whistle of "freedom," remains true today. "To break" must be reclaimed and revised between "as it is" and "as it [could] be," where so much Latino poetry makes its home.

Fronteras Americanas ends similarly, with Wideload asking the audience to reject an IBM advertisement celebrating the "smaller" world that moves "beyond borders." He wants "below" and "here" to supplant sanguine proclamations from "above" and "beyond": "Free trade all de way from Méjico to Chile—dis is a big deal and I want to say it is a very complicated thing and it is only the beginning. And I wish to remind you, at this crucial juncture in our shared geographies [. . .] under all this talk of Money and Markets there are living, breathing, dreaming men, women and children" (77). This entreaty against guiding abstractions, "Money and Markets," critiques the neoliberal relation between capital, for which the world *is* "smaller" and borderless, and labor, which breathes and dreams "under" its power. In his study of the Chicano movement revised for the fortieth anniversary of the student "walkouts" (or "blowouts") in East Los Angeles in March 1968, Muñoz points out that Latinos have "come a long way since the 1960s." But he adds that the counter-revolution has been "fueled by a backlash against the gains." "Whatever new vision emerges" in this era, he concludes, "it must be revolutionary in nature" (223, 228, 233). *Broken Souths* examines these "new visions" by heeding Wideload's demand, following poets who imagine "shared geographies" more than just those made by the "hundreds and hundreds" of corporations.

CHAPTER ONE

Hemispheric Otherwises in the Shadow of "1968"

Martín Espada's Zapatista Poems

The culture in which we live is perhaps the most claustrophobic that has
ever existed; in the culture of globalization [. . .] there is no glimpse of
an elsewhere *or an* otherwise. *The given is a prison. And faced with such*
reductionism, human intelligence is reduced to greed.
                                    —John Berger, *The Shape of a Pocket* (214)

With border-crossing products, persons, and capital, and with trea-
ties linking states under the auspice of market freedom, conceptions of
a hemispheric America are possible in myriad ways unimaginable even
to visionaries such as Walt Whitman and José Martí. But the neoliberal
incarnation of global capitalism has also augmented boundaries between rich and poor, citizens and the undocumented, and "you and I." If
"Room 5600" maps hemispheric integration and fragmentation, the January 2, 1994, edition of NPR's *All Things Considered* program juxtaposed
NAFTA—the sign and vehicle of integration—and a revolutionary "otherwise" to its logic. That a New Year's poem appeared on NPR is unremark-
able; that it was Espada's "Imagine the Angels of Bread," however, defies
NPR's moderation. With its anaphoric "This is the year" praising poetry's
capacity to facilitate change, the poem reverses relations between judges
and immigrants, capitalists and workers. Its template for a radical break
with the neoliberal order foreshadows scores of NAFTA-era migrants by
inverting their negative reception: "This is the year that those / who swim
the border's undertow / and shiver in boxcars / are greeted with trumpets
and drums / at the railroad crossing / on the other side" (*Imagine the Angels*
14). That NPR aired a subversive poem may be taken as anomaly, over-
sight, or the will of a defiant producer. That it aired "in the same broadcast

as the news of the Zapatista uprising," as Espada notes (*Zapata's Disciple* 125), and hours after NAFTA's implementation, is a striking irony.

Given no evidence Espada had advance notice of the Zapatista uprising while writing "Imagine the Angels of Bread," its allusions to borders, migrants, factory workers, plantations, and "rebellion[s] begin[ning] with [an] idea" pre-historicize rather than prophesy the rebellion against the triumphalist free-trade narrative: "if every rebellion begins with the idea / that conquerors on horseback / are not many-legged gods, that they too drown / if plunged in the river, / then this is the year" (16, 18).[1] The poem's compound conditional clauses ("if . . . if . . . then") connect "idea[s]" to the material conditions of possibility embodied by iterations of "to break" emerging from repetitive historical conditions of oppression. Similarly, when the Zapatista rebellion began on New Year's Day, many Mayan rebels used wooden sticks carved as mock rifles. Though some had guns, all were symbolically armed with the "idea" that "globalization" augments suffering rather than emancipates. Against NAFTA's promises of progress, competition, efficiency, and cheaper prices, the Zapatistas began their campaign chanting, "NAFTA is death." For the Zapatistas, Luis Hernández Navarro writes, "naming the intolerable" *as* neoliberalism required "constructing a new language" of resistance (65). Their bold act of belief called to account the heterogeneous "many-legged gods" of neoliberal globalization against which, the story went, resistance would be futile, by exposing them as "drown[able]" human creations and extensions of the conquest.

"Imagine the Angels of Bread" charts a hemispheric vision of a different freedom than that portended by "free trade," private property relations, and divisions of class, race, and nation. Its deictic anaphora "this" fortuitously pinpoints the year and day of NAFTA's implementation and the Zapatista rebellion. In this sense, NPR tacitly authorized the poem's advocacy of uprising, which it contextualizes in real time by suggesting the idea animating this uprising in Chiapas is akin to that against slavery, the Holocaust, and the destruction of indigenous peoples. Whereas the poem implicitly links neoliberalism to the conquest and puts the Zapatistas in the lineage of abolitionists, labor activists, and Puerto Rican independence advocates (*independentistas*), the Zapatistas' subcomandante Marcos explicitly views neoliberalism as extending conquest and colonization. He calls it "a world system" striving to conquer "new territory" (270–271). Klein defines it similarly as "an attempt by multinational capital to recapture the highly profitable, lawless frontier that Adam Smith, the intellectual forefather of today's neoliberals, so admired." Neoliberals, she continues, "set out to systematically dismantle existing laws and regulations to re-create that earlier lawlessness." "Where Smith's colonists earned their record profits by seizing what he described as 'waste lands' for 'but a trifle,'" she concludes, "multinationals see government programs, public assets and everything that is not for sale as terrain to be conquered and seized" (304–305).[2] Over three decades and nine original collections, Espada's poetry has emerged in response to this movement's conquests. "*The* Latino poet of his generation," as Earl Shorris proclaims on countless press releases, tracks neoliberalism's historical touchstones and defends the autonomy of Latina/o places by subverting its justificatory language and exposing its extralegal, antidemocratic violence.[3]

This discussion of "Imagine the Angels of Bread" underscores how Espada conceptualizes the *longue durée* of the struggle for dignity and daily bread in the Americas. In this chapter, I examine how Espada's entrance into what his friend and translator Pérez-Bustillo calls "the Mexican poetry world" and his desire to poeticize the Zapatistas accurately challenge his inter-American poetics, due in part to the fact that "dialogue with the South is much more important to Latinos in North America than it is to Latin Americans," as Coco Fusco writes ("Nationalism and Latinos" 159).[4] Espada's Zapatista poems create what Gruesz calls a "view of Latino identity grounded in a larger web of transamerican perceptions and contacts" rather than in nationality, genealogy, or language (*Ambassadors* xii), but they also show the limits of transnational solidarity in the face of capital's influence. Although set in Mexico, "Sing Zapatista" and "Circle Your Name" do not focus on the nation-state's imaginary power, as is true of his Chile poems. Rather, as Noel says of *The Republic of Poetry*, the Zapatista poems "remind us of how the Latino/a American experience can provide a strategic vantage point from which to think hemispherically, while attuned to histories of colonialism and oppression" (869–870). Espada's "vantage point" emerges from his firsthand view of the most iconic "otherwise" to neoliberal globalization, the Zapatista rebellion, and to his friend's intimate knowledge of their struggle.

José Rabasa writes that the Zapatistas embody a transhistorical "lucidity" linking neoliberalism to the conquest. They "respond to the specific conditions of postmodernity": "globalization, transnationalism, the 'demise' of socialism, [and] neoliberalism." Although the Zapatista revolt "is determined by these political and economic conditions," Rabasa argues, it "should not be reduced to a postmodern phenomenon." Rather, their "interpretation of the sources of their oppression," he concludes, has "a lucidity that has been from the start a part of Indian resistance to colonialism" ("Of Zapatismo" 420–421). A similar lucidity structures Espada's visionary poetics, with its pinpoint ironies and linguistic resistance to entrenched oppressions. Because hegemonic power uses euphemisms to "bleed language of meaning," he writes, "poets must reconcile language with meaning and restore blood to words" (*Lover of a Subversive* 95). This restoration requires clarity, and critics agree that Espada strives for "poetic diction more refined" than Nuyorican and Chicano poets who use spoken rhythms (Rivas 150) and that he achieves "methodical" and "rigorous" "historical reflection" (Salgado 205). What goes unremarked is the difficulty of creating this poetics, especially in writing "revolution." In actively advancing an otherwise, after all, the Zapatistas' teleological and epistemological orientations diverge from the progressive, meliorist course of "historical reflection."

Consequently, actionable resistance to neoliberalism, Arif Dirlik suggests, requires "formulat[ing] alternatives" to "the political defeatism if not nihilism of a ludic postmodernity" (16). Rather than creating possibilities for most people, as the theory insists and Pacheco's "1968" dramatizes, neoliberal globalization encloses them and creates "claustrophobia" instead.[5] Espada's lucid, robust poetics of restoration joins textual to referential contexts and ideas to actions by taking such alternatives seriously and by tending postmodern modes carefully. In the following pages, I argue that Espada's Zapatista poems develop a *lucid* place-based consciousness contesting the *ludic*, atomized individualism that reinforces neoliberal norms, and that Pacheco's "1968" captures and critiques their essential logic.

Place and Space in "Sing Zapatista"

The Martín Espada Papers paint an intriguing picture of the poet's visit to Mexico City and Tepoztlán, the setting of "Sing Zapatista," a small town two hours by highway from the capital, and his subsequent composition of the poem in the United States. By piecing together the contexts for the poem's composition and reading the poem's figures of place, space, and nature as resources for resistance, I answer a question returned to throughout *Broken Souths*: "What does it mean to be an 'author' in a distinctly transamerican sense?" (Gruesz, *Ambassadors* 13). For Espada, depicting the Zapatista caravan's March 6, 2001, stop in Tepoztlán en route to Mexico City to meet with President Vicente Fox means collaborating with others, using diverse textual sources, deferring to local knowledge, balancing humility and self-belief, and binding literary language and indigenous resistance to their places of emergence.

By conceptualizing the revolutionary production of space and place through ecological processes, "Sing Zapatista" "contest[s] the terms of capitalist spatial formation," as Brady argues of Chicana literature (6). Whereas critiques of Espada's poetry, and Latino poetry in general, tend to focus on identity formations and cultural resistance, an overarching ecocritical approach broadens his already capacious "poetry of the political imagination" (*Zapata's Disciple* 100). In mending the divide between humans and nature in capitalist logic and enlightenment thought, and the corollary divide between language and material referents in poststructuralism, ecocriticism shows how place and space are produced through social-economic relations, institutional arrangements, and ecological processes. Moreover, although "nature" is socially and ideologically constructed, ecocriticism argues that it is composed of material processes with agency of their own. At its most radical, ecocriticism critiques what Foster, Clark, and York call "the ecological rift" between humans and the natural world underlying capitalism's logic of conquering, controlling, and commodifying nature.[6]

In ecocriticism, as in much critical theory, place is often associated with labor and space with capital. Everyday work practices are grounded in place "from below"; mobile, flexible capital commands space "from above." Place is bounded and intimate; space is extensive but subject to human agency with sufficient resources. In his study of ecopoetry, for instance, J. Scott Bryson aligns place with stability, domesticity, security, and enclosure, and space with "wildness," "mystery," and the unknown. By seeing place and space as interdependent, he rejects the limiting preference "toward place and against space" in ecocriticism, nature writing, and environmental activism (8–9, 21, 69). Yet ecocriticism often implies that only certain types of place count as "place." This hesitancy to critique the capitalist mode of production as a driver of environmental devastation ignores how capitalists create place. Place-based movements like corporate research parks serve capital interests, and cities and states compete by marketing themselves as "good business environments." Developers and corporations are also "place-makers," in Bryson's terms, but as Espada's and Pacheco's poems show, they make place through displacement and erasure.[7]

In this sense, "place" has a perplexing corollary in the "local." Despite perceptions to the contrary, the "local"—like "place"—does not belong to the Left. Ursula K. Heise argues that US environmental movements have spent their "utopian capital" on "a return to the local and celebration of a 'sense of place.'" These essentialized, even reactionary, notions of place and the local have long been subject to antiessentialist critiques within postmodernist cultural modes (8). They instantiate illusory autonomies and exclude global imaginaries that might offer empowering conceptions of place. Heise argues against this stress on the local and for "environmental world citizenship" (10). But this approach, too, has limitations. In examining issues of representation and the local during the successful Tepoztlán uprising in 1995 against a luxury-tourist development project on communal lands, Rabasa argues that the global is "a determinant of local communities [that] contribute[s] to their deterioration, but it lacks the symbolic elements to institutionalize an alternative community" (*Without History* 77). He maintains the local "as the site of resistance to transnational interests and processes of globalization," even as he complicates the processes by which it can be represented (88). As he writes of "local" and "subaltern" (77), above/below, space/place, and global/local are relational rather than fixed concepts, and it is critical to keep them in tension with each other.[8]

"Sing Zapatista" emphasizes each pair's creative play and revisability by imagining place "from below" and space commanded by the creative resources of revolutionary thought and action. In order to disrupt neoliberal rationality's control of space, including its production of the absolute boundaries of private property, Espada uses poetic conceptions of space. For Henri Lefebvre, such "representational spaces" (or "spaces of representation") "overlay" the imagination onto material spaces shaped by dominant power structures. These representational spaces include "projects and projections, symbols and utopias," "complex symbolisms," and "the clandestine or underground side of social life" (*Production of Space* 12, 33, 39). Similarly, Michel de Certeau implies that "articulating a second, poetic geography on top of the geography of the literal, forbidden, or permitted meaning" (105) converts rational, tightly controlled spaces—in "Sing Zapatista," the town, plaza, street, and stage—into sites for emancipatory practice. Much as Brady sees Chicana texts disrupting conceptions of space as "inert and transparent" and thus natural and unchangeable (6), these "poetic geographies" in "Sing Zapatista" imagine place-based cultural practices wresting control over extensive, "inert" space from capital's grip.

The poem internalizes dialectical tensions between place and space and representational spaces and spaces of dispossession to create a conception of place produced from below that promotes radical resistance to capital and the state that serves it. In this capacity, place is a set of convergent and revisable processes, flows, and forces, in other words, an ongoing "project." When "place" is "conceived as project" (23), in Dirlik's terms, stability can be mapped to movement and metaphor to material reality. As a "project," place has a "topographical grounding" (22) that integrates theoretical, ecocritical, and poetic conceptions. Dirlik writes:

> Groundedness, which is not the same thing as immutable fixity, and some measure of definition by flexible and porous boundaries [. . .] are crucial to any conceptualization of place and place-based consciousness. Place as metaphor suggests groundedness from below, and a flexible and porous boundary around it, without closing out the extralocal, all the way to the global. What is important about the metaphor is that it calls for a definition of what is to be included in the place from within the place—some control over the conduct and organization of everyday life, in other words—rather than from above, from those placeless abstractions such as capital [and] the nation-state. (22–23)

"Sing Zapatista" models a place-based consciousness grounded in the natural world, diverse cultural resources, and local-global interfaces by viewing the resistant languages that emerge from place(s) as collaborative, mobile, and historically situated. To reenact the Zapatista defense of place, Espada imagines the collective singing of poetry in public space contesting the violent abstractions of global capitalism. This use of public space counters capital's conversion of places into "unending chain[s] of exchange-values" (Dirlik 18). In Marxist terms, preserving places for use-value against exchange-value models a mode of social relations promoting radical equality and everyday practices apart from capitalist valuation. In this mode, people meet face to face, paradoxically through Zapatista masks rather than fetishized relations, where the exchange of things conceals those between persons.

"Sing Zapatista" (*Alabanza* 216–217) builds this alternative communal formation by binding poetic form to the production of place "from within the place." Like "This is the year" in "Imagine the Angels of Bread," each of the poem's eight end-stopped quatrains begins with the anaphoric "Sing the word" followed by an italicized word and an image explicating it. This lucid device uses the imperative mood to exalt poetic language and to command continued singing. These eight iterations of "Sing the word" also foreground the chorus. Rather than a conventional refrain following verses, this chorus precedes the individual voice while maintaining the muscular initial command. The first line, "Sing the word *Tepoztlán*, Place of Copper," begins triangulating place, the poetic "word," and collective song. That *Tepoztlán* is the first "word" the poem "sing[s]" insists that the place from which a language draws its power is primary. This first quatrain views the town settled within its natural environment and the symbolic meanings inhering there: "Sing the word *Tepoztlán*, Place of Copper, / pueblo of cobblestone and purple blossoms / amid the cliffs, serpent god ablaze with plumage / peering from the shaven rock." These images bind literary ("sing[ing]"), cosmological ("serpent god"), and economic ("copper") forms and processes to cyclical and deep-temporal natural formations, including an icon of the Aztec god Quetzalcóatl, reputedly born near Tepoztlán.

Yet these images also skirt the language of travel guides. "Cobblestone and purple blossoms / amid the cliffs" conjures a decontextualized postcard and thus Tepoztlán's dependence on tourism, with its alternative religious centers, craft stores, hotels, and cafés. In an e-mail to Pérez-Bustillo, who advised Espada during the writing process, Espada admits as much: "the references in stanza #1," he writes, "come from Lonely Planet, which says that the translation of 'Tepoztlán' is Place of Copper" ("Mexico—'Sing'"). That said, these images are joined by the fierce, foreboding "serpent," "ablaze," "peering," and "shaven rock" that prepare the town's stunning topography—forbidding and nurturing in a deep valley—to defend place, with force, if necessary. The consonance on "Place" in "Tepoztlán," "copper," "pueblo," "purple," "serpent," "plumage," and "peering" reinforces the essential (and sonically potent) relationship between sound and space, as songs echo from cliff and cobblestone and mountaintop ruin acts as a Zapatista sentinel. These aural qualities reject the hegemonic media's misrepresentations of place. *All Things Considered* enters the fray again with its September 7, 1995, report on the aforementioned Tepoztlán uprising. The program's background "sound track for ambience" and patronizing depictions of local folklore, Rabasa argues, produce a "caricature" of the Indian uprising as a "lost cause" against the forces of "progress," here a euphemism for high-end golf courses and spas (*Without History* 85–87). The first quatrain may use the Lonely Planet guide as a Nahuatl dictionary, the Aztec/Mexica language spoken by over a million people in the area surrounding Tepoztlán, but it emphasizes Zapatista triumph. Their cultural-political practices become robust forces of resistance by reversing tropes of inevitable victory (Western "progress") and defeat (indigenous "lost cause[s]").

The poem's formal elements of alliteration, repetition, anaphora, and metonymy combine with thematic elements to contest representations of "lost causes." In Adorno's words, the "interpenetration" of form and content "captures the historical moment within [the poem's] bounds" (*Notes* 46), threading the individuated lyric mode to collective modes of resistance. This is apparent in the choral singing of eight metonymic keywords, which move from "*Tepoztlán*" through figures of indigenous resistance before ending with "*Marcos*." They "capture" the *longue durée* of the conquest from the sixteenth century to its iteration in the immediate "historical moment," the uprising against neoliberalism. In order, "*Tepoztlán*," "*Zapata*," "*Zapatista*," "*Félix Serdán*," "*comandante*," "*durito*," "*zapateado*," and "*Marcos*" connect the revolutionary Zapatistas of 1910 to neoliberal-era Zapatistas and both to ongoing dispossessions initiated with the conquest of indigenous peoples. Many of these Spanish-language words are Mexicanisms, with several derived from Nahuatl. The dissonance between singing Spanish and Nahuatl in an English-language poem registers acutely with Espada, as he explicates "the word," directly in the case of Tepoztlán, and indirectly elsewhere. Espada's lucid "translations" of these words are reinforced by archival documents showing his dedication to exacting detail and to communicating across languages. The core of these documents is a string of pre- and post-visit e-mails between Espada and Pérez-Bustillo, who was then a professor at the State of Mexico campus of Instituto Tecnológico y de Estudios Superiores de Monterrey (Monterrey Tec). In addition to discussions about Espada's readings in Mexico, the e-mails reveal the poet's private willingness to cede textual authority to Lonely Planet and his friend's knowledge. In an e-mail string ending on April 16, 2001, six weeks after the visit, Espada presses Pérez-Bustillo to translate and publish the poem in Mexico. He calls it what "came out of the Tepoztlán visit" and "proof that [his] time in México was appreciated and well-spent." Then Pérez-Bustillo praises it as an "incredible" distillation of their "all too brief all too disorganized taste of Zapatismo together" ("Mexico—'Sing'"). Although tempting, it is a mistake to read this correspondence as insight into how Espada's visit inspired him or how he torques the brevity of his visit, and of his knowledge, into seamless lyric. Instead, the e-mails contextualize how the poem connects "the word" to "place" to defend the latter against capital, which descends on and attempts to transform places into homogeneous spaces for accumulation.

The e-mails demonstrate Espada's belief that poems should depict place from local perspectives of resistance, which are necessary to "sing" well, even if the singing will mostly be heard far away. To this end, Espada asks Pérez-Bustillo what he calls "nitpicky" questions about Tepoztlán, Emiliano Zapata, Quetzalcóatl, the Zapatistas, and *bastones de mando* ("staffs of command" the Tepoztecos gave to the Zapatistas to authorize speaking on their behalf). Near the end of these e-mails, Pérez-Bustillo, a legal scholar who has studied and worked with the Zapatistas, calls it "our poem" and Espada's "first on the topic which has given structure and meaning to my life the last seven years" ("Mexico—'Sing'").[9] "Our poem" may test credulity but the archive reveals Espada's reliance on Pérez-Bustillo. Here he encourages Espada's cheeky rejection of bourgeois travel-writing tropes and provides autochthonous images of Tepoztlán. In a clever aside, Espada asks Pérez-Bustillo about the prominence of melons in Mexico to check the accuracy of the poem's depiction of Félix Serdán—its fourth "word[s]"—who rode with Zapata at age eleven and in 2001 stood on stage with the Zapatista delegation. Espada writes, "I know that there must be melons in México. The Lonely Planet tells me so" ("Mexico – 'Sing'"). Pérez-Bustillo responds, "Age 11 for Serdán sounds right from what I know, last I saw him he was 90-plus in 1997." And, yes, he adds, melons "definitely exist and are very popular here, delicious in fact" ("Mexico—'Sing'"). In the poem, Serdán is "witness to a century's harvest of campesino skulls / abundant as melons." As metaphors for the abundance of skulls produced by state-capital violence, this is an instance in which Espada checks his poetics against the realities of Mexico. Poetic melons require referential corollaries (actual melons) to meet local evidentiary structures rather than the expectations of travelers, even as he privately admits his status as a Latino outsider who supports the Zapatistas.

In deferring to local and commodified tourist knowledge, Espada resists converting the Zapatistas into universal symbols. Mignolo argues that the Zapatista uprising constitutes a "theoretical revolution" (124) enacting *"the end of abstract universals,"* such as communism and capitalism, *"competing for their superiority over others"* (144). "Instead of translating rich, diverse histories and knowledges into abstract universals," he writes, "the kind of translation called for in the world of many worlds," the Zapatistas' idea of the global that counteracts Berger's "claustrophobia," "would allow each its own dignity without reduction, and maintain the autonomy of local, non-dependent histories" (144). "Sing Zapatista" shows restraint in regard to such universals by deferring to local historical geographies of resistance, even as other Espada poems promote them. "Imagine the Angels of Bread," for instance, uses "evict[ion]," "rebellion," "refugees," "immigrants," "own[ers]," "landlords," "squatters," and "abolition" to critique property relations, and official metonyms of legal justice, like "files," "deeds," "wills," and "deport[ation]," to suggest the justice system's abuses can be reversed into contrary universals promoting the marginalized. Such language is absent from "Sing Zapatista," apart from "rebellion" and "rebels," which are descriptive rather than figurative or aspirational.

Instead, figurations of above and below invert power dynamics defining resistance to the powers of capital, the neoliberal state, and official history. Just as class formations are relational, these inversions replace universals with translocal communal formations between Tepoztecos and marchers from Chiapas. "Sing Zapatista" begins with cliffs (above) and cobblestones (below), yet the former's perched icon is not a global capitalist abstraction "peering" down from above, but an indigenous figure with significances literally and figuratively inaccessible to exchange-value. Ensuing quatrains present various images of above and below. Above: "the roof" of the Zapatista caravan, "the platform" where Zapatistas speak, the metaphorical "shoe" that "crushe[s]" from above, and Marcos speaking "above the crowd." And below: "railroad tracks," "cornfields," "the long rosary of blood / beaded and stippled across the earth," a "scarab on a banner," "the scarab-people cluster[ed] below" the banner, and a guitarist's "fingers skitter[ing] like scarabs." As in the first stanza, these images and tropes are not fixed binaries, and they subvert expectations linking "above" to oppressive power by showing the Zapatistas garnering collective strength from both above and below. These conceptions collide in the sixth quatrain: "Sing the word *durito*, hard little one, scarab on a banner / draped across the face of the church where bells bang / to welcome the rebels, as the scarab-people cluster below / shouting their vow never to be crushed by the shoe." This figuration of Zapatista supporters as a "cluster" of beetles "the color of earth," as an earlier line has it, meets the trope of the shoe, singular, powerful, and merciless, descending from above. These constructions pit the neoliberal metanarrative of placeless, mobile, consumer-based individualism (the shoe) against a collectivity (or "cluster") resolutely in place, connected to natural processes, and in motion in the "tap and stamp of the women dancing in the plaza." As Hopenhayn writes, such a relation between above and below portends conflict: "The reaction from below, to a violence that is institutionalized, or implicit in the unjust distribution of wealth will be superseded by a new pitiless counterreaction from above" (30).

If the shoe represents neoliberal globalization's goal of crushing alternative modes of organizing life, *durito* is a metaphor supporting the Zapatistas' "theoretical revolution." Whereas the previous words to be sung are people, places, and roles (*"comandante"*), *durito* is the diminutive form of the adjective *duro* (hard, tough), but it is also a scarab, or beetle. Marcos often uses it as an anthropomorphized theoretical construct, the talking beetle Durito, to critique neoliberal power structures. In Spanish, "beetle" (*escarabajo*) incorporates the notion of below (*abajo*). In one of his communiqués, Marcos depicts Durito holding a piano on top of his shell (254). This conceit has many connotations, but I see it in terms of the poem's celebratory vision of alternative collective formations embodied by the Zapatista visit to Tepoztlán. The impossible (a beetle holding a piano) becomes possible (an egalitarian society in which the small are strong) when one thinks figuratively: the seemingly powerless support the large and powerful and cultures of labor support high art (the piano). The play in the "vow never to be crushed by the shoe" converts the shoe's figurative power from the private property of the oppressive few "above" to the many "cluster[ed]" "below" in the plaza. These multiple "duritos" "tap" and "stamp" their feet on the ground; yet instead of destroying like "the shoe," these feet create culture. This conversion of the power of "the shoe" into "the percussion of [the] feet" reclaims the name Zapata, a masculine ending removed from *zapato*, Spanish for "shoe." Finally, the nominalized adjective *durito* undoes the rift between the passive, adjectival "broken" and the verb "to break" by turning its presumptive conditions of marginality (smallness, powerlessness, and connection to the earth) into forces for resistance. Muscularity drives such contestation, but strength does not map to size.

To understand this production of space from below, it is critical to see "how cultural practices both *produce* and *represent* space, rather than simply *happen within* space," as Derksen writes (12). "Space is a weak concept in neoliberalism," he argues, because it views space as inevitably "produced from above, by the forces of the market" (253). Espada sees the Tepoztlán plaza produced from below by linking poetry, music, and political struggle. The final quatrains of "Sing Zapatista" are set in Tepoztlán's main plaza, where a "platform" holds twenty-three "faceless / masked" Zapatista delegates and where "the scarab-people" "sing the word." This collective act of reclaiming the "word" from a power nexus descending from above is facilitated by producing the space of the plaza from below through active use, with dancing, percussive feet. Espada's recurrent figures of Latin American plazas convert the iconic spaces traditionally reserved for exercising hierarchical order through the nexus of church, state, and market power, into spaces for resistant subject formation.[10] The alliteration at the poem's opening continues in these quatrains, linking the production of "place" with "plaza," "platform," "percussion," and "scarab-people." The metaphor of "scarab-people" connects Zapata's rebellion and the Zapatistas. Each is "the color of earth," the former directly, the latter metonymically. The former "peasants of Morelos"—the state where Tepoztlán is located and where Zapata was born—are "husking rifles / stalk by stalk from the cornfields." This figure links nature and culture in the act of revolution and rebellion to harvest.[11] "Stalks" also contrast "skulls" aurally. As organic extensions of and from the earth each uprising is naturally constituted and justified in corn "stalks"; in contrast, "skulls" equate to hollow justifications of progress. These divergent conceptions of the production of place, one from below through "stalks" and the other from above through "skulls," counterpose sustenance with destruction.

Yet the neoliberal-era Zapatistas travel "without rifles" in a collective though rhetorically singular "caravan." Their "word" is a synecdoche for a collective language of resistance to neoliberal hegemony by a chorus of "singers." This multivocal "word" serves as a weapon in a "theoretical revolution" that establishes continuities between Zapata's struggle at the turn of the twentieth century and the Zapatistas' challenge to neoliberalism. Espada recuperates this historical dialectic, and its connectivity between past, present, and place-based communal subjects, from the erasures of global capitalism. The poem's relations between local scales of encounter, such as plazas and streets on which the caravan travels, connects the word, the earth, and the "scarab-people" against national and global forces that descend "from above" and produce "skulls." The poem thereby posits an alternative "word" to the neoliberal logos. This one is constituted in a figure of transportation, the collective, autonomous "caravan"—the Zapatistas' "bus panting" into Tepoztlán, "dangling ghosts" of history "from the roof"—that stands against the car, its singular, diminished linguistic form. Whereas neoliberalism's "word" is an individuated economic "freedom" unmoored from justice, equality, and the common good, "Sing Zapatista" models a multilingual, collectively created "word" between rural and urban; Chiapas and Mexico City; Zapata and the Zapatistas; and Nahuatl, Spanish, and English—and in Tepoztlán. As a plural, mobile logos constituted in place, this conception activates Doreen Massey's sense that place is "a particular moment" of "social interrelations at all scales." In this sense, Espada's Tepoztlán "includes relations which stretch beyond" it (5), from Chiapas to his e-mail server in Massachusetts. This eight-part logos resists the logic that neoliberalism ushers in "the end of history," where history is seen as the global triumph of capitalism and the ascent of the individual versus collective goals.

This logos is activated in a plaza, where the church's "word" presides. Yet its bells "bang / to welcome the rebels" "smuggling Mayan tongues to the microphone in the plaza." "Smuggling" parodies the free market's putatively transparent norms of equal exchange, and the church "drowses" as its "bells bang" in unison with the alternative "word." In the last quatrain, the poet's command to "sing the word" becomes a collective "chanting" of the sequence's final word: "Sing the word *Marcos*, el Subcomandante, and listen / when he says above the crowd chanting his name: / *Marcos does not exist. I am a window. I am a mirror. / I am you. You are me.*" While the individual's deference to the collective is a Zapatista strategy for focusing on the goals of the "scarab-people," the poet's deference to the collectively chanted word effaces the lyric speaker, allowing his words to be sung by readers and his singular voice to be replaced by a chorus. This move reinforces Rabasa's claim that "Marcos no longer defines his task as one of representation" ("Of Zapatismo" 422). The poem's imperative—to sing—is in this last case joined to another: to listen. Not only does Marcos follow the second one in deferring to collective goals, but the poem follows it by showing that poets must listen carefully to sing well. As such, Espada does not represent Marcos or the Zapatistas. Instead, his poem defers to them and cedes his voice to theirs, as we imagine the poet in "the crowd chanting [Marcos's] name." And although Marcos is literally "above the crowd," he is also *in* the crowd, within every "masked," anonymous, and singing person, including the poet.[12]

With these figures, "Sing Zapatista" conceives place as a "project" against the displacement of collective landholders that spurred the Zapatista uprising. This historical conception links Mexico City, where communal forms were dismantled in obeisance to North American capital, to collective *ejidos* in Morelos and Chiapas. Neoliberalism's version of the conquest converts communal spaces into privatized, absolute spaces for capital accumulation by destroying collective forms, including labor organizations and cooperative ownership. Yet in the neoliberal view, Indians were not dispossessed, they were incorporated into the free market. Their land was necessary—not *as* land for cultivating crops but as private property per se—for ensuring "progress." Thus in order to conform to NAFTA, in 1991 the Mexican government cancelled Article 27 of the Constitution, opening up *ejido* lands to privatization, including around Tepoztlán, and to foreign and domestic buyers. Under this Article, "Indian communal landholdings [*ejidos*] were protected from sale or privatization," but NAFTA reframed this protection as an "obsolete barrier to investment" (Hayden 82). In the run-up to NAFTA's implementation, moreover,

President Salinas's economic program followed neoliberal orthodoxy, gutting the public sector by privatizing banks and industries at cut rates (Harvey, *Brief History* 101). The Zapatistas, Harvey writes, rejected the goals of these "reforms" by "appeal[ing] fundamentally to notions of the rights and dignity of labor, of indigenous and regional ways of life, in the face of the homogenizing forces of commodification backed by state power." And they did so symbolically, by beginning the uprising "on the day that NAFTA took effect" to show that neoliberal ideology was "the root of the problems" (*Spaces of Hope* 74). "Sing Zapatista" celebrates "indigenous and regional ways of life" against the metaphorical "shoe" that harnesses "homogenizing forces of commodification" in order to "crush" them. In enacting the forms, figures, and metaphors of these ways of life, the poem attempts to preserve their aesthetic and epistemological autonomies.

As a "project," place grasps and resists these machinations from above that erase and rewrite in the image of capital. In "Sing Zapatista," this "project" begins not with federal statutes but below ground, in soil cycles, geological processes, and harvests that ensure the continued "husking" of corn and rifles. Using Dirlik's terms, Tepoztlán is constituted as a "place from within the place" through singing in the plaza but also in struggling against the proverbial "shoe." The poem draws "flexible and porous boundar[ies]" around Tepoztlán—"cliffs" and "shaven rock" enclose the town but do not prevent the arrival of marchers, the history of conquest embodied by the church, or the "century's harvest of campesino skulls / abundant as melons," the product of collusion between global capital and nation-states critiqued with a metaphor of market "abundance."[13] This place-based subjectivity resists displacement and commodification, contesting abstractions from above that transform "abundant" harvests into oppressive forms. Even so, alongside Espada's ironic, discrete use of Lonely Planet, the poem's byline indicates to readers that the town exists only on March 6, 2001. In this way, the poem suggests Tepoztlán is a place to be passed through en route to the next poem in the collection *Alabanza*, "Ezequiel" (218–220), whose subject is extralegal violence on the United States–Mexico border, or to Mexico City, which lends Tepoztlán meaning as a tourist retreat for middle-class Mexicans.

Espada's notion of a collective, intertextual project replaces the discrete, private, individual lyric self with choral, multiple, public poetic "singers." In explaining his composition of another poem, Espada writes that "the subject of the poem is, in a way, the co-author of the poem" (*Zapata's Disciple* 110). By expanding this notion, we can view Marcos, Pérez-Bustillo, indigenous musicians and dancers, and Lonely Planet as coauthors of

"Sing Zapatista." These multiple textual sources echo Rabasa's take on Marcos's identity as a textual collage. "'He,'" Rabasa wisely puts the pronoun in quotes, is comprised of "a series of communiqués, interviews, and speeches" rather than a "coherent and consistent self behind the statements." "These multiple subject positions," he continues, "have little to do with a celebration of a postmodern fragmented self," given that Marcos's perspective on the Zapatista place in history is "profoundly tragic" ("Of Zapatismo" 421). Reading "Sing Zapatista" through intertextual tensions between individuality and anonymity, individual and collective authorship, and aspirational collectivities and actual debasements of collective bonds animates this tragedy as well as the intellectual poverty of the "fragmented self." Celebrating a "postmodern fragmented self" is a mockery in this context, as neoliberal hegemony refuses the Indian a full self. This foreclosure of indigenous forms of life, including cooperative "ownership" and autonomy, is the tragedy Rabasa refers to and against which Espada's plural "word" countermands.

In this reading, "Sing Zapatista" enacts collective authorship against the interrelated modes of ludic and radical individualism. Other than Marcos's quoted, interpersonal "I," the poem lacks a lyric "I," and it never refers to its "author," even obliquely. As such, the poem expresses Pacheco's *ars poetica*, put succinctly in "In Defense of Anonymity": poetry is "anonymous since it's collective" (*Selected Poems* 179). Poems are composed actively between writers and readers and from numerous texts, and thus numerous writers and readers preceding them.[14] The Spanish ("anónima ya que es colectiva") makes the case more forcefully: because poetry is always already collective it must be anonymous, just as the Zapatistas were anonymous, as in invisible, before they were visibly anonymous as masked rebels. By making their invisibility explicit with masks, they gained collective influence. Yet Espada's poem carries his name alone. Although the poem praises and approximates the Zapatista model of autonomous, decentered, and collective decision making derived from lucid struggles, it should not be mistaken for them.

Espada's attempt to forge an alternative poetic word is nonetheless mediated by the literary marketplace. The archive reveals this discomfiting truth: e-mails show the poet as an earnest hustler, negotiating readings, appearances, honorariums, and book sales through Pérez-Bustillo's contacts in Mexico ("Mexico—Mexico City"). This is not to suggest that Espada is impudent, or driven by money and fame. Rather, when combined with other archival documents expressing concerns about disappointing sales, diminishing royalties, just-missed literary awards, his 1993 bankruptcy and foreclosure ("Bankruptcy"), and his wife's medical conditions and hospital bills ("Correspondence: Campo"), these pressures define the age of neoliberal rationality, when all literary value is subject to economic valuation, and writers must attend to Wideload's "Money and Markets" (77) in equal measure to what we might call "Literature and Poetry." An accounting of Latino poetics in the neoliberal era must extend Adorno's "social interpretation" of lyric poetry wherein poems are "brought into conjunction with bustle and commotion." Although, in Adorno's words, the "traditional" and still dominant "ideal of lyric poetry" in the United States "is to remain unaffected by bustle and commotion" (*Notes* 37), Latino poetry sings in, through, and because of "commotion."

A February 23, 2001, e-mail from Pérez-Bustillo to Espada shows the limits of the poet's resistance to neoliberal rationality ("Mexico—'Sing'"). In explaining his struggles organizing Espada's March 7 and 8 readings in Mexico City, Pérez-Bustillo depicts last-minute scrambling to secure arrangements, honorariums, and a well-known headliner for the first reading. He writes that he "reached out personally to every single major Mexican progressive writer (most but not all poets) to join us on March 7th," including Elena Poniatowska, Homero Aridjis, and Pacheco. Although he calls Pacheco "THE BEST in the Mexican poetry world," knowledge of Pacheco's "Contra los recitales" [Against poetry readings] (*Tarde o temprano* 153) might have spared Pérez-Bustillo the trouble. In any case, "progressive" suggests he searched for a fellow traveler. But he begins by telling Espada to "forget about courses," that "there is NO COURSE," presumably the visit's most lucrative possibility. He continues, "Your [plane] ticket will be covered, [but] the honorarium that is GUARANTEED has dropped because we don't have the course at Casa Lamm," the cultural center in Mexico City's Colonia Roma that "dropped the ball." Pérez-Bustillo's use of capital letters crests when he says, "PLEASE BELIEVE ME THAT I AM BUSTING MY ASS ON ALL THIS," acknowledging Espada's exacting standards and reasonable claims to fair compensation. In calling his readings "gigs," moreover, Pérez-Bustillo recognizes Espada's exhausting public reading schedule that often resembles a rock star's tour.

Ultimately, the e-mails show Pérez-Bustillo negotiating the literary marketplace on behalf of Espada and the challenges of creating what Gruesz calls "a web" of "contacts" between North and Latin America. The "big headliner" for the March 7 reading at USIU–Mexico City (United States International University, now known as Alliant International University) was the Chiapan poet Juan Bañuelos. As a member of CONAI (Comisión Nacional de Intermediación), the commission that mediated the San

Andrés Accords between the Zapatistas and the Mexican state, Bañuelos undoubtedly influenced Espada's understanding of the Zapatistas. Espada asks Pérez-Bustillo to send his translation "with the original to our friend Bañuelos," likely to "have good ideas about where it might be published in México." Then he adds, "I do like publishing abroad." This exchange reveals Espada's desire to find an audience and legitimacy for Latino writing in Mexico—which the translation of "Sing Zapatista" has yet to find—while Bañuelos's presence on the commission likely underscored for Espada the role of poets in Mexican society in comparison to the US. As "ONE OF MEXICO'S BEST KNOWN POETS," Pérez-Bustillo tells Espada, Bañuelos would "likely generate lots more income" at their reading, with its modest eighty peso (about eight dollars) admission price. "A paid breakfast with [E]nglish-speaking ladies from the 'American Society'" would presumably do the same ("Mexico—'Sing'"). It may be obvious that a Latino poet visiting Mexico depends on Mexican poets for his reception, but the power of "English-speaking ladies" is a disturbing moment of clarity regarding Latino poetry in Mexico.[15]

These are troubling realities for a poet who believes that poetry can promote emancipation. For this possibility requires a conception of poetry emphasizing its distinctive use-values. After decades of postmodernist delinking of "poetics" from poetry, as Virginia Jackson writes, "put[ting] the poetry back in poetics" (181) is essential to such a conception. "Sing Zapatista" follows the idea that for poetry to participate in changing the world (a politics) it must protect and nurture its linguistic and formal properties (a poetics). Jonathan Culler argues that poetry's "special tenses, such as the lyric present," produce a "distinctive lyric temporality" (205). This tense structures Espada's anaphoric "this is the year" and "sing the word" to buttress the present temporality of Indian resistance, as well as its continuity with past resistance, rather than as a "lost cause" always relegated to repeating defeat. Culler concludes that lyric enacts both "the bodily experience of temporality" and "the formative dwelling in a particular language" (205). Although this idea embeds representative, individuated bourgeois subjectivity, it also illuminates Espada's use of lyric to promote radical subjectivities "dwelling" *between* languages and *in* time. But poetry also has a capacity for reimagining place and space. This lacuna in many conceptions of lyric poetry in the United States is attributable, in part, to its being read doggedly in terms of "timelessness and placelessness" (Jackson 186 n. 4) and "inwardness" (Culler 203). Like many poems in *Broken Souths*, "Sing Zapatista" imparts meaning in time and place by trading the primacy of meditative "inwardness" for a collective orientation to "otherwises" that emerge from "bustle and commotion."

Inter-American Solidarity in "Circle Your Name"

Whereas "Sing Zapatista" directly depicts the Zapatistas with Pérez-Bustillo's assistance, "Circle Your Name" (*Alabanza* 211–213) addresses and is dedicated to Pérez-Bustillo. By asking him to *"Leave México"* after the state declares him a subversive for working with the Zapatistas, the poem makes him a character in an inter-American drama set in the years after NAFTA's passage. In depicting his friend riding a bus through Mexico City, moreover, Espada uses a common figure of the bus to examine literary and legal advocacy under neoliberalism's institutional, extralegal, and infrastructural violence.[16] Allusions to multiple texts in the opening lines connote the power of naming and the risk taken by those who challenge the neoliberal order and those who advocate for them. After an epigraph denoting a space-time (*"Ciudad de México, March 1996"*) and the dedication (*"for Camilo Pérez-Bustillo"*), the poem begins: *"Fingered: Two Hundred Enemies of the System* / says the headline in *Excelsior,* / and your name is on the list / of subversives counted by the state, / your name a strand / in the black braid of names on the page." Counting the title, these four iterations of "name[s]" subvert expectations for a poem dedicated to an individual. Their close repetition reinforces the visual metaphor: "strands" in a single rope convert the isolated individual into a collective of interlocking selves constituted as a subversive, if threatened, public text. This reconfiguration of the state's list of subversives responds to the Mexico City daily's provocative headline. What is often called the *prensa vendida* (the "sell-out" or bought press) in Mexico unwittingly organizes leftists, workers, and advocates into a collective of subversives. In figuring individual actions as compositional elements for collective texts, the poem foregrounds interpretive and revisionary actions—one text's "enemies" constitutes another's heroes. These bifurcated names create the official "headline" and the subsequent revision into a menacing "black braid," with the latter's consonance suggesting power, confrontation, and depth of voice in contrast to the surficial "fingered."

The name "Pérez-Bustillo" thus intertwines in "the black braid of names on the page" with those he represents. An expansive, corollary "black braid of names" spans an astonishing eighty-one dedications in

Espada's collections. Dedicated to poets, activists, and fellow travelers, these poems episodically distill collective modes of emancipation in praise of individuals and convert proximate "names" into collective "braids." Badiou's and Derrida's divergent thoughts on proper names in political movements clarify this relation between individual and collective resistance. Badiou argues for "the vital importance of proper names in all revolutionary politics." "Both spectacular and paradoxical," for him the proper name is a "simple, powerful symbol" combining the "unrepresentable" actions of scores of revolutionaries. Although "emancipatory politics is essentially the politics of the anonymous masses," "it is distinguished all along the way by proper names, which define it historically, which represent it, much more forcefully than is the case for other kinds of politics." "In these proper names," Badiou concludes, "the ordinary individual discovers glorious, distinctive individuals as the mediation for his or her own individuality, as the proof that he or she can force its finitude" (249–250). In Badiou's framework, "Circle Your Name" subsumes nameless Mayan Zapatistas, "bus drivers on strike," "union leaders," and "masked comandantes," under the proper name "Pérez-Bustillo," their advocate and symbolic figure of resistance. His "glorious, distinctive" courage stands in for theirs. In using this conceit of Whitmanian and Nerudian poetics, Espada risks the hierarchical problems of representation examined in Latin American subaltern studies. This dilemma resonates acutely in Espada's "poetics of advocacy," whereby poets speak for the voiceless.[17]

Contra Badiou, Derrida's insights facilitate a clearer, more libratory sense of Espada's rendering of the relation between "proper names" and anonymous subversives. Derrida argues for delinking the proper name from symbolic value to create value outside of (and anterior to) processes of representation. "A man's life, as unique as his death, will always be more than a paradigm and something other than a symbol," Derrida argues, "and this is precisely what a proper name should always name." But, he adds, "having recourse to a common noun" that encompasses and exceeds the "proper name" provides space for collective, symbolic value. Whereas Derrida's "common noun" is "Communist" (xiv), "common nouns" recur across Espada's collections, including "Zapatista," "independentista," "subversive," "compañero," "revolutionary," "Puerto Rican," "worker," "striker," "refugee," "migrant," "squatter," and "exile." His poems weave these common nouns into a textual "black braid of names." In this capacity, the individual "proper name" defers to and supplements the collective, anonymous "common noun," just as "Pérez-Bustillo" becomes "a strand / in the black braid of names on the page." The common yet single "strand"

and the singular "braid" composed of multiple names take precedence over the proper name, the collective text over the individual's act, and rebels (the Zapatistas) over poems advocating for them.

These "common names" portend danger to those who carry them. This is certainly true of the "subversive" Pérez-Bustillo, whom Espada urges to seek refuge in Boston. "Circle Your Name" stresses this invitation but soon moves to images of Pérez-Bustillo continuing his work. His rejection shifts the poem's locus from competing texts and names to Mexico City, where Pérez-Bustillo ignores his safety, "squeezing onto the same bus / every morning to sweat with all the others / who sweat on buses." Espada does not ask us to picture Pérez-Bustillo riding a bus to work each morning but to imagine him taking a *type* of bus—hot, crowded, and full of "all the others" who are condemned by poverty "to sweat on buses" again and again, in the poem's repetition. Whereas taking the bus "beyond the age of twenty-six" testifies to the rider's "failure," in Margaret Thatcher's unsparing dismissal of the vast majority of the world's population who does not own a car (Grescoe 8), in Mexico City the bus has endured as an especially pliable symbol of the city's turbulent history. "Urban transport in Mexico City has been so fundamental to the history of the nation and the experience of its residents," Diane E. Davis argues, "that it constantly emerges in the popular idiom and in literary works as a metaphor for political change and as a source of collective self understanding" (16). Writers have recently critiqued how top-down policy decisions, like highway projects, privilege private (cars) over public (buses, trains) transport. José Joaquín Blanco sees these "solutions" favoring the mobile individual's command over space: "The constructions favoring the individual transportation of the privileged not only take precedence over public transport for the masses but positively hamper it, making it even slower and more tiresome" ("Tacubaya" 198). Although the situation has improved somewhat recently, these observations outline the atomizing and controlling effects of cars alongside their registers of mobility and independence in comparison to "tiresome" buses and trains.

"All the others" is Espada's encompassing figure for those left behind by neoliberal plenty, consigned to one of thousands of *peseros*, Mexico City's privately owned microbuses used by the working poor, those in the vast informal sector, and those coming from or going to places the metro does not. Loosely regulated, often without official stops (but with fixed routes), they can be dangerous, uncomfortable, and unpredictable. *Pesero* stops, Blanco writes, are "blindly and randomly located alongside bridges and highways, surrounded by hulking stairways and tunnels, dusty footways, and hundreds of grimy vending stalls attracting customers who must dodge the powerful vehicles and conduits of the privileged." Like "all the others," these hard-working "leftovers," as Blanco calls outcasts from networks designed for car owners ("Tacubaya" 199), join the "braid" of the *pesero*. Espada pictures Pérez-Bustillo traveling with those he represents, his fate entangled with theirs and their solidarity creating a sweaty collectivity. This image figuratively "braids" together those Harvey calls "the discontented, the alienated, the deprived and the dispossessed" (*Enigma of Capital* 240), which would include lawyer-professors, poets, literary scholars, "all the others," and "leftovers." Together, the latter two symbolize the disposable masses of neoliberal globalization, thereby expanding Thomas Fink's claim that Espada's poetry speaks for a "broader potential coalition" of Latinos (212) to include not only the widely accepted "common names" like "worker" and "immigrant" but also those excluded even from radical Left movements, the "leftovers."

Such solidarities disrupt the state's monopoly on violence in support of corporate power. Pérez-Bustillo is subject to this violence "because" he defends "bus drivers on strike" and "union leaders [who] watch their shadows" on walls of jail cells; each group "need[s] [his] lawyer's words to translate / the echo of their empty mouths." Here Espada links the state's defense of neoliberal policies to the creation of political prisoners, "peasant grave[s]," and "empty mouths" of hunger and alienation. This violence and disciplining of labor were necessary for implementing free-market "reforms" in Mexico, Chile, and elsewhere. Allusions to these contexts for the Zapatista uprising follow the list of subversives as the de facto reason for their "fingering." The thrice repeated "because" in the first stanza echoes the thrice-repeated "name[s]" to dramatize the danger to Pérez-Bustillo. The last refers to the Zapatistas: "because you have seen the masked comandantes / in the mountains, and have sworn to them / that we will know of every peasant grave / shoveled by soldiers, where many fingertips / poke through soil like new shoots of grass."[18] The poem's dateline marks the month in 1996 when the subversives list appeared in *Excelsior,* just after the Zapatistas and the state signed the San Andrés Accords delineating basic tenets of indigenous autonomy and cultural rights that were never honored. Yet the poem was not published until 2001. This date suggests that the Acteal Massacre, on December 22, 1997, when state-sponsored paramilitaries killed forty-five unarmed Maya in a Chiapas village, denied culpability, and expelled human rights workers and journalists (Pérez-Bustillo 180), also explains the poem's urgent tone. Pérez-Bustillo's speech act of swearing to the "masked comandantes

/ in the mountains" also promises to advocate for the Zapatistas and those killed in Acteal.[19] In speaking to his readers, Espada emphasizes a process of rebirth from violence: after being "fingered" as "subversives," murdered, and buried, ecological processes of fertilization nurture new "fingertips" in defiance of oblivion.

This passage creates a transnational form of advocacy by triangulating "you" (Pérez-Bustillo), "them" (the Zapatistas), and "we" (the poet and his readers) into a subversive network united by common knowledge. In this sense, the poem produces embodied human beings from "fingertips" and fertile fields from mere "shoots of grass." Pérez-Bustillo advocates for workers, strikers, the Zapatistas, and "leftovers"; the poem advocates for Pérez-Bustillo by praising him; and "we" advocate for the Maya in what Borges calls "the aesthetic act" of reading (*Selected Poems* 267). This third tier of advocacy tests believability, for the task of translating empathy into action and solidarity into justice remains. A speaker in Pacheco's *I Watch the Earth* responds to the 1985 earthquake in Mexico City with such a question: "What good is my solidarity? / It doesn't clear rubble" (*City of Memory* 117). Indeed, what good is my solidarity to Acteal's victims? Does Espada ask us to imagine impossible, even exploitative, "braids" of solidarity? In critiquing literary-representational modes and the institutionalization of counterdiscourses, Georg M. Gugelberger favors imagining the "possibility of the impossible." In this case, "realizing what we cannot do" — "identify with the subaltern in a gesture of solidarity" — "is a worthy experience of learning" (18) and thus of poetry. Espada stresses the urgency and fragility of this necessary experience, insisting that "what we cannot do" is essential to imagine.[20]

The poem develops the direct, personal advocacy when the speaker "fax[es]" a letter on behalf of Pérez-Bustillo "to Amnesty International / and the Mexican Consulate in Boston." Espada's entreaties to both the state and a human rights NGO, which have proliferated in the neoliberal era as the state retreats from public duties, should also be read in conjunction with another, more nefarious and influential letter-writing campaign during the same time period. In 1995, Chase Manhattan Bank, a cog in the Rockefeller empire, sent a letter to the Mexican government advocating the "elimination" of the Zapatistas (Wypijewski 70). In light of this demand, the danger to Pérez-Bustillo is constituted, like NAFTA, across the Mexico–US border, and between states and global capital. Espada's exacting though largely suggestive imagery of these partnerships and their use of violence is embodied in the corpse of a "judge / who refused to sign an order arresting the strikers." These bullets reverberate from south to north, from Mexico City to Massachusetts, and from the Mexican government to Chase Manhattan's offices, when the judge's "skull bullet-burst like the lightbulb / dropped today on the floor of my kitchen." This simile depicts the threat to those who resist hegemonic power, suggesting a fundamental relation between skulls (in "peasant graves" and judicial chambers) and the products (lightbulbs) and privileges (electricity) of relative wealth delivered through uneven infrastructure.

Thereafter the poem shifts space-times to Chile in 1973 to stake equivalencies between an informant there "saying with a finger" whom to condemn and the one who "fingered" Pérez-Bustillo. This "finger" links the counter-revolution's violence in Chile to Mexico and resistance to it onto the shared common noun "subversive."[21] In the last stanza, the speaker commands Pérez-Bustillo to make a monument celebrating his "subversive" status: "Unfold the newspaper hidden in your desk. / Circle your name as the informer did. / Frame the headline and the black braid of names; / dangle the frame from a crooked nail." This act converts "the black braid of names" from the newsprint of the *prensa vendida* into a three-dimensional monument with dual registers. As a private one, it hangs in Pérez-Bustillo's office; public, it shape-shifts into a statue in a plaza: "The marble general on horseback in the plaza / will rear up, his mustache bristling with jealousy / at your unwanted prize."[22]

Although Espada does not name or place "the marble general," Mexico City's ideologically charged monuments suggest a symbolically resonant location: Paseo de la Reforma, the iconic avenue running from Chapultepec Park into the historic center, central plaza (*Zócalo*), and beyond. The Haussmann-style boulevard became a key vector for narrating Mexican national history and identity during the decades-long dictatorship of Porfirio Díaz at the turn of the twentieth century that ushered in and consolidated the capitalist era. During this reign, monuments to Juárez, Columbus, Cuauhtémoc, and Independence ("El Ángel") were built along Reforma. "The honor of announcing the boulevard went to Spain's Carlos IV, an inept king," Michael Johns writes. This statue was built in 1803 by Mexican royalists, and later moved to the Bucareli, "where Reforma would later begin." El Caballito, as the statue came to be called, depicts Carlos IV on horseback, with a sword and a laurel wreath (Johns 25). This "rearing equestrian statue" (Sheridan 150), a monument to official colonial history, approximates the representation Espada dismantles and appropriates for subversive means.[23]

The construction of monuments during the Porfiriato aimed to erase the contradictions of Mexican history. "Aristocrats," Johns writes, "took their history lesson each day as they rode along Reforma to and from Chapultepec Park" (27). Mauricio Tenorio Trillo describes this enduring "history lesson" as a palindrome that forecloses dissonance and pluralism: "the ideal city acquired a coherent set of icons that made the idea of nation discursively, ideologically and physically real." "Whether read from the Zócalo to Chapultepec or from Chapultepec to the Zócalo," he writes, "the Paseo de la Reforma told the same story, fulfilling the ideal of a patriotic history: to make history a perfect unmistakable palindrome, with no conflicts or contradictions" (97–98). Imagine, then, accompanying Pérez-Bustillo in a *pesero* along Reforma, monuments "rear[ing] up" as we pass. Imagine, too, the alternative "idea of nation" carried within the bus and promoted by the Zapatista resistance to "oblivion" in favor of "a world capable of containing all the worlds" (Marcos 284).[24] The contradictions contained in the *pesero*—between mobility and confinement, hard work and endless poverty, and being hot and crowded on a wide, shady boulevard, with sweaty "brilliant" skin shimmering like Reforma's glass hotels, condos, and offices—create not "a coherent set of icons" but a mobile monument to sweat, perseverance, and resistance to the logic that only market valuations matter. If Mexico City "coheres," Juan Villoro writes, it is "because it can be traversed" (124). In a fragmented, dispersed city, traversal in a *pesero* challenges any claims of equality and access for "leftovers."

The poem suggests how actual oppressions (overcrowded buses) and symbols of them (marble generals) might be converted to solidarities for rethinking city and nation as pluralist asymmetries rather than palindromes. This concept of collective liberation diverges from the exclusively economic freedom of neoliberal ideology. But it is not purely positive, just as the poet's act of advocacy remains insufficient for helping his friend and for changing economic and social conditions. The very acts of laborers "squeez[ing] in" and "sweating" each day ensure the "freedom" of the corporate, managerial, and owning classes. Rather than "failures," as Thatcher claimed, the bus riders are bondholders and trustees of this freedom, and the poem empowers their mobile, collective sweat into a textual figure of power. The bus, then, serves as a complex symbol for these contradictions of individual ownership and collective oppression. As a student in the 1968 Student movement told Elena Poniatowska, "We take over the buses because [. . .] buses don't belong to the people; they belong to the bus companies" (78). Moreover, in reading poems about Lima's buses, Kuhnheim writes, "The bus is a microcosm [. . .] of a certain portion of the city" in "bring[ing] together a conglomeration of people" (107–108).

She offers three possibilities for viewing the bus as a place: "its own place, another contemporary 'no-place,' or a mobile place that is a part of the city itself" (109). In Espada's poem, the bus is a moving vantage point from which to critique official narratives; it is also a space of slippage, where "perfect palindromes" of progress meet their exceptions. In the words of Bolaño's poem "Ernesto Cardenal and I," the bus carries "those who really truly / can't take it anymore" (*Romantic Dogs* 13) but heroically continue to do so.[25]

In mapping apparent mobility ("free trade," market "freedom," transportation) to actual confinement (graves, prison cells, crowded buses) and official texts (subversive lists, monuments) to extralegal violence (Acteal, labor suppression), "Circle Your Name" depicts marble and textual monuments serving the state's neoliberal policy goals of privatization, deregulation, and unrestrained freedom for capital interests. Although these monuments to surveillance, repression, and authoritarianism seem calcified, they are actually subject to subversion. As in the dancing feet in the plaza in "Sing Zapatista," "Circle Your Name" imagines such resistance emerging from the ground up, in "sweaty" collectivities traversing the city and in "new shoots of grass" in Chiapas and Morelos. Most powerfully, solidarity and collective memory circulate in a form of public transportation, the microbus, in a space—Reforma—where this memory and imagination are least welcome and most dissonant.

Rereading "1968," Mapping Blank Pages

Whereas "Sing Zapatista" models a mobile, multilingual defense of place, and "Circle Your Name" tacks transnational solidarity to the "common name" and the bus, Pacheco's "1968" maps a cartography of erasure, disordered temporality, and diminished humanity under neoliberal hegemony. If Espada "sing[s]" against "the shoe," Pacheco offers silence, not as Bartlebian protest but as the counter-revolution's enduring legacy. Whereas "timelessness and placelessness" certainly *serve* the neoliberal worldview, "1968" goes further to suggest that they *are* the worldview. The narratives of 1968 have had lasting effects on Latino and Latin American cultural production in general and on Mexican and Chicano literary practices in particular. The massacre of hundreds of unarmed young people in Plaza de Tres Culturas (Tlatelolco) in Mexico City, on October 2, 1968, just days before the start of the Summer Olympics there, and after months of marches and demonstrations led by the Mexican Student Movement, often serves as a metonym for a year of promise and devastation. Tlatelolco marked the beginning of the Partido Revolucionario Institucional's (PRI's) long demise, which (temporarily) ended with Fox's inauguration in 2001. But it also closed a brief era of utopian promise symbolized by the Student Movement. On the fortieth anniversary of 1968, the Mexican intellectual Carlos Monsiváis wrote that the year's events are frequently reduced to "the defenseless multitude in Tlatelolco" (*El 68* 237). He concedes this reduction's partial accuracy, given the movement's animation by potential "otherwises." "It is terrible to describe a movement by its victims," Monsiváis writes, but they "became victims for believing possible the creation of alternatives" (*El 68* 237).[26] Monsiváis explains that 1968 remains central to Mexican narratives through its grip on aesthetic imaginaries, as a store of symbols, images, and myths (*El 68* 29–30). 1968 retains a "revolutionary textuality," in de la Campa's terms (*Latin Americanism* 42), continually reconstituting historical memory as a poetics. Nearly every major Mexican poet, and many Latino writers, after all, has written about Tlatelolco. As Monsiváis says, books about 1968 cover "hundreds of miles," and poets play key roles in its ongoing importance (*El 68* 29).[27]

Expanding readings of 1968 beyond Tlatelolco, Mexican history, and civil rights movements in the United States frames the year's symbolic role in neoliberalism's hemispheric ascent. Many critics suggest the origins, motivations, and targets of neoliberalism emerged from the events of 1968. Harvey begins his history of neoliberalism by referring to the global urban uprisings of 1968, while Hopenhayn indicates that the "pitiless counterreaction from above" was in part motivated by 1968 movements (30). Recuperating "to break," the guiding leftist infinitive of 1968, in relation to "broken" spaces produced through neoliberal upheaval, contests neoliberal depictions of 1968 movements as aberrations, errors of judgment, and isolated attempts to promote outdated social models. Monsiváis argues that the neoliberal project ascended in the early 1980s in Mexico, with austerity, privatization, and deregulation, in part through its unrelenting ideological dismissal of the events of 1968 as "local" occurrences and student goals of justice and equality as "idealismo romántico" and "el delirio de la guerrilla" (*El 68* 235). As an imaginary, 1968's collective spirit of "to break" underlines ("subrayar") the current era's cynicism, which Monsiváis defines through the prefix "post-" common to postmodern and neoliberal ideological constructs. Such constructs promote a singularized "post-militante, post-activista, post-cívico" subjectivity (*El 68* 236) that mirrors the US version. In this strategic temporal break advanced by neoliberalism's defenders, including skeptics of solidarity, collectivity, and activism on the Left, the movements of 1968 become "premoderno," part of an irrelevant, idealistic past (*El 68* 236). As such, it is critical to retrieve what neoliberalism effaces in promoting itself as universal and progressive: the idea that other worlds *were* and *are* possible.

Pacheco's "1968" keeps this possibility radically open. Critics generally privilege temporality and postmodern textuality in reading Pacheco, but I see these features as components of a place-based ecopoetics that reconstructs Mexico City from a range of national, regional, and global literary geographies.[28] In Pacheco's texts, nothing is merely a "local" phenomenon, as in the neoliberal reckoning of 1968 that contradicts its "placelessness." "1968" is itself part of a suite of 1968 poems originally published in *Don't Ask Me How the Time Goes By* (26–29), which won Mexico's National Poetry Prize and arguably cemented Pacheco's reputation as "THE BEST" of the generation following Octavio Paz. The original "1968" invokes W. B. Yeats's "Easter, 1916." The first lines modify its famous refrain, "All changed, changed utterly: / A terrible beauty is born," by dropping its orders of magnitude ("utterly") and aesthetic discernment ("terrible beauty"). They emphasize the "break," capitalist modes of creative destruction, and indeed the logic of modernism: "A world comes apart / a world is born."[29]

Nearly all of the original poem's provocative language is gone by 2000. In his third edition of complete poems, *Tarde o temprano*, the twenty-five-line "1968" is diminished to two:

> Página blanca al fin:
> todo es posible.
> [At the end, a blank page:
> everything is possible.] (67; my translation)

As the remains of an ambitious poem, it is tempting to focus on what's been lost rather than gained. The cuts might be attributed to an extreme instance of Pacheco's practice of constant revision or as consolidated, momentary clarity following decades of neoliberal ascendancy. Whatever the case, this revision offers chilling lucidity, and it reinforces Ronald J. Friis's sense that 1968—the year—was a "political turning point" for Pacheco's writing (175). Underlying this lucidity are Pacheco's frequent figures of human depravity as corollaries to neoliberal conceptions of *homo economicus*. The revised poem, as a fragment of the original and a reduction of it, depicts the humanity wrenched from neoliberalism's "disposable" populations, in Henry A. Giroux's term. If the hope embodied in 1968 is diminished dramatically by 2000, the inverse applies for Mexico's extremely wealthy. In 1988, Mexico had two billionaires; in 2000, twenty-four. Just one equaled the income of the seventeen million poorest Mexicans (Bell Lara and López 23). To leave the poem in its original state would be to see poems as artifacts rather than living texts continually reproduced between writers and readers. Mary Docter argues that Pacheco "offers up his work as something not yet finished and searches for a reader to complete a process he could only begin" (374). This idea includes Pacheco as a reader of his own work. Because texts "necessarily produce yet other relations" over time, "not because the words have changed, but because *we* are different," Docter writes (388), "1968" reflects on its own textuality through diminution. For readers to finish the poem magnifies their own diminished civic roles as citizen-consumers, even as it empowers them to fill in the blank page with their own speculations.

With the symbolic registers of the "blank page" and the shift from the many (twenty-five lines) to the few, the revised "1968" captures the core logic of the neoliberal project. From Chile in 1973 to Hurricane Katrina, neoliberals have created and capitalized on disaster and state violence to institute sweeping free-market "reforms." With a blank slate, the thinking goes, it is easier to remake the world in the image of capital. This is why Klein uses "blank" to describe the logic: "This desire for godlike powers of total creation is precisely why free-market ideologues are so drawn to crises and disasters." "What has animated Friedman's counterrevolution is," she writes, "an attraction to a kind of freedom and possibility available only in times of cataclysmic change—when people, with their stubborn habits and insistent demands, are blasted out of the way—moments when democracy seems a practical impossibility" (25). Neoliberalism both requires and produces "Broken Souths," its alpha and omega. On this claustrophobic plane, the violent suppression of Tlatelolco and the Left's defeats (and tentative civil rights victories in the United States) in 1968 resonate symbolically as neoliberalism's initial conditions of possibility. This logic of erasing and remaking frames neoliberalism as a dystopian political project, where the ideal of the free market is often little more than an ideological apparatus justifying plunder.[30] Further, Pacheco's erasure of everything but the "blank page" and the perpetually present "todo es posible" signify the neoliberal rejection of historical, geographical, ecological, and social contexts.

Revising Espada, "this [was] the year" in which all seemed radically open on the Left and, in hindsight, the Right. There's the rub in Pacheco's revision. The latter version captures the spirit of utopian possibility bound up in the urban revolutions of 1968, but from the vantage point of their failure. The historically expansive title, the lyric present tense, and the radically inclusive "possible" create a dialectic between revolution and counter-revolution. These tensions are latent in the "blank page," hidden in traces under the erasures. The poem's proximity in the original collection to those about the conquest, the Vietnam War, Che Guevara, and Tlatelolco reminds us that the "blank page" applied to both Left revolutionary and Right counter-revolutionary (anti-communist) ideologies. Capitalism, in this sense, always has a "permanently revolutionary character" (Harvey, *Enigma of Capital* 127). "Revolution itself, that 'modern' idea," de Certeau writes, "represents the scriptural project at the level of an entire society seeking to *constitute itself* as a blank page with respect to the past, to write itself by itself" (135). This convergent thinking across the late 1960s political spectrum has profound implications for conceptions of place and space. Place is an impediment to be overcome, just as capital sees "barriers" (rather than "limits") to movement and accumulation. All places, moreover, become subject to identical economic laws (neoliberalism) or empancipatory historical forces (Left revolution). Neoliberalism's "vision of a singular economy, valid in all places and at all historical moments," after all, "scorns the historical, social, and political complexity of developing nations" (Valdés 275, 277). This does not suggest that the Left was equally scornful, just that it was unreceptive to place as a "project." Vanguard leftist movements also descended "from above." Part of what motivated 1968 movements, Badiou recalls, "was the conviction that [they] had to do away with places" and "spatial hierarchies" (60). In these contexts, a Latino Left, as Beverley writes of its Latin American counterpart, must develop a politics (and a poetics) without a modernist teleology ("Dos caminos"). With internal cultural diversities and place-based figurations of "to break" rather than a "blank page," the poetics of "Broken Souths" contests these "timeless," "placeless" universals.

Pacheco's "blank page" incorporates the possibility of revolution and counter-revolution but its flat affect foregrounds the latter's triumph. This dynamic between possibility and reality is, in part, a matter of language. When Hopenhayn says that "neoliberalism appropriated the word 'revolution,' stuffing it with the euphoria of worldwide capitalism in the making" (15), he suggests the triumph of neoliberal thinking over language, literary and otherwise. "This uncritical triumphalism," he concludes, "announces the end of ideologies and of utopias even as it tries to construct itself as the only ideology and utopia" (27). Pacheco clarifies this delinking of reality from representation by making the "blank page" a mystifying force. Badiou has this mystification in mind in positing: "the real outcome and the real hero of '68 is unfettered neo-liberal capitalism" (44). When neoliberalism is seen as the individuated "hero" of 1968, collective forms, including labor unions, social security, and public education, not to mention socialism, become political evils to eradicate. The "blank page" symbolizes the counter-revolution's goal of erasure. "This imperative," Klein notes, "was reflected in the dominant metaphors" used in the Southern Cone's neoliberal turn. Euphemisms of "cleaning," "scrubbing," and "uprooting" (Klein 129) are violent figures of the "blank page."

Yet the "blank page" also carries the possibility of radical literary creation within its neutral-sounding, though nefarious, source. On one hand, this means the emptied, free-floating "revolution" is used to market sodas and sneakers. On the other, Gaston Bachelard's idea that the poetic image "is not an echo of the past" but always "the sign of a new being" (xvi, xxix) takes the "blank page" as a suitable surface for the arrival of newness, a correlative trope of its "sign," or an energizing site of radical potentiality. Yet the revised "1968" testifies to the impossibility and undesirability of the "blank page," as well as the insurmountable challenge of any project that attempts "to write itself by itself." Whereas "todo es posible" includes the erasure of place, history, and memory as possibilities, Pacheco's remaining lines retain a lucidity testifying to neoliberalism's inability to destroy the possibility of other possibilities. If 1968 is "a sort of historical poem that gives us new courage," as Badiou proffers (44), what remains, the year *as* a revisable text, also conjures what's been erased.

And yet the revised "1968" maps the featureless cartography of a single blank page. Its putatively fixed, measureable dimensions dismiss relationality, margins, other texts, all contexts, the constraints and processes of the natural world, transgressions of all sorts, and the idea that "pages" themselves may differ. In this absolute space, the tyrannical godlike individual writes his script without regard to others. In this sense, the neoliberal conversion of 1960s struggles for more capacious individual freedoms into an atomized economic freedom of equal exchange was brilliantly conceived. Harvey writes, "The founding figures of neoliberal thought took political ideals of human dignity and individual freedom" as "the central values of civilization" and argued that they were threatened by state planning, unions, and all sorts of collective forms (*Brief History* 5).[31] This view has helped to produce "the neoliberal discourse of 'super individualization'" (Derksen 66), which foists full responsibility on the individual. In Pacheco's poetics, "super individualization" forecloses borrowing, intertextuality, and "collective" literary creation, his figures for the abiding interpersonal dimensions of cultural forms. His "'Yo' With a Capital 'I,'" for instance, laments how radical individualism diminishes literary language, empathy for others, and the common good: "'I' comes first, / and the other verb forms / are always diminished" (*City of Memory* 167). If the author, with a capital A, is the prototypically imperious individual who rules the "blank page," the foreclosure of collaboration is a tragedy that drastically limits human expressive capacity.

Because the "blank page" threatens the main tenet of Pacheco's poetics, the figure is his sharpest condemnation of neoliberal thought. The trope halts exchanges of ideas, intertextual borrowings and allusions, and interactions between and among texts, writers, and readers. Most of all, it undermines the idea that poetry is "collective." In Marxist thinking, changes emerge from extant material conditions. So too for Pacheco's poetics, which makes texts from other texts. As Docter shows, Pacheco writes "original poem[s] entirely from previous texts" (376).[32] When the "previous texts" are "blank pages," this type of writing is impossible. While Pacheco's "blank page" initially seems to share qualities with his trope of "anonymity," the latter effaces authorial presence in favor of texts and readers who "co-author" them anew. It is in this sense that Pacheco's poetics critiques complicity between neoliberal ideology and postmodernist cultural modes. De la Campa writes that both efface "the nitty-gritty nature of history" with "tropes that compress, or dismiss, social specificity" (*Latin Americanism* 11, 20). This compression converts Latin America's internal diversities into a homogenized "blank page" that reproduces "backyard" and "Convenience Store" constructs, as detailed in my introduction.

"The future," Derksen writes, is neoliberalism's "fatal flaw" (37). Without a past, and in a present bereft of alternatives, the "blank" horizon lacks ground for rebuilding. As the Student Movement crested in Mexico, in the United States, the Chicano movement was beginning and Herrera was starting a poetic project that would deploy, critique, and reinvent the images of each. Chapter 2 examines how this leading Chicano poet reconciles the collectivism of 1968 to the individualistic present and to the future of the United States, in which Latinos are ascendant. Like Espada, he depicts the Zapatistas from a transnational Latino subjectivity that emerges in revolutionary texts and images. Unlike him, however, Herrera eschews lucidity for restless, playful, and unpredictable experimentation.

CHAPTER TWO

Molotovs and Subtleties

Juan Felipe Herrera's
Post-Movement *Norteamérica*

*A baby molotov, at midnight—the East L.A. method. Good thing it didn't
go off. But, they got el mensaje. We invented Chicano Studies, con manos
limpias en las mañanas, demanding our rights (this sounds old now but
we did demand our rights). With our language, our home-poems, our long
walks and fasts for justice. [. . .] I can say this. This was our starting point.
[. . .]*

—Herrera, "How to Enroll in a Chicano Studies Class"
(*Notebooks* 127)

*Them or us, I would say: take your pick, I would say, ten million starving
children or a couple of bourgeois counterrevolutionaries. It was not a time
for subtleties.*

—Ariel Dorfman, *Heading South, Looking North* (96)

While Earl Shorris declares Espada *"the* Latino poet of his generation,"
Francisco A. Lomelí calls Herrera *the* "voice of the overall Chicano experience" (xv). They are indeed two "of the few Latino poets in this country
to have any kind of forum," as Espada describes his status ("'Taking Back'"
540). When Herrera was appointed poet laureate of California—the first
Latina/o to be so named—in the spring of 2012, he secured his standing
as perhaps the most visible Latino poet. This honor came on the heels
of a National Book Critics Circle award and a *New York Times Book Review* Notable Book of the Year honor for *Half of the World in Light: New
and Selected Poems*. Herrera and Espada represent the best of unique but
convergent strains of Latino poetry, with different historical-geographic
contexts, aesthetic practices, and influences. Herrera's improvisational
mysticism complements Espada's highly crafted materialism. Together,

they showcase the dexterous heterogeneities and figurative critiques of neoliberal capitalism in Latino poetics, from within Chicano and Nuyorican literary geographies, respectively.

As this chapter's first epigraph implies, Herrera navigates 1968's inventive language of collective agitation, with its locus in the Chicano movement, and the neoliberal present, where identities are produced in the market rather than through cultural nationalism and political solidarity. Whereas a masculinist, hierarchical nationalism malformed the Chicano movement's otherwise just aims for self-determination, as Monsiváis points out the "post-" era dismisses collective movements and revolutions as relics of a misguided, idealistic past or reserves them for other geographies (i.e., the Middle East). "Post-" constructions of hegemonic neoliberalism parallel mappings of Chicano (and Latino) poetry. Periodizing terms such as "Post-Sixties" (Dalleo and Machado Sáez), "After Aztlán" (Ray Gonzalez), and the customary "post-movement" divide the late 1960s to early 1970s from the present. Even the common "generation" has this implication. Oliver-Rotger writes that Herrera "straddle[s] generations" between movement nationalism and post-movement transnationalism, arguing that *Mayan Drifter: A Chicano Poet in the Lowlands of America*, a prose autoethnography of his travels in Chiapas, rejects the movement's "romantic emphasis" on Chicanos' indigenous roots (171–172). Herrera critiques simplistic *indigenismo*, but he writes passionately about indigenous cultures, and movement ideals and languages remain present in his texts, if in new, critical, and reflective forms. In fact, Herrera reconciles "molotovs" and "subtleties," provocative metonyms of the two eras, as dialectical poles in an animated, embodied poetics in which bold collective action and enticingly individuated artistic freedom converge. This poetics reconciles two primary Latino critical modes identified by Dalleo and Machado Sáez—collectivist "anticolonialist resistance" and individualist "multicultural synthesis" (10)—somewhat surprisingly by viewing "revolution" as a living historical possibility alternately repressed and animated by neoliberal capitalism.[1]

The division between collective forms ("our language") and "subtleties" (qualified individual responses to oppression) structures the epigraphs' reflections on the period 1968–73 from the "post-" revolutionary present. In *Heading South, Looking North*, a memoir of Salvador Allende's revolution and the coup of September 11, the Latino-Chilean exile Ariel Dorfman describes this divide by lamenting the appropriation and commodification of "the word *revolution*," which "has been relegated to ads for jogging shoes." "Cynicism," he continues, "is the prevailing attitude and amnesia is vaunted and justified as the solution to all the pain of the past" (261). Dorfman's breathy, exasperated prose captures the shift from collective outrage to pacified "post-history" ("amnesia") consumption. Whereas Allende's "peaceful road to socialism" remains a point of pride for Dorfman, its failure to build political-economic coalitions that might have prevented the coup offers harsh lessons on the utility of violence, whatever its ethical deficiencies. The epigraph's conditional clauses ("I would say") underscore this utilitarian view. Whereas his memoir dramatizes how complicated and nuanced revolutionary ideals were lived between 1968 and 1973, the conclusion is deceptively simple: "It was not a time for subtleties." Dorfman's implicit apologia for his youthful beliefs emerges from a putatively enlightened, realistic, and measured present defined by intellectual "subtleties."

As a keyword of the split between eras, "subtlety" approaches critical-intellectual consensus, apart from critics working in Marxist traditions. In reading Dorfman's memoir, for instance, Sophie A. McClennen never uses "capitalism," "capital," "free market," "neoliberalism," "labor," "union," or "socialism" and includes but three surficial references to "revolution." Omitting these words is possible only in a hegemonic "post-" framework that produces ahistorical phrases such as "the historical moment that destroyed the collective of which Dorfman was an active member." In this frame, the coup and its aftermaths are merely "moment[s] in Chilean history" scarring the individual (178, 186 n. 9), *not* epoch-making global events. Yet the commonsense claim "It was not a time for subtleties" is doubly specious. Not only were there subtleties then, but current conditions require overt actions. Should vast inequalities, bought elections, corporations-as-persons, environmental devastations, mass incarcerations of African Americans and Latinos, and legal defenses of torture produce "subtle" responses?[2]

Herrera's dialogic poetics reconciles "molotovs" and "subtleties" by finding innovative forms to express a spirit of direct, uncompromising action within the openings for individual expression under neoliberal citizenship modes and postmodernist aesthetics. His texts give new life to the displaced image stores and floating signifiers of "revolution" putatively left behind ("post-"). Extending Lomelí's terms, Herrera is an "alchemist" and "inimitable synthesizer" (xvi) of past and present subjectivities. In contrast to Dorfman's repeated "I would say," which reenacts a past speech act in conditional language, the prose poem "How to Enroll in a Chicano Studies Class" reinscribes the language discourses of "subtleties" obfuscate. Herrera's repetition of "demands" tacks the unequivocal, direct actions of the past to present languages. The poem's dateline, "Spring, '68," locates the foundational moment of the Chicano movement—the "blowouts" or "walkouts"—and the phrases "demanding our rights" and "we did demand our rights" match actions to ideals. In these ways, "long walks," "fasts for justices," and "home-poems" symbolize two fronts in the struggle to create a new collective identity through creative self-determination ("*our* language") and institutional agency ("we invented Chicano Studies").

When Herrera code switches to an image of clean hands ("manos limpias en las mañanas"), he symbolizes the movement's righteousness and the dawn of a new identity. This iteration of "to break" was a core belief of student movements: that new identities are born through collective action. "The Chicano Movement was a historic first attempt," Muñoz writes, "to shape a politics of unification" by Mexican American students and workers. "The movement," he continues, "rejected all previous identities and thus represented a counter-hegemonic political and cultural project" (22). Although Herrera's passage covers both fronts of this "project," like Dorfman he is hesitant, even apologetic, about the era's Molotov cocktails ("Good thing it didn't go off") and assertion of demands ("this sounds old now"). As such, he sounds uncertain even when putatively assertive ("I can say this"), as if trying to convince himself about the wisdom of his younger self. Tacitly admitting that subtlety trumps direct action seems to say *we know better now*. Yet these self-reflexive asides should be read within Herrera's reinscriptions of the past, which take three forms in his texts: reasserting demands that "post-" discourses erase the need for, critiquing the movement language of the late 1960s to early 1970s that misapprehends and displaces the realities of the present, and finding new forms to express demands again.

As "el mensaje" ("the message"), the "molotov" delivered a warning about the movement's commitment to action. But it is also the message's *symbol* that defined its revolutionary, improvisational, even reckless "method[s]." In this sense, the poem delivers a message to contemporary readers with a dialectical "method" that puts the past in dialogue with present realities ("this sounds old now"). Andres Rodriguez writes that Chicano "revolutionary activists of the sixties fail[ed] to pass on the lessons of struggle and pride" to later generations. This was partly an aesthetic failure, he claims, because movement poets had "the subtlety of howitzers." This implicit opposition between "message" (as "lessons") and "subtlety" (as "method") highlights how Herrera "pass[es] on" the movement's spirit by undermining specious dichotomies dividing the eras:

molotov/subtlety, direct/indirect, obvious/ambiguous, reckless/measured, active/passive, action/thought, violence/nonviolence, and revolution/ assimilation. Rejecting these "post-" binaries requires seeing "demands" as the cause of Latinos' substantive progress and the back story of neoliberal alienations and inequities. After all, gains by Latinos and other groups made through collective struggle in the late 1960s to early 1970s have animated a vigorous counter-reaction. "That era of revolutionary upheaval," Muñoz writes, "gave way to a conservative counter-revolution" focused on "market-centered neoliberal restructuring" and "fueled by a backlash against the gains" of oppressed groups (223).

As in Pacheco's "1968," this historical dialectic has roots in student movements' two fronts of resistance: the repressive state and capitalism. By the late 1960s the rich had seen their power, influence, and share of wealth diminish, in part through welfare-state redistributions. With its scorn for state intervention in the market and its belief in the capitalist marketplace as the sole guarantor of freedom, the counter-revolution took advantage of the first front of discontent. Milton Friedman and others demonized the state and, implicitly, gains made by Latinos, African Americans, and women through civil rights legislation, which required state intervention. The "neoliberal market-based populist culture of differentiated consumerism and individual libertarianism," Harvey explains, required "a practical strategy that emphasized the liberty of consumer choice, not only with respect to particular products but also with respect to lifestyles, modes of expression, and a wide range of cultural practices" (*Brief History* 42). In converting collectivist identities into consumer "lifestyles" bereft of the movement's revolutionary spirit, this shift helped to produce "Hispanicization," the process by which Chicano identity was consumed in an "all-encompassing category" that effaces differences between Latino groups (Libretti 139). Herrera calls the literary-economic arm of this process the "Hispanic Movimiento Advertising Machine," which has "spawn[ed] a new generation of 'melting pot' ventriloquists" (*Notebooks* 105). In this way, the backlash from the Right accompanied the subsumption of Chicano identity into a free-market, consumerist Latinidad, as another multicultural identity to be packaged and sold. In combination, they relegated collective struggle to an irretrievable past and left the "new generation" with "ventriloquist" rhetoric.

This story finds a new focus in Arizona's 2011 banning of the acclaimed Mexican American Studies program of the Tucson Unified School District. The program was deemed illegal based on Arizona H.B. 2281 (2010), passed with support from John Huppenthal, then a legislator and now the law's main proponent as Arizona's superintendent of public instruction. The law prohibits programs that "promote the overthrow of the United States government," "promote resentment toward a race or class of people," or "advocate ethnic solidarity instead of the treatment of pupils as individuals" ("Rejected in Tucson"). The breadth and depth of these three prohibitions are stunning, for they focus broadly on erasing histories of oppression and the texts that emerge from dispossession to challenge official narratives of progress that frequently exclude and exploit groups of people. The second and third tenets pinpoint the neoliberal project's logic and practice. The second protects official capitalist history, which deemphasizes (or elides) class relations. At the same time, it ensures the rights of the rich *as a class* to guide the education of working-class students and to be insulated from their distrust (and disgust). The third dramatizes the legacy of the counter-revolution, as outlined by Harvey and Muñoz. Collective identities must be legislated against vigorously when they challenge the free market's inclusiveness, particularly when their historical and economic contexts provide evidence of violence and exclusion. Herrera's texts anticipate these prohibitions by reconciling "pupils as individuals" to "ethnic solidarity." In his view, their convergence produces radical individual creativity and radical collective awareness of capitalism's harms.[3]

Against essentialized ethnic-national identities, which counter-intuitively reinforce inequality, Herrera creates dynamic forms and subjectivities to reinvigorate Chicano and Latino solidarities. Below, I explore how *Notebooks of a Chile Verde Smuggler* evaluates Chicano movement ideals and iconography. I then analyze how "One Year Before the Zapatista Rebellion" and *Mayan Drifter* meditate on "the Indian," "revolution," the Zapatistas, and the difficulty of writing about Mexico from the United States. Next, I discuss "Norteamérica, I Am Your Scar" and "A Day Without a Mexican: Video Clip" as pinnacles of Herrera's poetics of reconciliation. Respectively, they convert assimilation to resistance and commodified revolutionary signs to tools of collective struggle.

Measuring the "Event" of 1968

No Latino writer mines the territory between 1968 and the neoliberal present with greater skill and passion than Herrera. *Half of the World in Light* spans from his early poems (1969–73) and first collection (1974) to a surreal, haunting section of new poems. The collection opens with the

Chicano movement's iconography, neologisms, code switching, and spoken rhythms. "Moctezuma blood and spirit," Ipal Nemohuani (Huitzilopochtli, the god of war), Zapata, Tláloc, "maiztlán" (combining maíz and Aztlán), Quetzalcóatl, and "[A]merindia" showcase movement poetry's store of allusions (3–20).[4] Thereafter, Herrera's poems track what Rafael Pérez-Torres calls "the discontinuities that will mark the procession of Chicano culture" from the late 1960s to the present (*Movements* 76). The collection's last poem, "Let Me Tell You What a Poem Brings," consolidates his *ars poetica*: "the mist becomes central to your existence" (301). Contrasts between Herrera's "mist" and Espada's lucidity are substantial. Yet Herrera's poetry published in the interim creates continuities that keep Aztec gods present in "the mist" and "molotovs" exploding amid "subtleties." In Herrera, the past is omnipresent, if in traces. As such, he explores Pérez-Torres's questions about whether the movement created "real change": "Has it enabled Chicanas a degree of self-determination previously not possible? And if it has, has that empowerment led to a clearer inscription or greater erasure of Chicana culture and differentiation? [. . .] How can one address the relationship between cultural self-identification and the history of territorial dispossession from which it arises?" (*Movements* 76–77).

Even Herrera's "subtle" answers are explosive. Badiou's and Slavoj Žižek's conceptions of the "event" illuminate how he evaluates the movement by reconciling emancipatory and assimilationist identities. For Badiou, an "event" is "a rupture in the normal order of bodies and languages as it exists for any particular situation." Because it creates "new possibilities," "it is located not merely at the level of objective possibilities but at the level of the possibility of possibilities" (242–243). This enigmatic definition follows the logic of "to break": the "event" has material and philosophical dimensions, including the possibility of creating new ontological and epistemological formations. The Chicano movement's "events" include the "blowouts," the birth of Chicano/Latino studies, and an identity whose language and history fractures the "normal order." Now, when structural alternatives do not seem like "objective possibilities," the idea that "events" exist "at the level of the possibility of possibilities" reopens debates about how to create "ruptures." This strategy allows us to denounce the movement's patriarchal hierarchies and homophobia, as well as its tacit suspicion of reflective forms of political engagement, while reinvigorating its orientation toward collective liberation and structural change.

In contrast to Badiou, Žižek evaluates the "event" through its putative opposite, "the everyday," and by rejecting the binary between activity and

passivity common to 1968 narratives. "The key test of every radical emancipatory movement is," Žižek argues, "to what extent it transforms on a
daily basis the *practico-inert* institutional practices which gain the upper
hand once the fervor of the struggle is over and people return to business
as usual." He concludes, "The success of a revolution should not be measured by the sublime awe of its ecstatic moments, but by the changes the
big Event leaves at the level of the everyday, the day after the insurrection"
(153–154). To evaluate the "event," Žižek favors the criteria of "business as
usual" to "fervor" and "awe." According to this "test," the Chicano movement achieved some success, particularly in the distillation of cultural
pride into artistic forms. Although the recent attack on the Mexican American studies program in Tucson is a huge setback, late 1960s movements
transformed "institutional practices" in secondary and higher education.
Latino studies programs are prominent across the United States, but laws
in Arizona (S.B. 1070, 2010), Alabama (H.B. 56, 2011), and elsewhere
have funneled the collection of anti-immigrant tropes Leo R. Chavez calls
"the Latino Threat Narrative" into legal-institutional forms. Moreover,
gentrification and housing struggles are major problems "at the level of the
everyday" under neoliberalism's urban economic-legal regimes. In these
contexts, Žižek's "test" of radical movements begs a question that hounds
Herrera: how can Latino writers combine "fervor" (inspiration) and "the
everyday" (work, struggle) in the context of new (and old) oppressions?
Badiou's conceptions of the past in literary terms offer insight. As "the real
hero of '68," neoliberal capitalism's individualism and "garish world of all
sorts of consumerism" (44) forecloses collective "demands," "messages,"
"methods," and "events." Whereas Herrera's epigraph shows that there was
a clear "they" in 1968 ("they got el mensaje") when the antagonist was the
nation-state, now the "hero" is global capitalism. Where does a new movement make demands, and to whom? Because what remains of 1968 is its
literariness—as the "historical poem that gives us new courage" to fight the
"hero" (44)—Badiou suggests that collective aspiration and possibility are
the territory of a poetics of demands.

Badiou's conception of 1968 *as* a "poem" combines historical materialism ("the everyday") and inspiration ("courage") to "demand" essential
"rights" again. In reclaiming the spirit of the Chicano movement as an
"event" and critiquing and often discarding its forms ("methods"), Herrera reconciles political commitment and postmodernist aesthetics, narrative and lyric modes, and oral and written forms. In reviewing *Half of
the World in Light* and *187 Reasons Mexicanos Can't Cross the Border*,

the poet-critic Stephen Burt underscores bridges from movement to post-movement poetics: "Many poets since the 1960s have dreamed of a new hybrid art, part oral, part written, part English, part something else: an art grounded in ethnic identity, fueled by collective pride, yet irreducibly individual too." Herrera is, Burt concludes, "one of the first to succeed" in this poetic synthesis. I would argue that his success exemplifies the ways in which Latino poetry is experimental in the most basic sense, by testing languages and subjectivities thought irreconcilable (English/Spanish, written/oral, Mexican/"American") against each other in order to create new ones. By rejecting "flirtations with 'language' aestheticism" (*Notebooks* 105), thus distancing himself from Language poetry, the iconic North American postmodernist aesthetic, Herrera implies that experiment is the shared ground of convergent strains of Latino poetry. His poetics, he avers, emerges from "the gut" of Chicano collective history rather than from studied innovation (*Notebooks* 43).

Two recurring "entries" in *Notebooks* form extended prose meditations evaluating the Chicano movement as an "event" with two levels: literary languages and everyday institutional practices. Eleven "Undelivered Letters to Víctor," whose interlocutor is the writer Víctor Martínez, and seventeen "June Journals" are interspersed randomly through the sprawling *Notebooks*. The "Letters" map an incomplete and thwarted but intimate dialogue overheard by readers. The "Journals" are discursive private meditations to which readers gain access. In grappling with what Andres Rodriguez calls the Chicano movement as "a complex and fascinating icon," they dramatize the origins, successes, failures, and futures of Chicano literature. Rather than sites of longing and nostalgia, the images, tropes, and figures of the movement Herrera reinscribes sometimes reject the earlier forms outright and occasionally express exhaustion, even consternation, at the iconic symbolism. Yet they also recapture the inspirational, resolute spirit of the movement. As a dialectical poetics, the entries put pasts in play, with the titular "Letters" and "Journals" reminding us that the poet is also conversing with his former, past selves, including the one who proclaimed "Moctezuma blood and spirit."

Herrera's allusions to the movement can appear purgative rather than dialectical and recuperative. Under scrutiny, however, another view emerges: while the movement's tired iconography is an index of appropriation and commodification, its spirit must find new languages of emancipation that reconcile individual growth with collective empowerment. In "Letter #38" (105), Herrera lists the literary-aesthetic forms and strategies that reduce Latino identities to reproducible, debased commodities: "'ethnic folk drama'"; "'qualified' ethnic know-how, 'minority' bombast," "manifestos"; "keep[ing] it current, PC, and racy"; "a refurbished fem Virgen de Guadalupe"; "stay[ing] in the 'color' game"; "quasi-nationalism"; and "Aztec sloganeering." These "props" produce "writing" that is alternately "ranting," "harpooning," "huddl[ing]," and "install[ing]," all of which connote mechanical rather than inspirational processes. Because they reject multiplicity and complexity for rote reproduction of received forms, "you can't lean" on them, they "will not pull us through," and they are "not enough," "not sufficient," and "out of the question." All told, Herrera writes, they "will annihilate us."

"Letter #30" (42) amplifies these rebukes with the charged signifiers "young" and "new." Herrera asks Víctor: "Have you seen the young ones" who "spit out 'Aztlán,' talk about new stone idols, ring up workshop poetics" and declare "'Chicano power' and 'Quetzalcoatl' one more time?" Although "the gallon of hand-me-down nationalist sewage" the young recycle mechanically unnerves Herrera, he also admits "the New gnaws at [him]." The letter sees "the New" as the onslaught of history, with a terse allusion to "ground zero" communicating uncertainty about the impact of September 11, 2001, on Latino writing. But he also has in mind the narrow, exclusionary avant-garde in US poetry. As the Chicano poet-critic J. Michael Martinez and Jordan Windholz argue, when "the new" is used to define innovative, experimental poetry—the Language poets, for instance—it has imperialist, ethnocentric subtexts that confine already marginalized poets, especially Chicanos and Latinos, to a putatively passé identity-based poetry, regardless of their forms or contents. Most broadly, "young" and "new" destabilize late-1960s binaries. The Chicano movement rejected "old" identities, including "Mexican American," but "Chicano," new then, has now been defanged. Muñoz defines the movement by its use of "Chicano" as an oppositional identity and by its emergence from two social movement paradigms—identity politics and student activism (19–26). "Workshop poetics" indicates continuity with student movements, but it replaces poetry oriented toward activism, political struggle, and social justice with a cloistered poetry, wherein "the New" disavows collective ethnic identities. Instead of emerging from and being inspired by "the everyday" in the service of transforming it, Herrera suggests that "workshop poetics" detaches languages from material contexts. He critiques "workshop" and movement poetics by implying that each misappropriates "idols" from the historical geographies that give them meaning.

Yet in the late 1960s, Mexica/Aztec gods served the cause of Chicano self-determination, political power, and liberation, even if masculinist and exploitative of indigenous cultures. In the present, their purpose is unclear. These intersections between old and new stage meetings between past and present Herreras, subverting his former self and synchronizing it to his present self.

Herrera sees Chicano identity as "a complicated theoretical negotiation," in Michael Hames-García's terms, "constantly revised over the course of an individual life, rather than a process of 'discovery' with an identifiable endpoint" (473). As such, the poet's pronouncements about "endpoint[s]" yield to uncertainty and renegotiation. "Letter #30" ends with Herrera talking to himself, doubting his dismissals: "Wipe my face, squint, make sure I say what I mean." This halting construction creates tension between "meaning" (content) and "saying" (form) that equates to "message" and "methods." A similar expression concludes "Letter #9" (94): "You know Víctor, I am going to say it—no more movements, nothing about lines or metaphors or even about quality and craft; you know what I mean?" Although "Letter #38" declares "that boat ride is over baby," it ends: "[W]e got to keep close to all of our lives as they suffer, as they bleed all around us, the mission is on, Vic—I am wandering off, again, I know." Declaring an end to "movements" forces Herrera to mark the end of "an era." In "Letter #7" (134), the death of the writer and painter José Antonio Burciaga in 1996 offers this occasion: "Burciaga's death marks the end of an era, let me use these terms just once more—the end of an era." Herrera's worries about stagnation, over being stuck in "eras" or "movements" that have run their course, require constant revision, but they also require a "mission," a concept echoing the language of "demands" and "messages." "Letter #10" concludes: "All that"—the movement era—"is gone now and in some way it stays with us" (86). "Gone" and "stays" are dialectical tension points in the "complicated theoretical negotiation" of Herrera's poetics. For him, "the mission" is the same—liberation, creativity, dignity—but the forms to express it must change.

Against "stone idols," "sloganeering," "movements," "eras," and the cultivated detachment of "workshop poetics" and "Language" aesthetics, Herrera creates an elemental, affective base for Chicano poetry. This continual "mission" emerges in response to what he calls, in "June Journals 6-1-88" (43), "our Capitalism," which I understand as the specific, explosive intersection between neoliberalism and Latino identities on Žižek's "level of the everyday." "June Journals 6-1-88" sees Chicano literary history as a complex relation between artistic expression and collectively embodied, individually felt affective states. "As Chicano artists," it begins,

> we have always pulled out our images, landscapes and symbols from the gut to the page, from the bile to the open forum; historias terribles of our people, our time; historical suffering in vitro.

> It is time to quench another thirst, perhaps, a greater thirst, one that is more insatiable, delicious: pull out the monsters from the Colossal Inside, North America; the gargoyles of power, our soft-spoken and concentric-eyed representatives; much better than the familiar grimacing representations of ourselves. (43)

Period markers like the portable, transhistorical "always," "our time," and "it is time," situate an affective imaginary within a *longue durée* of "historical suffering." Because "our" appears obsessively in the letters and journals, *Notebooks* takes a collective measure of individuated literary modes. The act of "pull[ing] out" literary language "from the gut to the page," and placing historical consciousness "in vitro," gives aesthetics origins in the body, not in abstract rationality. This shared historical body of suffering is internalized in individual Chicanos.

Whereas rational Cartesian modes "intellectualize human experience [and] understanding," "turn[ing] processes into static entities" (Johnson 11), affective modes of knowledge creation ("from the gut to the page") buttress Hames-García's formulation of Chicano identity as a process of theoretical negotiation. "Emotions," Mark Johnson writes, "are not merely subjective, private feelings." Because they are embedded in lived, material spaces, they are fundamental to "communal well-being" (67). This entanglement of individual subjectivity and collective health underlies Herrera's critique of 1968 and the necessity of reconstructing its spirit in the present, where radical individualism trumps all. In lamenting the recycling of "nationalist sewage" in "Letter #30," he wonders whether "we never did fall, truly alone and shivering, into the furnace of an authentic experience and explosion of community across assigned boundaries and voices, into the colossal and marvelous thing called change" (42). Here, Herrera proposes Žižek's "test" of the movement: "to what extent [did] it transform" the everyday? Together, "June Journals 6-1-88" and "Letter #30" join embodied affects ("gut," "bile," "suffering in vitro," "thirst," "insatiable," "delicious," "grimacing"); affective metaphors ("fall," "shivering," "furnace," "explosion"); and figures that elicit emotions ("monsters," "gargoyles"). As an affective index to the transformation of "the everyday," the "thing called change" remains uncertain. The inability to reconcile intellect ("subtlety") and affect, collective "we" and individual "alone"—symbolic binaries of two eras—prolong this uncertainty.

"Our Capitalism" subsumes the collective Chicano "our" under its logic. "June Journals 6-1-88" raises this issue in the interrogative mode: "What have we learned from our Capitalism? The decapitation of our joys? The desire for simulations of consciousness?" Of Herrera's many idiosyncratic phrases, "Our Capitalism" stands out in denoting a specific *type* of capitalism: *Chicano* Capitalism. In this mode of production, what accumulates is not capital but representations of Chicanos. "Our" denotes complicity in a hyper-acquisitive ideology, implying that Chicanos (and Latinos) buy and sell "ourselves," in terms of both labor power and cultural identity. Images of Chicanos become cheap commodities, mere exchange-values. Similar constructions ("all of our lives," "our people," "our time," "our soft-spoken and concentric-eyed representatives," and "our images, landscapes and symbols") mark a collective syntax and pronominal form that simultaneously militate against radical individualism and are totally subsumed by its logic. "Our" thus cops to capitalism's inherent contradictions: servitude and freedom, violence and progress, exploitation and inspiration: *these* are the movement's legacies as an "event." In North America, Herrera's "Colossal Inside," neoliberalism economizes every sphere of life. Like each "you and I" in Cardenal's "Room 5600," the collective "Our" struggles to detach from "Capitalism" and to create subjectivities apart from the discrete individual successes that are the currency of multiculturalism and identity politics.

Consecutive poems in *Notebooks*, "Chican@ Literature 100" and "How to Enroll in a Chicano Studies Class" (126–127), imagine Chicano studies curricula under "Our Capitalism." They remind us that in early 1968 "Chicano Studies was still a dream" and that Latino studies is now institutionalized. Because their lessons require historical perspective, the first poem tells the hypothetical student to help her grandmother "if she still lives," and to "go back and find the seed-voices," "the ones that raised you" and "the ancient songs way deep inside." These intergenerational bonds underlie a Chicano studies reconciled between activist origins and an institutionalized, professionalized, and individuated present. Rather than using the images and languages of the past, the present generation ("you") must figure things out on its own ("alone and shivering") while revering—but not imitating—the ancestors. That *we* invented Chicano Studies," as the second poem says, implicitly asks the student in the first: what are *you* going to invent? This Chicano studies model has no syllabus or canon, but it requires an anticonsumer ethos: "First of all, you are not going to find this stuff at the mall, in one of those flashy pendejada shops" (126). Rather than reading Alurista or Anzaldúa, the first poem prescribes actions: *quiet down, listen, walk, paint, try, make, rake, do, dig, carry, leave, go back*. This cyclical verb sequence begins with "quiet" and "listen" and ends with "leave" (behind) and "go back" (to the beginning), demonstrating how Herrera's poetics learns from, reinvents, and recycles past "messages" in new forms. The second poem's final sentence—"Breathe in, breathe out, this green wind, makes you strong"—suggests that 1968's "wind" continues to blow. Herrera only asks Chicanos to breathe it in and to exhale with "blowouts" appropriate to current struggles.

Unwriting "Chicano," Writing the Zapatistas

Whereas *Notebooks* evaluates the Chicano movement as an "event," "One Year Before the Zapatista Rebellion" (*187 Reasons*) considers the challenge of representing the signature "event" of resistance to neoliberalism. Given that Herrera's experience of the movement coincided with his awareness of "grenadiers in Tlatelolco" (*Notebooks* 20), it is unsurprising that his view of Chicano identity changes with the Zapatistas. The essay begins with the character Juan's question to Maga, his partner, "How can I write about Mexico?'" (175). In their conversation, Maga and Juan sort through shifting scales and identity markers to rethink Herrera's trips to Chiapas in 1970, 1982, and 1993 from the aftermath of the Zapatista rebellion.[5] Early on, Juan admits that "Mexico" signifies capaciously in the United States and in Chicano literature. This fact makes literary representation daunting: "Juan was well aware that when he talked of Mexico, he was actually talking about Latin America" (176). Espada's Zapatista poems efface the poet's presence to create a hemispheric poetics momentarily placed in Mexico; in contrast, Herrera's meditations on the Zapatistas emerge from the premise that Mexico is a stand-in for Latin America in the Chicano imaginary. The first "equation" of his list poem, "Fuzzy Equations," highlights this metonymy by suggesting that "Latin America" is derived from a "fuzzy" calculation: "Humility + oppression + a Virgin − territory = Latin America" (*Notebooks* 74). In collapsing Mexican and Chicano allegiances to Guadalupe into a universal Latin American icon, this "equation" effaces "the Indian," who is oppressed, dispossessed of territory, and stereotypically humble. Finding a literary language to write "revolution" and "Mexico" in this context requires Juan to explore his US Americanness.

Herrera describes "unearth[ing] the stories about the Chicano and Latin American experience" as a "key concern" in his books (*Night Train* xii). These frequently disjunctive "stories" help him "to rethink America, to rethink [him]self, and to rethink American writing," a "trinity" he questions even as he asserts it (*Mayan Drifter* 8). Nowhere is this unearthing more dissonant than in Mexico, the home country of his parents. In "Pyramid of Supplications," for example, Herrera reshapes his identity with dissonant figures of belonging. Both "from here" and "a stranger that never left," he is a "swanky Chicano boppin' down" Mexico City's streets and "chang[ing] into someone else," the dimensions of which shift constantly in his work. The poem imagines "mak[ing] a deal with the literary honchos" of Pérez-Bustillo's "Mexican poetry world" by asking them, "How about a special supplement on New Raza Poetry / From California, the Southwest?" The parenthetical question that follows, "(Who would travel so far to get published?)" (*187 Reasons* 261), teases Chicano desires for legitimacy in Mexico, Espada's aspiration of publishing there, and relations between bourgeois "travel" writing and literary value.

Mayan Drifter interrogates romantic concepts like "discovery," "the search," and "Traveling Men" (4, 169, 107) to critique ethnographic and travel writing tropes and to renegotiate Chicano identity. In reading this subversive "auto-ethnography," Oliver-Rotger suggests that the title dramatizes contradictory trajectories in Herrera's poetics: his commitment "to place-based communities and historical origins" meets metaphors of "drifting" and "rootless wandering" (172, 178). This dialectic guides his meta-reflections on how Latino identities, "Chicano" in particular, signify unevenly across the hemisphere, especially in Mexico. "One Year Before the Zapatista Rebellion" asks: What happens when "the Indian" becomes a mediating figure between Mexican and Chicano? When "Latin America" is the mediating idea between Latino and US "American"? When the internally diverse "Mexico" becomes a metonym for an even more diverse "Latin America"? These confusions cause Maga to lament the difficulty of "'speak[ing] of a fettered Indian Latin America barely breathing'" as "'the World Bank [and] Mexican billionaires'" toast "'with NAFTA teacups'" (184). By destabilizing "the Indian," "Mexico," and "Latin America," and seeing them as "quicksilver placeholders for globalized corporate interests" (182), Juan stresses the urgency of using them carefully and restoring the agency of those saddled with their historical weight. Oliver-Rotger argues that Juan and Maga's conversation is "a detached metareflection on the contingency of the position of the Chicano travel writer and poet within the[se] global realit[ies]." In short, Herrera turns the ethnographic lens on himself in order to examine his self-construction (183).

Yet a broader subjectivity is also at stake: the Latino writer redeeming the political commitment of 1968 in the "globalized corporate" present. To this end, the conversation eventually focuses on how to comprehend Juan's personal experience of indigenous Chiapas within the conceptual frame of "revolution." Herrera's claim that "I want to say something about me" at the outset of *Mayan Drifter* (6) enmeshes subject ("I") and object ("me") within the unstable registers of "American," "Indian," "Chicano," and "Latino." Rather than his role in the Chicano movement or his child-hood in migrant labor camps, his visitor's experience of Chiapas is "his initiation into the complex of his identities as Chicano, Latino, mestizo, Indian, American—most of all American." In other words, traveling south fleshes out his identity by pointing up its constitution in the North with the South in mind. This process counter-intuitively produces an abiding US "Americanness." "No doubt about it," Juan concludes, in Chiapas "he had found his Other home too" ("One Year" 179). This reinscription of "American" identity as a supplemental, placeless "Other" strains his cred-ibility in writing about revolution. When he asks, "'Can the writer truly speak of revolution?'" he means a certain type of writer, one with "status [. . .] prospering in the ganglia of a superpower" ("One Year" 175–176).

This epistemological and geographical privilege maps Juan's individual experience of Chiapas to a tentative conception of collective revolution. Forms of "to know" appear throughout the Zapatista essay, often in nega-tive constructions conceding his inability to understand Chiapas, Mexico, and the internal logic of the Zapatista uprising, rather than its causes and motivations. This pointed figure of the traveler's privilege admits to igno-rance: "He had not the slightest inkling a campesino and Indian revolu-tion hiccupped in the shadows of his fancy-colored backpack" (180–181). When he learns of the Zapatista uprising (perhaps on NPR's *All Things Considered*) one year after leaving Chiapas, he realizes his blindness in and to the place he thought he knew. The visibility and tractability of "revolution," he concedes, eluded his Chicano lens. Whereas "revolu-tion" often serves as a stylized rhetorical gesture in post-movement Latino and Chicano writing, in Latin America, de la Campa notes, "revolution" approaches metanarrative. The Zapatista uprising was thus able to gain traction in its counter-critique of neoliberalism as a metanarrative (*Latin Americanism* 29, 56). This latter metanarrative extends centuries of pater-nalistic conquest. Maga's lament that "'every time we say "Indian culture"

we lose ground'" (184) pinpoints the shortcomings of representational literary modes, which mirror centuries of official, paternalistic promises of
salvation, preservation, and incorporation through benevolent representation. Maga ultimately taunts Juan with a practical question further undermining his textual authority: "'You think you are a suburban Zapatista,
don't you? Let's see your ammo'" (184). Because Herrera's "ammo" is
literary language, both figurative and representational, it is complicit in
these histories. The essay's final pages thus forgo theoretical questions to
render Juan's experiences in Chiapas's Lacandon jungle and to pine subtly
for the false clarity and wholeness of his past.

Throughout *Mayan Drifter*, Herrera approaches these entangled questions as a poet reliant upon "intuition" to render "what he sees" (33) rather
than with the scholar's or anthropologist's systematic, putatively detached
methodology. Whereas Oliver-Rotger focuses on the genre of *Mayan
Drifter*, as an "auto-ethnography," travelogue, and "postmodern ethnic
autobiography" that "resists the generic codes of travel writing and interrogates the epistemological position of the traveler" (174), his prose reflections can also be read as statements of poetics and affective meditations on
literary representation. In these ways, he calls *Mayan Drifter* his "offering
as a poet to Mexico's Indian peoples and to all those who want to think
about and reimagine America" (3). Yet he knows the gift's initial recipients
may not want or need his "offering." This admission pinpoints the challenge of creating what Kevin Concannon, Lomelí, and Marc Priewe call
"'in touch'" textual "negotiation and dialogue" between North and Latin
America (5) rather than facile, paternalistic "gifts." This disjunctive relation between Chicano poet and indigenous Mexicans finds resonance in
the book's trope of "gathering." When Herrera's "gathering" of images,
senses, and signs of Indians striving for autonomy (40) is viewed as a counterpart to the "offering," the text seeks to return the guiding questions, revolutionary possibilities, and "Indian culture[s]" to Indians. Although both
are mediated, as they have been for over five hundred years, through "the
eyes" of a well-meaning outsider, Herrera "do[es] not seek to build a revolutionary 'character' either in the text, the reader, or in [him]self." Instead,
he insists "questions of revolution must be posed by a deeper and more
critical set of currents—the people themselves, across the Americas" (6).

This idea suggests uncertain dynamics between Latino poetics, North-
South relations, and "Indian culture" differently than Espada's seamless
lucidity in the interest of solidarity. This is due in part to Herrera's version
of post-movement poetics. Oliver-Rotger argues that he "undermines the
Chicano nationalist myth of the journey into the depths of indigenous

cultures" as a way to instantiate "the pre-Columbian origins of Chicanos" (188). Yet his critique also reinvents the myth *as* a poetics. *Lotería Cards and Fortune Poems*, which joins Herrera's poems and the Mexican artist Artemio Rodríguez's black-and-white linoleum prints of the traditional Mexican game of chance, was published in 1999, two years after *Mayan Drifter*. The book's biography of Herrera illuminates how he triangulates "Chicano," "Latino," and "indigenous" into a mythic, even shamanistic, transnational poetics. It begins with a concept echoed in "Sing Zapatista," where Espada learns "the word" of indigenous resistance: Herrera "was initiated into the Word by the fire-speakers of the early Chicano Movimiento." "In 1970," it goes on, Herrera's "project to redefine *a Latino poetics* and *dramatic political form* led him to the indigenous cultures of Mexico," where he "filmed" and "recorded" "rituals," "songs," and "daily life" (213; my emphasis). This marked shift from a "Chicano" to a "Latino" poetics emerges from careful listening to and observation of Mexican indigenous cultures through ethnography, with the goal of broadening, reinventing, relocating, and *repoliticizing* his poetics.

In critiquing the exclusionary methodologies of history and anthropology, Rabasa suggests that *poetics* participates in the resistance to neoliberalism as it is embodied in the practices of those "without history," like the Indians of Chiapas. "Subaltern insurrections," Rabasa writes, are "ruled by the imagination, marvel, civil society, and poetics, which the prose of counterinsurgency—that is, history—has sought to neutralize" (*Without History* 141). In these terms, Juan and Maga's skepticism about the articulation "Indian culture" can be located in its effacement of "the continuum of Indian communalism" from pre-conquest to the present. This lens suggests how "Indian culture"—in scare quotes—conjures nostalgia that reduces contemporary iterations of Indian resistance, like the Zapatistas, to "lost causes" and "degraded manifestations of the ancient grandeur" (*Without History* 2). Juan and Maga's dialogue makes self-reflexive poetics the Latino imaginary's path to restoring "marvel" to its rightful holders: Indians and revolutionaries. Even so, the absurd echo between suburban and subaltern underscores the challenge of replacing *ludic* with *lucid* forms to contest neoliberalism.

Citizenship and the North American Scar

If Herrera's meditations on the Chicano movement and the Zapatistas are interrogative, "Norteamérica, I Am Your Scar" (*Night Train*) and "A

Day Without a Mexican" (*187 Reasons*) use the declarative mode to claim Chicanos as rightful citizen-subjects of North America. Like *Notebooks*, "Norteamérica, I Am Your Scar" locates Chicano identity under the intense pressure and scrutiny of US power. Its figure of "the scar" recuperates a form of solidarity within an order that militates against collectivist modes, and its affective, hemispheric map of "our Capitalism" from the scar's perspective depicts the transnational dimensions of Chicano identity on "the level of the everyday," when things enter a state of "business as usual," in Žižek's metric. On this level, the Chicano power of survival and the seeming inevitability that Chicanos, and Latinos in general, will transform the United States from within, ultimately testify that the premise of H.B. 2281 is impossible: that historical "scars" are erasable.

Starting with the title, Herrera's first-person speaker addresses "Norteamérica" from its "scar." The initial term locates Chicano identity within a continental formation whose historical-geographic dimensions are both ambiguous and precise. In refusing to name the United States as such, the poem rejects an "America" that narrowly refers to the United States, promoting instead an oppositional viewpoint common in Latin America whereby "Norteamérica" challenges US hegemony. Even so, a "North American" scale for Chicano identity supersedes hemispheric, nationalist, and border frameworks. The poem's publication date underscores this nominal act. In 1994, NAFTA made "North America" an official economic bloc united by the ideology that "competition" increases "freedom" for all. In Gloria Anzaldúa's genealogy, the ancestors of Chicanos migrated across the Bering Strait, then went south to what is now the US Southwest, then to the Valley of Mexico to establish Tenochtitlán, and then went back north under pressure of further conquests (26–35). Chicanos thereby constitute an historical "scar" spanning NAFTA's geography, from Canada in the north to Chiapas in southern Mexico.

Herrera converts Anzaldúa's figure of Chicana/o identity as an open wound that "hemorrhages" "before a scab forms" (25) into a visible "scar" signifying durability. As an affective, embodied sign of a wound that has healed, at least minimally, the "scar" is felt individually but shared collectively. The "scar" puts divergent stories about its origin into dialogue, with the speaker's apostrophe "you," lyric's conventional mode of address to an absent or distant interlocutor, relating the official version of the scar's origins:

[. . .] the phosphor crescent on your palm, this scar
you say you got from hunting wild game

somewhere in the South, when you used to dream
about saguaro and when you towered over
the wire coils across the endless borders
and military bridges into my anguish,
into my resentments. (99)

The geographically indeterminate "somewhere in the South" spans the expansive US imperial project, from the Treaty of Guadalupe-Hidalgo to occupations of Cuba, Puerto Rico, and the Dominican Republic; interventions and coups in Chile, Guatemala, Nicaragua, and El Salvador; Plan Colombia; and structural adjustment, privatization, and deregulation. The effects are physiological ("anguish") and metaphysical ("resentments"), and the stories emerging from "broken" subjects first dispossessed then incorporated into Norteamérica *through* capitalism quietly warn the United States from within its damaged, violent body politic: "Listen to me. / Your scar speaks to you" (100). The official origin story, the "scar" warns, converts to "wild game" the very subjects who create US power and wealth with their labor.

Whereas "June Journals 6-1-88" asks Chicano writers to turn from self-representation ("ourselves") to "the Colossal Inside, North America," these disarmingly gentle commands ask the United States to be introspective about its constitutive margins, dispossessions, and exclusions. This dialectical relation between self-reflexive interiority and externalizing collective consciousness vis-à-vis hegemonic power pinpoints what Pérez-Torres sees as "a central tension" of "postrevolutionary" and "post-sixties" Chicano identity. Although Chicanos have "penetrated" US space, "that national space has likewise traversed the 'Chicana/o.'" As such, he identifies two polar possibilities: that "Chicana resistance to exploitation" facilitates "the development of a more complex and totalizing capitalism" or that Chicanos are "new players in history who, by resisting, force that economic system against the direction of its own internal logic" (*Movements* 76). In depicting Chicanos as historical subjects who resist *and* sustain capitalism (by working for it to earn a daily wage), "Norteamérica, I Am Your Scar" complicates Pérez-Torres's poles, suggesting that the neoliberal project will withstand Chicano resistance so long as it remains oppositional. In this sense, the "complex and totalizing capitalism" encompasses but is not coterminus with Herrera's "our Capitalism." Only by meeting the United States on its own neoliberal ground and within its logic of market-based incorporation, rather than in a *res publica*, or democratic body politics, can this collective historical subject—the "scar"—transform the body.

The poem imagines the scar transforming the body with highly figurative, lyrical, surreal, and compressed images. Its brief, opening declarative sentences of physical struggle precede a one-line stanza, "It is hard to walk, like this." The floating deictic "this" gathers images of pain shared by a plural "we," who "grab at their shoulders / at odd times"; endure "something eating at the[ir] ligaments," "a stranger's blue wool weigh[ing] on [them]," and a "crazy quill" and "barbed hook" "undulat[ing] inside the small of [their] back"; "crouch as if in a snow blizzard"; and see their "portraits hang[ing] on the precipice" (97). Emotions, as Johnson notes, are not simply bounded private states, they are embedded in shared "situations" created by material forces. Figures like "our back" make "walking" under duress a powerful collective act of survival. Whereas figures of walking in *Notebooks* and "A Day Without a Mexican," as seen below, represent activism, this one connotes the (meta)physical conditions of life *as* the scar.

The scar's relation to the body has a delicately and surprisingly rendered, if predictable, political economy. A pleading conversational passage with another detached deictic depicts the scar as a space for exploiting and alienating collective labor power: "You see, this is what we have; / all we have. You know this." Here, *this* includes "undershirts," "a wishbone, a toothpick, [and] something / that we've kept for ourselves," minimal possessions appropriated by Norteamérica. "Your daylight thefts" of "our small icebox," "our fender," and "our dishrag" suggest the appropriation of the means of sustenance (icebox), transportation (fender), and labor (dishrag) (99); that each of these figures is a synecdoche, a part detached from a functional whole, moreover, suggests that Norteamérica's demand for Chicano labor disavows labor's access to the means of subsistence. In this regard, near the poem's end the speaker declares this "the age of the half-men / and the half-women" (100). This period marker prefigures ones to "the era" in *Notebooks*, but unlike those this one pins down a cornerstone of neoliberal ideology, *homo economicus*, which reduces subjects to rational economic actors, pure and simple, strategizing for individual gain. While this figure diminishes rather than augments individual Chicanos, collectively the situation is even more urgent. Yet again a referentless deictic envisions this condition: "This is my village, full of crosses, swollen, dedicated to your industry, / groomed in your spirit of bank flowers and helicopter prowls" (99). The "village" may be "dedicated" to capitalism and "groomed" in its "spirit" of commodification, but it still requires surveillance. The poem's totalizing figurative depiction of Chicano life in terms of dispossession and exploitation turns on this critique of how "our

Capitalism" creates a state of simultaneous fullness and emptiness. Playing by the rules guarantees but meager possessions dependent on luck ("wishbone"), a consolatory religion and death ("crosses"), and an artificial ("swollen," as in an inflammation) temporary prosperity. These features define the "scar" *as* a place.

An emancipatory Chicano literature emerges under these constraints on movement and agency. Like "June Journals 6-1-88," the poem depicts an embodied affective imaginary that moves "from the gut to the page." But here Chicano art achieves greater grace and vigor by blending what Lauro Flores and Oliver-Rotger call "the strange and the everyday, the primitive and the modern, and the mystical and the real" in Herrera (172). "Somehow," the speaker states with surprise, "we still lift / our delicate fingers; / a true gentleness moves." When they "sing, at last" the song resembles "a fang with lightning," "a desert of terrible ink," and an "unfinished stone fist novel unraveling all its wetness" (97, 98). These figures of artistic creation under duress replace movement poetry's monumental, individual icons—living revolutionaries as well as Aztec gods—with collective, anonymous ones. In "Letter #1" (18), for instance, Herrera responds to the underlying warrant of identity politics—"if one Chicano or Latina makes it, then we all make it"—by recalling how "we hoisted up Che Guevara and Lolita Lebrón as our American figures" and "chanted" *América* at movement-era meetings and demonstrations. The warrant shows the limits of identity politics: individual representation supplants structural change, with the individual who "makes it" serving as the evidence for, and sign of, Chicanos having become "authentic Americans," as "Letter #1" puts it. Additionally, because "*our* American figures" also emerged from the Cuban Revolution and the Puerto Rican independence movement respectively, Herrera implies that they did not adequately illuminate Chicano aims for self-determination. "Norteamérica, I Am Your Scar" envisions instead "our American figures" as a collective, nameless narrator who shifts between "I" and "we."

As a multivalent, paradoxically grounded (*in* North America) and portable "scar" capable of enduring tremendous suffering and of transforming the US body politic, this collective runs from the skin down into the circulatory system of the hemisphere, from "somewhere in the South" to "somewhere in this curled-up nation" (99, 100). This latter figure implies that diminishing workers, the marginalized, and Latinos broadly also diminishes the nation-state. Herrera makes this suggestion in "Letter #7," when he claims, "America speaks louder than our tiny books" (134). If Chicano books are "tiny" in relation to North America's neoliberal project, and in relation to its impacts in Chiapas and throughout Latin America, as "Letter #7" concludes, they are nonetheless bound to the project, as a scar is to its body. As such, "Norteamérica, I Am Your Scar" directly expresses a revolutionary desire—"I want to say good-bye Big Man. / I want to say farewell Holy Jaw" (99)—replete with "subtleties" supposedly incompatible with such a politics. This desire is difficult to instrumentalize given how Latino votes are solicited ("you say you are campaigning. / I received the champagne bottle and the bow tie" [98]) and the common fate shared by the "scar" and "Norteamérica." As the speaker says, "[W]e are so tied to you" (99). If "Holy Jaw" represents Chicano incorporation into the body politic through maceration, "Big Man" symbolizes both the United States' and the Chicano movement's masculinist cultural nationalism. "The twinned and linked forces of heterosexism and assimilation," Libretti writes, undermined the movement's emancipatory politics (139). It equally defines the US imperial project.

With stark monosyllables connoting patriarchy and monumentality and demanding obedience, "Big Man" and "Holy Jaw" serve as figures of tradition, narrowly as in the Chicano movement, and broadly as in the United States' history of "hunting" in Latin America. We might imagine these nominalized entities as "Big Man, Inc." and "Holy Jaw, Co.," corporate bodies that must be obeyed and served because we are bound to them, like a scar to a body. In these ways, Herrera satirically channels Adorno's sense that "one must have tradition in oneself, to hate it properly" (*Minima Moralia* 52). To hate tradition "properly," Herrera consumes and internalizes each tradition—movement poetics and economic imperialism. His reworked movement iconography in *Notebooks* covers the first; second, his Americanness emerges in Chiapas, where it is symbolized by a backpack perhaps bought at a "flashy pendejada shop." "You will find me," the speaker addresses North America, "in a shape so familiar, so close to you; // in your language" (100). This admission tracks Herrera's career arc; like many Latino poets, he began writing bilingual and Spanish-language poems and now largely writes English-language poems. The "wild game," he reminds the hunter, has learned to speak the hunter's language. This metaphor conjures the poor migrants crossing the United States-Mexico border who are now subject to billions of dollars of high-tech military surveillance. Even so, the speaker entices *Norteamérica* with a seemingly acquiescent, conciliatory invitation. After "tak[ing] your hand / in the shape of my hand" (99), he says, "Let's walk together in this light" (100). However, because when "your hand bleeds," it covers "our roofs / like a reconnaissance map" (99), and because "this light" is created by "the scar

[that] lives with its bulbous velvet root on fire" (100), the invitation is also a threat.

These contexts stage the poem's ending, where the speaker says he will "celebrate / when we shall walk with two legs once again / and when our hands shall burst from your hands" (100). This figure reconciles molotovs and subtleties, revolution and assimilation, by turning "half-men" and "half-women" into fully embodied humans. This is possible when "you" and "I"—the body and its "scar"—join hands. *Norteamérica* is now no longer a thief but also not an equal partner; rather, the scar on its palm is a stage for Chicano liberation. "Burst[ing]" depicts a revolutionary event that transforms the state from within rather than overthrowing it. By returning the scar to an open wound, this "burst" seems to say: *If you do not allow us, even help us, to change you, you will continue to diminish, and it will not be because we had a revolution but because we did not.* As "a rupture in the normal order of bodies"—in the poem's images of ligaments, backs, fingers, hands, legs, and scars—the event occupies "the level of the possibility of possibilities" (Badiou 242–243). This concluding "event" ruptures the oppressive order between the scar and the body politic, with the scar liberating the body from its own violence. Subtly and deceptively, the figure of speech *in the palm of your hands* undergoes a reversal: what is in the palm—the scar—controls the hand rather than vice versa. Because the scar is located on Norteamérica's palm, it tells the fortune of the United States as much as it does the fortune of Chicanos.

With its crafted figurative language, refined political consciousness, and dual capacity to surprise and to make familiar, "Norteamérica, I Am Your Scar" is one of the most innovative, capacious, and haunting Latino poems published "under the neoliberal sign." I. use "crafted" cautiously, as Herrera views the concept with suspicion. "June Journals 6-25-88" proposes a stark choice Chicano writers face between the "North American Literary Order that is 'Craft'" and the "Sabotage" of "official gatekeepers" and "word gendarmes" (104). Yet like Espada, Herrera reconciles these oppositions. Espada's "poetry of the political imagination" combines "craft and commitment" to create "an *artistry* of dissent" (*Zapata's Disciple* 100). Whereas Espada brings "Craft" to the act of "Sabotage," Herrera "sabotages" the cold polish and putative purity of "Craft" by writing both tightly crafted and messy, improvisational, and verbally excessive poems. "A Day Without a Mexican" (*187 Reasons*) is a prime example of the latter. The twenty-page poem depicts the immigrant rights march in Los Angeles on May 1, 2006, in which 400,000 marchers protested the federal anti-immigrant bill H.R. 4437. The title alludes to the "Great

American Boycott" and "Day Without an Immigrant" protests; the satirical film of the same name; and "the Latino Threat Narrative," which names all Latinos "Mexicans."[6] With its proliferating protest signs, fragmented lines, and lack of punctuation, the poem trades "craft" for abandon. The poet collects these signs, self-consciously recording the "event" "with notes & camera" (45). Unlike *Notebooks* and *Mayan Drifter*, this "gathering" restores images of the late 1960s through Latino subjects negotiating "super individualization," commodification, and contradictory desires for citizenship within the "scar." Contrary to the "blank page" of counter-revolutionary logic, the poem catalogues the proliferating textual traces of 1968, 1970, and 1973—the key space-times of revolution and counter-revolution—repurposed in 2006 in the immigrant rights struggle. Myriad signs cited repeatedly in the text—on posters, banners, flags, t-shirts, hats, and handkerchiefs—carry displaced, ungrounded, and iconic images of resistance that collectively map the market-produced heterogeneity and consumer-based activism of the neoliberal present.

Even more so than *Notebooks*, "A Day Without a Mexican" is a text about texts, charting a polyvocal, unscripted, and collective poetics in comparison to Espada's unified, scripted chorus of "singing." It thus affirms Badiou's belief that 1968 persists as "a sort of historical poem that gives us new courage" (44) but with a caveat: 1968 endures as a collage of fragmented texts that emerges from appropriative consumer modes. Herrera's poem gathers slogans and symbols from the following historical geographies of struggle, which the neoliberal counter-revolution has sought to erase and relegate to the past (symbolized in "post-" articulations) or to subvert, appropriate, and commodify: (1) Mexico City, 1968 (54); (2) the Chicano movement (55, 66); (3) the United Farm Workers movement (52, 56); (4) Allende's socialist revolution (52); and (5) the Zapatistas (53, 58, 61). Practically speaking, these signs reflect the fact that "many of the organizers of the boycott and the protest marches were veterans of the 1960s Chicano Movement and the Farm Workers Movement" (Muñoz 227). This fact reinforces Noel's sense that the poem "underscore[s] the failings of documentary poetics" because it is "always embedded in the documentarian's emotional investments," in this case Herrera's "wistfulness somewhat tempered by hope" (861). As this chapter shows, however, these "emotional investments" structure Herrera's poetics overall; "A Day Without a Mexican" is but one search for new forms to recast and reinvent them. Most suggestively, the signs create a subtle conceit underlying the poem—that all of the movements above can be seen as Indian uprisings, whatever the actual subject positions of their participants (53, 61).

When the civil rights movement is included—Herrera calls the train he and other marchers take to Los Angeles "a Mexican freedom train" after finding common ground with an African American passenger (44)—they can be seen as uprisings of peoples "the color of earth," in the image of "Sing Zapatista." The 2006 march may not be part of "Indian culture," but Herrera sees Indian features and "style" everywhere (53). This imprecise conceit nonetheless captures the poem's sense that lucid polyvocal resistance and the spirit of 1968 infused the march. "The past," he writes, "becomes the present where we march" (58).

Whereas transhistorical Zapata allusions, for instance, pay homage and create lineages,[7] the march's proliferation of images across North-South geographies might be termed *recycling the revolution*. On one hand, recycling is a bourgeois, consumer-based mode that fails to disrupt the destructive ideology of endless growth. On the other hand, marchers reuse a repertoire of potent symbols that escaped the "blank page" in lieu of new resistance symbols of their own. As neoliberalism's main form of citizenship and socialization, consumer identities circumscribe revolutionary subjects before their articulation. Herein lies a difference between the movements of the late 1960s, the rural, subaltern Zapatistas, and the (sub)urban marchers of 2006. Whereas the former two rejected market identities as a matter of course, the latter have had to embrace them because they embody them. The poem's abundant market signs, after all, cover their bodies. They include sports teams (44, 57), brand names (a "South Pole T" [57] and "a Harley shirt" [68]), US cultural symbols ("Spiderman cap" [55] and "Superman capes" [56]), and symbols of Mexican heritage tourism ("a Teotihuacan T" [66]). They also include two commodified symbols of resistance, the Zapatistas (53, 61) and Che Guevara (53, 63). All these symbols are doubly worn: worn and worn out. Guevara has nearly become his t-shirt image, and Marcos seems headed for a similar fate. Yet these poses have substance. Herrera describes a Chicano waving a Zapatista flag with a "Mexican flag / wrapped around his face," as having "Subcomandante Marcos style / Chiapas style Indian style revolution style" (53). Herein lies the poem's basic question about resistance under neoliberalism: how does "style" convert into substance, image into action, and noun into verb?

Herrera's rhetorical question—"Could the symbols mesh?"—expresses a similar concern in response to the image stores of late 1960s and mid-1990s protest marches (*Mayan Drifter* 69). A different question—*Could the individuals mesh?*—more usefully augurs the need for intergenerational bonds to overcome atomization. "The net result" of neoliberal restructuring, Robert W. McChesney argues, "is an atomized society of disengaged individuals who feel demoralized and socially powerless" (11). The passage from "One Year Before the Zapatista Rebellion" cited in my preface to this book imagines this demoralizing atomization with metaphors of travel, tourism, and transience. "In every room" of the border "hotel," Herrera writes, "there is an [individual] Indian" (183). Whereas each gazes across the border from a separate room, the crumbling, "broken" walls between them indicate latent possibilities for revolt, a "to break" incorporated in the structure of the "hotel," by definition a space of transition.

"A Day Without a Mexican" converts this atomization to an interwoven collectivity. To my revised question, it envisions an otherwise produced by aggregating atomized consumers with similar struggles. The beginning of the poem (p. 49) announces the march is "without" "leaders":

> everyone everyone   alone   is a leader woven
>   everyone is   here

This spacing, lack of punctuation, and amphibology continue throughout the poem; here, the syntax suggests "everyone" is a leader, which is in keeping with neoliberal individualism. Yet "woven" and the repeated "everyone" make the interpersonal paramount, stitching each "leader" into a whole constituted "here" and now *as* a march. The poem's subtitle, "Video Clip," advances this idea. Not only does it conjure how films turn single, still frames into a moving picture and fragments into a whole, the aggregated "video clip" "woven" from fragments is a metaphor for refiguring what Žižek calls neoliberalism's "privatization of the social." This process undermines collectivist modes by producing "new enclosures" that turn modes of belonging once negotiated in public space into privatized, monetized consumer forms (144), as in the "hotel" rooms preventing collective bonds. The marchers' worn-out, individuated consumer images facilitate connections to past struggles, and their joining in public space turns their bodies, as the very signs of enclosure, into a "woven" form of collective belonging.

This complex dynamic operates through the idea of "without." The preposition appears in the title, the passage about "leaders," and Rabasa's theory of indigenous insurrection. He argues that "the specter of history" has two modalities: repetition and immanence. The first "exposes the work of history itself as haunting the present." The second "carries the promise of liberation in the 'life history' of individuals and communities that history cannot access or delimit" (*Without History* 9). Herrera's work negotiates the first modality constantly: questions like "How can I write about Mexico?" and "Can the writer speak of revolution?" implicitly grasp how "the work of history" obviates indigenous forms of life. Because this historicizing impulse is subsumed under state narratives of citizenship, inclusion, and consumption it has limited use for many emancipatory projects. In contrast, the second modality can constitute an outside to history, a condition "without history" that may resist the logic of capital and the state. To be "without" historical subjectivity, to be denied a place in history, and paradoxically to be relegated to the past (history) as "a lost cause" are tragedies, as Rabasa says of Marcos's view of the Zapatistas, but they also open spaces for contestation. Herrera's "without leaders" questions representational and historical modes, while the title, "without a Mexican," marshals an existential threat to neoliberalism, which functions by driving down labor costs, exploiting temporary and migrant workers, and by opening borders for capital. The poem thus undermines the idea that immigrants threaten US prosperity, as Leo R. Chavez distills it in the tropes of "the Latino Threat Narrative," by implying that they produce it. These "withouts" may not mesh easily with indigenous subalternity but they conjure and reject the "illegal alien" (not only without status, but without humanity) lashed on (undocumented) Latinos.

This idea brings us to the inter-American echoes subtending Latino poetics in the neoliberal era. The march was designed to draw attention to those "without" citizenship. Signs such as "Hoy marchamos mañana votamos" / "Today we march tomorrow we vote" (55); "We are Americans" (51); and "We are not criminals" (61) assert belonging within the United States' borders. Herrera reads the last sign as the "credo" of "a nation // in formation" (61). Although this definition turns on negation, absence, and consent to and incorporation into the state, the "nation // in formation" is both a pan-Latino state within the US nation-state and a transnational Latino state that spans the Americas. In this perspective, Herrera's phrase "Citizenship after centuries of labor" (68) restores the long history of Latinos in the United States as a Latino imaginary's starting point. This imaginary is theoretically and figuratively hemispheric if practically statebound. It finds its immanent historical geography in the sign, "Yo nací en América soy Americano ok" (62). The dual claim that being born in the American hemisphere produces rights as a US citizen takes to task the unhindered movement of capital across borders under free trade, and its resultant command over space, as the inspiration for labor's equal claim to space and belonging across it.

The idea of state "citizenship" further unsettles Herrera's (im)possibility of writing about "revolution." The word appears often in "A Day Without a Mexican" as if to highlight dissonance between revolutionary signs and citizenship discourses. It is not that the crowd's "words against multinationals words big words / revolution words" (65) are insincere but that calls for incorporation may silence those to autonomy and structural change. When Herrera sees Chicanas "reclaim[ing] the revolution" he follows it with the unpunctuated question "what revolution" (58). Revolution in the air—in signs, slogans, chants, and "styles"—is *not* a revolution. And yet Herrera shows a poetics of "gathering" guiding "revolution" into dialogue with "citizenship." "The revolt" against hegemonic power, he writes, "is ancient, cyclical, and at times hemispheric." His textual iteration of this "revolt" aims "to disassemble" "the lexicon" of "Indian culture," "America," and "Mexico" (*Mayan Drifter* 8) by thinking through the hemispheric registers of Latino citizenship. As a cautious Chicano guide to Latin America, his textual form of "to break" ("to disassemble") builds a revolutionary poetic subject through fragments by refusing to name and represent it as such. Because "neoliberalism only supports forms of artistic expression that subject themselves to the hegemony of the market," as Rabasa notes (*Without History* 143), Herrera knows that the task of creating a poetics resurrecting the late 1960s in the neoliberal present must operate from within literary culture and ultimately within the nation-state. "How can [he] write about" those forms that do not submit to the market—the Zapatistas—in forms—essay, poetry—that certainly do? "How can [he] write about" the appropriation of nonmarket forms by market ones, revolutionary subjects by t-shirts? "A Day Without a Mexican" answers by simply affirming continuing action: "we walk that is all" (49). This movement rejects both a teleology of progress and mere "drifting," promising only the collective bonds of "walking" while waiting for a moment to "burst."

From "blowouts" to Zapatistas to May Day marches, Herrera's "events" challenge the neoliberal order while finding space in it for joy, levity, and dignity. As a multivalent field, Latino poetry spans what Herrera calls the "many Americas" (*Notebooks* 134), a literary history bridging events, national groups, traditions, languages, molotovs, and subtleties. Yet Herrera's foreword to the superb anthology edited by Aragón, *The Wind Shifts: New Latino Poetry*, maps Latino poetry differently. As in "Chican@ Literature 100," Herrera uses the increasingly common "Latin@ poetry." This symbol memorably (and usefully, one might argue) combines masculine and feminine endings, but it also homogenizes Latinidad in hyper-capitalist cyberspace. Moreover, Herrera uses the concept of "microhistories" to locate "Latin@ poetry" after "political" poetry and after the influence of Alurista and Anzaldúa, the avatars of movement and border poetics. Even "the question of identity," Herrera says, "belongs to a past generation of poets" (xv). These points effectively articulate the expansive aesthetic range of new Latino poetry. This is no accident: Herrera and Espada have both been instrumental in promoting some of the most exceptional Latino poets of the new generation. Herrera selected J. Michael Martinez's beguilingly beautiful, vanguard *Heredities* for the Walt Whitman award from the Academy of American Poets in 2009, and Espada has helped to launch the careers of Aracelis Girmay and John Murillo. Yet Herrera's choice of terms also subsumes Latino identity under neoliberalism's atomized individualism, separates poets from the scar's overlapping collective histories, and nearly relegates "Chicano poetry" and "Nuyorican poetry" to artifacts. In stressing Latino studies' activist origins, Saldaña-Portillo argues that Puerto Ricans' and Chicanos' direct experiences of US colonization and annexation demand their continued principal status in Latino studies (509). In this light, Herrera's claim that "all borders" in Latin@ poetry are "'unidentifiable'" (xvii) begs a question: Are we really "post-border" too? If so, inequalities between neoliberalism and a more just political economy, billionaires and disposables, citizens and "illegals," and between (and within) Latino groups will be erased not by subtleties but by the blunt "post-" triumphalism of neoliberal rationality. In spite of its timeless, placeless global logic and the false allure of a "post-border" world, the symbolic and practical power of the nation-state persists. Chapter 3 turns to an examination of how Bolaño's and Espada's textual "countries" contest the violent formation of the first neoliberal state.

CHAPTER THREE

Against the Neoliberal State

Roberto Bolaño's "Country" of Writing and Martín Espada's "Republic" of Poetry

What would have happened if September 11 had never existed? It's a silly question, but sometimes it's necessary to ask silly questions, or it's inevitable, or it suits our natural laziness. What would have happened? Many things, of course. The history of Latin America would be different. But on a basic level, I think everything would be the same, in Chile and in Latin America.

—Bolaño, "A Modest Proposal"
(*Between Parentheses* 88)

Whoever writes is exiled from writing, which is the country—his own—where he is not a prophet.
—Maurice Blanchot, *The Writing of the Disaster* (63)

"Silly questions" provoke consideration of the inconceivable. If the definitive narrative of Bolaño's life, literature, and nation had not happened, surely history—Bolaño's, Chile's, and Latin America's—would be different. This is how epoch-defining events are narrated. Yet Bolaño posits that the historical otherwise—the coup of September 11, 1973, never happened—would not have produced an alternative future. Instead, the event that seemingly determined everything determined little. In this view, the neoliberal counter-revolution would have prevailed without Pinochet. If not Chile, Friedman's free-market fundamentalist project, guided from the Rockefeller-funded economics department at the University of Chicago, would count another nation as its coup de grâce. This is how empirical experiments work. As a "laboratory" for the first neoliberal state, "the Chilean miracle," as US media persist in calling the Pinochet years, became an export model, even as Chile remains one of the world's most unequal states.[1]

But September 11, 1973, *did* happen. Allende's "peaceful road to socialism" ended with the US-backed coup; the Chilean acolytes of Friedman, "Los Chicago Boys," implemented economic "shock treatments"; and Pinochet's state disappeared, murdered, imprisoned, and tortured thousands. Whereas the direction of Latin American history might have been the same, the event's content and forms were determinate. Just as the "blank page" threatens Pacheco's poetics, which revises previous texts, Bolaño's "inevitable" question challenges his narratives. Like 1968, moreover, 1973 remains a key archive of symbols for writers across the Americas, and eerie concurrences between them underlie Bolaño's literary project. The narrator of *Amulet* recalls her confinement to a bathroom stall during the police takeover of the National Autonomous University of Mexico (UNAM) in the weeks before Tlatelolco: "And the dream of September 1968 reappeared in that September of 1973, which must mean something, surely, it can't have been purely coincidental" (75). For Bolaño, who lived in Mexico City as a teenager, from 1968 to 1973, and then again following his exile from Chile after returning there just before the coup, 1968 is an iconic moment of defeat that "flashes up" in 1973, as Walter Benjamin says of historical memory, like a bad "dream." This pairing haunts Bolaño's poetic depictions of the Right's depravities and the Left's idealistic fervor, forms of oppression and liberation developing together, inversions between revolution and counter-revolution, and the violence constitutive of each. For Bolaño, 1968 and 1973 paradoxically determine absolutely nothing that follows and every last word said about it.

Bolaño and Espada each represent September 11, 1973, as a form of "disaster" that continues to "flash up." For Blanchot, disaster "escapes the very possibility of experience" while setting "the limit of writing." Although "the disaster de-scribes," it is "the force of writing" and cannot be "excluded from it" or seen as "extratextual" (7). As a force that inscribes itself in texts while making its articulation impossible, disaster is both the condition of writing and something that writing attempts to exceed. On this point, Bolaño's claim that "plots are a strange matter" and that "a story chooses you and won't leave you in peace" (Boullosa) can be mapped to the disaster's effects on literary subjectivity. Comprehending the Pinochet years is a "complex task," the Chilean writer Diamela Eltit claims, "because the total or partial suspension of the rule of law penetrated, circulated, and lodged in the body of the subject" (1801). In Bolaño's view, the "penetrated" "body of the subject" negotiates narrative ("plot," "story") and form. Whereas narrative "chooses you," form is a "choice" "belong[ing] to you" (Boullosa). Because September 11 is *the* story that chose Bolaño, that "won't leave [him] in peace," his lyric subjects navigate forms of "broken" and "to break" produced by the coup. In 1998, eight years after Pinochet's reign ended, Bolaño wrote: "Sometimes I get the feeling that September 11 wants to break us. Sometimes I get the feeling that September 11 has already irrevocably broken us" (*Between Parentheses* 88). Tensions between forms imposed by historical violence and forms chosen by poets structure Bolaño's narratives of the coup and its aftermaths. If the form of history feels "irrevocabl[e]," even its key events effects rather than causes, then texts emerge between narrative (story) and lyric (form). In this poetics, disaster can be momentarily *dis*lodged from lyric subjects.

Bolaño and Espada create imagined "countries" through intertextual reflections on "disaster," as the "story," and "revolution," as a possible "form" of belonging. If Bolaño's "silly question" conjures alternative pasts and dismisses potential otherwises, his poems use subversive romantic tropes of "dream" and "nightmare" to reflect on the utopian promises of 1968 and Allende's election in 1970 and their violent ends. Because youth is revolution's condition of possibility for Bolaño, "to break" is not confined to the past; as the provenance of youth, it is omnipresent but doomed to defeat by "irrevocabl[e]" maturity. In depicting the coup and postcoup Chile with moments of lucid awakening, Bolaño makes figures of "dream" and "nightmare" the dialectical "limits of writing," the parameters of revolution and counter-revolution, and the contested terrain of 1968 and 1973. This poetics captures Hopenhayn's sense of the current era's "awaken[ing]" from the "pleasant dream" and the "nightmare" "called revolution." "To abandon the image of a possible revolution," he concludes, is "a peculiar way to die" (1, 2). These "peculiar" deaths and "abandon[ed]" images structure Bolaño's poetry, from the title poem of *The Romantic Dogs* to his epic "The Neochileans." All told, Bolaño creates what Hopenhayn calls a "map of the revolution's orphans" (16) with laments of defeat, challenges to the neoliberal state's ideals, and reflections on the Left's failures.

Given the Left's failure to transform the nation-state, it is unsurprising that many Latino and Latin American literary practices are now delinked from politics. Today's individuated market-based modes contrast the entwined literary and social movements of the late 1960s and early 1970s. Reflecting on this era, Beatriz Sarlo writes: "Something socially significant was at stake in those theories which posited a connection between literary and revolutionary practice. Almost all the writers of that period had to make some pronouncement about this connection" (25). Under neoliberal ideals, compulsory links between aesthetics and politics have shifted into a "post-" ideology of artistic autonomy in which such "connection" is retrograde. Reclaiming "to break" requires recovering the literary "stake" in political-economic life. Bolaño and Espada complicate "connection[s] between literary and revolutionary practice" while insisting they are necessary and invigorating. As gestural utopias emergent from dystopian historical geographies, Bolaño's "country" and Espada's "republic" model textual state forms to establish these "stake[s]" and "connection[s]." Their "countries" are not reproducible or instrumental. Instead, they critique and reformulate state practices and values. Whereas Bolaño's Borgesian trope of the "library" *as* a "nation" subverts nostalgic, nationalistic state forms (of the Right and Left), Espada's vision of "poetry" *as* a "republic" replaces the capitalist state with one run by poets, including line cooks following poetic "recipes" and baboons who "scream for joy" when read poetry (*Republic of Poetry* 3). Each reconciles individual pleasure ("joy") to collective transformation ("revolution") and rewards dissent and difference in egalitarian, pluralist spaces legitimated by homage, empathy, and idiosyncrasy, rather than by normative canons or compulsory citizenship roles.

Three ideas guide Bolaño's and Espada's aesthetic critiques of the neoliberal state form. First, the neoliberal state mobilizes a new governmentality. Under neoliberal rationality, Brown argues, the market regulates and controls the state, thus reversing the state regulation of the economy in classical liberalism, Keynesian and welfare state models, and socialism. As such, state legitimacy is measured by profits, and citizenship is reduced to consumerist entrepreneurialism (41–42). Second, this latter form, *homo economicus*, promotes the "individualized owner-citizen" (Derksen 16), a rational actor motivated solely by material gain. Third, in depicting the first neoliberal state as a disaster that implemented and enforced these ideals through violence and repression, Bolaño and Espada challenge this legitimacy and underscore neoliberalism's "most basic feature": "the systematic use of state power to impose (financial) market imperatives" (Saad-Filho and Johnston 3). Although debate exists about whether the neoliberal state apparatus weakens or strengthens the nation-state, its indisputable goal is "to facilitate conditions for profitable capital accumulation." This goal, Harvey writes, requires "a radical reconfiguration of state institutions and practices" governing relations between centralized authority and decentralized corporate power (*Brief History* 7, 78–80).[2]

Despite the rise of globalism and transnationalism, the state remains the guarantor of individual rights. Under neoliberalism, Harvey shows, "rights cluster around two dominant logics of power," the territorial state and capital. Because states must enforce rights, they are "derivative of and conditional upon citizenship" (*Spaces of Global Capitalism* 180). Although Bolaño's and Espada's texts model what Harvey calls a different "bundle of rights" than market-based rights enforced by states, it is easy to see how a transterritorial "library" or "republic" may not ensure basic conceptual protections for the illiterate and subjects "without history." In claiming "the only country for a true writer is his library, a library that may be on bookshelves or in the memory," Bolaño dismisses the benefits of state citizenship and rejects exilic nostalgia as the "refrain" of a "lie" (*Between Parentheses* 43). In addition to revising Cruz's map of "exile[s] from broken / Souths" toward consolatory "otherwises" produced through reading and writing, this conception also rejects Pinochet's repression, wherein citizens became obedient consumers nostalgic for the "order" preceding Allende's election. September 11, 1973, may have chosen Bolaño, but the nostalgia for "revolution" that "flashes up" in his poetry balances his disgust for the exilic nostalgia produced by its failure. In contrast, Espada consistently chooses the coup as a key image store, and his reverence for Chile follows his veneration of Neruda.

Under neoliberal norms, the nation as an "imagined community," Benedict Anderson's term for how the nation was made conceivable to dissimilar citizen-subjects through print media, becomes a state of passive, atomized viewers produced by what Leo R. Chavez calls the "image-producing industries," dispersed multimedia technologies that create exclusionary norms of citizenship and belonging (4).[3] Against the coercive market-based inclusion and violent enclosures of this "imagined community," and against the demise of print forms, Bolaño and Espada recuperate material culture—physical texts—with "poetry" as an embodied historical agent. They democratize poetry by including the nation-state's constitutive others (i.e., prisoners, exiles, the young) and by confronting violence as the supposed outside of poetry and the effaced constitutive inside of the neoliberal state. Rather than promoting "'Yo' With a Capital 'I,'" Pacheco's imperious individual, and the corporation with "individual" legal rights, these "countries" gather texts into a collective "library." This figure elevates use-value over exchange-value, reading over writing, and shared borrowing rights over private property. In countering the "blank page," it figuratively rejects the "*blanqueo,*" which is, as Brett Levinson notes, the logic of post-Pinochet neoliberalism that erases memories of state violence and links between dictatorship and the free market. "The reason for Pinochet's installation," Levinson writes, was "the imposition of the free market" (101, 98). This erasure, Klein concludes, "fail[s] to hold the ideology accountable for the crimes committed in its first laboratory" (158). In the following pages I examine how Bolaño and Espada take literary accounts of these crimes.

Bolaño's Library-as-Nation

In his meditations on disaster, Blanchot observes that "writing" is a "country" in which the writer is marginal: "Whoever writes is exiled from writing, which is the country—his own—where he is not a prophet" (63). Bolaño's library-as-nation enacts Blanchot's ideas that writing is a writer's own country, a country of exile, and a country where the prophets are others. In this "country" of texts, citizens are exiles and the nation-state is a lost idea. To make this "country," Bolaño gathers texts into a portable library that constitutes an alternative space of belonging. As a pretext to citizenship in "the country" of writing, exile facilitates critiques of the state. "I don't believe in exile," Bolaño once said, "especially not when the word sits next to the word *literature*" (*Between Parentheses* 38). In his "country," prophets include Borges, Nicanor Parra, and "Poetry" itself; in contrast, the forces unleashed on September 11 become a singular imaginary "beast," *the* disaster. The beast pits the neoliberal state made through violence and ensured by surveillance against its unintended consequence, the country of "writing" as a library of those who would contest this state's cold, instrumental logic. This approach to Bolaño's haunted exilic representations of Chile offers an essential counterpart to the scholarly focus on his fiction, so much of which follows the lives of poets.

Bolaño envisions the imaginary beast in "A Modest Proposal," an essay found in his papers by Ignacio Echevarría, the editor of *Between Parentheses*. This posthumous collection compiles Bolaño's essays, reviews, columns, and speeches, from 1998 until his death from liver failure in 2003. Bolaño wrote the essay after visiting Chile in 1998, his first time back in the country since 1973; although it was likely published while he was alive, where and when remain uncertain (*Between Parentheses* 374–375). Before considering the "silly" but "inevitable" question, the essay introduces the imaginary figure through which Bolaño *reads* September 11. The densely allusive figure conjures the event's enduring power. "September 11, 1973," he writes, "glides over us like the penultimate Chilean condor or even like a winged *huemul*, a beast from the *Book of Imaginary Beings*" (*Between Parentheses* 87). This three-part figure carries many intertextual traces, including titular echoes of Swift's "A Modest Proposal" and references to iconic, endangered Andean animals: the huemul, a breed of deer, and the condor. The latter's iconography was used by the notorious Chilean secret police, DINA (Dirección de Inteligencia Nacional), who established "Operation Condor" in November 1973 to track leftists and Allende sympathizers across the Southern Cone. But the guiding allusion comes from Kafka via Borges. Bolaño cites in full "An Animal Dreamed by Kafka," an entry in Borges's "anthology of fantastic zoology" (xi), *The Book of Imaginary Beings*, which was first published in 1967:

> It is the animal with the big tail, a tail many yards long and like a fox's brush. How I should like to get my hands on this tail some time, but it is impossible, the animal is constantly moving about, the tail is constantly being flung this way and that. The animal resembles a kangaroo, but not as to the face, which is flat almost like a human face, and small and oval; only its teeth have any power of expression, whether they are concealed or bared. Sometimes I have the feeling that the animal is trying to tame me. What other purpose could it have in withdrawing its tail when I snatch at it, and then again, waiting calmly until I am tempted again, and then leaping away once more? (*Between Parentheses* 87–88)

In adapting Kafka's language ("Sometimes I get the feeling . . . ") in the essay, Bolaño uses an imaginary form to depict an "abject" (*Between Parentheses* 87) collective subjectivity constructed through fear and impotence. By replacing "the animal" with "September 11," "trying" with "has," "to tame" with "to break" (and "amaestrar," *to master*, in the Spanish), and "me" with "us," Bolaño represents September 11 as an ongoing "forma irreversible" (*Entre paréntesis* 82). The disaster never ends, terrifying and "breaking" subjects in its path, frustrating attempts to halt its thrashing, and mocking efforts to understand it. As a figure of DINA's helicopters and the coup's bomber planes, Bolaño's imaginary being revises Kafka's earthbound imaginary animal thrashing its tail to one hovering above, haunting and stalking those below.[4]

Bolaño's reinscription of "An Animal Dreamed by Kafka" depicts the product of Pinochet and the Chicago Boys' laboratory experiment—a purportedly "free market" abjectly dependent upon authoritarian violence. This unmanageable product has a visage "almost like a human face," which signifies how its unnatural dimensions approach but do not achieve human characteristics. This is in keeping with *The Book of Imaginary Beings*, which "deliberately excluded [. . .] legends concerning human transformations" (xiii). As the counter-revolution's disfigured product, the imaginary beast consolidates Bolaño's disruptions of rational, detached portrayals of the coup and its aftermaths with forms and narratives of violence and disorder.[5] In addition to contesting depictions of the era as an "economic miracle," this figure mocks what the character Verdecchia encounters before traveling to Chile in *Fronteras Americanas*: "under Pinochet," he reads in a Fodor's travel guide, "Chile enjoys a more stable political climate than it did in the early seventies" (37–38). Rather than the Chicago Boys' ideologically neutral "scientific" models to stimulate growth, create stability, control inflation, and create economic freedom, the imaginary animal, *as* the free market, controls us, not as an impersonal force, as the theory goes, but as a terrifying monster. It "tames" us but not as classical political economy and neoliberal theory hypothesize it, where the market discourages violence in noncoercive ways. Unregulated and cyclical, the beast flings "this way and that," without purpose other than to elude those who would moderate it. "Only its teeth have any power of expression," and these exist to prevent control or regulation. Rather than a benevolent, meliorist invisible hand, a vicious, visible tail suggests a diminished humanity—from human hand to animal tail—created by the coup and counter-revolution.

Bolaño's reworking of Kafkaesque and Borgesian modes of reordering perception conjures the role of "animal spirits" on September 11 and after. Although the term is often attributed to Keynes, I have in mind Marx's "animal spirits" unleashed when workers labor together. Through cooperation and competition they raise their productivity, exceed their capacities as individuals, and create new modes of collective power. Because man is a "social animal," Marx writes, when "working together he strips off the fetters of his individuality, and develops the capabilities of his species" (*Capital* 447).[6] In this light, the imaginary being is produced not by Pinochet or "dictatorship" narrowly but by stanching these animal spirits and releasing more violent ones. The Pinochet regime "declared political activity irrelevant" and "heralded an individualism regulated only by free market forces" (Valdés xi). Both were designed to crush the animal spirits of worker cooperation, labor power, and the very idea of revolution, which "suppose[s] the full integration of personal with communal life" (Hopenhayn 2). Neoliberalism's limited view of species being promotes individual competition over collective cooperation, while torture, disappearances, arrests, and political repressions destroyed the Left's organization and limited its access to public space. Bolaño's imaginary being dramatizes how the neoliberal state reshaped the individual-state relation at the nexus of centralized authoritarianism and decentralized economic "freedom."

Matthew Hart and Jim Hansen argue that the state is no longer "organized around territory, the law, or the body of the sovereign but around systems of surveillance" (495). As texts, cultures, and people increasingly transgress national borders, states intensify this nexus with "ever more panoptical forms of protection and control" (506). With its ubiquitous presence, this control frustrates resistance and "tame[s]" the individual, in part by producing isolated subjects with the overwhelming sense that alternatives are infeasible.

These authoritarian animal spirits produced torture but also the "rational" and "scientific" dismantling of state services in the name of "freedom." "The reduction of 'freedom' to 'freedom of enterprise' unleashes all those 'negative freedoms,'" Harvey writes. "In its pure form," he continues, neoliberalism "threaten[s] to conjure up its own nemesis in varieties of authoritarian populism and nationalism" (*Brief History* 80–81). This "nemesis" is the imaginary beast that terrifies in order to coerce the consent of the terrified. Pinochet's repression and neoliberal theory cooperated to stimulate a particular type of animal spirits—the energy of capitalists and their supporters—to unleash the market *on* the state. In this sense, Juan Gabriel Valdés suggests, Chile was not only the first but the "most radical case" of neoliberal state formation. Rather than privatization and austerity imposed by international institutions and banks, as in Latin America thereafter, the Chilean state "literally dismantled itself" (4) by privatizing most everything. The Chilean neoliberal project was thus a true revolution. The animal spirits contained in, and unleashed by, the imaginary beast that haunts Bolaño's textual nation conjure a disturbing, unpredictable symbol of total upheaval, the prototypical "disaster."[7]

Total upheaval underlies Bolaño's figures of Chile's disordered temporality. As a state stuck in the year "1973," over which disaster hovers and literary subjectivity remains captive, Bolaño's "Chile" animates Blanchot's sense that "the disaster is perhaps passivity, and thus past, always past, even in the past, out of date" (3). While the beast "glides" above, on the ground below Bolaño's lyric subjects struggle against passivity by following repeating "tracks," "trails," "paths," and "roads" that struggle to emerge from the past. The opening, title poem of *The Romantic Dogs* (3) introduces the autobiographical figure of the "twenty-year-old Chilean" who follows the "paths." This corollary to the "real" Bolaño, who was born in 1953 and who inhabits the collection's "Self-Portrait at Twenty Years" (5) and "The Worm" (23), animates the romantic and Borgesian archetypes structuring his poetics, including "dream," "nightmare," "love," "spirit," and "labyrinth." "The Romantic Dogs" begins: "Back then, I'd reached

the age of twenty / and I was crazy. / I'd lost a country / but won a dream."
This bathetic declaration parallels Bolaño's sense that revolution, "true
poetry" (*Romantic Dogs* 63), and "dreams" are bound to the territory of
youth. He wants to remain "with" and "alongside" "the romantic dogs," a
figure of collective, grounded animal spirits countering the singular beast
haunting from above. Not only is the "dream" located "alongside" these
"dogs," "with" them it detaches from the territory of the state, to which
it had been closely bound in the concept of "revolution," and follows the
paths, trails, and texts of exile. Even so, "the nightmare" reminds him
he "will grow up," emerge from "the labyrinth," and eventually "forget."
In the neoliberal era, Hopenhayn writes, "a resurgence of romanticism
shouldn't be surprising," especially when "redemption through revolution" is deemed impossible (10). Bolaño's indecorous romantic tropes are
wary of redemption and maturity, serving as paradigmatic instances of this
"resurgence" in revolution's void.

"The Romantic Dogs" combines figures of submission, romantic emotion, historical fixation, and negation in echoing Blanchot's semantic connections between "passivity, passion, past, [and] *pas*" (16). They reach
apotheosis at the conclusion, when the speaker-poet insists—hopelessly,
given his past-tense reflection on 1973—that he is "going to stay" "with the
romantic dogs." "But back then," he prefaces this final reflection, "growing
up would have been a crime." This temporal "back then" opens and closes
the poem; at the end, however, "but" ("pero") qualifies the phrase. The
conjunction "pero" echoes "perros" ("dogs") and offers insight into the
conjunctive, intertextual "paths" the latter travel through Bolaño's texts.
Recurrent, variable paths map his revulsion for Chile post-1973, but "the
dog's path" also integrates metaphysical and material struggles against displacement. Like Bolaño's spatial figures of Chile as a "hallway," this path
is symbolically narrow and isolated.[8] In "Dirty, Poorly Dressed" (*Romantic
Dogs* 41), where "the dog's path" appears, the image stores of 1968 and
1973 fail to console: "A Chilean educated in Mexico can withstand everything, / I thought, but it wasn't true." Moreover, "no one wants to go"
on this path, and "poets travel" there only "when they have nothing left
to do." In other words, when they have been defeated and are "grown
up." Yet the path of "perros" is also that of "pero," where animal spirits
and conjunctions exist, where the "but" of exception, otherwise, and contingency remains. The twenty-year-old Chilean ultimately follows these
"paths" and "hallways" to other texts and writers and to encounters between his "soul" and "heart." Together, "paths" and "hallways" comprise

the mobile "shelves" of a library constituted between Chile and Mexico and the "dream" of youth and the "nightmare" of defeat.

Within these affective "limits of writing," in Blanchot's terms, Bolaño challenges the idea that poetry belongs to an educated bourgeoisie who simultaneously eschew emotion for rational economic calculation, imagination for material wealth, and incalculable "dreams" for quantitative acquisition. For Bolaño, these citizenship norms sacrifice passion and creativity to order and decorum. To critique them, he follows the path of Parra, whose surname echoes *pero* and *perro*, and which "Parra's Footsteps" (*Romantic Dogs* 129–131) explicitly announces. Like Parra, Bolaño converts poetry into "Poetry," a suspicious character who frequents dark alleys and shady motels, interacts with hustlers and prostitutes, and offends conventional decorum.[9] As the guiding anthropomorphic figure of his imaginary state's inclusiveness, "Poetry" antagonizes aesthetic codes by celebrating marginality. Bolaño's post-1973 Chile and post-exilic library-as-nation emerge in part from reading Parra, whom he calls "the best living poet in the Spanish language" (*Between Parentheses* 72). His respect for Parra's poetry can be distilled to two factors: its capacity "to wear out the public's patience" and its urgency.[10] To Bolaño, "Parra writes as if the next day he'll be electrocuted" (*Between Parentheses* 100–101). Both apply equally to Bolaño's writing. The first stresses his indecorous subjects, and the second makes pending defeat the prime mover in the "country of writing." Because "Poetry" is "braver than anyone," as Bolaño twice asserts (*Romantic Dogs* 7, 21), it becomes the country's idealized but troubled citizen. This allegorical character incorporates youthful "dreams" of revolution and mature reflections on defeat. It reclaims language from "the writing of the disaster," which in Blanchot's reckoning means more than how disaster is "communicated, attested to, or prophesied." "The writing done by the disaster" also "ruins books and wrecks language" (Smock ix). Transferring the knotty lyric self, written in part *by* disaster, onto a notion of collective "Poetry" stresses how texts exhibit more "braver[y]" and cooperation than other human actions. As a mock-heroic exile searching for meaning amid the disaster's recurrent violence, this conceit elevates readers and the act of reading above writers. "Reading," Bolaño insisted in interviews and essays, "is always more important than writing" (Boullosa). Without readers, the library-as-nation and "Poetry" are inconceivable.[11]

These conceptions of "Poetry" and "disaster" reach tragic registers in "The Neochileans," an epic free-verse poem of approximately five hundred short lines (*Tres* 76–113). Bolaño's representations of Chile as a powerful *idea* frozen in time in 1973 and as haunted place presided over by dogs and imaginary beasts in the present converge here into a collective condition of illness and death. On one hand, Bolaño's biography emphasizes his return to Chile from Mexico City in the weeks before September 11 to "help build socialism" and his subsequent imprisonment, for eight days, after the coup. The cover flap of *By Night in Chile* uses this history to market the figure of Bolaño's self-fashioning in relation to the coup, "the twenty-year-old Chilean."[12] On the other hand, Bolaño depicts Chile as a place to leave, permanently. "The Neochileans" evokes the new Chile produced by Pinochet and the counter-revolution. This idea of "the new" underlies the poem's exploration of the psychic landscapes of "the revolution's orphans." It asks, "How can so much evil exist / In a country so new, / so miniscule?" (89). This guileless tone enfolds inchoate idealism into tacit critique of youthful blindness in order to grapple with the signs of newness, including the neoliberal "new," "the end of history" that makes the present a "blank page." The poet Forrest Gander writes that Bolaño disavows "making it new" as a gesture of humility before "poetry" (42), but he also rejects this aesthetic ideal because of the consequences of the new in neoliberal Chile. The poem's critique of "the end of history" and the constitutive violence of "the new" follows Parra, who ridicules the claim as a non sequitur proceeding not from history but from its absence (*After-Dinner* 7, 45, 367). For Parra, there has never been "history" if it is defined as progress toward a better state of affairs; to end, it must have begun. In these ways, neoliberalism produces the new Chile and signifies the second coming of the New World, a conquest bathed in repeating violence in which the "new" in Neochilean and neoliberalism converge.

Figures of transportation symbolize the "new" Chile. By the end of Pinochet's reign, "the nouveaux riches, roaring through traffic in their expensive sedans, seemed to mock those left behind, trapped in fuming buses" (Constable and Valenzuela 245). Contrasts between "roaring" in "expensive sedans" and being "trapped" in "fuming buses" depict the dramatic inequities in wealth and mobility after "the end of history." The band of approximately twenty-year-old Chilean musicians named "The Neochileans" negotiates these poles, leaving Chile in a "camioneta" (van). Rather than conspicuous consuming or crowded commuting, they initially travel with uncertain purpose. Dunia Gras calls "The Neochileans" "un *road-poem*" where the characters journey toward an idealized North in search of themselves and artistic freedom (67). The term "road-poem" captures the poem's allusions to an inter-American, cross-genre literature in which travel, "the road," and youthful rebellion contest bourgeois norms. But it also reinforces the ideological "packaging" of Bolaño in the United States. The cover flap of the New Directions translation of *Tres* proclaims "The Neochileans" "a sort of *On the Road* in verse," a comparison obscuring its tragic tone. Sarah Pollack argues similarly that in calling his Chile novels "Southern Cone dictatorship novels" and that in saying *The Savage Detectives* is full of "'adolescent' idealism," presses and reviewers help readers "discover in Latin America [. . .] an adventure undertaken in the earnest belief of the saving power and transcendental meaning of action and poetry" (16). This marketing erases the US's historical support of dictators in Latin America and the Caribbean in the names of stability, market freedom, and business environments friendly to North American corporations, while also ignoring how Bolaño's poetry reveals the magnetic horror of "the road."[13]

Unlike the packaging of *The Savage Detectives* that produces "a Bolaño" for US consumption (Pollack 355), "The Neochileans" subverts transcendence. It begins when the "dream" has ended and "nightmare" rules night and day. That the "dream" remains a structuring device in the poem underlines how its absence haunts the present. Figures of "terror," "horror," and "madness" appear throughout, and a nefarious presence is palpable. Whereas the band drives "Always heading / North" (79, 85), a vague, idealized marker for "freedom," they move more surely toward a collective fate: to die young.[14] Because revolution is now impossible, the Neochileans move for the sake of moving. And when these "survivors" (111) of the counter-revolution survive, it is momentarily and by fate: "we realized / The Neochileans / Would be forever / Governed / By chance" (111). A frequent Bolaño figure, "el azar" (chance or fate) resides in the North rather than in Chile, or in the South in general. This external force "governs" the new Chileans in place of the state, like the imaginary beast hovering above them.

These themes frame "The Neochileans" as an allegorical journey through and out of neoliberal Chile. First, the band's journey begins suspiciously. The first-person narrator says they "boarded" their van with resignation, suggesting withheld forms of grief, as if they are being loaded up, driven to prison, and disappeared. "In a sense," he declares, "the trip was over / When we started" (79). Moreover, a "manager" who goes unmentioned thereafter rents their van, and they seem not to know where they are going, except that they are leaving Santiago and heading toward the Atacama Desert, the location of Chacabuco, Pinochet's most notorious concentration camp. Finally, the "north" is "foretold" in a "white kerchief / Sometimes covering / My face / Like a shroud." As they travel through surreal Chilean towns and countryside, they seem guided ("governed") by nightmare and fever. The first signifies through figures of mobility and confinement "projected" like a horror film onto the screen of "the white kerchief": "My nomadic nightmares / And my sedentary nightmares" (79). And fever determines the poem's increasingly haunted imagery, as the band's singer, Pancho Ferri, also known as Pancho Relámpago ("Lightning") and Pancho Misterio, grows delirious with a high fever. Thereafter the fever serves as the van's gas and compass; the speaker wonders "if Pancho Misterio's / Fever / Were our fuel / Or our navigational device?" (99). As a deregulating and disordering force of the body's navigation processes, fever is a chilling counterpart to Verdecchia's broken compass. To revise Verdecchia's terms, the Neochileans only appear to be "heading north" when they are actually heading "backwards" into the psychosis of neoliberal Chile. If nightmare and fever act as navigational devices to map the era, from 1973 to 1989, when the poem begins, what does it say about the subjects produced under the neoliberal sign? That they are defined by a shared, misguiding illusion of control over their own fate.

Being guided by their elder leader's illness is the fate of "the revolution's orphans," who were governed by the competing fever dreams of revolution and counter-revolution. Blanchot's notion that "fervent commitment to infinite progress is valid only as fervor, since the infinite is the end, precisely, of all progress" (63), negates "the end of history" thesis as conjuring content-devoid, infinite "blank pages." But it also indicates how the Neochileans' travels are validated through the feverish navigation device that "always spins in crazy circles," like Verdecchia's compass. The poem ends with the van crossing into Ecuador, and then with the revelation that Pancho was twenty-eight or twenty-nine "and soon he would die." The final lines brim with pathos halting their travels north: "And none of the Neochileans / Was over 22" (73). As an animal spirit fueling their shared passion for music and literature, the fever misapprehends texts as exclusive realms of narrative history, which "chooses you." Under the mastery of fever, the freedom of form, "a choice made through intelligence" (Boullosa), disappears. After leaving Arica, the last town in the Chilean Atacama, and presumably escaping their pasts, they enter Peru, crossing "the border of Reason" and following "pure inspiration / And no method at all" (95, 81). Whereas the Chicago Boys claimed to follow models of rationality and dispassionate science, the Neochileans favor "inspiration." Their animal spirits are the territory of youth; as Bolaño insists, "only the young are brave, only the young are pure of heart" (*Between Parentheses* 100). This is a tragedy of Bolaño's "country": dream and nightmare are entangled territories of passion that leave little space for the counterweight of poetic intelligence. Intellect emerges only postdefeat, post-exile, and with maturity, when the "fever" has already done its damage. In this reckoning, Bolaño's work narrows the Chilean Left's historical diversity. In 1960, C. Wright Mills wrote that the working class in the developed world was being replaced by the young (students, intellectuals) as the "historic agent of change." "Who is it that is getting disgusted with what Marx called 'all the old crap?'" he asked presciently. Yet he was careful to note a difference in Latin America. With his exilic sensibility, Bolaño seems not to have recognized it—his "youth" totally supplants the working class. Allende's revolution, after all, brought together workers, peasants, students, and intellectuals. That's why, in part, it was met with such violence from the Right.[15]

As orphans guided by a fevered singer-poet in search of inspiration, the Neochileans make their literary pilgrimage under uncertainty. Before leaving Santiago, they make a drunken visit to the monument to Rubén Darío, the Nicaraguan *modernista* who spent many years in Chile. After this marker of influence, such touchstones become hazy, intermittent, and bleak, but one stands out. While the band is in Lima and reading Peruvian poetry, Pancho mentions a forgotten Chilean novel, which they describe as *"nec spes nec metus"* (107). The Latin *without hope without fear* structures the poem's view of the new Chile and its literary landscape: fear is so ever-present it is the norm, a state of abjection effacing both dream and nightmare. As such, it only appears to be without fear and thus only without hope. If there is hope for Chilean poetry, the poem implies, it lies in the lack of fear, the rejection of nationalism, and the idea of the library-as-nation. The fever, after all, eventually guides the Neochileans to a collective identity with transnational registers. Near the end, the Neochileans call themselves "Lucky Latin Americans," without the "neo-" prefix (111). If the Neochileans are governed *by* ("por") fate, the latter travel *with* ("con") luck; each decouples collective identity from collective agency, but at least the latter is tentatively celebratory. Born New Chileans just before the coup, at twenty-two, at the turn of the 1990s, they are Latin Americans, the Neoliberal fever having gone continental. The fever, as *Broken Souths* shows, was on the verge of dramatically jumping scales. "The Latin American [neoliberal] right," as Bolaño wrote a decade later, was "now globalized" (*Between Parentheses* 100).

The transition from Chilean to Latin American subjectivity under-lies many of Bolaño's texts. He sees nationalism, especially Chilean, as a "wretched" form that "collapses under its own weight." He explains the expression viscerally: "imagine a statue made of shit slowly sinking into the desert: well, that's what it means for something to collapse under its own weight" (*Between Parentheses* 45).[16] Sadly, the same might be said of the band the Neochileans, who collapse under the weight of their fever-ish passion without firmer material to support it. This notion undergirds Bolaño's conception of the library-as-nation. It rejects nationalism and reframes Chilean writers, such as Parra, within a portable literary geogra-phy emphasizing the physical space of the library. Yet "the twenty-year-old Chilean" ultimately becomes the aging, displaced Latin American gather-ing texts below the hovering imaginary beast of his past. "Parra's Footsteps" indexes this idea by renaming revolution "Atlantis," which is "ferocious and infinite" but "totally pointless." The poem's solution to this paradox echoes the end of Herrera's march poem, "A Day Without a Mexican": "Get walking, then, Latin Americans." It ends by imploring them to "Start searching for the missing footsteps / Of the lost poets." On this path all that can be heard are "Parra's footsteps / And the dreams of generations / Sacri-ficed beneath the wheel / Unchronicled" (*Romantic Dogs* 131). Whereas Bolaño's "trails" follow Borges, Kafka, Parra, and the Beats, among other writers, those "sacrificed" to progress and "unchronicled" by it, along with "Poetry" itself, are the citizens of Bolaño's nation. Their plural dream of "to break" may seem "pointless" in the wake of 1968 and 1973, but their *unwritten* texts also create his inclusive, just country, where the "unchron-icled" move from the past's margins into future texts.

Near the end of "A Modest Proposal," Bolaño proposes raising statues not of "shit" but of Parra and Neruda, with their backs to each other, in Santiago's Plaza Italia. He concludes by imagining the confused public reception for this image, and he mocks the innuendo cast at him: "Bolaño says that Parra is the poet of the right and Neruda the poet of the left." The next and final sentence is biting: "Some people don't know how to read" (*Between Parentheses* 91). This complaint serves as meta-critique in Bolaño's textual nation: Pinochet, fascists, and neoliberals are nothing if not poor readers, for they prefer bad fictions of freedom, nationalism, and justice. His dismissal suggests high standards for grasping irony and satire, as well as his frustration with submitting writers to a Left-Right calculus, when simply viewing the statues from the opposite side reverses their ide-ologies. In other words, only open, careful readers who balance passion with reason and story with form hold passports to Bolaño's library-as-nation.

Espada's "Republic of Poetry"

Whereas Bolaño's Neruda symbolizes the fraught relation between poetry and politics, Espada's Neruda is a talisman for the capacity of "Poetry" to threaten hegemonic power. In Espada's "republic," Neruda's monumental antagonist is September 11, as a composite symbol of the United States' interventionist history in Latin America and Neruda's death eleven days after his friend Allende's. Although Espada composed the cycle of twelve Chile poems in *The Republic of Poetry* after traveling there with other poets for the Neruda centennial, unlike his Mexico poems discussed in chapter 1, it culminates a long investment.[17] Longo argues that Espada's "poetic praxis" is "grounded in Neruda" (Introduction xxiv), but it is also grounded in resistance to this interventionist history, including its recent iteration, neoliberalism. She cleverly converts the Salvadoran poet Roque Dalton's Nerudian ideal of "poetry like bread" into "poetry like Wonder Bread" to signify the marketing of Neruda for mass consumption in the United States, in a "packaging" that prefigures Bolaño's. Espada's "republic" deconstructs this packaging by reclaiming Neruda's leftist politics bleached out (like Wonder Bread) in popular representations that make him a consumable image of Latin American abundance. Longo's claim that "Espada's vision of the people [. . .] is less utopian than Neruda's" ("Post Wonder Bread" 147) registers Neruda's muscular fisherman and miners but comes under pressure in Espada's near-conversion of Neruda himself into a utopic figure of an idealized Chile. "Espada's is the mythic Chile of yesteryear," Noel says, "not the neoliberal Chile of today" (869), with its new student movement protesting the near-total privatization of education. For the Right, after all, Chile means neither Neruda nor Pinochet but free-market triumph. Corporate commodification, as in "bread" to "Wonder Bread," erases both versions.

Whereas Bolaño elegizes the dream of revolution and decries the violence symbolized by the dictator filling its void, Espada confronts neoliberal deprivations by filling Neruda's absence with other poets. In twenty-six poems, *The Republic of Poetry* features ten approximate temporal markers delineating the neoliberal era, practically launched with the coup and Neruda's death. The clearest allusion appears in "The Soldiers in the Garden" (12–13), when Pinochet's soldiers invade Neruda's house. Although they "apologize to señor Neruda" after he threatens them with the sole *"danger"* there—*"poetry"*—the poem ends solemnly: "For thirty years / we have been searching / for another incantation / to make the soldiers / vanish from the garden." Throughout the book, temporal phrases like "for thirty years" combine with spatial figures, as in the depiction of Estadio Chile, the Santiago stadium converted to a prison after the coup, where "thirty-one years are measured" by victims' "last breath[s]" (10). These space-times make the next "incantation" multiple voices from the South, where poetry has libratory possibilities stanched in the North. This plural "incantation" reclaims "the garden," a literary-ecological construct in Neruda, Cardenal, and Pacheco (DeGrave 90–92), from trampling by hegemonic power, preserving it for the cultivation of an emancipatory ecopoetics.

Unlike the Neochileans, who drive north, Espada's opening, title poem makes a pilgrimage south to gather these "incantations." "In the republic of poetry," it begins, "a train full of poets / rolls south in the rain" (3). In the United States, when things go badly, it is a commonplace to say they "went south." This directional figure portends bad fortune. Espada, like many Latino poets, reverses this compass. His movement south, away from the United States, nonetheless occurs "in the rain," a portent of struggle and hindered vision. As a reader of Latin America from a Latino North comprised of displaced "Broken Souths," the poet reads and travels with limited sightlines. To reach the "South" from the North, this figure suggests, one must endure the obscuring rain of "estereotypes," "subtleties," and historical violence. Espada's texts repeatedly establish "South" as a literary-material space for contesting inequitable relations. They reinforce Mignolo's position that Hegel's "natural" division between North and South "is being inverted," as social movements in Latin America "indicate that democracy and respect for human rights are increasing in the South, while totalitarianism, violation of human rights, the use of violence to achieve domination, and extreme conservatism are on the rise in the North" (158–159). This is fraught ground: to write "North by South," a Latino poet must borrow and praise the South's literary resources while avoiding misappropriation and decontextualization. In arguing that Espada "seems to offer the poets of the South [. . .] as the heroic counterforce to the North's imperialism," Gruesz implies that he fails to do so. This North-South binary, she writes, "discourages historical nuance" about oppressions in the South ("Walt Whitman" 164). Yet Espada also troubles the binary by composing his "republic" with convergent, overlapping souths, including those in the North, rather than with a monolithic South that serves the North's corporate or literary interests.

Although Chile and Neruda are its setting and inspiration, the republic's citizens are the "unchronicled," the disappeared "without history," and those "disgusted with what Marx called 'all the old crap.'" Their representatives are poets, most from multiple souths. The collection alludes to or makes dedications to Cardenal,[18] the Chilean poet Raúl Zurita, the Chilean singers Víctor and Joan Jara, the South African poet Dennis Brutus, Whitman, and others. The dedication—"*This book is dedicated to Darío*"—alludes to a five-year-old Chilean boy named for the poet. The boy's "searching" eyes haunt the poem "Black Islands" (14), where Espada meets him "between Neruda's tomb / and the anchor in the garden." Moreover, "The Face on the Envelope" is dedicated to the Puerto Rican poet Julia de Burgos. When a Puerto Rican inmate, one of the "unchronicled," reads her in a Connecticut prison, he is so moved he draws her portrait on an envelope that eventually reaches Espada's "astonished hands" (35). Even one of two poems dedicated to a nonsouthern poet (global and US Souths) ends "somewhere near the border with México" (31), where Robert Creeley died. "You Got a Song, Man" has Creeley converse with Thoreau, who was jailed for "refusing tax for the Mexican War" (32). Others are dedicated to southern African American poets Jeff Male and Yusef Komunyakaa. In Virginia, "Confederate ghost-patrols" haunt Male (29), while "No Words But Hands" depicts the difficulty of consoling the Louisiana-born Komunyakaa, who accompanied Espada to Chile shortly after his wife and son died.

Transportation figures set these souths in motion to converge on the contested state of Chile on September 11, 1973. Trains, cars, boats, helicopters, and planes appear throughout the collection, from the title poem's first and final lines, which occur in the airport, to the Chile cycle's last poem, which begins with Pinochet's limousine and ends with him "scurrying away with his bodyguards" (25). "Not Here," the book's second poem (5–7), uses figures of ships, planes, and cars to depict the coup from disjunctive North-South geographies. Its multiple space-times map a "North by South" perspective on neoliberalism's foundational event. They include September 11 in Santiago and Valparaíso, "on or around" the same day in Washington, D.C., 1982 in the air above New York, and July 2004 in Santiago, the poem's "today." Beginning with the title, "Not Here" suggests displacement, yet it also contains multiple elsewheres in the dual roots of utopia, Greek for "no-place" and "good place." First, "Not" indicates somewhere else, a "no-place" demarcated from *here*. Second, the full title follows the poem "The Republic of Poetry," which is a quintessentially "good place." As such, "not here" is always theoretically *there*. The utopian possibility of converting unjust spaces to "good places" subtends Espada's poetics. Yet the extant critical focus on his advocacy for Latino, working-class, and migrant cultures often misses how "good places," or "spaces of hope," Harvey's term for how critical geographic practice can renovate utopian thought, emerge under oppression. Harvey argues that utopian forms must account for "the production of space and time." Most utopianisms, he shows, focus on space or time, modeling either "spatial form" or "social process" (*Spaces of Hope* 182). The former isolates an ideal space from the historical-geographical processes that actually create spaces, while the latter (as in the "blank page") ignores the spatial forms through which historical processes work. "Not Here" critiques this delinking of form and process by interlinking "here" and "there" and "then" and "now." In this way, otherwises can be built through the passive "broken"—a given spatial form—and the active "to break"—a historical process.

As a constant negation of present space, place, and time, "Not Here" reflects on relations between violent past places and potentially redemptive future space-times. These geographies of possibility are bound to antagonistic North-South formations across which Darío's "searching" eyes seek new "incantations." In the North, President Nixon asked his advisors to "make the [Chilean] economy scream" after Allende's election in 1970 (Grandin 59). In the South, Rubén Darío's image of US imperialism as a "deep-seated tremor" following "the enormous vertebrae of the Andes" conjures the coup and its aftermaths as powerfully as it did Theodore Roosevelt's "big stick" (150–153). These North-South geographies warn against equating the actually existing nation-state of Chile with the utopian "republic." Although the title poem begins with the dedication "*for Chile*," this approach mistakes the form of the ideal state for the actual, neoliberal one from which it conceptually emerges. In other words, "here," "there," and elsewhere become entangled, and Chile becomes the material location where the struggle for the utopic space-time of the latter is enacted. In this way, the title poem contrasts the brutality of "Not Here" with depictions of poetry's usefulness that appear throughout the book. Not only do poems create "joy," but they are "useful as a coat to a coughing man" (30), providing comfort and protection to the suffering and marginalized.

This conception of use-value guides the title poem, as the basic needs of cooking and eating are removed from the market calculus of exchange-value. Instead they reproduce collective poetic values: "kitchens in restaurants / use odes for recipes / from eel to artichoke, / and poets eat for free" (3). Because five year olds and line cooks are also poets in this republic, these lines stake a claim to radical egalitarianism and everyday practical transformation, in which poetry is as essential as cooking and eating. They allude to Dalton's claim "that poetry, like bread, is for everyone," which

Espada cites in *Poetry Like Bread*, his anthology of political poets of the Americas that includes Cardenal, Dalton, and Herrera (20). By subtly linking Dalton's claim to Nerudian odes to eels and artichokes, "The Republic of Poetry" expands the expressive palate of literary production. These everyday practices are spaces of radical possibility creatively legislating new norms. The republic thus poeticizes "resistance to the idea that authenticity, creativity, and originality" are the product of the capitalist class rather than "working class, peasant or other non-capitalist historical geographies" (Harvey, "Art of Rent" 108). As an anti-capitalist imaginary, the republic critiques systemic features promoting and reproducing capitalist domination in general. Emphasizing use-value, the realm of quality, rather than the abstracted quantitative calculus of exchange-value, which does not distinguish bread from napalm, as Cardenal's "Room 5600" shows, substitutes coats and recipes for fetishized forms of appearance. The republic thereby makes poetry—as a use-value exchanged for free that sustains as bread rather than Wonder Bread—the state's form of fellowship.

Like Pacheco's "collective" poetry made between writers and readers, and Bolaño's "Poetry" as collective liberation from imposed "stories," Espada's "co-authorship" includes excluded others in the composition process. If "the subject of the poem is, in a way, the co-author of the poem," as Espada writes (*Zapata's Disciple* 110) and as I discussed in chapter 1, his intertextual republic has many "co-authors"—other poets, five year olds, cooks, prisoners, families of the disappeared, and Brooklyn public-housing residents. This idea converts poems' "subjects" from objects of literary gazes into lyric speakers. "Not Here" is dedicated to Zurita, the poem's "co-author" and one of Espada's guides to Chile. Although Zurita's poetics trends much more experimentally than Espada's—the cover of *Purgatory*, his first book, calls him "a postmodern master"—each poet reveres Neruda, who is their common ground.[19] "Not Here" excerpts and italicizes lines from Zurita's *Anteparadise* that respond with "love" and "dancing" to his torture under Pinochet. Whereas "multiple configurations of utopia" in *Anteparadise* map "the radical dissolution of intersubjectivity" (Weintraub 228–229), Espada creates radical intersubjectivities between North and South and among Latino and North and Latin American poets to contest official narratives of the coup. And if Zurita "reconstruct[s] the 'imaginary community' of the [Chilean] nation" (Kuhnheim 80), Espada makes Chile the site for launching an imaginary transnational "republic." In juxtaposing poetic languages from the Latino North and the Chilean South and as plural responses to the US-backed coup, "Not Here" and the "republic" provide exemplary instances to support Longo's idea of a canon comprised of Latina/o and Latin American poets ("Poet's Place"). Espada thereby converts his own formative "canon" into an inter-American "republic" connecting "Broken Souths" across space-times that he believes all writers of conscience must eventually confront.

Whereas binaries such as here/there and above/below produce canons by separating nations and "high" cultures from "low" cultures, "Not Here" redraws spatiotemporal relations between D.C. and Chile, North and South, Latino and Chilean, by collapsing time frames, tenses, and locations. It begins with the lyric present tense: "The other poets tell me he tried to blind himself." This line occurs in the poem's "today," in July 2004, as Zurita and Espada walk "through the courtyard / of the presidential palace," and as the latter reflects on being told by other Chilean poets at the Neruda celebration about Zurita's attempt to poison himself.[20] The poem then shifts to "September 11, 1973," then back to the present, and then to 1980 ("seven years later"), when Zurita wrote *Anteparadise*. Subsequently, the poem returns to "today" before moving to the years "*after the bombing, after the coup*" when, as Zurita says, Chileans had to grieve Allende in silence, "heads down, hands in pockets." This image represents "the suffering of our time," in Blanchot's terms: "'A *wasted man, bent head, bowed shoulders, unthinking, gaze extinguished.' 'Our gaze was turned to the ground*'" (81). Espada replaces this asymmetric relation between suffering and empathy with intersubjective "searching" eyes that parallel Bolaño's "searching" for "missing footsteps."[21] Finally, the poem shifts back to the present tense and, in the last stanza, to "on or around the night of September 11, 1973," when the poet is sixteen, "ten miles away" from the White House, intoxicated, and joyriding in torrential rain.

To reorder these geographic grammars and lyric tenses, "Not Here" uses visionary figures of the elements introduced in the title poem's rain and airport images. They embody emancipatory and oppressive potentialities, being subject to contestation by "subversives" like Zurita and by metonymic forces of oppression: "warships," "knuckles," "*steel-toed boots*," and "the plotters." No element is controlled by either side; rain is equated to knuckles but also to the "tongue" and thus to poetry. Given that the coup appears in metonyms, glances, and insinuations, it approximates Bolaño's "imaginary being" flinging its tail back and forth. Such power is difficult to locate or still; neither here nor there, it eludes comprehension and capture, residing behind warships, knuckles, and boots but not in them.[22] In contrast, Zurita's embodied presence is "forged" in fire, from the materials used to torture him. He was held for two months, "a prisoner of circumstance" deemed suspicious as a student carrying a folder of avant-garde poems (Kuhnheim 72–73). Because he was tortured "deep in the ribs of a navy ship," and his "beard is forged in gray, the steel of a navy ship," his poetry, and by extension Espada's, emerges from symbols of water and fire. "Today," in July 2004, "only the water knows how many" were disappeared after "warships invaded the harbor of Valparaíso / and subversives staggered at gunpoint / through the city of hills down to the dock." Yet the palace's "fountain" also "speaks in the water's tongue" as the poets walk beneath it. The "speaking" fountain circulates the harbor's knowledge and eventually circulates through the republic's poets, who speak in and through the elements. "Not Here" makes this idea explicit: "Zurita knows what the water knows, / what the sky will not confess even to the gods / who switch the electricity on, off, then on again." The poet's knowledge matches the water's, but it exceeds both "the gods" of nature and Pinochet's "gods" of torture. Although the former "gods" control "electricity," orchestrating passages from day to night into perpetuity ("on, off, then on again"), and the latter wield cattle prods of electroshock, both types of "electricity" course through Zurita's body. "The other poets tell" Espada *"electricity was involved"* in Zurita's torture. Whereas the passive voice disembodies his torturers, Zurita's knowledge is "lodged in [his] body," to use Eltit's words (1801). His poetic project is grounded in sensory experience and the strength to withstand the "shock treatment" also figuratively given to the Chilean state and body politic by the Chicago Boys. Zurita thus speaks through the "water's tongue" to "co-author" a "republic" that turns metonymic tools of torture into emancipatory elements. Rather than descend as "electricity" from above, this poetics emerges from below, from the depths of oceans and prisons.

Espada also subverts symbols of above/below with images of the sky drawn from contestatory literary formations under Pinochet. Zurita and Eltit were members of Colectivo Acciones de Arte (CADA), an art collective formed in 1979. Of their many public installations and "happenings," ¡Ay South America! "involved scattering 400,000 pamphlets over Santiago from six civilian aircraft" (Eltit 1803).[23] Espada's title poem likewise transforms iconic images of descending bombs into "poems on bookmarks" that "bombard the national palace" from "rent[ed]" helicopters (4). "Not Here," moreover, alludes to Zurita's "sky-writing" project. In 1982, the year Espada published his first collection, *The Immigrant Iceboy's Bolero*, Zurita was flying over El Barrio, Manhattan's Puerto Rican/Latino neighborhood where many Espada poems are set, "writing" one-line poems. Whereas Zurita's poems were literally "written in the sky" and reproduced as photographs at the beginning of *Anteparadise*, Espada's republic emerges figuratively from convergences between above and below, sky and earth, literary and popular cultures, canonical poets and unnamed prisoners, North (as above, in conventional cartographic maps) and South (as below, in said maps). His poem "bombing" rewrites the army's bombing of the presidential palace on September 11, and poems gently "fluttering from the sky" further counters DINA, which "dispose[d] of some victims by dropping them into the ocean from helicopters" (Klein 110). Espada thus follows CADA and Zurita in redeeming the elements from their use for murder and concealment.

"Not Here" revises representations of the coup by replacing monuments, a form of historical memory fundamental to nation-states, with lyric poems. "Today," Espada writes, "Allende is white marble outside the palace, / mute as a martyr, without a free hand to wave / from the balcony, without a voice to crackle / his last words in the radio air." Like Valparaíso harbor, Allende's monument cannot speak, and his September 11 radio address is inalterable. For similar reasons, Lefebvre argues *"against the monument."* "Essentially repressive," it converts historical memory from active process to rigid object. Yet Lefebvre also reserves theoretical space *"for the monument"* because it incorporates a "u-topic" collective "sense of being *elsewhere"* (*Urban Revolution* 21–22). Lefebvre's understanding of space as absolute, relative, and relational underlies how collective memory is unpredictable. The Allende monument, like private property forms, is in absolute space. It has boundaries, measurable height, weight, and density, and a location outside the presidential palace, among other quantitative metrics. However, Harvey writes, this notion "helps not a whit with the question" of how it enfolds disputed meanings (*Spaces of Global Capitalism* 126). The statue also has relative dimensions—its proximity to the balcony from which Allende gave his final address and the palace where he died along with its similarity to other statues. Not until we consider relational space-time—the realm of subjective memory—can we parse competing claims on history. Harvey writes of Ground Zero:

> If the site is merely historicized in relative space (by a certain sort of monumentality) [i.e., it happened *here*, not *there*] then this imposes a fixed narrative on the space. The effect will be to foreclose on future possibilities and interpretations. Such closure will tend to constrict the generative power to build a different future. Memory, on the other hand, is [. . .] a potentiality that can at times "flash up" uncontrollably at times of crisis to reveal new possibilities. The way the site might be

lived by those who encounter it then becomes unpredictable and uncertain. (*Spaces of Global Capitalism* 137–138)

The forces that produced September 11, 1973, and 2001, Harvey argues, require an "accounting" that allows creative space for reinterpretation and the contingencies of subjective memory (138). Espada's "republic" models a monumentality that eschews "fixed narrative" and "closure" for Benjamin's flashes that open spaces for imagining otherwises, and the multiple space-times of "Not Here" need readers to map their relations and to interpret their logic and consequences. For Espada, poems, rather than monuments, "crackle" with subversive, utopic possibilities.

"Not Here" integrates relative and relational concepts of space-time to make a poetic "accounting" of the disaster. The last stanza's transportation figures reassess the North-South symbolism of "here" and "there":

I am the one navigating the night without stars.
On or around the night of September 11, 1973,
at the age of sixteen,
I was vandalizing a golf course in the rain,
fishtailing my car through the mud on the ninth hole
as beer cans rolled under my feet.
Ten miles away, at the White House,
the plotters were pleased; the coup
was a world in miniature they painted by hand,
a train with real smoke and bells
circling the track in the basement.
The rest of us drank too much, drove too fast,
as the radio told us what happened
on the other side of the world
and the windshield wipers said
not here, not here, not here. (7)

The two absolute space-times of September 11, 1973, are clear departure points for unpacking the stanza. In Valparaíso, Zurita is "in the ribs of a navy ship," while near D.C. Espada is "fishtailing [his] car through the mud." If September 11's space-time is unequivocal in Chile, even the day itself is uncertain for the teenager. "On or around" the same day, he "navigate[s] the night without stars." Plunged in darkness in the White House's figurative shadow, he lacks a compass (even a "fever") to locate himself and his memories. The relative conception of space-time points to differences between "here" and "there," D.C. and Chile, and the proximity of the golf course, a symbol of leisure, to the White House. But a relative dimension in size also exists: the title poem's "train of poets" is diminished to a model train in a basement. These images disorder above and below, but they also point to the consequences of models. Like neoliberal monetarist models of inflation mitigation, the model train has "real smoke and bells." After all, neoliberalism's goal is "not to make a model that is more adequate to the real world"; rather, it contorts the world to fit the model (Clarke 58). Espada finds an apt figure for the restrictions on humanity in such models, and his "train full of poets" figuratively enlarges, democratizes, and pluralizes the miniature train.

The idea of relational space-time offers the most provocative valence on these divergent memories of September 11, 1973. Lived, relational spaces of experience, or "spaces of representation," in Lefebvre's terms, "overlay" the imagination onto material spaces shaped by hegemonic power. They contain "affective kernel[s]," which are the provenance of unpredictable memories, dreams, visions, phantoms, and psychic states that threaten official narratives (*Production of Space* 39, 42). If differences between memories of torture and joyriding are obvious, their shared "affective kernels" of transportation vehicles and ecological elements resonate between South and North. In Chile, a boat. In the United States, a car. In Chile, the sea, a fountain. In the United States, rain, beer. In Chile, the "radio air" carrying Allende's eloquent last words.[24] In the United States, vapid radio news. These subjective, relational aspects reinforce the power of poetic insight even as they denounce isolation and ignorance produced in the shadow of the White House. Zurita speaks with the "water's tongue," the sixteen year old speaks with beer's sloppy imprecision. Windshield wipers, moreover, clear water to improve the driver's vision, but "what the water knows" is swept into gutters. The squeaking sound of wipers, *"not here, not here, not here,"* may be a byproduct of protection from the elements, but it hides the teenager beneath a shield of ignorance, a fiction of disconnection orchestrated "ten miles away," where the White House argued that the coup produced "freedom" and "order." Orlando Letelier, Allende's ambassador to the United States, wrote in 1976 that there was instead "an inner harmony" between terror and repression and the establishment of free-market "reforms," in contradistinction to US government and corporate claims that they had nothing to do with the "economic freedom" Pinochet brought to Chile. DINA agents later assassinated Letelier in D.C. for exposing this inverse relation between economic and political freedoms (137, 142).[25]

Espada similarly converts neoliberalism to "anti-communism" to evacuate its idealism. In defending Neruda to a conference panel hostile to political poetry in general and Neruda's politics in particular, he uses this lens: "Communism was not the great political scourge of Latin America in the twentieth century; it was anti-communism. The ideology of anti-communism fueled the bloody military coup in Chile." He then catalogues the neoliberal counter-revolution's violence in the Southern Cone's Dirty Wars, Central American "slaughter[s]," and "the continued colonial occupation of Puerto Rico." Like Bolaño's imaginary beast, "the ghost of anti-communism is always with us" (*Lover of a Subversive* 91). This link finds nuance in "General Pinochet at the Bookstore," the final poem in the Chile cycle (25). The epigraph places it in Santiago, in July 2004, when Pinochet's "limo" drops him to "browse / for rare works of history" in a bookstore ironically called "La Oportunidad." No evidence of his guilt remains: "There were no bloody fingerprints left on the pages. / No books turned to ash at his touch." But the poem unexpectedly declares that the reality is, in fact, "Worse: His hands were scrubbed." This variant on the "blank page" alludes to imprisoned student leaders whose 1985 protest poem, "Our hands are clean," became a symbol of struggle against Pinochet (Constable and Valenzuela 263). The image also refers to Neruda's *Canto general*, with its images of hands, and Espada's poetic catalogue of hands. Here, Espada converts the symbol of labor to Pinochet's ability to avoid trial and punishment. By linking his "clean" hands to leisure ("browse"), consumption (shopping), class power ("limo"), luxury ("rare"), and the threat of violence that protects these privileges ("bodyguards"), the poem joins authoritarianism to the means and the ends of the neoliberal project while also suggesting the necessity of texts ("bookstores") to call such power to account. It ends with the gathered "crowd" "jeer[ing]" the aged dictator, who is "so much smaller in person." The relational question—*smaller than what?*—goes unspoken. Are dictators always "smaller" than both "the crowd" and the global forces ensuring their power?

"Not Here" makes these nuanced links with a figure of "the other side of the world." This shifting, relative geography finds its form in the squeaky windshield's illusory *"not here,"* which symbolizes the ideological disconnection between state terror and market freedom. If September 11, 1973, was horrifyingly outsized for Chile, it "was a world in miniature" the White House "painted by hand." Such illusion defines the teenager's car as an ironic figure of isolation, confinement, and stasis against the car's conventional symbolism of mobility and freedom, as in metaphors of "the road." Whereas the windshield is clear, rain falls all around the car. The car, moreover, fails to deliver "the news," as Creeley insists poets must do in "You Got a Song, Man." "*Drive*," he tells Espada, "because poets must / bring the news to the next town," not to mention "the other side of the world."[26] This passage helps work out the remaining paradoxes of the poem's conceptions of "here" and "there." Given that "here" is a constantly shifting deictic that requires contextualization, it follows us wherever we go. On the other hand, "not here" is always "there" and someone else's "here," just as it is always the "today" of the poem when it is read. This syntactical role of "here" recalls Berger's claustrophobia and absolute space but also constant movement. Neoliberal globalization, after all, produces extreme inequality and all sorts of enclosures, but it also opens possibilities for connections across plural iterations of "here." "The other side of the world" now seems more connected to "here" than it must have in 1973. This is not to a posit a "flat" world or agency unconstrained by class or race, for instance, merely that access to knowledge has increased across geographic scales, and that even local and antiglobalization movements often operate globally. In "Not Here," the here/there binary is a fictional disjunction that serves neoliberalism's power structures and official stories. "Not here," in this sense, is like "the dog's path"— where poets must go to "bring the news" of both disaster and possibility.

Espada's republic ultimately makes "the news" of September 11, 1973, and 2001 neoliberal-era cornerstones. His multiple temporal markers spanning the three decades between these events extend what Longo calls Espada's use of Neruda to "rethink" the "common understanding" of US history ("Post Wonder Bread" 146). In this sense, it is difficult for US readers to read "September 11, 1973" without also seeing "September 11, 2001." Even implicit juxtapositions conjure neoliberalism's key contradiction: disaster facilitates the implementation of free-market reforms. Bolaño's and Espada's "countries" emerge between these events, and the republic's constitutive linkages between North, *as* here, and South, *as* there, provocatively shift their meanings. Beverley writes that September 11, 1973, initiated a period of right-wing ascendancy in which Latin America and the United States were integrated "under the neoliberal sign." September 11, 2001, in contrast, began a new era in Latin America, with leftist electoral triumphs and new social movements. Echoing Hegel and Mignolo, Beverley believes this dichotomy will lead to further North-South confrontations ("Dos caminos"). Espada seeks to head off such confrontation by imagining an inter-American "republic" comprised of poets and laborers from overlapping "Broken Souths" who critique and remake the North.

For Espada, confrontation is not inevitable nor is it definitive, but we need new "incantations," and fast.

His republic reorients these North-South relations by equating September 11, 1973, to September 11, 2001, in global significance. This historical geography of the second event reveals free-market fundamentalism as a leading cause of terror. Espada's relation to Dorfman illustrates this idea. In the acknowledgments of *The Republic of Poetry*, Espada thanks him "for reading the Chile poems." Whereas little can be gleaned from this acknowledgment about Dorfman's influence on the poems, his essay on September 11, 1973, and 2001 offers some insight. Dorfman is well positioned to understand the relationship between the events. Before being exiled from Chile after working for Allende, he spent much of his childhood in New York. "Haunted by the need to understand and extract the hidden meaning of the juxtaposition and coincidence of these two September 11s," Dorfman posits a "commensurate disorientation" that creates a systemic historical geography in "the multiple variations of the many September 11s that are scattered through the globe" (2–3, 5). In this sense, Espada's September 11, 2001, poems ("Alabanza: In Praise of Local 100" [*Alabanza* 231–232], and "Return" [45] and "The God of the Weather-Beaten Face" [48–50] in *The Republic of Poetry*) combine with his September 11, 1973, poems to bookend those about dispossession in the United States, Mexico, Nicaragua, El Salvador, Puerto Rico, and elsewhere in the intervening years as "variations" of neoliberal disaster. Like Bolaño's "silly" question, these "heres" of neoliberal-era violence deconstruct and reinforce each event's monumentality while reframing US readers' "common understanding" of "September 11" as one disaster among others.

In *Heading South, Looking North*, a title recalling Verdecchia's "backwards" walking from north to south, Dorfman concludes that September 11, 1973, marked the end of an era animated by revolutionary spirit and the concomitant beginning of neoliberalism:

> Pinochet was preparing the world as we know it now, more than twenty years later, where [. . .] greed has been proclaimed as good and profits have become the only basis to judge value and cynicism is the prevailing attitude and amnesia is vaunted and justified as the solution to all the pain of the past. [. . .] Allende's revolution, rather than being the wave of the future, was the last gasp of a past that was dying, [. . .] we were the dinosaurs, we were the ones buried in the past, we were the

ones who wanted to resist globalization, we were the ones who wanted to base our lives on something other than neo-liberal competition and individualism. (261–262)

Pinochet readied "the world as we know it now," when "freedom" and "free markets" conceal imperial wars, state violence, and plunder. Bolaño and Espada critique the "attitude and amnesia" structuring this reality by calling out state violence and by imagining "something other than neo-liberal competition and individualism" as state norms. In Chile, "transitology," a primary approach to viewing the post-Pinochet state, largely brackets the preceding violence (Rowe 281), while the banning of Tucson's Mexican American studies program erases the imperial histories behind immigration to the United States. Dorfman's take on the inevitability of defeat, moreover, reinforces Bolaño's "everything would be the same" version of Latin American history, while his lament for "buried" otherwises finds balm in Espada's republic. Bolaño's and Espada's mapping of intertextual "countries" via this violence ultimately counters the "post-" rhetoric Dorfman finds so intractable. This rhetoric is advantageous to the neoliberal state, which was born in violence and continues to utilize and profit from it. Despite ample talk of the nation-state's obsolescence, it retains imaginary allure and powerful influence. Neoliberal ideology, Derksen rightly argues, views the state "as the unwieldy outmoded social apparatus that burdens the market," yet it retains the state's role in "reregulating" the political economy toward corporate power and in producing the nation as a "powerful affective symbol" (23). After all, Chomsky writes that the rhetoric of rugged individualism and self-reliance is "selectively employed as a weapon against the poor, [as] the wealthy and powerful will continue to rely upon state power" ("Notes on NAFTA" 20). These ideas collectively pinpoint the Tea Party's contradictions (nationalistic fervor and antigovernment rage) and the essence of the neoliberal project: class power.

Bolaño's "country" and Espada's "republic" emerge from exile north and travel south, respectively, and from broken bonds with their states of origin. If states function by shared norms and rights, theirs cluster around those of writers and readers: imaginative flights; free expression; unlimited access to books; compassion for the outcast and defeated; abiding respect for the hidden, buried, and forgotten; and the youthful hope that is the *sine qua non* of "Poetry." Levinson reminds us that any cultural mode that does not acquiesce to market logic is a poetics. The same is true of texts such as Bolaño's and Espada's that reject the state's acquiescence to the market. "Such a poetics *es muy poco*: it is not enough," Levinson writes, "[b]ut it is nonetheless the horizon of possibility" (98). Chapter 4 moves from the state to the region within the state, exploring how Appalachian Latino writing expands Latino poetry's own "horizons of possibility."

CHAPTER FOUR

"Andando entre dos mundos"
Maurice Kilwein Guevara's and Marcos McPeek Villatoro's Appalachian Latino Poetics

[T]he rise of the violentologists enunciates the perversity, persistence, and obliqueness of terror as constructor of modern life in Colombia.
— Santiago Villaveces-Izquierdo,
"The Crossroads of Faith" (307)

One test of whether Appalachia retains its distinctive image in the twenty-first century will be whether the children and grandchildren of Spanish-speaking immigrants find their identities as Latinos or as mountaineers.
— John Alexander Williams, *Appalachia* (394)

While browsing a bookstore in Bogotá's Eldorado International Airport in 2010 after visiting friends, I noticed a book bearing the name of Colombia's former president amid the typical airport fare: travel guides, detective novels, self-improvement tracts, celebrity memoirs. Juan Manuel López Caballero's provocative title, *Alvaro Uribe: El Caballo de Troya del Neoliberalismo* [Alvaro Uribe: The Trojan Horse of Neoliberalism], was exciting but dissonant. With Uribe's approval rating hovering at 80 percent following the demise of the FARC (Revolutionary Armed Forces of Colombia), I knew I had just benefitted from security improvements. The book also reminded me that, as a US citizen, my taxes financed Plan Colombia, the "war on drugs," and the economic-military aid that supported the "Trojan Horse." It also symbolized the visibility of anticapitalist discourse in Colombia in comparison to the United States, where it often elicits condescension and scorn. Finally, just as Espada ends his Chile cycle with

Pinochet browsing a bookstore for "works of history," as if to remind us that dictators also read, and Bolaño locates his "country" within a portable library, Santiago Villaveces-Izquierdo situates the critical legacy of "violentology," the institutionalized study of violence in Colombia, within a bookstore as he browses "varied and multiple" texts about violence. The violentologists, he writes, embraced the study of "our heaviest burden but also our major constructor of national identity" (305).

Although violence has decreased markedly, it remains a symbol of Colombian identity, particularly in the United States. The airplane is a pliable figure of this violence, as in cartel drug planes, Plan Colombia crop dusters, and drug mules.[1] In Kilwein Guevara's *Autobiography of So-and-so: Poems in Prose*, a collection of surreal prose poems that graft Colombian history onto Appalachian historical geographies, the life of the Colombian Pittsburgher "So-and-so" unfurls with airplane figures marking formative turns. The consecutive poems "Why I Return to Colombia" and "Clearing Customs" depict the narrator returning to Colombia for the first time since leaving Belencito, a tiny pueblo in the Andes north of Bogotá, for Pittsburgh, as a child. Descending into Bogotá, his airplane diminishes to a moth: "Returning took thirty years: I fly into Bogotá at night. Landing in the Andes is like a moth dipping into the side of a starry bowl" (50). This otherworldly metaphor emerges from a delicate figure of nature. From above, the narrator casts hyper-urbanization as the gentle, nurturing warmth of an inverted cosmos, a source of sustenance ("bowl"), and a countervailing force to invasive security and surveillance measures symbolized by a customs agent examining the narrator's typewriter and his claims to being a poet with suspicion.

Kilwein Guevara's airport figures subtly participate in revising the narrow expectations of what Verdecchia's Wideload calls "estereotypes," which the character uses to critique North American images of Colombia and the "war on drugs" and to reeducate the "Saxonian community" about Latinos (60–63). Popular images of Appalachia similarly miseducate by concealing economic and ideological structures. "Estereotypes" in particular limit understanding by reproducing the either/or logic found in John Alexander Williams's "Latino"/"mountaineer" binary in the epigraph above. Against this logic, Kilwein Guevara and Villatoro merge Latino and Appalachian identities, often by using transportation figures and by critiquing invidious stereotypes. While Kilwein Guevara enigmatically reworks Colombian and Appalachian images in northern Appalachia, Villatoro rethinks Latino subjectivity in light of the rural US South's haunted racial history. Together, they develop an Appalachian Latino poetics by drawing from and transforming Latino, Latin American, and Appalachian traditions and practices.

Whereas the airplane connects places from above, this emerging Latino literature also "walks" between them. Villatoro's first collection, *They Say that I Am Two*, features images of walking that symbolize the restlessness of being in between languages and histories. The section titled "Central America: Walking the Sweet Waistline" mobilizes Neruda's image of "La dulce cintura de América" (7) with "walking" as a means of practical traversal and reverent pilgrimage. Whereas Herrera's "A Day Without a Mexican" underscores the potential of Latinos walking together, and Bolaño directs readers to walk in search of his generation's "missing footsteps," Villatoro emphasizes the individual Latino's negotiation of multiple historical geographies. This conceit crests in "Oda a Selena," his Spanish-language ode to the murdered Chicana pop star. The poem's speaker believes that Selena was, and he *is*, "andando entre dos mundos / como si fueran uno" [walking between two worlds / as if they were one] (*On Tuesday* 73; my translation). When paired with his idea that Latino split subjects are unified through the body's circulating blood, that "blood knows only one body," as his first collection's title poem puts it (77), this walking trope situates Villatoro's and Kilwein Guevara's Latino identities on the ground, in the body, and within the metaphors of a poetics, as suggested by "como si" ("as if").

Similarly, Kilwein Guevara's first collection, *Postmortem*, links its two sections, "America I," which takes place in Colombia, and "America II," located largely in Pittsburgh and northern Appalachia, through "The Bridge" (31). The poem refers to the latter locations as the "new America." It ends when "everything / begins to shake and roar" and the five year old's mother warns him of the "*ferrocarril*" (train). Images of transportation, mountains, blood, and bodies "bridge" Kilwein Guevara's and Villatoro's poetic settings. The "walking" Latino gathers these "worlds" into one body by animating de Certeau's equation of "pedestrian processes to linguistic formations." The "walking" body remaps North-South relations by creatively "weav[ing] places together" and by forming idiosyncratic "paths [that] give shape to spaces." Yet for de Certeau, "to walk is to lack a place" and to search constantly for stability (97, 103). These contradictions locate the Appalachian Latino body "walking" figuratively between worlds to "weave" them together into a new "shape," even as this movement recalls both displacement and absence.

Two shared contexts situate Appalachian Latino poetics in motion between "two worlds / as if they were one." First, imaginary constructs guide US relations with Appalachia as an internal region and Latin America as a world region. Second, uneven geographies of capitalist development reinforce and benefit from such constructions. As *ideas*, "Appalachia" and "Latin America" remain broken "compasses," to extend Verdecchia's figure of inter-American confusion, which misguide as often as not. It is no coincidence that scholars see each "idea" similarly. De la Campa views "America" as a contested ideological terrain of competing "locations" and "myths" that underlie the dissonance between the continental formation, as seen from Latin America, and the exclusionary US national identity. Constructions of "America" and "Latin America," he writes, are "arbitrary exercise[s] in location" and "sites not far from the lines of utopia and nostalgia." Their "myths," moreover, "are abundant and prone to constant revision" ("Latin, Latino, American" 373–374). Like "America," "Latin America" is partly an invention. Although "Latin America" is often "too large and diverse to be a useful category" for critical analysis (Chasteen xiii), its imaginary contours shape popular and literary perceptions, in the South and in the North.[2]

The idea of "Appalachia" likewise emerges from contested "myths" and "locations." Ronald D. Eller argues that Appalachia was "created by urban journalists." And like "Latin America," the idea of "Appalachia" serves as "a counterpoint" to US ideals of "progress" (1). Although "Appalachia is one of the oldest names on North American maps, dating from the early Spanish explorations" (Williams 9), disagreement remains about its contours and whether it is an invention.[3] Because political borders efface natural ones, Williams writes, "most scholars turn to cultural markers when they try to determine just where Appalachia begins and ends" (11). Similar questions guide US "American" studies and studies of the Americas paradigms. Was "America" "discovered" or "invented"? Is it one continent or two? Where does it begin and end? When did it begin? Is it an emancipatory or oppressive idea, or both? Like "Appalachia" and "Latin America," "Latino" is also a "fictive construct" (Gruesz, *Ambassadors* xi) with diverse "cultural markers." Kilwein Guevara's and Villatoro's texts are valuable partly because they expand the "cultural markers" for "Latino" from the "bridges" between Latin America and Appalachia, as shifting ideas and locations in relation to "America," the United States' imperial register.

"Latin America" and "Appalachia" are ideologically constructed as differentially scaled regions in relation to the United States. Whereas one is a world region and the other a region within the state, this scalar discontinuity belies how each interfaces with US power similarly. Whether one views this relation in terms of economic imperialism, colonialism, or uneven development, both are popularly viewed as the United States' "others." "Like Latinos in the United States," de la Campa writes, "Latin America is often forced into a conceptual or political unity as a hemispheric or civilizational 'other' to the United States" ("Latinos and the Crossover Aesthetic" xv). A similar claim can be made about Appalachia. Williams explains that modernist approaches define a region as "a territory set apart from others," thus foreclosing interpenetrations of culture and capital and internal variability. As such, drawing Appalachia's "official" boundaries in 1965, the federal Appalachian Regional Commission (ARC) "slice[d] across the mountains, valleys, and plateaus [. . .] as if those features had no geometries of their own" (10). This production of "region" rejects topographical groundings of place, in Dirlik's terms, and imposes "blank page" development models. In contrast, postmodern modes view a region as "a zone characterized by the interaction of global and local human and environmental forces" (12). This notion of "region" exposes conceptual unities and civilizational others as ideological constructs serving hegemonic power. In stressing interdependence and permeability, this idea guides Appalachian Latino poetics, which critiques negative Appalachian images and imagines Latino cultural geographies producing "Appalachia" differently.

As "place[s] apart" (Williams 8) from the United States, Appalachia and Latin America remain essential to its identity. Not coincidentally, government, financial, and corporate discourses have long used similar terms to portray Appalachia and Latin America as "the other America," in need of outside capital and expertise to fuel development. Whereas Latin America is referred to as the United States' "back yard," with its many demeaning connotations, Appalachia is the "backcountry" (Williams 16). The former relies on political and economic determinisms, the latter environmental determinism wherein mountain geography produces poverty and perversity. Each carries a portable, binary image store of "estereotypes." *Fronteras Americanas* suggests that North America reads "Latin America" through the hyper-masculine male—embodied by the "Latin Lover," Che Guevara revolutionary, and violent, idealistic cartel leader—and the desperate, dim *mojado* (wetback) who invades the orderly North and steals jobs from (white) citizens. Wideload archives these images in one character. The Appalachian corollary pits the self-sufficient mountaineer against the backward, barbarous hillbilly (Williams 17).[4]

Williams's sense that Appalachia is "a territory of images" (8) applies equally to popular North American perspectives of Latin America and Latinos. *Fronteras Americanas* compiles, satirizes, and *predicts* the contours of this "territory," with dictators, "third-world theme parks," coups, border fences, *mojados*, coyotes, gangbangers, drug mules, and "anchor babies." Such images of deprivation, violence, and lawlessness point to how "Appalachia" is used as a trope for depicting Mexico. Given that all Latinos are frequently "lumped with" Mexicans in the United States (Chavez 16), this popular construction converts stereotypes into vehicles for facile cross-cultural understanding. Two examples demonstrate. First, *Virginia Quarterly Review* includes this statement in its "war on drugs" issue: "Dominated by the Sierra Madre Occidental, Sinaloa is seen as backward back-country, Mexico's own Appalachia" (Apter 11). Second, an article in the *New Yorker*, that iconic index to urbane, liberal culture, relates how a "senior American diplomat" refers to a cartel in Michoacán—two states south of Sinaloa—as "'hillbilly-hero moonshiners of Mexico's Appalachia'" (Finnegan 46). Neither article questions the shared pivotal term of their analogies.

Equivalent imaginaries of Appalachia and Latin America as backward "Broken Souths" double the pressure on Latinos in Appalachia. As Latino and Appalachian, they are "the other America" twice over. Kilwein Guevara's and Villatoro's Appalachian Latino poetics enmesh these "others" by revising their image stores. This strategy contests civilized/backward and either/or binaries, locating cultural resources at convergence points between "others." Current iterations of these fraught regional imaginaries emerge from the development discourses of the 1960s that neoliberal-era uneven geographic development has magnified. The "war on poverty" aimed to mitigate Appalachia's asymmetric relation to US "progress." Yet it too was a Trojan Horse, concealing processes designed to extract wealth, strengthen class power, and perpetuate dependency. Eller notes that development officials, like the ARC, equated Appalachia and Latin America (73). His description of Appalachia's asymmetric "deficiencies" and "resources" echoes Mignolo's critique of the "idea" of Latin America as a "convenience store": "The perceived economic and cultural deficiencies of Appalachia allowed entrepreneurs a free hand to tap the region's natural resources in the name of development" (2). Activists have consequently likened Appalachia to a "banana republic" that receives "foreign aid" and where "absentee corporations" plunder "just as surely as they stole the riches of Central America" (Eller 136). As a "colonial possession" of corporations, the Appalachian poet-activist Don West adds, Appalachia endures euphemistic subterfuges. A true "war on poverty," he writes, would require "a total reconstruction of the system of ownership, production, and distribution of wealth" (68–69).

Whether the colony is internal to the state, as in Appalachia and Puerto Rico, or external, as in Latin America, these relations follow the logic of what Harvey and Greg Grandin call "the new imperialism," wherein diffuse legal, institutional, nongovernmental, and corporate powers replace centralized state control and military might. "Accumulation by dispossession" underlies how the new imperialism reproduces massive inequalities within the United States and between the United States and Latin America. Marx called this type of accumulation "original" or "primitive" due to its role in consolidating class power and the means of production at the beginning of the capitalist era. Capitalists had to start somewhere, often by violently appropriating collective lands in order to accumulate their "original" capital and to incorporate peasants into the wage-labor force. Yet this type of accumulation continues apace. Harvey defines accumulation by dispossession as "the wholesale appropriation by capital of all manner of things which it has little or nothing to do with creating" and the "external coercion by some superior power," such as corporations, to penetrate "pre-existing social order[s] and geographical terrain[s] to the advantage of that power." Not only are these processes "necessary" to the "survival" and "stability" of capitalism (*Spaces of Global Capitalism* 91–93), but accumulation by dispossession often utilizes coercion, fraud, and violence, as in privatized public lands, public education converted to for-profit enterprises, predatory foreclosures, dissolved pension funds, and eminent domain displacements, among other examples.[5]

Corporations have long viewed Appalachia and Latin America as regions from which to extract resources while leaving behind "externalities," like destroyed ecosystems and tainted water supplies. Because both regions, broadly speaking, have weak labor and environmental protections, extraction is often facilitated by exclusive access rights and generous tax breaks. In Appalachia, mountaintop removal mining and subsurface mineral rights are instances of "suppression of rights to the commons" and capital's "perpetual search" for resources as production inputs and independent surplus values (*Spaces of Global Capitalism* 43, 91–92). While Appalachia is a "national sacrifice zone,"[6] the Amazon and Andes are "multinational sacrifice zones" for corporations. "Sacrifice" turns the euphemism of "development" to "destruction," clarifying power relations between "region" and nation. In some parts of Appalachia, after all, corporations "control up to 90 percent of the surface land and 100 percent of the mineral resources" (Eller 199, 168). Eller thus writes that Appalachia has "always been tied to national markets, despite popular images of the region as isolated" and that "the long pattern of wealth flowing out of the mountains" continues unabated (223). Neoliberal keywords conceal these consequences in triumphal terms of economic "freedom," job "creation," energy "independence," and "clean" coal.

Alongside processes of dispossession that produce "region" and "place," migratory patterns have brought more Latinos to Appalachia. Although the Appalachian Latino population remains small relative to the US Latino population as a whole (1.3 percent) and to the total Appalachian population (2 percent), between 1990 and 2000 the Latino population in Appalachia increased 239 percent to 465,000. Several features distinguish this group from the US Latino population. Whereas Mexicans comprise 66 percent of the overall Latino population, they comprise 55 percent of Appalachian Latinos (Hayden 298; Barcus 298–299, 302). As of 2000, 49 percent of Latinos in Appalachia were born outside the United States, whereas 40 percent of US Latinos were foreign born (Barcus 298–299). And Kilwein Guevara's depictions of western Pennsylvania and Villatoro's of northern Alabama reflect the fact that "high-growth [Latino] counties are clustered in peripheral areas in [Appalachia's] northern and southern subregions" (Barcus 298).[7] In positing that the current Latino influx is "no more exotic" than earlier waves of migrants (394), including Scots-Irish, southern African Americans, and Eastern Europeans (Barcus 303),[8] Williams implicitly (if awkwardly) counters "the Latino Threat Narrative," Chavez's term for the mistaken set of "common sense" assumptions that Latinos are unlike previous groups due to their refusal to assimilate to US culture (2–3). Below, I trace a literary geography of Kilwein Guevara's northern and Villatoro's southern Appalachia, including a reading of "When the Paw Brought Us Down," Villatoro's poem about Immigration and Naturalization Service (INS) raids in northern Alabama that dramatizes the nefarious power of this fictitious "threat." I conclude with thoughts on how their inventive texts expand the historical, geographical, and aesthetic parameters of Latino literary studies.

Kilwein Guevara's Northern Appalachia

From *Postmortem*, *Poems of the River Spirit*, and *Autobiography of So-and-so* to *Poema*, Kilwein Guevara's collections enact increasingly sustained, experimental encounters between Latino, Appalachian, and Latin

American literary geographies.[9] His abiding interest in the power of images emerges in conjunction with his lyric speakers' intuitive apprehensions of Colombian and Appalachian historical conditions. As "a territory of images" constituted between Colombia and Appalachia, childhood sense perceptions and intertextual allusions, his poems use the surreal, disjunctive, unpredictable, and nonlinear to disrupt negative imaginaries. As in other "Broken Souths" poems, vehicles are prominent, from an "old, borrowed Dodge [that] has broken down in the middle of mountain" "on the road from Belencito to Bogotá" to Pittsburgh's "dirty yellow streetcars," "train[s] in the night" (*Autobiography* 24, 22), and "56C" buses (*Poems* 37). These figures accompany images of mountains, hills, and rivers, as well as decaying infrastructure (bridges, public housing stock, mills, and mines), in Colombia and in and around Pittsburgh.

Yet Kilwein Guevara's inter-American "territory of images" does not represent places or histories. Rather, he seeks to represent the images and symbols that purport to represent the realities. That is to say the "territory" is explicitly textual. This idea registers acutely in poems about Colombia in "So-and-so's" hemispheric "*Autobiography*."[10] "Why I Return to Colombia" ends with a ruminative question about images *as* texts: "What if all the stories you knew about the past fit into tiny photographs the size of slides, black & white with crenulated borders?" (49). The question recalls an earlier allusion to family photographs "at the airport in Bogotá on the day [they] all left Colombia" (27). These paired images of images (photos) render memory and perceptions of space and time functions of diminishing scales and flattened affects, as if to ask the appropriate scale for accessing "the past." Conspicuous spatial terms ("fit," "tiny," "size," "slides," "borders") and indicators of departure ("airport," "left") rather than place-based groundedness depict history and memory as atomized, portable images consolidated into decorative, delicate ("crenulated"), miniaturized packages for consumption. But by whom? The inquisitive apostrophe ("you") puts pressure on images to tell "the stories." In other words, lyric must do the work of narrative; it must be both Bolaño's "story" and "form." This idea implicates readers/viewers as consumers of images. By addressing "you" in the manner of Wideload, as if channeling his "You people love dat kinda *shit*," where "shit" is not a "third world theme-park" but its generative affect, nostalgia, Kilwein Guevara suggests that North American readers/viewers, including Latinos, readily consume packaged ("crenulated borders") images of Latinos and Latin America. These "borders" are purely for show, easily torn apart. What invokes nostalgia more stereotypically than "black & white" photos with faded, decorative borders? "The Latino Threat Narrative" emphasizes the supposed Latino resistance to leaving behind (and the inability to leave behind) cultures of origin to assimilate. Kilwein Guevara's "autobiography" undermines this idea by rendering it as an inverted nostalgia whose object is not the past but nostalgia itself. In the eyes of "So-and-so," leaving places behind is primarily what Latinos do—it is the very condition of his Latinidad.

A similar question underscores the US relation to Appalachia and Latin America, Colombia in particular. What happens when the public store of knowledge about a country or region can be condensed to "tiny photographs"? In one sense, Kilwein Guevara implies that using his work as a guide to Colombia, which then serves as a prism through which to view Latin America and Latinos broadly, produces not clarity but "smoke," in Herrera's image. And like Espada's figure of traveling south to Chile, Kilwein Guevara suggests that the journey will commence figuratively "in the rain." In another sense, he extends Verdecchia's deconstruction of stereotypes. Unlike Verdecchia, however, Kilwein Guevara examines them indirectly. At the outset of *Postmortem*, the poem "Violentólogo" (8) subtly initiates this project. In linking neoliberal-era violence to the conquest ("the moment of that first Spanish sword"), the poem echoes many of the preceding critical and creative perspectives. The poem's tight-lipped, minimally explanatory endnote, "Now the study of violence is a formal discipline in Colombia" (77), empties out critiques of violentology like Villaveces-Izquierdo's and leaves US readers with a discomfiting mixture of curiosity and reinforced stereotypes.

This purposeful mixture negotiates the pressure on Latino writers to produce rote magic realisms for US readers. Kilwein Guevara's critique of this pressure parallels Espada's response to a *New York Times* book review of *Alabanza*, with its obligatory remark about the collection's supposed magic realism. The review, he tells the Cuban American poet Rafael Campo, "reads like bad travel writing: it's a quick take on a foreign country (namely, me) full of little mistakes and an insulting cultural stereotype or two" ("Alabanza" and "Correspondence: Campo"). "Violentólogo" gestures toward the stereotype's logic of "if . . . then," as in *If he's from Colombia or if he's Latino, then he must be a magic realist*, which it breaks tentatively and obliquely. It follows an Indian "backfalling" at the "first Spanish sword" by negating the false restorations and transfigurations of historical violence underlying misapprehensions of magic realism. Its phrases "no magic then from the open bloody mouth" and "no green

spirit stalk or sudden flowering" reject expectations put on Latino writers by publishers and reviewers, even as the phrases fulfill them as nega-
tions. The publishing industry, Cruz writes, "package[s]" Latino texts by
"throw[ing] the label 'magic realism'" on them. His dual conclusion mimics these cynical, top-down evaluations of Latino cultures: "it's gotta be
magic, unreal sells well as exotica" and "'if you've read one Latino [text],
you've read them all'" (*Red Beans* 90–91).[11]

The epigraphs to *Postmortem* and *Autobiography of So-and-so* critique
this dynamic by broadening and constricting, respectively, conventional
expectations about Latino writing. If one were to read Kilwein Guevara's
collections chronologically, Cruz's proclamation, "We're all immigrants to
this reality," would constitute the initial encounter with his poetics. This
piece of paratext questions what constitutes "reality" by stressing metaphysics over the essentialized dimension of Latino experience, immigration,
which the quote transforms into a universal human experience. When Kilwein Guevara shared the source for this epigraph with me via e-mail it became clear that it pays homage to Cruz by formalizing the improvisational
spirit of astonishment in Cruz's poetics. It also suggests Kilwein Guevara's
desire to be read as a poet qua poet, not just as a Latino poet: "This must
have been around 1990 at Woodland Pattern Book Center in Milwau-
kee," he writes, "Victor was reading with Robert Creeley, as I recall. Victor
was speaking extemporaneously between poems when he remarked that
all humans are immigrants to this amazing reality of being alive." The
epigraph to *Autobiography* comes from Gabriel García Márquez: "I returned to this forgotten village, trying to put the broken mirror of memory
back together from so many scattered shards." Why would Kilwein Guevara allude to the most famous Colombian and iconic master of magic
realism to introduce the "autobiography" of an anonymous ("So-and-so")
Colombian immigrant to Appalachia? Homage is part of the story but
insufficiently explanatory. Whereas García Márquez is a key cipher, like
the drug mule, of external perceptions of Colombia, and thus serves Kilwein Guevara as a primary figure in his "territory of images," a Borgesian
thread ultimately connects the two epigraphs. The archetypes of Borges's
metaphysical poetics, such as the mirror, indicate how Kilwein Guevara
imagines metaphysical "breaks" in Latino subjectivity.[12] Like Verdecchia's
compass, "the broken mirror" is internalized in the Latino subject. Both
create faulty memories, bad directions, and distorted reflections, but unlike the compass that spins subjectivity on a North-South axis, the mirror
fragments and multiplies subjectivity to create a dispersed interior geography. As the lyric self becomes "many scattered shards," a "broken mirror"

supposedly brings years of bad luck. Chance and fate, archetypes obsessed over by Borges and Bolaño, link metaphysics to historical geographies of exile and return in Kilwein Guevara's poetry.

Because "the broken mirror" requires new ways of seeing and multiple places and positions from which to see, Kilwein Guevara proposes, tests, and models ways of seeing outside the narrow confines of stereotype, convention, and expectation. This process begins with a self-reflexive examination of his constructed Colombian-Appalachian Latino self. "Self-Portrait," the first poem of *Autobiography*, participates in the practice of the literary *autorretrato* (self-portrait) common in Latin American writing, as in Bolaño's "Self Portrait at Twenty Years" (*Romantic Dogs* 5). And like Pacheco's "José Luis Cuevas: a self-portrait," in which the Mexican painter Cuevas begins by "studying [him]self from the outside" (*Selected Poems* 87), Kilwein Guevara's narrator studies himself "from the outside." On "the canvas," he is "the size of a railroad spike," "naked, head shaved to the bone," his eyes "about to open." In order to see him, he says, "you need to walk to the other part of the canvas and get down on your knees" (9). This "self-portrait" disrupts narrative conventions, implicating the reader ("you"), who must get on the ground ("on your knees") to produce the marginal, abjectly objectified narrator on the canvas.

This approach extends and alters the ways in which Latino poets depict marginality in ways anterior to postmodern forms of engagement.[13] The narrator of "The River Spirits" (*Poems* 3), for instance, is a rat. Like the similarly detested cockroach, a metonym for exclusion and predation in Espada's poetry, Kilwein Guevara's rat gathers the voices of Pittsburgh's working-class immigrants. The prose poem "Rata's Preamble" (*Poema* 59), moreover, follows a rat-narrator as he goes "to work at a desk in Bogotá and later in a ditch in Pittsburgh." The rat's class-conscious expression of deprivation—"Ours would be a history of chronic needs"—links urban spaces and spheres of work ("desk" and "ditch") from south to north through a collective voice of dispossession. Such marginal figures speaking from below require forgoing detached gazes from above; their voices and subject positions are only comprehensible "on your knees" and "in a ditch." This meeting of above and below guides the juxtaposition of "*Autobiography*" and "*So-and-so*" in Kilwein Guevara's title. Whereas the subversive self-portrait of insignificance initially seems to reinforce a pliable rags-to-riches trope, the collection proves otherwise, as "so-and-so" connotes anonymity, disposability, and indifference. If an "autobiography" suggests the telling of a significant public life, "So-and-so" does not merit the attention of either publishers or readers.

The second poem of *Autobiography*, "Reader of This Page," subverts expectations further. It begins: "I had a dream in my mother's womb three days before I was born." After recalling his former name, his "different mother," and other aspects of his dream, the narrator asserts, "Then comes the part where I am burned alive on the second day of February, 1614." He then uses apostrophe to address the reader directly: "I remember you, reader of this page, as I remember the soldiers in the dream leading us through the streets to the plaza of Cartagena de Indias" (13). These metaphysical ruminations, oneiric challenges to empirical norms, disordered temporalities, textual disjunctions, and implication of readers in the production of meaning construct "So-and-so" through multiple displacements. Together with "Self-Portrait," the poem locates the ensuing Appalachian Latino "autobiography" in generative Latin American cultural, historical, and geographical space, whereby the future Latino subject is constituted interpersonally, with multiple names, mothers, fates, and readers, through far-reaching dreams of his origins. As in *Postmortem*, the subsequent Appalachian narrative emerges from Colombia, but in a more surreal manner, in which the diminishment in scale—from towering Andes to smaller Appalachians—finds an inverse relation to the proliferating image stores of Appalachia.

"Late Supper in Northern Appalachia" consolidates this trajectory from Colombia to Appalachia and from colonial violence in Cartagena to the narrator's "discovery" of a new "America" in Pennsylvania. The poem appears near the end of *Autobiography of So-and-so* (70), where the critique of Appalachian stereotypes extends the poet's meditations on the North American image bank of Colombian-ness. Because "Late Supper" comes between poems about mining disasters, it is also haunted by the dispossessions of resource extraction, which define the political economies and topographies of Appalachia (coal, natural gas) and Colombia (gold, emeralds) as it did those of the conquest alluded to in "Reader of This Page." "Late Supper" begins by staging images of rural Appalachia:

> Mise en scène:
> The relief check is shimmed between the salt and the
> pepper shakers.
> The mother stirs the pot of stars with a wooden spoon. The
> father goes whistling for the children like an ambulance in the dark.
> Out of the thickets they run, shirts on fire because they have been
> playing with matches again. (70)

"Mise en scène" means "putting on stage" and invokes an arrangement of characters for theater. This reenactment interrogates staged, sensationalist constructions of Appalachian-ness for the consumption of outsiders, stereotypical "culture of poverty" depictions of Appalachia that render it picaresque and outside of time. "What renders such efforts problematic," Mary K. Anglin writes, "is not their emphasis on regional culture but the degree to which they have written this as extraordinary, existing outside the narratives of history and advanced capitalism" (566). These "efforts" actually serve capital, in part by effacing capital's role in reproducing underlying structural conditions.

The poem's "mise en scène" notably focuses on the members of a nuclear family at a dinner table on which a "relief check" serves as centerpiece for "brackish stew, chunks of deer meat and the isotropic glow of corn and carrots." This jarring image does not reinforce neoliberal disgust for the welfare state (or, pejoratively, the "nanny" state) but instead critiques the critique, particularly its use of images of backwardness and incompetence to support its pernicious intentions. The poem does not depict unemployment benefits doled out to the undeserving poor, who lead lives of comfort with *your* hard-earned money, as in the company-line critique of the welfare state. Rather, it suggests the deindustrialization of northern Appalachia. The ensuing image of the family's "morning dove in the bamboo cage" suggests capital flight to cheaper labor markets in Asia. By confining the symbol of peace to a cage, moreover, it hints at the violent enclosures produced by the outsourcing of industrial jobs.

As in "Reader of This Page," the poem's direct challenge to the "reader" ("you") prescribes the audience's position vis-à-vis the family. But, critically, it does not determine "your" response to them or to the image that reproduces them for your consumption. The poem ends with an apostrophe, an iconic stereotype of Appalachia ("the trailer"), and further stress on the role consumers/viewers play in constructing stories through commodified images: "Reader, they've set a place for you at the table. 'You're welcome,' the mother says. Inside the trailer, the narcotic buzzing of cicadas drowns out everything except the story you came for." Like "all the stories you kn[o]w about the past" condensed into tiny, nostalgic photographs in "Why I Return to Colombia," the trailer constrains the reader's vision and implicates him in the reproduction of inaccurate images. The equivocal conclusion puts pressure on the reader's assumptions and prejudices, and the preposition that ends the poem emphasizes "your" ongoing entrance into their space. What story is it, exactly, that "you came for"?

By making the reader consume, or eat, his own construction, to enter the stage of his own stereotypes and sit at the table where these images have material impacts, the poem shifts the blame for poverty from the hard-working family to those who construct the view—those who "set" the stage rather than those who "set" the table. Because "you" only see what "you came for" poverty's quotidian dimensions become manipulative performance with a powerful confirmation bias. The welfare check is in plein air as if to say it creates invasive visibility rather than relief. "Shimmed between the salt and the pepper shakers," it reproduces the family every day. But it also provides flavor for guests/consumers, even as their "pot of stars" implies that the means of subsistence are more imaginary than material. In this sense, images of backwardness and ignorance ("the dark," "the thickets," and "playing with matches") conceal economic conditions that produce poverty by unfairly justifying its construction. These are ignorant "hillbillies," not self-sufficient "mountaineers." Yet the family displays more dignity than the putatively more sophisticated consumer of images (and poems), as the guest receives charity (a free meal) from the generous family that is itself consumed by a voracious national appetite for coal and images of the "other." Finally, the "pot of stars" echoes Bogotá as a "starry bowl" to suggest shared imaginary and material conditions across uneven North-South and rural-urban geographies.

Whereas a Latino poet might be expected to betray misgivings about Appalachia, with its relative paucity of ethnic and cultural diversity, Kilwein Guevara's poems revere its marginal voices. His empathic poems about impoverished Appalachian persons model a poetics of close listening to distinctive regional syntax, diction, and pronunciation. "Grimm the Janitor" (*Autobiography* 39) transcribes the vernacular speech patterns of a Vietnam War veteran with unflinching opinions and "one arm that didn't work completely." It documents the poet's immersion in this language, and his keen hearing of it, during the teenage narrator's summer as Grimm's assistant. He begins with a verse paragraph introducing Grimm's fourteen quoted pronouncements to follow, each of which begins with the anaphoric "Grimm said." "The whole time I worked for him," the narrator recalls, "he said *yes* and *nope* and *warsh that* and *move it* and *poosh that there* and very little else except for the day there was a thunderstorm; then he talked nonstop for twenty-five minutes." Grimm's first words, "Stay in school, boy," hint that this peculiar list-poem documents the narrator's education, and his second line humbly stresses Grimm's sensory, intuitive knowledge. "I ain't educated, see, but least I got eyes," recalls Darío's "searching" eyes in Espada's "republic" as unprepossessing repositories of potential revelation. Grimm's class- and place-based sightlines illuminate the contours of the neoliberal era in northern Appalachia. His direct pedagogy, like Wideload's, partly explains the Latino apprentice's deference to him and his use of Grimm as a guide to Pittsburgh, Appalachia, and the workings of hegemonic power.

This approach to reading "Grimm" makes his critique of the Vietnam War secondary to a structural analysis of neoliberalism voiced by one of its anonymous, disposable lives. Even so, Grimm views the "anti-communist" Vietnam War as fundamental to the logic of capitalist exploitation. He relates that "one day the government come knocking on my door and says, boy, now you got to get in a plane and fly a whole day and get off and kill some people you can't even talk to." For Grimm, the Vietnam War was not an isolated event but part of a pattern of global political-economic forces that dispossess the poor of life choices, dignity, and their own bodies. He tells "the talk show man on the AM radio" as he eats his "frozen dinner and drink[s] [his] Iron City" beer that "war is rich old men spilling out the blood of the young and poor." After alluding to his own horrific acts of violence in Vietnam, he complains: "French marigolds bring the lady bugs that eat the aphids on your tomato plants. And the aphids came here in the first place because they should have kept them Norway maples in Norway where they belong." This antiglobalization sentiment defends place in the name of ecosystem health, and its topographical grounding of place, in Dirlik's terms, prefers barriers to permeability. The string of unintended consequences, moreover, suggests the inertia underlying the implementation of market solutions to problems created by the market, while the monocausal logic creates an endless string that condemns cross-cultural human migrations by their proximate characteristics.

Such unpredictable and generally unintended convergences of natural forms, images, ideas, and cultural vernaculars have intensified under neoliberal globalization. Like Cruz's ecopoetics, which insists "the earth is migration" and celebrates languages "constantly breaking into each other like ocean waves" (*Red Beans* 87, 89–90), Kilwein Guevara's poetic bridge making is possible because his texts do not stay "where they belong"—say, in a narrow literary tradition or genre. Rhetorical constructions such as "they should have kept them [. . .] where they belong" are the province of the far Right, with its reactionary discourse emanating from spectral plural pronouns ("they" and "them") that view "belonging" in the individualistic, exclusionary terms of "the Latino Threat Narrative." Yet Grimm's comment is not metaphorical. Rather, it addresses his means of subsistence, the interrupted native food ways that leave him dependent upon the state and corporations he despises. His cultivated, specific knowledge of horticulture indicates idiosyncratic, independent thinking and experiential knowledge rather than parroted right-wing radio talking points. Grimm, moreover, seems to treat the teenage Latino immigrant as a confidante, while his ire is also directed at the most lily white of symbols, the Scandinavian state. Nonetheless, his logical sequence is followed by racist subtext—"them city problems started with that bussing"—that mistakes a government solution to spatialized segregation as the cause of urban dissolution. In Grimm's reasoning, buses are not a symptom of city problems but the cause for them. His denigration of the bus as a symbol of and vehicle for mitigating racial segregation recalls the civil rights movement and landmark Supreme Court cases. In conflating causes and effects, he reveals his mind's limitations as well as the bus's fraught symbolism.

Ultimately, "Grimm the Janitor" investigates how languages of dissent and discontent register across dispossessed groups, in this case immigrant Latinos and poor white Appalachians. In this sense, the poem conjures how resistance to neoliberal capitalism also emerges from the far Right. Yet it also enacts a powerful rejoinder to those who would dismiss Grimm as an ignorant hillbilly. His dynamic, contradictory spoken language is couched in, at the very least, a type of post-traumatic stress disorder and visceral class consciousness. Additionally, like the "you" referenced throughout *Autobiography*, Grimm, too, is a "reader of this page," and thus complicit in authoring its "territory of images." His last substantive comment, "I read where the whole mine just flatten like a pancake," is one of the book's free-floating allusions to mining disasters. But this allusion turns the poem authoritatively, if precipitously, to capital's abuse of labor as a disposable source of wealth creation. The mine is exhausted, workers are consumed like "pancake[s]," and Grimm is mangled by war. Appropriately, he stops talking when thunderstorm and poem end and they return to work: "Rain stop, boy. Poosh that there." His fragmented, dissociative stream of consciousness thus threads together disconnected and bizarre observations ("Ever skin a rabbit in the sunshine?") through the narrator's anaphora ("Grimm said") and the laborer's mangled body. This broken body fuels a global economic engine run by real abstractions ("rich old men" and "the government") that control wars, resource extraction ("the whole mine"), the production of nature ("marigolds" and "maples"), and global trade.

As a source for Kilwein Guevara's poetics, and one derived from careful close listening within the contexts of devalued labor and marginalized working bodies, "Grimm" offers a counterpart to identity-based Latino literary critiques of exploitation. Espada's "Jorge the Church Janitor Finally Quits," for instance, offers a similar class perspective expressed through the voice of a dispossessed immigrant janitor. As a first-person Latino narrator, however, Espada's "Jorge" invokes the actual Jorge, a Honduran janitor in a Cambridge, Massachusetts, church in 1989, as the poem's byline tells us. Jorge's ironic *autorretrato* begins with a statement of invisibility that deconstructs liberal pieties of multicultural inclusion and cross-cultural generosity in the shadows of Harvard. Jorge laments, "No one asks / where I am from, / I must be / from the country of janitors" (*Rebellion* 92). Whereas the church members lack interest in Latino languages, histories, and geographies when embodied in a janitor (rather than in an intellectual), the Appalachian Latino narrator listens carefully to Grimm, a presumptive Other, who in turn teaches him. He learns where Grimm is from, what he listens to, reads, eats, and believes. He pictures Grimm coming not from "the country of janitors," nor from what Jorge calls "a squatter's camp / outside the city / of their understanding" but from a city, region, and country the narrator sees through Grimm's eyes.

Unlike Jorge, Grimm is partly an allegorical character. Against the common name Jorge and his pious position as "Church Janitor," "Grimm the Janitor" recalls the adjective "grim," the metaphorical "Grim Reaper," and *Grimm's Fairy Tales*. These linguistic echoes have complex epistemological registers. If it is feasible to view Jorge and Grimm as speaking subalterns, what should poets, intellectuals, scholars, and readers learn from them? If fairy tales offer instruction, what claim does Grimm make on Latino intellectual and aesthetic cartographies under the neoliberal sign? Together, Grimm and Jorge are laborers "who really truly / can't take it anymore," in the words of Bolaño's poem "Ernesto Cardenal and I." More specifically, they suggest the frequently antagonistic relation between intellectuals and workers. By ceding control to the dispossessed rather than representing their interests, intellectuals relinquish their storytelling roles. This act creates relational spaces for criticism that are, by necessity, open to discomfiting ideas. Not only is Grimm's take on busing anathema to the Left, but Jorge's sardonic admission — "What they say / must be true: / I am smart, / but I have a bad attitude" — tests norms of discipline and productivity widely held across the political spectrum. In some sense, then, each poem's absence produces epistemological resonance. Whereas the dispossessed speak in each, Espada's lyric monologue lacks an interlocutor and Kilwein Guevara's interlocutor withholds moral judgment. These silences allow complexity and contradiction to stand while challenging readers to see through Jorge's and Grimm's eyes. In relation to Espada's lament for cross-cultural ethical engagement, Kilwein Guevara's poem displays the listening key to begin building class-based alliances across disparate groups who would confront the neoliberal order.[14]

In "Grimm the Janitor" and "Late Supper in Northern Appalachia," these forms of absence serve as indexes to ethical presence. Their indirect constructions of Latino identity through contact with marginalized Appalachian others create an implicit, aggregate *ars poetica* that crests in *Poema*, one of the most fully realized avant-garde collections published by a Latina/o poet.[15] Its "Poema without hands" (80) begins with the claim that a poem consists of absence: "Whatever it is that is wanting / is poema." The poem then lists multiple images: "families in the unventilated / truck"; "Guevara's / hands from Bolivia"; "painted frog[s] from Boyacá," the Andean state where Bolívar led the victory for Colombian independence in 1819; and "mountaintops near Caney Creek / in eastern Kentucky." Asphyxiated migrants, revolutionary limbs, endangered species, and amputated mountains require reconstruction by an absent "you," the "reader of this page" who breathes life into the text, without whom the poem would be nothing more than "the narcotic buzzing of cicadas." Kilwein Guevara's poems depend on readers to weave his cartography of the Americas together, from Colombia, to "unventilated / truck[s]" figuratively enjambed between the United States and Mexico and captivity and mobility, to the Appalachians. This "territory of images" revises relations between here/there, absence/presence, above/below, and broken/to break to create an in-process Appalachian Latinidad. The "starry hills" of Pittsburgh and the "starry bowl" of Bogotá (*Autobiography* 22, 50) form an intertextual, inter-American cosmology in which the Andes and Appalachians are omnipresent even in their absence.

Villatoro's Southern Latino Mountains

Whereas Kilwein Guevara is primarily a poet, Villatoro is a prolific multigenre writer. His autobiographical novel, *The Holy Spirit of My Uncle's Cojones* and two poetry collections (*They Say that I Am Two* and *On Tuesday, When the Homeless Disappeared*) distill questions of Appalachian Latinidad present across his books.[16] Born in 1962, Villatoro was raised in Rogersville, Tennessee, and describes himself as a "Latino Southerner," a "Latino Hillbilly," the product of a "blue-collar, coal mining" father, and a writer whose "people are from El Salvador and the Appalachian Mountains."[17] These assertions notwithstanding, Villatoro betrays greater ambivalence about Appalachia than Kilwein Guevara does. This is partly attributable to Villatoro's muted stress on class-consciousness, as well as his texts' locations in southern Appalachia, where 73 percent of Appalachia's Latino population resides (Barcus 304). From this fraught territory, Villatoro depicts Latinos enduring threats, adapting, and revising and renewing their identities.

Like Espada's "republic," *They Say that I Am Two* sees Neruda as a foundation for Latino poetics. Its four odes, including "Ode to an Avocado" (63) and "Ode to Pablo Neruda" (83–84), pay homage to Neruda's odes. Most pertinently, "Ode to D" (75) connects Appalachian and Latin American souths through "the D chord." Unlike Kilwein Guevara's stress on images, Villatoro's poetics proceeds from musical language, and his poems frequently evoke the senses through aural modes. In "Ode to D," Tennessee's iconic state song and the traditional rural folk song popular throughout Latin America converge: "D ends an easy round of Rocky Top / only to begin a chorus of De Colores." Although the first-person speaker "plays" and "tease[s]" the D chord from guitar strings, the "easy" transition from saluting Tennessee mountains to celebrating Latin American harvests belies fraught convergences in Villatoro's work and actual contacts between native Appalachians and Latino immigrants. The latter song's political valences, including its use by César Chávez and the United Farm Workers, instead indicate disjunctive concurrence and Villatoro's aspiration for less troubled transitions between his "two worlds."

Tony, the Appalachian Latino narrator of *The Holy Spirit of My Uncle's Cojones*, remarks similarly about the "easy" adaptation of his accent based upon his location: "I noticed my own voice as it slid away from Latino lilts into the groove of Appalachia" (25). This sociolinguistic self-monitoring contrasts the difficulties Tony experiences moving between Chicano and Salvadoran worlds in California and Appalachia, where he is a solitary Latino. As a Latino Bildungsroman charting his growth from teenage uncertainty in East Tennessee to lengthy trips to visit family in California and Mexico, the novel inverts Kilwein Guevara's literary geographies of departure from Colombia, arrival in Appalachia, and temporary return to Colombia. Rather than fluid transitions between linguistic and cultural codes, Villatoro envisions an Appalachian genesis, departure, and return empowered with a Latino identity nurtured through the narrator's psychological explorations in northern Mexico. The resultant, robust convergence of a well-played chord in two languages simultaneously incorporates his "two worlds" into a single, mobile Latino body tentatively confident of his places and languages.

For Villatoro, "playing" in two languages is a conscious aesthetic choice. But if the goal is reconciliation or convergence, his statements often suggest "worlds" running in parallel. His website emphasizes identity markers such as "Latino-ness" and "Appalachian-ness" and "Latino and Appalachian worlds," both of which imply duality. Tensions between parallelism and convergence underlie the divergent dual-language strategies of his collections. *They Say that I Am Two* includes ten back-to-back Spanish and English versions of poems; of forty English-language poems, one-fourth have Spanish versions. One could consider this relation the other way around: ten Spanish-language poems have English "approximations," Pacheco's term for translation's impossibility. In contrast, thirteen of thirty-nine poems in *On Tuesday* are in Spanish without English versions. With these poems, Villatoro joins a growing if still relatively small number of Latino poets publishing Spanish-language poems, without English versions, as a primary practice.[18] Like many Latino poets, Villatoro and Kilwein Guevara code switch between English and Spanish; yet whereas the English-language poems in *On Tuesday* are textured with Spanish, two consumer products and one place name are the sole English "words" in the thirteen Spanish poems. Spanish, in this sense, is a discrete, autonomous aesthetic choice.

The strategy of his first collection models duality and inclusion, and the second formalizes pluralism, autonomy, and nontranslatability. This divergence creates a productive dissonance between Villatoro's self-presentation and how his texts engage readers and create meaning. The back cover of *On Tuesday* suggests his view of the second approach and the unexpected dimensions of these relations. The description ends: "A final section of poems is presented in Spanish only—a statement of ascendance, a strategy of identity preservation, a gift to the cognoscenti." The thread tying these three features together is the provocative "Spanish only," which inverts the nefarious "English Only" movement. If the contours of "identity preservation" are easily discernible in this context, "statement" and "gift" complicate matters. What or who is in "ascendance"? Who is the "cognoscenti"? How is a section of poems a "gift"? Is this "gift" similar to Herrera's "offering" to the Indians of Chiapas? If so, for whom is it intended? Together, these questions examine how Latino writers and publishers of Latino literature negotiate economic imperatives and constraints. As a marketing tool, the cover of *On Tuesday* aims for overlapping audiences. In this implicit logic, "ascendance" marshals Latino demographic growth in the United States, "identity preservation" echoes the language of the Chicano and Nuyorican movements in order to create a bridge to the late 1960s, and "cognoscenti" woos intellectuals. This is not a critique of Villatoro's writing or of the University of Arizona Press's Camino del Sol series, which includes some of the best Latino poetry published in the last decade, including Francisco X. Alarcón's *From the Other Side of Night/Del otro lado de la noche*, Kilwein Guevara's *Poema*, Herrera's *Half of the World in Light*, María Meléndez's ecopoetic collection *How Long She'll Last in This World*, and Valerie Martínez's *Each and Her*, which I will discuss in the coda. This "Latina and Latino Literary Series" began in 1994 with a focus on Chicana/o literature, at the height of the "culture wars," "English Only" movements, and NAFTA's free-trade triumph. Against this background, the cover blurb's keywords map to uneven resistance to neoliberal logic. On one hand, they counter "English Only" with "Spanish only," mocking the nativist fear of a Latino *reconquista* of the US Southwest. On the other, they make Spanish the territory of the "cognoscenti." A discomfiting class consciousness grumbles beneath this term as a measure of prestige; it does not suggest the exclusion of English-only readers as much as a gated community of elite ones with superior educations. In this sense, the "gift" registers as a supplement to the text proper, which is in English. As a literary bonus track, it implies that in poetry publishing in the United States, Spanish is an avant-garde literary language rather than one suitable for a more accessible lyric poetry or, for that matter, everyday use by the multitudes.[19]

As a way to "revitalize progressive politics by thinking *through* the market," in Dalleo and Machado Sáez's terms (11), this marketing tactic comprises a deeply contradictory politics. Although the Latino population in Appalachia and as a percentage of the United States as a whole is in "ascendance," is there really a Latino "cognoscenti" in Appalachia? Who is the Latino "cognoscenti" in general? Is Spanish really its language? If so, why use an Italian word? If the cover captures Villatoro's belief that Spanish-only poems constitute a strategic move "to break" the dominance of English as the only legitimate literary language in the United States, as he suggests in his essay "In Search of Literary *Cojones*," then it exists uncomfortably with the connotations of "cognoscenti." It also contradicts Villatoro's poetics, which frequently uses popular references, such as those to Selena and "a Starbucks parking lot" (*On Tuesday* 8), a fact that Teresa Longo foregrounds in her essay on Villatoro. In these ways, the jacket statement about *On Tuesday*'s Spanish poems points to the challenge of writing across dispersed Latino literary forms and for diverse Latino readers, many of whom do not read Spanish. Compare, for instance, how Espada introduces his dual-language collection, *Rebellion / the Circle of a Lover's*

Hands/Rebelión es el giro de manos del amante, with inter-American and pan-Latino solidarities: "We [Espada and Pérez-Bustillo] have translated this book into Spanish in an effort to communicate with the peoples of Latin America who are the inspiration for many of these poems, as well as to bridge the gap between those Latinos, born in the U.S., who speak English as a primary language, and those more recent immigrants who speak predominately Spanish" (7). And then compare this to how Francisco Aragón introduces his bilingual collection, *Puerta del Sol.* In describing his "personal decision" to include his own Spanish "versions" of his original English-language poems, Aragón prefers the term "elaboration" to "translation" and disavows "faithful[ness] to the English" (xii–xv). Even though Villatoro, Espada, and Aragón intend (and deserve) to reach broad audiences, emphasizing an intellectual avant-garde, transnational class solidarity, and a self-aware personal poetics of rewriting, respectively, frames Latino poetry's multiple languages in divergent ways.[20]

This discussion rests in part on how publishers sell Latino poets and on how Latino writers see themselves and promote their counterparts. If "magic realism" has become a trope for marketing Latino literature, "Neruda" and "Borges" are close behind in frequency and pliability. Espada's book jackets, press releases, and reading materials refer to him as "the Pablo Neruda of North American authors," a statement made by Sandra Cisneros but similar to those made by Campo and Ilan Stavans.[21] Whereas Villatoro's first collection cultivates a Nerudian genealogy, *On Tuesday*'s cover describes the poetry as "combining Borgean [*sic*] logic" with "the grit of Neruda." This combination putatively joins Nerudian modes of political commitment to Borgesian intellectual poetry. This task is even more daunting than bridging Latino and Appalachian identities, never mind that Villatoro's previous collection evinces scant interest in Borgesian modes. This self-presentation bridges his first collection's largely narrative modalities to the more experimental, image-driven metaphysical poetics of the second. "Neruda" and "Borges" have unsurpassed cultural capital for Latino, if not Latina, poets. They presumably attract the "cognoscenti," who know at a glance what each signifies. And yet each writer's enormous, variable body of work signifies "Everything and Nothing," to borrow the title of Borges's prose poem about Shakespeare (*Selected Poems* 86–89). Whereas de la Campa shows that Borges's Argentine and Latin American identities are often erased in the United States, where he represents a foundational postmodernism (*Latin Americanism* 34), Villatoro's cover implies the opposite as it concerns Latino poetry. There "Borges" is a cipher for a nonpolitical Latin American vanguard and "Neruda" for political poetry. Gruesz writes that Neruda "codes as both 'populist' and 'popular' in the US" ("Walt Whitman" 164); in contrast, Borges "codes" as "postmodern," "apolitical," and "intellectual." As overflowing rather than empty signifiers, these Latin American icons are marketing keywords arbitrating Latino literary value. This is not to deny their influence on Latino poetry but to insist that literary and economic languages are deeply enmeshed and often convoluted.

Longo approaches this accounting in arguing that the shared "poetic praxis" of Villatoro, Espada, and the poet-critic Julio Marzán counters corporate misappropriations of Neruda. This practice joins Nerudian representational modes to "the tendency, prevalent in *testimonio,* to tell a personal story that contains a message from a subordinated group involved in a political struggle" (Introduction xxiv). Villatoro reinforces Longo's point in explaining that he learned "the art of the *testimonio*" when his "mother told [him] stories about hiding in a donkey-driven cart in a Salvadoran village while machine guns clattered in the distance" ("In Search" 165). But he also attributes his storytelling to his "Appalachian side" (Minick 206).[22] In laying groundwork for mapping "Broken Souths" across these North-South literary geographies, Longo writes that the "California-based novelist and poet, Marcos Villatoro" "map[s] a new poetic territory wherein U.S. Latino writing, like work produced in Chile, Mexico or El Salvador, may be read as part of the Latin American literary canon" ("Poet's Place"). Yet omitting "McPeek," locating him in California, and mapping his "poetic territory" *in* Latin America effaces both Appalachia and inter-American relations. Elevating a Latin American over a Latino canon, moreover, maintains a troublingly persistent status hierarchy that also has the paradoxical effect of blurring the lines between Latino and Latin American literary practices.

Two Villatoro poems ("Cuando nos tumbó la pata/When the Paw Brought Us Down" and "Fathers on the Water's Edge") map this "new poetic territory" within southern Appalachia, where Latino forms and Appalachian cultural practices create a place-based poetics. "When the Paw Brought Us Down" (*They Say* 70–71) depicts a June 1995 INS raid on Latino migrants in Appalachian Alabama, where Villatoro was then working as an advocate and organizer. With its incendiary acronym Protect American Workers, "Operation South PAW" resembles a "state of siege" that disrupts precarious Latino settlement. Villatoro's mise en scène of the "siege" foregrounds vehicles. Whereas *La Migra* (INS) descends from above in helicopters, Latino farm workers are confined to "truck[s] / filled with pillows and blankets." This image of the truck-as-home constitutes place portably. As a compromised figure for freedom of movement, it reinforces the poem's recurrent images of "closets" in which migrants hide. In contrast, images of nurturance evoke perseverant Latino home making in the mountains. Taken together, interactions between nature, transportation, and gender produce a tentative Latino place: "The children nestled into breasts / of mothers who kept vigil over / the nocturnal noises / running through the mountain." These "running" sounds follow migrants fleeing *La Migra* under the natural sounds of mountains at night, while the figure of vigil keeping produces the "affective kernel" defining Lefebvre's representational space. This "directly *lived*" space resists prohibition, interdictions, and bans, the main foundations of the given space for Latinos in Alabama "closets" (*Production of Space* 42, 39, 35).

These figures of threatened Latino place and the INS command over space critique the conflicting narratives of anti-immigrant groups and INS raids. The former groups have referred to the presence of Latinos in northern Alabama as a "Mexican invasion" (Mohl 57–58). This use of "Mexican" as a hostile synecdoche for Latinos the "color of earth," in the figure of "Sing Zapatista," is part of "the Latino Threat Narrative" that insists that immigrants steal the jobs of (white) Americans. This idea effaces the fact that most Appalachian Latinos identify as white (Hayden 298, 303–304) and that neoliberalism claims to be race- and ethnicity-neutral ("post-racial"). The passage of Alabama's drastically punitive law, H.B. 56 (2011), symbolizes the nativist Right's recent victory and the need for many undocumented Latinos to stay "in the closet," to repurpose a euphemism.[23] Rather than a "Mexican invasion," "Latino threat," or "brown peril," Mike Davis's term for how Latinos are depicted as the "equivalent of the obsolete red menace" (*Magical Urbanism* 90), upsetting putatively harmonious social-economic norms in the US South, "Operation South PAW" enforces the neoliberal goal of disciplining workers of all ethnicities. The INS controls the sky and ground, a "crazed serpent" with an "evil eye" that "squeez[es]" and "br[ings] down" by entering "closets" and "backroads," the private, hidden spheres of migrant labor. These figures join a pan–Latin American superstition ("evil eye") to an Appalachian spatial vernacular ("backroads") in the Christian serpent personifying the fallen nation-state's obeisance to capital. Operation South PAW raids of carpet mills in southern Appalachia "not only raised [anti-immigrant] tensions to new levels," they protected corporations employing "hundreds of undocumented immigrants" (Zúñiga and Hernández-León, "Appalachia" 264). Instead of "protecting American workers," the INS colluded with the media to create the appearance of "the recovery of / five hundred jobs stolen by Mexicans," most of whom returned to work with the tacit approval of the corporations that stood down during the raids.

The poem's narrator documents this return via communication and transportation routes between Mexico and Alabama. Although a US citizen safe from deportation, he is nonetheless "impotent" and immobile ("I made no moves") as others "fled into the woods." Although citizenship does not guarantee agency, it allows the narrator to be an intermediary who links the geographically shifting *here* and *there*. Remaining family members "tell [him] that deported cousins" are on their way back from Mexico, and he traces their trip from Monterrey to Houston to "a Birmingham truck stop." The poem ends with mountains figuratively awakened by foodways persistent through the night's deportations: "The mountains here? / They awoke to the hidden odor of tortillas / and the rising steam of boiled beans." Although the Latino presence may be "hidden" from sight, it is accessible to olfactory senses. Like the D chord, corn tortillas and beans differ in processing and preparation from cornbread and pinto beans, stereotypical staples of rural Appalachia, but they are substantively identical. This shared means of subsistence connects Latino to Appalachian practices by foregrounding the recurrent Latino *here* in the mountains and the routes from *there* (Monterrey, in this case) converging on them. In these contexts, "rising steam" has many registers: the byproduct of boiling water, the figurative anger of nativists, and the "ascendance" of Latinos in Appalachia.

"When the Paw Brought Us Down" dramatizes Latino migrants living between worlds and pressing for their convergence, tasks complicated by divisions between citizens and the undocumented. "Fathers on the Water's Edge" (*They Say* 78–80) narrates from a different angle, where Latinidad is revised by engaging nativist threats. Assertions of southern-ness and Appalachian-ness stand out in the Central American settings of *They Say that I Am Two*. In the first half of the poem, the speaker-poet walks alone in the near past ("yesterday") on the banks of the Mississippi River, where repeated "I know" and "I have no fear" constructions culminate in a proud affirmation, "I am, after all, a Southerner." Yet the affective timbre lies in the second half, as he considers how cultural practices are reproduced across generations and in the place-based relation to nature. In this part, the poet recalls his childhood on East Tennessee's Big Creek, where his father taught him to fish and hunt. His past-tense recollections then move to the lyric present with a resonant "here": "Here, I escape. / In the woods / and on the riverbanks / Dad blessed his son with / squirrel blood / and cool water from Big Creek." Like "When the Paw Brought Us Down," this passage views "here" as a natural refuge from the speaker's otherness in Appalachian cultural contexts. But "here" is also a space for expressing a shifting Latino identity. As such, the latter poem enfolds ontological and epistemological ("I know") formations into the woods and creeks of the mountains, where the Scots-Irish Appalachian father passes on place-based practices to his Latino son.

To become "neonatives," Williams's term for settlers "who developed strong attachments" to Appalachian communities (355), the poem implies that Latinos must immerse themselves in Appalachian practices that create specific conceptions and uses of nature. In this sense, the deictic "here" positions the speaker within culturally produced "woods" and "riverbanks." "The chord / of the arched bow" used for hunting echoes the D chord, and his father's teaching him to "skin [. . .] a rabbit" recalls Grimm's "ever skinned a rabbit in the sunshine?" The unsettling "I escape" following "here" completes the objectless sentence, forcing us to draw our own conclusions about what the narrator must escape *from*. If what he escapes *to* echoes migrants fleeing "into the woods," the stanza preceding "Here, I escape" suggests that "the woods" offer safety from "petty anger," "cursing," and the "memory of shame," metonyms for prejudices faced by Latinos. The engagement with nature allows father and son to "measure our own time / neither slow nor fast." This proprietary, autonomous temporality faces pressure in the alarming final lines: "He taught me survival techniques / against our own." The conflation of the first-person "me," which connotes individual Latino subjectivity, and the first-person plural "our," which signifies collective Appalachian identity, suggests that Latino perseverance in Appalachia relies on both/and rather than either/or practices. In Grimm's words, "where they belong" is "here," a shifting inter-American signifier of Latino place, even as the "blessing" by "blood" conjures the possibility of reactionary violence from the speaker's "own" Appalachian culture.

In navigating Latino and Appalachian identities, Villatoro, like Espada, sees violence as a key integer of the calculus of migration and cultural collision. Whereas deconstructed regional and national stereotypes underlie Kilwein Guevara's poetics, "When the Paw Brought Us Down" and "Fathers on the Water's Edge" depict Latino cultures emerging in Appalachia and Latinos undertaking iconic Appalachian practices. This nascent Appalachian Latino identity negotiates threats to create place, but a trinity of state and nativist violence, fundamentalist religion, and hyper-masculinity ultimately bridges Appalachian and Latino cultures in Villatoro's work. Although "The Holy Spirit of My Uncle's Cojones," *On Tuesday*'s poem version of the novel, suggests the superiority of California's Latino cultures to the "distant Appalachian lair / Moist with incestuous kin" (32), the concurrence of violence often draws them close. The novel's narrator admits that he "had been brought up in two God-fearing cultures—Appalachian and Latino, a double-whammy of lightning-wielding" (132). "In both my cultures," he says, slurs like "*cabrón* had a deep, hot sting" (27). This parallelism may obscure how dispossession links Appalachians and Latinos, but Villatoro's tackling of stereotypes facilitates his assertion of an Appalachian Latino "here" through the purgative power of curses and reclamations. "I'm from here," the novel's narrator says. "Part of my blood is this place, the place I so quickly cursed" (17). Whereas Kilwein Guevara interweaves South and North, Villatoro builds spaces for comparing the forms of *here* and *there*, as if "this place" might one day be more fully formed from their intersections.

Revising Latina/o Literary Geographies

Kilwein Guevara's and Villatoro's texts revise dominant Latino literary geographies along two vectors. First, they expand the "history of locations," as Santa Arias calls the collection of Latino migratory routes and settlement patterns exemplified in Espada's poetry. The inclusion of Appalachia, particularly southern, is increasingly important given the recent geographic shift in anti-immigrant politics. State laws passed in the ARC states of Alabama, Georgia, and South Carolina in 2011 make the more publicized Arizona law seem tame in comparison; they are unsurpassed in their capacities to conduct surveillance, to harass, and to punish. Second, Kilwein Guevara's and Villatoro's innovative poetics extend the expressive range of Latino literary practices. Although their poems often diverge in location, language, and form, they share similar subjects and thematic concerns. If their sustained interest in marginality, migration, poverty, and injustice defines the spectrum of Latino poetry, their oblique and uniquely positioned approaches to split subjectivities emergent under such conditions uniquely contribute to the Latino literary archive. Their margins, as it were, are other margins. Rather than iconic Latino literary spaces such as the border, barrio, and bodega, Kilwein Guevara and Villatoro poeticize spaces—creeks, mountains, coalmines, and "backroads"—shared across similarly disquieting regional constructs.

Kilwein Guevara's poetry in particular destabilizes and multiplies the contours of "Latino" and "Latino poetry." *Autobiography of So-and-so* responds with idiosyncratic anonymity to the hegemonic ideology that we live in a "post-racial" and "post-identity" era. Within this official story of equal incorporation into global capitalism and the nation-state, "So-and-so" must create himself with disjointed, unmoored images of com-modified multicultural identities. As the title of a poem in *Poema* suggests, "So-and-so" (and the poet) sees himself as a "Pepenador de palabras," a scavenger of words (56). The poem opens with a two-word chant, "Land-scape, landfill," that initiates the garbage picker's search of a landfill to find, sift through, and appropriate cultural detritus. This trope of "scav-enging" through the explicitly textual-material leftovers of culture revises Herrera's "gathering" of signs in *Mayan Drifter* and "A Day Without a Mexican" and locates Kilwein Guevara's poetics in the underbelly of con-sumer culture—the settlements rising on landfills in Mexico City, Bogotá, and other cities in the global South—aligning "So-and-so" with the survi-vors on capitalism's constitutive margins. His scavenger cartographies map the mobile terrain of Latino poetry, as the literary geography of allusions and places subtending it shifts unpredictably, from the Aztec god Huitzilo-pochtli, Oaxacan graffiti, and Plan Colombia crop dusters, to Gertrude Stein, the folk singer John Prine, and the Clarion River and French Creek in Appalachian Pennsylvania, full of "mine acids and heavy metals // tiny moons of oxygen," and "dark motes of human sewage," all references in *Poema* (57, 38, 35, 30, 50, 60–61).

Both poets' Appalachian locations broaden the principal Latino liter-ary geographies. These spaces are concentrated in Texas, California, the Southwest, and the border region, in territory ceded from Mexico in 1848; Florida, with its influx of Cubans at the end of the nineteenth century, Cuban exiles during the Revolution, and new settlement of Dominicans, Puerto Ricans, Colombians, and Argentines; Chicago, with large Puerto Rican and Mexican populations; and New York, with Puerto Ricans, Do-minicans, Colombians, Ecuadorans, and a growing Mexican population. Within these spaces, four internally diverse groups—Chicanos, Puerto Ri-cans, Cuban Americans, and Dominican Americans, each with its own "history of locations"—have defined the field of Latino literature. While these literatures and their canonical writers are well known and need no elucidation here, and demographics partly explain why these groups dominate Latino publishing and scholarship, it is useful to consider how Latino writing in and about Appalachia affects the guiding constructs of Latino literary studies.[24]

Kilwein Guevara's and Villatoro's convergent Latino and Appalachian rhythms, textures, and allusions trouble fixed historical groupings and caution against predicting future Latino literary forms. That the former is Colombian and the latter Salvadoran suggests the unpredictability of Latino migration, demanding prudence in either institutionalizing Appalachian Latino literature as a subfield or dismissing it as an anomaly. Even though both writers revise Latinidad within Appalachian contexts, and increasing immigration to Appalachia, particularly to the South, portend more Latino writers to come, Latino writing from Appalachia will not substantially impact these literary formations until more writers emerge in the mountains. The number of Latinos in Appalachia is likely to remain relatively small (Hayden 305), but southern Appalachia, and the US South in general, may yet produce unexpected Latino literary forms, given that these locations are "unlike traditional Latino immigrant destination areas, where one group initially dominated" (Odem and Lacy xvii). Villatoro and Kilwein Guevara also urge restraint. The narrator of *The Holy Spirit of My Uncle's Cojones* laments the lack of "reminders in Tennessee for a Latino youth to see himself in" (291), while *Postmortem*'s "The Bridge" symbolizes Appalachia's relative cultural pallor with a snowfall, the young Kilwein Guevara's "first surprise in this new America." But they are not quite alone: the Puerto Rican poet Ricardo Nazario y Colón, who was born in the South Bronx and lives in Kentucky, for instance, identifies with the Affrilachian Poets collective rather than as a Nuyorican poet. His collection, *Of Jíbaros and Hillbillies*, combines Puerto Rico's and Appalachia's rural folk icons.[25]

By shifting Latino literary geographies from urban centers (Los Angeles, New York, Chicago, Miami, San Juan, Santo Domingo, and Havana), the migrant labor fields of the Southwest and California, and the US-Mexican border to another marginalized region, Appalachian Latino writing inserts further interstices and scars into the purview of Latino literary studies. This additive value meets de la Campa's challenge to scholars and writers to develop "new ways of imagining the Americas within, as well as between, nations" ("Latin, Latino, American" 383). If the Americas are emerging "within" Appalachia and Latino Appalachia is emerging between North and South in the United States, and between Latin and North America, it is feasible to consider Appalachia an iteration of Mary Louise Pratt's "contact zones," where cultures meet under conditions of uneven power, agency, and access to resources. As a "contact" region *within* the United States, Appalachia expands the types of spaces where literary innovation occurs. "One could conceivably argue that [Latino] poetic vanguardism happens precisely, or that the conditions for poetic innovation are at a premium," Maria Damon writes, "in the interstices of geopolitical boundaries—in islands (Manhattan, Puerto Rico), on coasts (San Francisco Bay Area, Los Angeles), [and] on national borders (the length of the Rio Grande)" (480). Kilwein Guevara's and Villatoro's texts add a putatively isolated, backward mountain region to this list of spaces for poetic innovation.

An expanded "history of locations" delineates possible paths for revising the sources and uses of "Latino." In assessing the term's "validity," Juan Flores argues that "there is 'Latino' only from the point of view and as lived by the Mexican, the Puerto Rican, the Cuban, and so forth." "Without denying the congruencies and threads of interconnection among them that the term implies," he continues, the term "Latino" "only holds up when qualified by the national-group angle or optic from which it is uttered." "There is a 'Chicano/Latino' or 'Cuban/Latino' perspective, but no meaningful one that is simply 'Latino,'" he concludes (8). Appalachian Latino literature troubles critical and creative approaches using *a priori* national groupings as epistemological and ontological departure points. What happens when regional scales and locations precede or exceed national groupings in significance? Should "Appalachian/Latino" or "Colombian/Latino/Appalachian" accompany "Colombian/Latino" in this typology? Should nominalized scales of Latino experiences be multiplied across local-regional-national-transnational locations? If so, "Latino" also "holds up when qualified by" a range of geographic as well as national subject positions, even as it folds under the pressure of multiple identity markers. This line of thought depends on powerful, extant regional imaginaries. If "Appalachian Latino" registers critically because of overlapping, contested imaginaries informing each of its terms, a "New England Latino" imaginary, for example, makes little sense. In Appalachian contexts, constructs such as the "Mexican invasion" and "Latino Threat Narrative" show how "Latino" is employed as a negative singularity. In stereotypes, the only "meaningful" term is "Latino" minus the "national-group angle or optic," among other characteristics rendering Latinos humans rather than types. These constructions efface unique histories to emphasize Latino otherness. As such, it is critical to incorporate local and regional Latino identities into national ones to counter empty uses of "Latino" and to retain its empowering valences.

Together, Kilwein Guevara's and Villatoro's literary practices are an "ethos under formation," Flores and George Yúdice's seminal and ever-useful articulation of Latino poetics. By negotiating the ethical considerations of contact and by keeping the parameters of identity open and flexible, Appalachian Latino poetics constitutes a *"practice* rather than

representation of Latino identity" (60–61). The latter suggests a narrow
referential process in which literature reflects settled, preexisting identities, which it then demonstrates to readers. The former, on the other
hand, connotes an ensemble of revisable processes that actively produces
places, transnational cultural modes, and potentially emancipatory identities. Kilwein Guevara's and Villatoro's use of multiple poetic forms
practices possible Latino identities and searches for new combinations of
inter-American sources. In addition to free verse, which remains a favored
expressive mode in much of Latino poetry, they use experimental, avant-
garde modes; Anglo-European forms, such as villanelles, sonnets, sestinas,
and prose poems, commonly favored in recent North American poetry;
lyric-narrative conventions of Latino poetics, including code switching;
and Nerudian and Borgesian modes. Their formal poems track Latino
poets' growing use (and revision) of traditional Anglo-European and
Spanish-language forms, with the bar set by the diverse range of sonnets
in Alarcón's *From the Other Side of Night,* Campo's *What the Body Told,*
and Ada Limón's *Lucky Wreck,* and by Urayoán Noel's bilingual, multi-
register formal virtuosity spanning from *terza rima* to Spanish *décimas.*[26]
Most capaciously, Appalachian Latino poetics shows that "an 'author' in
a distinctly transamerican sense" (Gruesz, *Ambassadors* 13) searches for
convergent forms to contest misconceptions and dispossessions with creative, often unpredictable reinscriptions. Although their poetics should
not be mistaken for Espada's "artistry of dissent," Kilwein Guevara's and
Villatoro's texts are deeply invested in places defined by injustices and
the struggles against them. In Latino writing, moreover, nothing is more
political than language itself, as persistent talk of "English only," "illegal
aliens," and "anchor babies" painfully attests.

These threads bring us back to neoliberalism. Beverley concedes that
the market-based organization of society produces a compromised form of
radical heterogeneity ("Dos caminos"). It might be said then that Appalachian Latino literature is possible only under the neoliberal sign, with its
uneven, unpredictable deterritorializations. This chapter's texts, after all,
grapple with some of the counter-reactions and contradictions that arise in
these conditions. In their sights, the free-trade euphoria of NAFTA meets
the fallacious "protect American workers," "English only" is transformed
into "Spanish only" in an odd piece of marketing, the "Mexican invasion"
and "Latino threat" are countered by Latinos learning cultural practices
from those in whose names the threats are made, and "So-and-so" exemplifies the devaluation of (im)migrants as anonymous cogs in a machine.
In the Appalachian "contact" region, as in other "Broken Souths," Kilwein

Guevara and Villatoro humanize those who would resist the neoliberal order while making do with, and even taking advantage of, heterogeneous possibilities for making place opened up by free markets and their frequently illusory mobilities. Whereas the Appalachian Latino is an individual figure of inter-American contact under neoliberalism, chapter 5 examines how Nuyorican poetics maps Puerto Rico as a collective symbol of neoliberal upheavals, migrations, and false choices.

CHAPTER FIVE

"*MIGRATION . . . IS NOT A CRIME*"

Puerto Rican Status and "T-shirt solidarity" in Judith Ortiz Cofer, Victor Hernández Cruz, and Jack Agüeros

It's hard to imagine a worse candidate for admission to the Union than this Caribbean Dogpatch.
— Don Feder, "No Statehood for Caribbean Dogpatch"

No matter how far we perceive ourselves as being embedded in a particular culture, the moment we participate in global capitalism, this culture is already de-naturalized.
— Slavoj Žižek, *First as Tragedy* (144)

Two weeks before the island plebiscite on December 13, 1998, in which a majority voted for "None of the Above" over "Independence," "Statehood," "Commonwealth As Is," and "Revised Commonwealth," the *Boston Herald* published Don Feder's column opposing Puerto Rican statehood. Neither his odium for Puerto Ricans, Latinos, immigrants, and the poor, nor the response by advocacy groups such as LULAC (League of United Latin American Citizens), deviated from the basic contours of Right-neoliberal and Latino center-Left positions. Feder's virulent neoliberal ideology and blindness to the island's colonial status underlie his pitch-perfect iteration of "the Latino Threat Narrative." He cites the pliable bogeymen of more crime, "unassimilable immigrants [*sic*]," "non-English speakers," "welfare recipients," "alien culture," and "multiculturalis[ts]" accompanying Puerto Rican statehood. For its part, LULAC condemned the piece as racist and "un-American." What went unremarked by critics, scholars, and by Feder himself was the column's convoluted guiding analogy: that Puerto Rico is the Appalachia of the Caribbean. Feder's conceit combines the most trenchant stereotypes of black deviance—he points out that the island is poorer than Mississippi and has a higher murder rate than New York City, two unsubtle castigations of African American criminality—and of poor white hillbillies. "Dogpatch," the picaresque Appalachian Kentucky setting of the comic strip *L'il Abner*, stands without comment or explanation in the column's final sentence.[1]

As Feder's odd coup de grâce, "Dogpatch" is a bulwark of neoliberal logic and a testament to his willful misapprehension of historical relations between the United States and Puerto Rico. By pitting the shibboleth of "American culture" against the specter of a "Caribbean Dogpatch," Feder's column reinforces the infamous Supreme Court ruling that Puerto Rico "belongs to but is not part of the US" and the Jones Act (both 1917) that gave Puerto Ricans US citizenship but not full political incorporation. These forms of ambiguity were formalized in 1952 with the Estado Libre Asociado (ELA), or "commonwealth." Feder thus unwittingly depicts Puerto Ricans' US citizenship as always already second class. As Mike Davis notes, Puerto Rican poverty compared to other Latino groups "rebuts the facile claim that citizenship provides a magic carpet for immigrant success" (*Magical Urbanism* 123).[2] In this way, both Feder's column and "commonwealth" status submit citizenship to the logic of the market rather than to that of the nation-state. Given that "American culture" hews closer and closer to "global capitalism," it is already denaturalized before Feder and his ilk, including Tea Party–backed state legislatures in Arizona, Alabama, and elsewhere, attempt to preserve it with punitive anti-immigrant legislation. Herein lies a contradiction between neoliberal ideology and actually existing global capitalism. The Caribbean harbors "alien culture" so should be enclosed even as it offers tax havens and offshore banking essential to the consolidation of wealth and power under neoliberalism. The "Dogpatch" offers cheap labor and resources as well as a useful, barbaric Other to the threatened civilization of "American culture."

Feder's column pinpoints what Edward J. Carvalho calls "the two sides of neoliberalism" that he locates in the "proto-neoliberal" forms of the US occupation of Puerto Rico in 1898 and in Operation Bootstrap fifty years later. This dialectical tension between "cultural separatism" and economic incorporation has parallel effects. First, Carvalho traces the current rhetoric about "illegal" immigrants "leeching off of the system" to these earlier ethnocentric and racist colonial stereotypes of Puerto Ricans as lazy and shiftless. The second part of the equation—that cheap, industrious Puerto Rican bodies "could be used to maximize economic efficiency by increasing the return on investments and reducing the burden of labor costs" (12)—is unsurprisingly effaced in Feder's ahistorical account. Feder's hyperbolic final repartee thus dramatizes a guiding metaphor of free-market ideology that runs counter to the actual functioning of neoliberal policy arrangements. As a "candidate for admission," Puerto Rico competes in the marketplace and will be successful if its brand and product are of sufficient quality. This metaphor ignores the market's barriers to entry, unequal starting positions, and uneven command of resources. It also erases histories of colonization and obscures the asymmetrical freedoms of "Caribbean Dogpatch" residents and defenders of "American culture." Feder's desire for freedom *from* Latinos reveals an abiding fear that the relation of dependency actually runs the other way around. In this sense, economic "freedom" relies upon the isolation, unfreedoms, and lack of historical agency of those confined to Dogpatches.

Feder, however, is right on one point. It is indisputable that "Puerto Ricans have a national consciousness," even if the second part of his claim—that this consciousness is "incompatible with statehood"—has an expanding, hazy horizon and, in any case, colonizers give not a whit whether the conquered culture is "compatible" with the dominant one.[3] Although he cares little what this "national consciousness" *is* compatible with, and he happily consigns Puerto Rico to oblivion, this hanging question also structures scholarly studies of Puerto Rican cultural production in recent decades. The modalities of "national consciousness" turn on assessments of the place of Puerto Rico in the global order. Is Puerto Rico's ambiguous status emblematic or unique? Is the nation-state growing or diminishing in importance under neoliberal globalization? What sort of critical language best articulates how Puerto Rican cultural forms are constituted across geographical space, in motion between the island, New York, and other US locations? The only consensus, Flores notes, is that Puerto Rico is a colony (35). While Appalachia is an internal colony, "a national sacrifice zone" producing energy for capital accumulation, Flores and others follow work in the vein of Néstor García Canclini in viewing Puerto Rico as a "lite" colony and "trans-colony," designations that capture, with a measure of ironic distance, processes grounded in market-based consumption rather than in fixed territorial power structures. This difference between production and consumption suggests the flexibility and placelessness of the latter, which shifts and turns with each new "revolution" in consumer technology, product lines, and brand names.

If the disjunctures, upheavals, ambiguities, migrations, and reverse migrations of Puerto Ricans are "paradigmatic," according to Flores (15), and "part and parcel of contemporary life throughout the world," as Frances Negrón-Muntaner has it (10), it is also important to retain a difference. The nugget of neoliberal theory in Feder's dismissive final sentence points to this unique positioning. Negrón-Muntaner's sense that it matters little how we choose to name the conditions and structures of "contemporary life"—"call it postmodernity, globalization, the era of transnational capital," or "the global era" (10)—overlooks how neoliberalism has its own globalizing logic that differs from other capitalist eras that were also "global" in scale, logic, and practice. In comparison to recent "blank" and protest votes in other places she cites as versions of the "none of the above" strategy that makes Puerto Rico emblematic rather than unique (11–12), the fact of the status vote suggests a difference. (This difference might be one reason that Puerto Rico is omitted from accounts of neoliberalism such as Harvey's *Brief History*, as Carvalho carefully shows, even as Carvalho's own study excludes any discussion of the status issue.) Puerto Rico *is* a "candidate for admission" as a US state. This putative choice through official means, the decades-long COINTELPRO (the FBI counter-intelligence program) suppression of Puerto Rican *independentistas* notwithstanding, comprises a unique position from which to test "choice," the neoliberal keyword. As an ideological subterfuge, "choice" comes in the guise of heterogeneous market freedom, in which the citizen-as-consumer chooses between a plethora of options, whether for political representatives or soda brands. "School choice" is the dominant language of education "reform," just as the neoliberal assault on any reform of the health care system repeats the default position that market-based care gives patients (*as* consumers) greater "choice" of providers and treatments. Yet rational choice neglects the fact that individuals have little to no control over the available options. What's more, the choice of system is radically foreclosed. Because "there is no alternative" to neoliberal capitalism paired with limited forms of democracy, choices exist under strong restrictions. "The model neoliberal citizen," Brown writes, "is one who strategizes for her- or himself among various social, political, and economic options, not one who strives with others to alter or organize these options." Under these constraints, "The body politic ceases to be a body but is rather a group of individual entrepreneurs and consumers" (43).

In the context of neoliberal "choice," Puerto Rican status debates take on differential resonance. Negrón-Muntaner's sense that "the lack of adequate policies and political imagination" create conditions under which "none of the above" wins is correct (12), but the questions surrounding choice hew more closely to Carlos Pabón's lament for "the reduction of

the political and politics to the status issue." Although it dominates discussions, in part due to persistent romantic conceptions of the state and
national sovereignty, Pabón calls it a "nonsense dilemma" (65). While he
may intend to incite with this dismissal, he rightly suggests that global
economic structures mediate all of the options, if unevenly. After all, he
insists that the logic of the territorial nation-state, with its discourses of
sovereignty and limited forms of representative democracy, fails to incorporate numerous subjects, like refugees, the undocumented, and immigrants, along with those internally excluded from national projects, like
the poor, homeless, and mentally ill (70). Žižek's point is instructive here:
"No matter how far we perceive ourselves as being embedded in a particular culture," be it Puerto Rican or even Feder's purportedly natural
and irreproachable "American," "the moment we participate in global
capitalism, this culture is already de-naturalized." This is not the place to
flesh out Žižek's "de-naturalized," but his idea that there is a "moment,"
or breaking point, in which global processes overtake, rather than merely
penetrate or influence "particular culture[s]," reassesses the status issue in
terms gestured at by Pabón. The logic of territorial sovereignty misapprehends the scale and character of the dilemma: all options (independence,
commonwealth, statehood) exist under the neoliberal sign; the form of
each "choice" is subject to the machinations of global capitalism. In this
reckoning, "none of the above" is a constitutive outside, a Puerto Rican
iteration of the "without" Rabasa argues has the capacity to confront the
hegemony of capital and the state. In this sense, Puerto Rican "national
consciousness" *is* incompatible with the neoliberal state *and* US statehood.

This point brings us to the Nuyorican literary projects with roots in the
late 1960s and the broken/to break dialectic particular to Puerto Rican
historical geographies. In discussing divergences between the Nuyorican
movement and neoliberal individualism, Arlene Dávila points out that
"Nuyorican cultural nationalism" was "meant to challenge" the dispar-
agement of Puerto Ricans in "American culture" and mainland Puerto
Ricans' supposed debasement of island-based Hispanophone norms (72).
The goal of collective self-determination was animated in part by the
ideal of a break from capitalist relations; the Young Lords' radical activism remains a powerful, if somewhat forgotten, symbol of this possibility. Although the literary forms that emerged from these contexts were
"anchored" in Nuyorican "cultural expressions," as Dávila notes, they are
"now synonymous with U.S.-based" practices (72). This scale jumping effaces contested New York spaces from "Nuyorican" and "Puerto Rican"
from the same term now often narrowly associated with the Nuyorican

Poets Café, which sadly has traded cultural nationalism and radical innovation for performance poetry's predictable modes of multicultural individualism.[4] Rather than serve as exemplars of a movement with a set of aesthetic practices, this chapter's diverse literary forms model a mobile place-based consciousness that illuminates Puerto Rico's simultaneously unique and archetypal dimensions under neoliberal restructuring. This approach emphasizes New York as a locus of potentially emancipatory "Broken Souths," where a translocal sense of Puerto Rico emerges from the city's neoliberal restructuring in the 1970s to consolidate a broader class-based Latino imaginary.

Such an approach reframes the relation between "broken" and "to break," the passive condition produced by migratory upheaval and the active verb of collective struggle. This tension underlies theories of Puerto Rican cultural identity in ways that diverge from other places at the beginning of the neoliberal era. In *La memoria rota*, for instance, Arcadio Díaz-Quiñones uses "broken memory" as an extended metaphor of Puerto Rican identity under the upheaval of migration, reverse migration, and commonwealth status. Flores, moreover, calls the widespread migration to the mainland (largely New York) in the decades following World War II "the most pronounced break in collective memory" (50). It is fitting that Cruz's "The Lower East Side of Manhattan," published in 1997 at the apex of financial deregulation and the demonization of social safety nets instantiated in welfare "reform," historicizes the massive 1950s-era migration that was then being extended, magnified, and concretized into a logic of upheaval and hyper-urbanization that glorifies mobility. Plural "Broken Souths" are thus rooted in the paradigmatic Puerto Rican "break," and they have become the archetypal neoliberal forms of upheaval, displacement, and deterritorialization.

Whereas Cruz's ecopoetic essays join other Nuyorican texts in seeing potential emancipation in brokenness, his figure of the island unmoored from its tectonic plates in "Old San Juan" (*Red Beans*) depicts a negative "break" on a scale far exceeding the individual's capacity for agency. If "Dogpatch" is a displaced regional slur, Cruz's essays grapple with neoliberalism's global order, which wholly subjects human relations and the natural world to the logic of capital. The subservience of ecological, geological, and biological processes to economic ones presents an existential threat on a global scale, but for Cruz it also opens up space to rethink migration and rural/urban and North/South binaries. His essays about *tabaqueros* (cigar rollers) and campesinos praise modes and practices that thrived in Puerto Rico before the neoliberal era and its precursor,

Operation Bootstrap's midcentury liberalization. In wondering that "the immensity of a whole island moving had no way of being understood," "Old San Juan" configures the broken memory's lack of continuity with these pasts. "The land has made like the mind, it has finally joined the confusion," Cruz writes. And like the mind, it has "broken in half" (123). This breaking point locates the possibility of recuperating alternative forms of life within the constant circulation of capital, labor, ideas, and products in the current iteration of global capitalism. As such, the essay attributes to Puerto Rico a fragmented economic index of dispossession—the island is a "real estate chunk" (125)—and an ecological identity as an "enchanted traveling garden" (131). For Cruz, the question is how to preserve the latter against the pressures of the former. This negotiation between commodification and the creation of places for nurturing growth other than economic structures a unique Nuyorican poetic dialectic between dispossession and enchantment.

In the tumultuous summer of 1968, when the eleven-year-old Martín Espada met Jack Agüeros, the poet, translator, and future executive director of El Museo del Barrio, the iconic museum of Latino and Latin American art in New York City, he was enchanted by Agüeros's recent hunger strike demanding economic and political rights for New York's Puerto Ricans.[5] His individual sacrifice for collective goals—Agüeros said he was "eating anger instead of calories" ("Dismissed Official")—symbolizes the contrast to the present, when atomized consumers advertise "revolution" on t-shirts, as in Herrera's "A Day Without a Mexican." The narrator of Espada's "For the Jim Crow Mexican Restaurant in Cambridge, Massachusetts, Where My Cousin Esteban was Forbidden to Wait Tables Because He Wears Dreadlocks" (*Mayan Astronomer* 23–24) expresses this problem in addressing a Mexican restaurant's all-white wait staff: "I am aware of your T-shirt solidarity / with the refugees of the Américas, / since they steam in your kitchen."[6] "T-shirt solidarity" is a consumer mode of activism that converts Espada's cousin, a sculptor with "the fingertips / of ancestral Puerto Rican cigarmakers," into a roller of tortillas consumed by the well-meaning liberals of Cambridge, who might also sit in Jorge the Church Janitor's pews. As a type of García Canclini's "cultural citizenship," "T-shirt solidarity" fails to create structural change. Latino workers literally and figuratively "steam" in the kitchen, angry but largely powerless.

This chapter examines critiques of such consumer modes, which have struggled to fill the shared psychological voids created by Puerto Rico's ambiguous status and colonized condition. First, Judith Ortiz Cofer's "The Latin Deli: An Ars Poetica" dramatizes the troubling relations

between freedom, consumption, and transportation across convergent Latino souths. Next, in rethinking migration and human relations to nature
and place, Cruz's virtuosic ecopoetic essays animate Adorno's theory of the
essay as a fragmentary form that critiques false ideologies. Then, Agüeros's
sonnets playfully mock neoliberal claims to class mobility with figures of
confinement. I conclude with thoughts on Nuyorican poetics as the vanguard of poetry of the Americas in the neoliberal era.

False Transport in "The Latin Deli"

In Nuyorican poetics, figures of movement, transportation in particular,
often depict neoliberal "freedom" and "choice" mapping to confinement
rather than mobility, alienation over empowerment, and exclusion instead
of access to resources. In this regard, Nuyorican poetics follows Latino poetics in the neoliberal era. Yet the mobility afforded by Puerto Ricans' US
citizenship and status "choice" pressures the "formal promises of freedom
and equality," in Brown's terms, within economic structures that often
produce neither. Like Harvey's "bundle of rights," Brown's "alternative
table of values" illuminates how Nuyorican literary forms poeticize the
search "not for wealth or goods but for beauty, love, mental and physical
well-being, meaningful work, and peace" (57). As with tensions between
broken/to break and here/there, transportation figures have additional
symbolic resonance in Nuyorican poems due to massive migrations from
the island, frequent reverse migrations, and New York's topography of cars,
taxis, buses, trains, tunnels, and stations. "To attend to the 'break' that
migration has meant in Puerto Rican history," Flores writes, "it is necessary to remember the whole national 'project' from the perspective of
the breaking-point itself, from aboard the *guagua aérea*, the proverbial 'air
bus'" (51). Fittingly, Nuyorican transportation figures feature panoramas
and descents, in comparison to the grounded figures of, for instance, Villatoro's "truck / filled with pillows and blankets," Kilwein Guevara's "unventilated / truck," and Herrera's "migrant Mexicans, in the sorcery / called
thirst. Inside train cars. Doubled up / behind the axle of an Oldsmobile"
(*Half of the World* 149).

As a meta-poetics on transportation, "The Latin Deli" depicts consumerism's limited ability to connect people across space. The lyric-narrative
free-verse poem opens *The Latin Deli* (3–4), Cofer's collection of prose
and poetry about life in and around the Paterson, New Jersey, "Puerto
Rican tenement known as El Building" (7), from the 1960s to the present.

As a specifically Latina/o *ars poetica*, the poem examines how poetry uses language, produces meaning, and critiques conditions of migration, exile, poverty, and isolation. The poem's overarching modalities of space (here versus there) and time (the speed of modern transportation compared to Villatoro's figure of "walking between two worlds") foreground the *idea* of transport. Variations on *acá* (here) and *allá* (there) frequently serve as shifting spatial figures in Nuyorican writing, as they also do in Villatoro's work in chapter 4. Flores notes that these concepts facilitate "new mode[s] of identity-formation freed from the categorical fixity of place" (59). This notion offers an alternate means for creating place-based consciousness to topographical groundings of place in ecological and geological forms. In "The Latin Deli," however, "here" and "there" are fixed, the former in Paterson, the latter in the multiple "Broken Souths" of Paterson's Latinos. Because transportation takes someone from here to there but cannot unite them in space and time, the deli's commodities symbolize a consumer-based imagination's limits.[7]

The deli's proprietor, a "Patroness of Exiles" presiding over a "formica counter" and an "ancient register," must guide each customer away from Paterson and transport them south. The deli draws various Latino groups; only Puerto Ricans, Cubans, and Mexicans are named in the poem but the title suggests numerous national origins. Given this responsibility, the proprietor takes on mythical qualities. She is "a woman of no-age" occupying space but not time. This atemporal spatial logic conforms to the constraints of calcified historical memories: "no one / has been allowed to die and nothing to change" in each place of origin. This fixity is the antithesis of capital's logic. Once capital stops moving, stops producing new capital, and thus changing form from capital to money to capital, it ceases to exist *as* capital. This is not to say that the poem is explicitly anticapitalist but that it imagines shared Latino desires to stop the capital flow in which their lives are caught up. This desire produces willful miscalculations that do not consider inflation and other economic indicators. "It would be cheaper to fly to San Juan," they believe, "than to buy a pound of Bustelo coffee here." If this price comparison is technically inaccurate, and the relation between there and here misapprehended, so too is the proprietor's task. By "conjuring up products / from places that now exist only in their hearts— / closed ports she must trade with," the poem does not insist that ports are "closed" in the economic sense, nor that places (Cuba, Mexico, or Puerto Rico) have vanished off the map. It implies something subtler but similarly nefarious: that Latino (im)migrants, as labor power, are also consumable products. As such, they cannot be returned to the ports from which they were exported. Because the possibility of return to idealized spaces of origin is "closed," hunger for place can only be nourished by consuming "canned memories."

Published in 1993 during the run-up to NAFTA's implementation, the poem suggests that neoliberal-era trade is rather unfree. Its final lines close rather than open ports, emphasizing the barriers to entry that prevent many from participating directly in global trade, a key tenet of free-trade agreements. "Closed ports" echoes the opening of Herrera's "Exile," with its departure locations "at the greyhound bus stations, at airports, at silent wharfs" (*Half of the World* 23–24). "Closed ports" and "silent wharfs" remind us that the consumer-based formation of place erases labor's visibility from the production process. In "The Latin Deli," the producers of "culture"—in factories, workshops, kitchens, and fields—only consume. "A feature common to atomized 'communities,'" García Canclini writes, "is that they cluster around symbolic consumption rather than in relation to productive processes" (*Consumers* 159). This triple alienation—from others, the country of origin, and production—finds more empathy in Cofer's pairing of "products" and "hearts" than in Bolaño's rejection of tropes of nostalgia and return. Whereas Bolaño distrusts the fetishization of the lost nation, Cofer evinces wariness for the retrenched commodity fetish, in the Marxist sense. In the deli, relations between people, as among customers and between customers and "Patroness," appear as relations between things, the commodities on the shelves that transport consumers to imagined countries. In concealing the economic relations underlying the products, the commodity fetish recalls Žižek on global capitalism: Latinos "pass[ing] through" the deli have tenuous grips on the particular cultures subject to global repositioning.

Yet in "The Latin Deli" consumption serves as a mode of transterritorial citizenship that recasts the Puerto Rican cultural nation as pan-Latino. Although studies show that mainland Puerto Ricans "see themselves as part of a distinct nation [who] share a specifically Puerto Rican, not American or Latino, identity" (Duany 57), the poem insists on this broader network of "translocal" Latino groups. The Puerto Rican "Patroness" serves Latino dreams and "disillusions," "smil[ing]" with "understanding" at their needs because they resemble hers. Entangled positive and negative consequences emerge from this dynamic. In one sense, it brings disparate groups with convergent histories into a common space. For García Canclini, neoliberal-era identities are shaped by dispersed, transterritorial economic networks. As the main mode of exercising citizenship, García Canclini sees consumption as "good for thinking." Individuals, the argument goes, do not consume blindly but consciously and carefully, an idea Cofer's poem supports. In another sense, however, García Canclini concedes it is "difficult to think" through consumption because of its "capitulation" to a brutal "game of market laws" (*Consumers* 45). The fact that customers seek "the comfort / of spoken Spanish" points to the transitory manner in which consumption creates "comfort."

"The Latin Deli" views these limitations through contradictory fetish objects and figures of diminishment. Although customers cannot access the object itself ("there," the place of origin) and must replace it with material symbols that momentarily "conjur[e]" the object, the deli offers a space for reconstituting "Broken Souths" on a smaller scale. Later in the book, the narrator claims, "El Building had become their country" (93). This diminished scale structures the text: from island to "El Building," Latin America to Latin Deli, and variable collective historical memories to mass-produced "canned" memory. Yet identity is also reformed through face-to-face contact with the "Patroness" rather than in the dispersed hyperspaces of television and the Internet. This limited increase in intimacy nonetheless meets with "closed ports" when the customers leave the store. In these conditions, the idea of the nation "survives," García Canclini suggests, "as an interpretive community of consumers, whose traditional—alimentary, linguistic—habits induce them to relate in a peculiar way with the objects and information that circulate in international networks" (*Consumers* 43). Consumption, that is, becomes the sine qua non of neoliberal-era citizenship and attachment to the nation *as* idea replaces the political state, with its rights and protections.[8]

The possibility of collective identity formations across groups indicates how "The Latin Deli" aspires to *ars poetica*. Because the poem occupies the territory of deeply personal, solitary exchanges, it is primarily an elegy to asymmetrical losses that converge on collective recognition. "The Latin Deli" ascribes determinate cultural significance to economic transactions by suggesting the incompatibility between use-value and exchange-value. In this case use-value far exceeds value in exchange. Much of the poem's imagery suggests cheap, mass-produced products bought to satisfy emotional states such as longing and "hunger." Even though an item "would cost less at the A&P" than at the deli, buying it there "would not satisfy / the hunger of the fragile old man lost in the folds / of his winter coat." Products do not transport consumers; where they are bought and from whom come closer. This gesture toward Latino autonomy finds credence in the "ancient register," which shows continuity with the past and little interest in where money is stored. In other words, money does not become capital but "register[s]" as an interpersonal exchange between exiles. By creating place from displacement, the deli opposes the "non-places" proliferating under globalization. Corporate supermarkets and chain restaurants look similar everywhere; defined by "solitary contractuality," they exist "to be passed through" and are thus "measured in units of time" rather than of space (Augé 94, 104). The "old man" may avoid the "non-place" A&P, but the deli is also "pass[ed] through," echoing the exact function of non-places, even as it suspends temporality and a split North-South spatiality fixes Latinos in a grid of "closed" possibilities.

"The Latin Deli" ultimately critiques the shifting contours of textuality under neoliberal restructuring. Its modes of insufficient transport map a nefarious substitution: to consume commodities is to desire literature, love, joy, and belonging in place—that elusive "alternative table of values"—but instead to sort through "plastic," cans, packages, "stale candy," and "wax paper" in search of a product to transport you elsewhere. This shift maps literary culture narrowly to capital, consumption, and brand recognition, even as it has the potential to turn everyday practices into poetic gestures. After all, the deli's "narrow aisles" resemble lines of verse; a customer's "list of items" is "like poetry"; "the labels of packages" invoke "the names of lost lovers"; and Mexicans enter "talking lyrically / of *dólares* to be made in El Norte." If consumption is "good for thinking," lyric poetry is also a mode that "helps us think" (Terada 196). As an *ars poetica*, "The Latin Deli" helps us consider how refuges, like the deli, emerge under forces that sever here from there and reconnect them through de-based, exploitative commodity chains. It also renders a verdict on relations between Latino poetics and consumer-based citizenship, the neoliberal civic form. On the back cover of *The Latin Deli*, Ilan Stavans claims that Cofer "may well be the most important Hispanic writer in English today, the one who will happily leave behind ethnic writing to insert herself and her successors in a truly universal literature." Make no mistake: her deli is Nuyorican and Latino. Its *ars poetica* critiques the mark of distinction ("a truly universal literature") used to sell the book by searching for a pause button on *the* "truly universal" culture—global capitalism. Stavans's desired transition from "ethnic" to "universal" implies that the most successful Latino writer is the one least recognizable as such. This idea recalls Espada's justifiable anger, as he expresses it in a letter to the Lovelock Paiute poet Adrian C. Louis, at being praised by a critic for "liberating himself" from his Puerto Rican roots ("Correspondence: Louis"). And it belies the "happiness" created by cultures being diminished by the "blank pages" of the universal measure of value: money.[9]

Breaking Languages in Cruz's Ecopoetic Essays

Whereas "The Latin Deli" invokes claustrophobia with "narrow aisles" and "closed ports," Cruz's expansive essays imagine alternate modes of production and conceptions of nature as otherwises to neoliberal globalization. As meditations on migration, environmentalism, and the dissolution of peasant, indigenous, and rural forms of life, the essays offer consonant theories of poetry and the human relation to nature. For instance, he depicts "chin-chales," the cooperative workshops of tabaqueros, nurturing creative freedoms rooted in diachronic place-based practices. While Cruz's poems enact and improvise upon these theories, the visions of harmony emerging from dissonance in the essays complement the lyrical innovations of the poems with a pedagogical acuity.[10]

As a foil to Espada's lucid lyric materialism, Cruz's ecopoetic essays favor atmospheric impression held together by a supple broken/to break dialectic. Adorno argues that essays operate through "fragments" and "breaks" distinctly capable of assessing social reality. These discontinuities differ from the otherwise similar functions of lyric and essay in Adorno's thought, as each has the capacity to critique ideology and uncover social antagonisms. But they do so differently. Whereas the poem moves from the individual lyric subject to the "collective undercurrent" so that poetic subjectivity comprehends social reality, the essay begins with the complex whole in order to reveal it as ideological, transitory, partial, and in service to hegemonic power. In the first instance, "the poetic subject" "always stands for a far more general collective subject" that uncovers "the entirety of a society" (Notes 46, 38–39) rather than the poet's psychology or individual perspective. In contrast, the essay "requires that one's thought about the matter be from the outset as complex as the object itself." Unlike the poem, it has a direct "object" and "serves as a corrective to the stubborn primitiveness that always accompanies the prevailing form of reason." In "shak[ing] off the illusion of a simple and fundamentally logical world, an illusion well suited to the defense of the status quo," as Adorno puts it (Notes 15), Cruz's essays critique the ambiguities of the status "choice," the deception of radical individualism, and the ruse of neoliberal common sense. He shows obliquely and inferentially that more is not better; economic growth is often destructive; progress should be delinked from a futurist horizon; individuals, including artists, defer to the collective rather than vice versa; and market rationality fails to produce positive outcomes. And all the while he finds joy and beauty.

Cruz's frequent figures of "broken" and "to break" symbolize tensions between problems and possibilities. The radically open, fragmented essays, with breaks in syntax and logic, half-completed thoughts, run-on and spliced sentences, and jarring fragments enact what Flores calls "the broken tongue" (57). Carmelo Esterrich argues that Cruz's poetry "forces" Spanish and English "through phonetic, morphological and syntactical deformations" to "produce a new language composed of the[ir] ruined remains" (44). Cruz's essays recompose these "ruined" fragments more powerfully due to the essay's inherent formal features. Fragments, for Adorno, structure the essay:

> it has to be constructed as though it could always break off at any point. It thinks in fragments, just as reality is fragmentary, and finds its unity in and through the breaks and not by glossing them over. An unequivocal logical order deceives us about the antagonistic nature of what that order is imposed upon. Discontinuity is essential to the essay; its subject matter is always a conflict brought to a standstill. (*Notes* 16)

Cruz's claim that "poetics is the art of stopping the world" (*Red Beans* 7) echoes Adorno's idea that the essay "breaks" from the world and renders it more clearly by exposing its conflicts, fragmentations, and false constructions of wholeness. By "think[ing] in fragments" and mapping "unity in and through the breaks," Cruz's essays negotiate contradictions to find power in "Broken Souths." Created by mutual interaction, antagonism, and transformation, these "breaks" contrast constructs of cultural assimilation like "melt," "dissolve," and "blend" (*Red Beans* 89–91). Whereas these verbs entail loss, those of "to break" preserve partial contours, shapes, and outlines of spatial forms, much like "the remains" of the "collision" of languages Esterrich sees in the poems (55 n. 7). Cruz prefers collision to dissolution because it retains rather than effaces incongruities. Concepts such as "tripolarity" (*Panoramas* 15) keep the cultural inheritances of African, European, and indigenous sources in a flexible Latinidad without "blending" them into a facile mestizaje. Moreover, the "nature" of Latino places, Cruz suggests, is produced through "dislocation, geoconfusion, territorial crisscrossings," and "geodisplacement" (*Panoramas* 119, 120). These spatial neologisms catalogue the expressive capacities of Latino writing through morphologies of plurality and fragmentation.

"Mountains in the North: Hispanic Writing in the U.S.A." (*Red Beans*) finds a guiding figure for these breaks in a stormy, irregular natural force. Cruz has more than code switching in mind in "Spanish and English breaking into each other like ocean waves" (89–90). This "breaking into each other" is unequal but unexpectedly so. Subsequent images imply that the calculus of two languages is shorthand for South and North rather than for competing literary languages; this distinction recalls that many Latino writers compose largely if not completely in English. To mine the indeterminacies of the collision of cultures in the Americas, Cruz views changing North-South relations through the prism of broadly southern cultural dynamism and North American industriousness, acquisitiveness, and material wealth. Although this frame seemingly duplicates outmoded Latin-Anglo binaries (i.e., Hegel, Thomas Jefferson, José Martí, and Domingo Faustino Sarmiento), Cruz uses it as a screen to project bifurcated Latino writers as guides to the South in the North and as vehicles to transform the North from the South. "Mountains in the North" dramatizes this unique duality. In writing the South for North Americans—"weirdos" and "electric freaks" ruled by "sterility" and "television clichés"—Latinos can transport them places "North American authors [a]re only able to write about from the position of tourists" (89). Cruz thus sees Latino writers changing "American literature" by replacing "tourists" with experienced guides and "sterility" with "mobility" and "spice" (88).[11]

These defiant articulations take on a collective Latino identity: "We will be the first group that does not melt" (91); "our ingredients are raw the Anglo fire is not hot enough to dissolve them" (91); and "[we] have not blended into Northern Americana because our roots stay fresh" (89). Here North-South geographies facilitate challenges to the United States' power to reshape (im)migrants in the image of the dominant culture. "Due to the close proximity of the Americas," Cruz writes, "rushes of tropical electricity keep coming up to inform the work and transform the North American literary landscape" (89). This prose figure distills the "tropicalizing impulse" in Cruz's poetry, Urayoán Noel's rendering of Frances Aparicio and Susana Chávez-Silverman's concept of "tropicalization" in Latino writing (859). Although the figure may misleadingly suggest that the South is all "tropical," when "rushes" of "electricity" are understood as the forces of an atmospheric, climatological ecopoetics they also encompass and carry the highland cultures Cruz praises repeatedly. In this way, Cruz's circulatory "proximity" echoes Rabasa's "without" as a differential, mobile epistemological space to challenge hegemony, preserving an outside to empire and indicating that the United States is not part of the Americas but a place, idea, and "literary landscape" to be "transform[ed]" by them. Moreover, the nostalgic "roots" are tough to package *as* nostalgia when they are "raw" "ingredients" and thus in-formation rather than mass-produced "Wonder Bread," as discussed in chapter 3. Finally, reserving the space of inspiration as southern in origin and geographically located in multiple souths echoes Espada and Herrera, but Cruz also risks essentializing Latino writing and displacing it from potentially generative North American contexts.

Cruz's ecological sensibility ultimately bridges these literary geographies. He sees lyric qualities in natural forces and ecological dimensions in literary practices; as such, all production, including literary, is grounded in nature. This idea has theoretical implications for reconstituting "Broken Souths" at convergent "breaking" points of language and culture. For Cruz, tabaqueros and campesinos testify to capitalism's commodification and destruction of peasant, communal forms. Yet such disappearances also happen "naturally," so they gesture toward a poetics constituted in the constant "breaks" of ecological, geological, and biological processes. As an archetypal "break," migration paradoxically integrates the scales and spheres of human experience—individual and collective, natural and social, literary and improvisational—into a holistic Latino poetics both stable and dynamic. "Mountains in the North" begins with a soaring declaration that strives toward this poetics: "The earth is migration, everything is moving, changing interchanging, appearing, disappearing. National languages melt, sail into each other; languages are made of fragments, like bodies are made of fragments of something in the something" (87). That this fluid, repetitive syntax enacts constant movement in praise of the fragment and fragmentation is clear. That it also praises ambiguity, indeterminacy, and the unnamable is borne out by similar integrative declarations across the essays. But it also links natural processes and Cruz's conceptions of cultural formations. "Nature should always be regarded as intensely internally variegated," Harvey writes, "an unparalleled field of difference [. . .] in perpetual flux" (*Spaces of Global Capitalism* 87). For Cruz, literature follows, replicates, and even improves on this quality of nature.

Cruz's statements on this issue emphasize migration as a complex type of "transit." As process, event, and idea, migration bridges the particular and the general, human and global scales: "Migration is the story of my body, [and] it is the condition of this age," the individual is "an entity of constant change," and "in migration populations relieve themselves of their own heaviness" (*Red Beans* 4, 10, 5). The capitalist-era rift between humans and nature finds balm in Cruz's notion that natural processes of change correlate to those in human culture. "The events that manifest themselves in nature," he writes, "also declare themselves in us: revolution, migration, exile" (*Panoramas* 124). In these calculations, the dynamic cultural outcomes of migration might outweigh their losses, while the natural, biological fact of migration across the earth's species provides an ecological framework overlaying negative political-economic valences. In writing about ecopoetics, Jonathan Skinner suggests that the autonomous "travel" of plants and biological forms "unsettles much common sense about 'nature'" (19). By using ecopoetic registers to assess the postmodern condition wrought by structural changes in global capitalism, the neoliberal story writ large, Cruz seems to provide a ready-made justification for disruptions of populations and ecosystems. But "revolution" is also a manifestation of "nature." Cruz's ideal that cultural codes, processes, and sources work "in transit through each other" (*Red Beans* 9) rather than compete for limited territory charts an idea of revolution that makes the processes of nature a model for a different world, even as this idea falls short of a total "break" from capitalist logics of power. In these articulations, there is scant critique of injustice or inequality; Cruz, after all, searches for metaphors, figures, and images from natural processes of change to understand cultural-economic ones. If his ease with contradiction, conflict, and brokenness seem to celebrate "the condition of this age," closer examination reveals underlying dispossessions.

This point brings us to Cruz's conceptions of relations between place, space, and nature. In claiming that Latino writing is well equipped to understand "the condition of this age" due to shared experiences of "this motion, this tremendous coming and going, this here and there" (*Panoramas* 122), he foregrounds expansive spatial constructions over "grounded" local experiences of place. Nuyorican poetry, Edrik López argues, is "obsessed with space." In choosing "space" over "place," López rightly views "spatial constructions" as "the critical sites of contention" for contesting dispossession in New York (205–206, 210). Yet with their lyric ecology of migration, Cruz's essays require a broader engagement with the theoretical contours of place, space, and nature; after all, they disordered place-space and local-global articulations before much of the spatial turn in critical theory. Cruz sets figures of place in motion across space (i.e., from Puerto Rico to New York), with rural and urban "breaking into each other" and natural and literary "languages" interpenetrating as mutually reconstituting forces. Whereas critics generally view such deterritorializations as "the weakening of the ties between culture and place," Ursula K. Heise stresses its possibilities for creating global imaginaries (21). "The challenge for environmentalist thinking," she argues, "is to shift the core of its cultural imagination from sense of place to a less territorial and more systemic sense of planet" (56).

Cruz's essays proceed according to a version of this logic. If deterritorialization threatens island-based cultures, it also strengthens ties between culture and space, reconstitutes cultural practices across migratory patterns, and acknowledges the ecological/natural registers of migration. Seen this way, Cruz's view of deterritorialization multiplies cultural encounters and disperses fragments, which he sees as the core elements of cultural innovation. In this sense, his work is thoroughly postmodernist: his qualified praise of upheaval, nomadism, dislocation, and fragmentation nonetheless combines with disgust for technological innovation. But his aesthetic insights precede the current discussion of environmental criticism. Heise writes that ecocriticism "has not connected to the foundational idea in much recent cultural theory that identities are at their core made up of mixtures, fragments, and dispersed allegiances" (42–43). Cruz's ecological imaginary suggests that greater attention to Latino writing's environmental sensibility might yield beneficial insights, one of which counters the absence Heise laments. This is particularly true in his concept of "migration" as a natural and literary phenomenon in addition to a process of political-economic dispossession. Heise criticizes writers who "associat[e] geographical mobility with 'nomadism' [. . .] rather than with the more ecologically grounded concept of 'migration.'" In her view, as in Cruz's ecopoetics and in Bolaño's "library," to "ground" or "root" thinking in place is theoretically and artistically limiting (31).[12]

Does this approach put place at the mercy of space, making local cultures sites for anachronistic nostalgia? Where does it locate Puerto Rico, the ambiguous scale in a local-global dialectic, where "migration" may have ecological corollaries but is produced through an imperial political economy? Cruz's answers are appropriately celebratory and ambiguous. He echoes "The Latin Deli" on displacement and place consciousness— "Often the sense of place of those displaced is greater than those in place"— but immediately adds that "exile is the aerial view" (*Panoramas* 125). This reframing of above/below reinforces Bolaño's sense of exile, makes the *guagua aérea* a space to view the arc of migration, and locates Cruz's impressionistic view of place from the expansiveness of space. Yet the figure of the island floating north, on the water, far below "the aerial view," happens concurrently. Given that Puerto Rico, in this figure, is "the first country that became a floating mass, that became mobile," there is substantial pressure to conceptualize space *as* place, motion *as* stability. "Now that we are nowhere," Cruz writes, "we have a better sense of what somewhere could be like" (*Red Beans* 125, 127). This "nowhere"/"somewhere" pairing equates loosely to space/place: a "mobile" Puerto Rico necessitates the formation of a place-based consciousness through Heise's "sense of planet" rubric, which takes deterritorialization as the "ground" for identity and literary forms. If space is commanded by capital (from above), Cruz sees migration opening up possibilities for rethinking discontinuity *as* continuity, and space *as* a mobile positionality for imagining "somewhere" *as* the disordering of above and below.

Migration produces foundational encounters between place and space in Cruz's poetics. "The encounter between rural and urban landscape, a debate released through migration, a discussion of spatial tempos," he writes, "is the center of metaphor, the sharp contrast that keeps one in northern metros aware of a profound elsewhere" (*Panoramas* 21). Read through the defensive lens of adaptability, this "metaphor" transforms mountains into skyscrapers and Taíno cave paintings into urban graffiti.[13] Tested against utopian thought, however, "somewhere" and "profound elsewhere" have limitations. Linking spatial and temporal conceptions in actual places is key to utopian forms. In Cruz's take, "a profound elsewhere" can never be located *here*, in place and in time. Although this emphasis on the spatial component of elsewhere keeps multiple souths alive "in northern metros," Cruz sees place as necessarily insufficient for cultural innovation. In this way, constant change is a type of continuity, wherein political-economic subservience paired with illusory freedoms and privileges (citizenship, mobility, "choice") limits potential change. Rather than a place-based consciousness, Cruz creates a space-expansive consciousness with Latino "fragments" that reconstitute North-South cultural interactions. This makes for innovative "poetic creations" but potentially limited models for resistance and for achieving social justice.

As exceptions to these limits, Cruz's depictions of tabaqueros and campesinos contest capitalist logic while paradoxically providing creative sources for its constant renewal. Although Cruz's emphasis on space over place and movement over groundedness offers a conceptual alternative to local and antiglobalization movements, these depictions assert localized, place-based desires for autonomy and preservation. These meditations make pre-conquest indigenous cultures antecedents to contemporary Latino migratory patterns and literary forms. "Wandering from country to country was the destiny for many Latino poets," he writes, "as it was for the indigenous tribes of the Americas" (*Panoramas* 122). Praised as possibility by Heise and lamented by environmental writers and critics of neoliberalism's disregard for place and working-class cultures, for Cruz this "nomadism" is a simple fact. Whereas this construction ignores the settled urban cultures of the Incas and Atzecs (though the former was a "wandering" tribe that settled in the Valley of Mexico), it creates a gestural continuity with a past Cruz tries to recuperate in the essays, often by claiming capaciously that Caribbean cultures have the world's cultures as source materials.

"Some Thoughts as We Approach the 500th Anniversary of the Discovery of the Americas" (*Red Beans*) lays groundwork for celebrating campesinos and tabaqueros by making ecological thinking, radical activism, and cultural exchange key to preserving threatened modes of life that have been under threat for five centuries, as the title implies. In praising "the richness" of Puerto Rican languages, characterized by "strong expressiveness" and "proverbs and folktales," Cruz uses a conceit common in his texts: that these languages have "poured down from the campesino mountains" (136). This figure of overwhelming movement and influence—it "pour[s]" rather than trickles down, to take the neoliberal supply-side ideology for justifying inequality and low taxes on the rich—attributes linguistic innovation not to professional poets but to "campesino mountains." This phrase shows culture being shaped from above not by capital or in ivory towers but by landless peasants. Moreover, it makes "campesino" and "mountains" inextricable; rather than campesinos *in* or *from* the mountains, Cruz conjures natural abundance (a downpour), as if campesinos carry mountains into cities with them. As such, he insists that "poetry is a river in the language" (*Panoramas* 112, 116) because it is constantly changing and changed by nature. For Cruz, poetry refreshes language just as nature sustains cities, rather than the bourgeois construct wherein nature serves as a supplement, or outside, to civilization, and wherein poetry is a luxury item peripheral to daily life.

More pointed is Cruz's sense that in the aggregate campesinos—rather than corporations, marketers, film producers, publishers, or authors—keep language creative on a global scale:

It is the campesinos who keep particular vernaculars alive and pumping worldwide. Language seems to stagnate in the cities, where it is cut off from agriculture and thus from rhythm; in the cities people sing less. Peasants are nowadays an endangered species being replaced by individuals who are products of the industrial-technological processing age. Ecology-minded radicals should take up their cause, for of what good is it to have a good green earth if a bunch of jerks are going to be the ones to live in it. You can see the human rootlessness in the form of the Yuppies who now fill most large North American cities. Career freaks who opinionate nothing but go out and pay $6.00 for an avocado sandwich. In Puerto Rican terms that is a financial disgrace. (136)

Cruz's tone becomes angry infrequently. His disdain here converges on a single idea, "human rootlessness," with emphasis on the modifier. This rootlessness differs from the "tremendous coming and going" of migration; whereas the latter is rooted in and grounded by cultural formations and ecological processes, the former is produced by an individualism unmoored from even the production and consumption of food. At its core, the passage rejects *homo economicus*, neoliberal ideology's prime mover. Cruz disdains this "form" of humanity as irrational, wasteful, and uncreative. "Individuals," he insists, are "products" of a transitory era in history—capitalism—a "processing age" in which "financial disgrace" equates to unthinking consumption. Tragically, these individuals are replacing the peasants who grow for pennies the avocados they consume at inflated prices. Here Cruz shows the commodity fetish concealing relations between people as between products (avocados) and those who consume them far from their source. The inequality concealed therein animates "career freaks" and acquisitive "Yuppies" who do little other than fulfill "the form" of their economic being. Whereas they "fill" and "pay," peasants are "alive and pumping" despite their endangerment. Yet a contradiction underlies this critique and Cruz's poetics in general. His skepticism about language in urban space finds little support in his own writing. Cruz's innovative poetics emerges from the encounter between city and mountains, New York and Aguas Buenas, his birthplace and home in Puerto Rico.

What Cruz really rejects is bourgeois urbanity, just as his texts reject refinement as a bourgeois principle, like Herrera's and Bolaño's poems do but unlike Heise's intellectual "eco-cosmopolitanism." The environmental movement finds similar stakes for Cruz. Without incorporating peasant, campesino, and indigenous cultures, it will remain subject to criticism for catering to "Yuppies" and "career freaks" with views of "nature" as fundamentally apart from human settlements, as a "wilderness" to escape to on weekends. Whereas this construction underlies the capitalist conception of nature and thus animates conservation movements, different motivations guide the environmental justice movement, which focuses largely on harm done to the poor, minorities, migrant workers, and urban residents who confront drastically greater threats from pollution. Therein lies the power of Cruz's claim that "a good green earth" is of little use if "a bunch of jerks" ("Yuppies," "career freaks") are the only "forms" of humanity to occupy it. He therefore gestures toward an alliance between "ecology-minded radicals," campesinos, and the working class; such pairings are essential to challenging the neoliberal order and to pushing the environmental movement (particularly in the United States) in bolder directions. But does this alliance, given the phrase "take up their cause," follow hierarchical representational structures? Perhaps, with one caveat: peasants, not intellectuals, are primary sources of language and culture, the keepers of the "river" flowing through language.

The essays find their most suggestive register in the tabaqueros of Aguas Buenas. Infused with music, literature, and politics, their cooperative craft serves as a foil to the narrow, instrumentalized "form" and "career[s]" of *homo economicus*. These tabaqueros are the heroes of the opening essay of *Panoramas*, "Home Is Where the Music Is," a portrait of the poet's childhood. In meditating on issues central to Latino poetics, particularly how to model an "alternative table of values," including forms of "freedom," Cruz's idealized representation of tabaqueros focuses on the human relation to nature. "In transforming our environment," Harvey writes, "we necessarily transform ourselves. This is Marx's most fundamental theoretical point concerning the dialectics of our metabolic relation to nature" (*Spaces of Global Capitalism* 88). This mutual transformation informs and animates Cruz's tabaqueros, who in reshaping nature with their hands remake themselves and their political-aesthetic practices.

Like Rabasa's view of subaltern insurrections, Cruz's portrait of tabaqueros replaces history's evidentiary structures with a poetics. Syntactical forms such as "it seems" and "it is recounted" use subjective memory, oral tradition, and the speculative character of hearsay and innuendo. These strategies follow Cruz's atmospheric poetic geography, "aerial view" of exile, and desire to preserve threatened cultural practices key to Puerto Rican identity. His account proceeds from a respect for traditions rooted in place and for the politics and aesthetics of his forbears, particularly his grandfather, "Julio El Bohemio," an Aguas Buenas tabaquero. The "good green earth" passage above also ends by stressing "the importance of tradition in life as well as literature, for without it there is no real freedom" (*Red Beans* 136). The tabaqueros serve as a site of tradition and a repository for "freedom" as a relational concept rooted in cultural practices and constituted interpersonally rather than fixed in atomized individuals. It must be reiterated, then, that this version of "freedom" is diametrically opposed to bourgeois "lifestyle" *as* freedom, which Cruz dismisses as "barking about having the freedom to do whatever nauseous things their lifestyles call for"

(*Red Beans* 88–89). So although the historical record is more complicated and less celebratory, Cruz's account gives lyric testimony to a mode of production that challenges capitalism and locates freedom in tradition rather than in "progress," a teleological concept Cruz finds deeply suspicious. For him, a "junkyard" symbolizes "a heap of progress" (*Panoramas* 137). Gruesz writes that Cruz's critique of "progressive temporality" emerges from his inter-American "political project" that exceeds "the imperative of retelling lost and occluded histories." This project "critiques the narrative direction of modernity and its characterization of certain groups and spaces within the Americas as 'backward' and 'underdeveloped'" ("Walt Whitman" 170). Unlike Espada, who follows this "imperative of retelling" to create a dialectic in which emancipatory futures — *as* progress — emerge from historical wreckage, Cruz rejects modernity's guiding principles of mechanization, efficiency, and amelioration. No case dramatizes this critique better than the tabaqueros.

In "Home Is Where the Music Is," Aguas Buenas is animated by communalism, political consciousness, and passion for music and literature. Its workshops are hubs of energy generated by animal spirits, Marx's conception of men and women working together to exceed their individual capacities. Cruz recalls being taken to a *chinchal* as a child by his grandfather or uncle (14); given that Cruz was born in 1949 and migrated to New York in the mid-1950s this would have likely been in the early 1950s, a time of intensive migration. "The center of town," as he remembers it, "was full of tobacco workshops known as 'chin-chales' in the island vernacular" (13). Cruz's nonlinear narratives make it difficult to historicize his temporal constructions. The language of oral history is handy instead: "It is recounted by those who lived during this epoch that the tabaqueros were paid well" (14). By most accounts, the "golden age" preceded Cruz's birth by decades. At the end of the nineteenth century, an era of consolidation, massive infusions of US capital, and US annexation, wage-labor factories started replacing independent artisans and small workshops (Baldrich 147, 155). Nonetheless, in Cruz's reckoning, the *chinchales* were idealized anticapitalist spaces well into his childhood.[14] He calls them "active," "notorious" places and points out that tabaqueros were largely socialists, anarchists, rebels, and *independentistas* (13). The Puerto Rican Socialist Party, founded in 1915, was especially influential. Cruz writes: "It seems that all the tabaqueros in Aguas Buenas were socialists. It was the party of my grandfather Julio El Bohemio." He continues, "They were all that way through some kind of popular spirit and not as intellectuals inspired by some economic ideals they had read about" (17–18). The tension between "intellectuals" and an egalitarian, communal "popular spirit," a common trope in Cruz, finds dissonance in the tabaqueros' love of literature and philosophy. "They were all that way," it seems, by both shared "spirit" and intellect.

This popular-intellectual combination was a form of cultural citizenship that triangulated nature, literature, and production. "Old and young" tabaqueros "worked side by side, telling stories" and singing "Cuban, Mexican, Argentinean, [and] Chilean songs" (*Panoramas* 13–14).[15] In "Home Is Where the Music Is," this singing transforms nature, themselves, the production process, and the product, as "their songs entered the leaves" and "spic[ed] the rolling of cigars" (17–18). Cruz's pride in learning the art of poetry from these "philosophers of the masses [and] dramatic declaimers of poetry" (13) symbolizes mutual transformations between natural and literary forms in his work. "The rolling of cigars" correlates to the writing of poems; each transforms raw and received materials into sources of pleasure, "spirit," intellectual engagement, and to be fair, danger. Cruz also depicts the tabaqueros as consumers, but of texts, as well as producers. "In the mornings," he writes, "the tabaqueros would put a little money together and hire a reader to come in and read the newspaper." "Other times," he continues, "the tabaqueros would hire a reader to come and read them a chapter of a book a day" (17–18). Espada's great-great-grand uncle Don Luis was one, reading "newspapers in the morning, / Cervantes or Marx in the afternoon," addressing "labor and capital, as the tabaqueros / rolled leaves of tobacco to smolder in distant mouths" (*Alabanza* 224–225). These are striking historical facts. A. G. Quintero-Rivera reports that tabaqueros had a 59.7 percent literacy rate compared to the general rate of 22.7 percent but explains that "literacy rates underestimate the artisans' real level of education" attained through oral readings. "It was a common practice among cigarmakers working together," he writes, "to pay someone to read to them while they worked." "The reading program," he continues, "was established by the cigarmakers themselves and included local newspapers, international periodicals," usually from unions, "social novels," and "social philosophy," including Proudhon and Marx (27). This collective practice praised by Cruz and Espada contrasts the individuated modes of "The Latin Deli." The tabaqueros' forms of literacy link intellect to craft, and their self-directed "reading program" gives literature everyday use-value, wherein literature is not a supplemental leisure pursuit for "career freaks" or a paternalistic "program" to educate, represent, or control workers.

Cruz's praise of alternative economic relations firmly rejects radical individualism. Although "individual experience" is the starting point of consciousness, Adorno writes, it is "mediated by the overarching experience of historical humankind." For Cruz, that means mediation by collective migration and natural forms. That "historical humankind" "is mediated and one's own experience unmediated is," Adorno concludes, "self-deception on the part of an individualistic society and ideology" (*Notes* 10). Cruz's critique of this self-deception reworks human-nature interfaces. For instance, dedicating *Panoramas* "to a rock and a tree respectively," a boulder in the River Borinquen and "an old man Ceiba rooted in the valley between Caguas and Aguas Buenas" (9), replaces typical dedications (as in Espada's "black braid") with natural forms apprehended as individuals. In Taíno practices, Cruz writes, "to walk the mountains was to encounter the trees as individuals" (11). These "individuals" do not symbolize anthropocentric, individuated freedoms; rather, they are natural forms with autonomous agency. This ecopoetic cornerstone derives from Cruz's reverence for indigenous conceptions of nature.

The anticapitalist spatiotemporality of the *chinchales* in "Home Is Where the Music Is" ties together Cruz's ecopoetic essays. Though skilled artisans, their "leisurely work pace" is essential for "freeing their minds for contemplation and aesthetic flight" (13). This mode of daily transport ("flight") contrasts with "the iron bird" (19), the *guagua aérea*. The tabaqueros, Cruz tells us, "constituted a strong force in this first wave of migration" to New York early in the twentieth century. Counter to Cruz's ecologically grounded migrations, this wave was "one of the most one-dimensional of human exoduses," determined not by nature but by capitalist class structures. "It was not the upper classes that had to leave," he writes, "the bourgeois never leave where they are milking" (19). As US capital flew south to mechanized factories, surplus labor, including tabaqueros, flew north, where they found a different spatiotemporality.[16] Rather than seasonal work for six months, after which "the whole town went into a slumber" (14), rather than an "island economy" that is "a slow-moving snail" (*Red Beans* 5), and rather than the "horizontal" posture of siestas, they found speed, verticality, and an ideology of productivity in service to "the economy," abstracted, godlike, and seemingly neutral. In New York, this "horizontal" repose makes "you lazy, or worse, useless to the economy" (12–13), while "flashing" and "darting" "cars, buses, subways" paradoxically create "a new vertical comprehension" (21). Cruz celebrates mobility, but he sees its underside. He challenges us to align the freedom of "slumber" to the biological and ecological rhythms of "migration," to promote an ecological economy of communal forms over exchange-value and individual consumption, and to resist the hyper-productive ideology symbolized by nonstop urban transportation.

The News from Agüeros's New York

In *Sonnets from the Puerto Rican*, Agüeros uses such transportation figures to great effect. With frequent references to "the headlines," including ones related to neoliberalization from the late 1980s to the mid-1990s, the sonnets bring "the news" (42) about "the new liberals" (30), a clear if idiosyncratic reference to neoliberalism. If "it is difficult to get the news from poems," as William Carlos Williams, the Puerto Rican modernist and Paterson resident, wrote (318), Agüeros's sonnets deliver "the news" in accessible but denaturalized form, with humor, lyricism, honesty, and irreverence.[17] That Agüeros marks his sonnets as "from the Puerto Rican" begs the question of the preposition's function. Does it indicate derivation, that "the Puerto Rican" supplies source material? Might it suggest a particular viewpoint? Does it entice the dubious reader who thinks Puerto Ricans do not, cannot, or should not write sonnets? Such thinking, Espada reasons in an essay on Agüeros, narrows Latino poetry's range; the sonnet, this thinking goes, is insufficiently "authentic" and "urban" and thus inappropriate for representing Latino experiences (*Lover of a Subversive* 47). By explicitly titling each sonnet a "Sonnet," and by following the basic form, with fourteen lines and the conventional problem (in loose *octaves*) and resolution (in loose *sestets*) structure, while generally eschewing rhyme and iambic pentameter, Agüeros creates a dialectic between "sonnet" and "Puerto Rican" to transform both the traditional form and the expressive range of Puerto Rican subjectivity.

In reading contemporary sonnets, David Caplan argues against the prevailing idea that the sonnet is foreign rather than "American" (11). Agüeros insists similarly that the sonnet is thoroughly Puerto Rican, with its tropes of sadness, loss, unrequited love, and what he calls "Captivity" to the type of freedom in capitalist class, property, and productive relations. Because the sonnet is "often assumed to be the sign of aesthetic and political conservatism," Caplan writes that the "striking alliance of 'traditional' prosody and 'radical' scholarship has yet to receive the attention it deserves" (63). Caplan focuses on queer poetics, including Campo's sonnets, but the notion also applies to Agüeros's sonnets. As Caplan notes, critical binaries between "conventional" and "experimental" forms often map inaccurately to right- and left-wing politics respectively. "Assigning stable values to poetic forms," he concludes, ignores shifting contexts, perspectives, and contents (11).[18] Agüeros's "Sonnet for Ambiguous Captivity" highlights the convergence of traditional form and radical critique. Here, false neoliberal freedoms extend Puerto Rico's "ambiguous" colonial status:

> Captivity, I have taken your white horse. Punctilious
> Death rides it better. Dubious, I try to look you in
> your eye. Are you something like old-time slavery, or
> are you like its clever cousin, colonialism? Are you
> the same as "occupied," like when a bigger bird takes
> over your nest, shits, and you still have to sweep? Or
> when you struggle like the bottom fish snouting in the
> deep cold water and the suck fish goes by scaled in his
> neon colors, living off dividends, thinking banking is
> work? Captivity, you look like Ireland and Puerto Rico!
>
> Four horsemen of the apocalypse, why should anyone fear
> your arrival, when you have already grown gray among us
> too familiar and so contemptible? And you, Captivity, you
>
> remind me of a working man who has to be his own horse. (41)

As is typical of his sonnets, lines have twelve to fifteen syllables and five to six stresses, with the exception of the final two. The sardonic apostrophe, relentless enjambment, frequent caesura, high number of unstressed syllables per line, and antic subjectivity structure the sonnets. Although the book's dedication acknowledges a debt "for their tutoring" to Shelley, Shakespeare, Browning, cummings, and Millay, and to a public school teacher in El Barrio "who introduced" Agüeros to sonnets (9), his poems also feature typical Spanish-language prosody. With the exception of the lines ending with "or," "Or," "you," and "horse," all lines end on weak beats, and these often feature elision with the previous syllable, traits common to *coplas* and *décimas*. Finally, the sonnets often end with couplets, but nearly as often the final line stands alone as a compressed, mock-aphoristic but rarely obvious or packaged conclusion. These final two lines stand out with seven strong beats apiece, and the enjambed final line and a half satirically captures the delusions and injustices of neoliberal ideology.

In these lines the collection's frequent subway trains, cars, and bicycles give way to the horse. The "working man who has to be his own horse" consolidates a critique of the outcomes of neoliberalization with a figure for the difficulty of upward mobility. Amid the ambiguity about Puerto Rico's status, it symbolizes compromised freedoms of movement, labor's alienation from the means of production, and the laborer as an appendage of the machine. It interweaves the poem's figures of economic exploitation, which collectively act as a metaphorical index to neoliberal-era inequality. To begin, the metaphor "like when a bigger bird takes / over your nest, shits, and you still have to sweep" captures the process and outcome of accumulation by dispossession, especially the corporate strategy of externalizing costs, like pollution. Second, "the bottom fish" and "the suck fish" competing for resources recalls the now-aphoristic rejection of the capitalist ideal of equal exchange, that *nothing is more unequal than the equal treatment of unequals*. This figure of unequal class relations turns on the binary of above/below. At "the bottom," one fish is "snouting" and "struggl[ing]" in the "cold" in order to survive, while above "the suck fish" vacuums resources and wealth upward. Another figure of accumulation by dispossession, this one suggests the shift from a manufacturing, industrial base toward the financialization of the capitalist economy. In the past three decades, the post-Fordist model of capital accumulation has "the suck fish" "living off dividends," conspicuously consuming flashy goods in "neon colors." The poem's mockery of the fish's claim that "banking is work" hints at the ways in which the leaders of neoliberal plunder, particularly in the financial sector, proclaim that they deserve to be praised and honored for their hard work and contribution to society. Yet "the suck fish" takes from rather than gives to "the bottom fish." This sucking up rather than trickling down symbolizes the redistribution of wealth and resources from the bottom to the top under neoliberal policies. The competing fish indicate different registers for the freedom of movement: one is "snouting" for daily sustenance, the other "goes by" in leisure. This is freedom in a fishbowl governed by "suck fish," democracy controlled by corporations. The final line mocks pull-yourself-up-by-the-bootstraps individualism. To be your "own horse" follows a similar illogic to equate "freedom" with "captivity," and as with "The Latin Deli" and the status issue, any "choice" is made in a fishbowl of options and with scant resources.

Like "Sonnet for Ambiguous Captivity," the twenty "Landscapes" opening *Sonnets from the Puerto Rican* use transportation figures to imagine the diverging fates of capital and labor under neoliberalism. The mobile "landscapes" of "Sonnet for the #6" and "Sonnet for Heaven Below" are grittier and more "urban," to recall Espada's mock critique, with frequent subway trains, streets, and parks. Here the quotidian lives of Nuyoricans, Latinos, and the poor glimpse transcendence through defeat. Here homeless sleeping in subways are "actually angels fatigued from long hours and no pay," as in the latter poem's figure of the inverse relation between hard work and financial reward (17). Here, almost invariably, are tensions between freedom and captivity, mobility and confinement. Agüeros's poems, as Espada writes, are "bewildered by the spectacle of movement without progress" (*Lover of a Subversive* 38). In the poem preceding "Ambiguous Captivity," the older poet puts this figuratively: capital has "free transportation," with deregulation, privatization, open borders, and nearly unfettered access to legislators and to the media. "Isn't it shy Peace" rather than "Red-Horsed War," he asks us, "that deserves free transportation?" (40). Labor, in contrast, has only the body, which must also be its "own horse."

This relation is summarized in the concluding line of "Sonnet: News from the World, Tompkins Square Park, & the Metropolitan Transit Authority," a "Landscape" tackling the events of 1989, gentrification, and differences between "the captains of Wall Street" and the homeless. Its pithy exclamation—"Ah, Capitalism! The three-card monte master" (21)—wonders at capitalism's power to conceal underlying structures in forms of appearance. Such insight into Brown's sense that "neoliberal subjects are controlled *through* their freedom" (44) depicts capitalism as a confidence game in which the rules are rigged to benefit those in control, "the suck fish." Capitalism's brilliance comes in creating the appearance that the game is free and fair with equal, transparent rules for all. In this scenario understanding how and why one has lost is maddening. Juxtaposed to the workhorse, this con game figure underscores Brown's freedom-as-captivity and Žižek's sense that capitalist societies pair "personal freedoms" with "slave-like work discipline." "What makes capital exceptional," he writes, "is its unique combination of the values of freedom and equality and the facts of exploitation and domination" (124–125). Agüeros imagines this combination with accessible, humorous figures of awe. In their acute grasp of capitalism's seemingly intractable injustices lies the challenge of confronting them except with puzzled admiration.

The power of his paired sadness and joy makes the critical neglect of Agüeros puzzling but ultimately understandable. His quasi-formal poetics, existentialist religious themes, dark comedy, and adept negotiation of Nuyorican and Latino experiences alongside near-universal themes of love and death make Agüeros, as Espada proffers, "a prime candidate for crossing over into mainstream literary acceptance" (*Lover of a Subversive*

46). In grasping for explanations, Espada posits that Agüeros symbolizes the general disregard for Puerto Rican writers. "In a community full of neglected writers," Espada laments, "the neglect of Agüeros seems particularly unjust." This is especially "inexcusable" in New York, he writes, given that "the Puerto Rican community has been a significant presence in New York—the literary capital of the country—for more than seventy years" (*Lover of a Subversive* 46). Puerto Ricans' minimal cultural capital in comparison to other Latino groups, especially Latin American exiles, influences which writers are neglected and celebrated.[19] In my view, however, the compelling logic is that Agüeros's graceful, accessible, and formal anticapitalist poetics confounds definitions of Latino writing in a "post-" era that deems anticapitalism passé. Further, they are not didactic "protest" poems (and thus unfairly dismissed), "perfect" formal sonnets (and thus praised in some circles), or written from a critically sexy identity position, each of which makes it difficult to assess the sonnets under prevailing critical models. They are fully realized critiques of the neoliberal order through the lens of Puerto Rico's ambiguous, often invisible, status.

On September 12, 1968, two months after Agüeros's hunger strike, an event symbolized relations between US capital and Puerto Rican cultural formations. As the Student Movement crested in Mexico City, the megamall Plaza Las Américas opened in San Juan. Once the biggest in Latin America, it remains the Caribbean's largest. Its provocative logo (Figure 2) depicts Columbus's three ships, and its two-part motto ("the center of it all" and "the center of your life") reinforces neoliberal globalization's continuity with the conquest, the centrality of corporate capital to organizing everyday life, and the role of consumption in structuring individual ("your") identity. "Sonnet for Ambiguous Captivity" expresses conquest's continuous presence: it is "already grown gray among us / too familiar and so contemptible." Rather than an "arrival" or "discovery," the sonnets take the indigenous view of the conquest as an "apocalypse" and perpetual "center of it all" that constitutes life from birth to death. Apocalyptic imagery appropriately guides Agüeros's Columbus sonnets, "Sonnet after Columbus, I and II." They imagine "the stiff starched sails" (14) depicted in the megamall logo crushed by a "diluvial tidal wave swamping the Santas, / Pintas, Niñas, [and] Boeing 747's" (27). The Appalachian writer and activist Wendell Berry describes capital's current conquest in terms of the former: "it is as if the future is a newly discovered continent which the corporations are colonizing" (58). One may use boats and the other airplanes but each creates "familiar" and "contemptible" outcomes.[20]

Figure 2

Agüeros's "Landscapes" pinpoint these outcomes with provocative "Banana Republic" figures. While it is unsurprising that Plaza Las Americas has a Banana Republic store, that paragon of dispossession made status symbol, Agüeros's claim that the United States has become a banana republic due to a governing plutocracy and increasing wealth inequality might be. In 2012, on the heels of Occupy Wall Street, this claim found in both "Sonnet for Saturday, October 6, 1990" (25) and "Headlines from America, Banana Republic, Spring 1995" (42) looks prescient. The latter begins with the prosaic, "One percent of Americans own forty percent of the wealth," and proceeds to give six lines of supporting evidence. The shift comes in line eight, where a modified sestet resolution begins "That's the news, here's the editorial" and ends with an apostrophe to "Captivity": "Banana Republic, exhume your revolutionary Declaration now!" This "editorial" on "the news" is dismayed at conditions Latinos migrate north to escape, according to the popular perception. But it also expresses hope that below ("exhume") every banana republic is a latent revolution. The term "banana republic" enfolds historical nation-states, of which the United Fruit Company's Guatemala is the paragon; clothing stores symbolizing the necessity of conspicuous consumption to capitalism; and satires rejecting the criminalization of Latinos. As such, Agüeros's "Banana

Republic" sonnets join Bogotá's satirical "Banana Republic" t-shirts cited in the preface to *Broken Souths* in insisting that "MIGRATION . . . IS NOT A CRIME" and that revolutions based on dignity, daily bread, and useful work must eventually supplant "T-shirt solidarity."

These multiple, disputed "banana republics" resonate in popular constructions of islands as paradises. The poet Muriel Rukeyser's "Islands" memorably mocks radical individualism in exasperation at this view: "O for God's sake / they are connected / underneath" (544).[21] Given that islands are separated by water and "connected / underneath" by submerged landforms, this figure usefully maps Latino groups to one another while maintaining their autonomies. In Nuyorican literary forms, moreover, Puerto Rico is both an isolated anomaly (captive *and* free) and a paradigm of neoliberal-era dispossession. This "island" connects spaces of resistance to the neoliberal order from below, revealing how Latino poetry is "connected / underneath" by historical geographies of upheaval, exile, and struggle. Mapping "underneath" is a unique capacity of Nuyorican poetics, with its array of forms, including lyric-narrative free verse, ecopoetic essays, and anticapitalist sonnets, among so many others. Like Bolaño's and Espada's "countries" of writing, Cruz and Agüeros circumvent neoliberal enclosures by including campesinos, tabaqueros, the homeless, public housing residents, prisoners, prostitutes, and the working-class artists, musicians, boxers, taxi drivers, seamstresses, teachers, and journalists depicted in the thirty-two "Portraits" concluding the sonnets. While the sonnets are nominally "Puerto Rican" and nationality remains the "binding principle" for Latino groups (Flores 212), Nuyorican poetics demonstrates the countervailing benefits of a shared Latino imaginary that connects even seemingly insular forms.

In introducing *The Wind Shifts: New Latino Poetry*, Francisco Aragón claims that "the bedrock of Latino poetry is Chicano poetry, both in proportion and subject matter" (1). In New York, however, the volatile geology of the "bedrock" shifts. In addition to the poets discussed here, poets ranging from Julia de Burgos and Clemente Soto Vélez, to Nuyorican movement poets such as Pedro Pietri, to their innovative successors such as Edwin Torres, to younger poets such as Noel and Aracelis Girmay, make Puerto Rican poetry another "bedrock of Latino poetry."[22] Multiplying Aragón's claim further across plural "Broken Souths" assembles spaces and forms of poetic innovation that contest neoliberal ideals. Katherine Sugg argues that multiethnic US literatures, including Latino, require "rigorous skepticism toward the 'singularization' of communities, texts, and critical schools." She emphasizes instead pluralist processes for mapping literary fields along multiple axes (240). A similar approach guides my mapping of "Broken Souths" poetry. Like the writers in this chapter whose practices move between North and South, across Latino groups, and within marginal, working-class, and threatened forms of life, these souths resist singularization. With remarkable internal diversity, Nuyorican poetics is the vanguard of poetry of the Americas. It too is "none of the above" when the choices are US, "American," Latino, Spanish-language, English-language, island, and mainland. The next chapter moves from multiplicity to Mexico City, a singular "monster" produced through neoliberalism's processes of total urbanization.

CHAPTER SIX

Godzilla in Mexico City

Poetics of Infrastructure in José Emilio Pacheco and Roberto Bolaño

The large city has but a single problem: number.
　　　　　—Henri Lefebvre, *The Urban Revolution* (92)

When Lefebvre's digressive manifesto for urban studies, *The Urban Revolution*, was published in 1970, Mexico City's population was eight million. Due to massive rural-to-urban migration, the population now approaches thirty million and Lefebvre's modeling of urban space as a simultaneously discrete and comprehensive field for the coming era of "complete" urbanization is increasingly apposite (*Urban Revolution* 1). This idea foreshadowed the ascendant "planet of slums," in Mike Davis's terms, where millions move to cities monthly. If Lefebvre's cheeky assertion renders all theoretical and practical questions of urbanism functions of scale and magnitude, Victor Hernández Cruz's reckoning of this "number" as "infinite Mexico City" pinpoints a principal Latina/o and autochthonous literary perception of the city (*Panoramas* 150). In the Americas, nowhere has urban growth magnified neoliberal outcomes more than in Mexico City, the cultural capital of Latin America and the stereotyped Other of presumptively finite, measurable US cities. The city's "infinite" scale exceeds many nations and pressures the literary imagination to grapple with particular, localized experiences of the city in relation to the city as a conceptual whole.[1] In introducing *The Urban Revolution*, the critical geographer Neil Smith observes that a profound shift in images of large cities accompanies the transition from industrial models of urban development to the production of urban space through heritage tourism, telecommunications, financial services, and service, cultural, and entertainment industries, the post-Fordist modes of capital accumulation scorned in Agüeros's sonnets (xi). In Mexico City, moreover, an intractable counter force obscures the "single problem," multiplying its registers, images, and measurement difficulties. Pollution, both literal and figurative, underlies numerous literary conceptions of the city, by Latino, Mexican, and Latin American writers alike. In this obscuring lens, the metric shifts from "number" as the "single problem" to the material and immaterial valences of "pollution."

Among Latino representations of Mexico City, Cruz's "If You See Me in L.A. It's Because I'm Looking for the Airport" (*Panoramas*) depicts this dynamic most suggestively.[2] In imagining Mexico City's pollution from Los Angeles's comparatively less polluted freeways while searching for an exit to the airport, the speaker ponders Los Angeles's history of conquest and profoundly Mexican cultural dimensions. "What would the Mexicans want / L.A. back for?" he asks (104).[3] The antic, oblique answer—"They got Mexico City / And can give lessons / On how to perfect / The pollution" (105)—tends toward synecdoche in the United States, where the infamous smog obscures nearly everything else about the Mexican capital. From this perspective, smog serves as a figure in which the part—"the pollution"—substitutes for the whole, a complex set of economic, political, cultural, geological, and ecological forces. García Canclini, perhaps the most influential cultural theorist of Mexico City, deadpans "Is Pollution All There Is to See?" in discussing the role of Mexico City's museums in its "improvised" globalization (82–83). This rhetorical question sardonically replies to Cruz's mock-critique of the stereotypical US view, which overlooks, among other things, how Mexico City has more museums than any city in the world. This "pollution" of perception combines with actual pollution to render an affirmative response to García Canclini's question from the United States. After all, the nation whose name Mexico City shares remains the "Broken South" par excellence in the hegemonic US perspective and in the corollary "Latino Threat Narrative," which operates through a metonym wherein "Mexicans" stand in for all Latinos. When combined with the perception that Mexico City, weighted with the nation's name, is overrun by cartels, criminals, and swine flu the US view of the city as a "Broken South" has been augmented.

The US perception has not always been unfavorable. Before the neoliberal ascendancy, Mexico City was considered a natural wonder and ideal destination for North American writers and artists. Jack Kerouac's *On the Road*, for instance, depicts the drive toward Mexico City as a descent into the "magic *south*" (253).[4] Whereas the shift from "magic" to "broken" is uneven, partial, and always dialogic, and it obscures deep structural inequalities comprising Mexico City before neoliberalism, such literary figures foreground the power of literary (mis)perception as well as the literally clean air of the 1950s. This environmental shift is embodied in Carlos Fuentes's novel of Mexico City, *La región mas transparente del aire* [*Where the Air Is Clear*], published in 1958. In contrast, *La región menos transparente* [The Region with the Least Clear Air], a centuries-spanning anthology of poetry about Mexico City, inverts Fuentes to account for the "perfect" pollution under which it was published in 2003. The editor and poet Héctor Carreto's title foregrounds "the pollution" as a literary signifier of the city. But the anthology also suggests the centrality of poetry to its identity, from preconquest poets to contemporary writers such as Juan Bañuelos and David Huerta. This literary geography begins with the Nahuatl poet-warrior Nezahualcóyotl, who ruled Texcoco, part of present-day Mexico City, alongside the Aztec Tenochtitlán. His name now graces one of the world's largest slums, known by the diminutive "Neza."[5] An up-to-date literary geography of the city's iconic poets would also include Bolaño's sprawling novel *The Savage Detectives*, which follows "all the young poets of Mexico City, those who were born here and those who came from the provinces, and those who swept here on the current from other places in Latin America" (205).

Among the poets "born here," Pacheco remains the preeminent voice on "the pollution." His "Badland" recalls the era conjured in Fuentes's title, when "from any corner you could see mountains." Yet because the mountains were so visible then, residents did not notice them until "an unbreathable curtain" of smog "from the incessant millions of vehicles" and other pollutants fell and they became conspicuous in their absence (*Selected Poems* 181). Pacheco's urban ecopoetics uses literary language to measure these hazy empirical realities, including the smog that literally obscures mountains while figuratively constituting the linguistic and literary processes charged with representing them. His intertextual ecopoems examine how language represents and obfuscates economic and ecological processes, and his alert weariness counterbalances "those who swept" into a city long a haven for literary, artistic, and political exiles. Among the poets "swept here," Bolaño is perhaps both the most famous and uniquely positioned, viewing Mexico City through the dual historical lenses of 1968 and 1973.[6]

In this chapter, I read their depictions of "the pollution," infrastructure, and the built environment to theorize an emergent urban poetics under neoliberal forces. This approach revises cultural and literary studies perspectives on Mexico City, which combine two convergent themes. First, the events of 1968 are a pivot point in Mexico City's historical geography, political economy, and literary subjectivity. Second, problems exacerbated or produced by hyper-urbanization—pollution; unreliable water access, supply, and delivery; scant legal employment opportunities and burgeoning informal sectors; inadequate and dilapidated housing; crowded, inaccessible, and expensive transportation networks; growing wealth inequality; and lagging capital investment, to name a few—have created a near consensus that the city as a whole is impossible to map, narrate, and understand. "Urban theorists have argued that one of the key aspects of the modern city," Rubén Gallo writes in analyzing Mexico City's cultural dimensions, "is that it cannot be represented in its totality" (21). Instead, models of fragmentation, disjunction, and dispersal dominate theoretical conversations. Because of its incorporation of surrounding villages and its topographical spread across the mountains and plateaus of the Valley of Mexico, Mexico City has been especially fertile ground for such theories. García Canclini exemplifies these approaches in calling it "a disassembled jigsaw puzzle" with loosely networked, dispersed centers (*Consumers* 56) divided by *delegaciones* (districts or boroughs), *colonias* (neighborhoods), and freeways. The city's nominative range, including the popular "DF" (for the Distrito Federal), visceral "Mancha Urbana" (Urban Stain), and menacing and affectionate "El Monstruo," formalizes the city's constitutive, linguistic multiplicities.[7]

At the same time, cultural studies approaches following critics such as García Canclini and Angel Rama read the Latin American city as a singular text with manifold registers, voices, and sensibilities. Even García Canclini uses "the city" as an active agent signifying myriad urban processes. "When the city invades the desert, the forest, the mountain, everything that surrounds and embraces it," he writes with Mexico City in mind, "it breaks into pieces, losing its sense of space" (*Consumers* 60). Such dissonance between active whole ("the city") and disassembled, "broken" parts ("pieces") produces numerous interpretive dilemmas.[8] To map the transformed "sense of space," this chapter reworks the broken/to break dialectic through its hyper-urban dynamic between broken parts and conceptual whole. Unlike previous chapters, this "to break" also serves as the infinitive verb of "complete" urbanization, with the city as an expanding whole "breaking" as it grows. My readings of infrastructure and the built environment engage with this break by examining how poems negotiate the contradictory linguistic and material dimensions of "the pollution." If scholars and critics are bound by theoretical and empirical methods, poets are freed to articulate Mexico City's intuitive totality, which they often do by considering specific, localized forms and movements within the "single problem," *the* city. For instance, Mexico City poems often locate images of cars, taxis, buses, metro trains and stations, neighborhoods, streets, monuments, plazas, buildings, and landforms within the confounding whole.[9]

These poems depict tensions between global and local forces, mobility and confinement, and ground-level street views and abstractions from above. But their unique contributions are revelatory figures of infrastructure, which the extant, corollary "scholarly infrastructure" struggles to comprehend. This inadequacy, Patricia Yaeger argues, prevents literary studies from understanding cities, particularly hyper-urbanized agglomerations in the global South. Although often ignored in favor of critically sexier social relations and identity formations, infrastructure is perhaps the fundamental component in the functioning of urban space and the health and well-being of urban residents. As such, Yaeger's "poetics of infrastructure," or "metropoetics," remaps the urban imaginary by emphasizing how literary texts reflect differential access to infrastructure. Infrastructure's highly literary "play of surface and depth (subways, water mains) [and] of hypervisibility (bridges) and invisibility (the electric grid)," she posits, makes it "tempting to imagine that the deep structures of city texts might mirror the deep structures of cities." She discovers, however, that infrastructure is often "barely visible" in urban poems and novels, and that "you have to dig to find" representations "of people's massed relations to infrastructure." "This absence," she concludes, signifies "infrastructural privilege," ignoring "where it takes you, who uses it, who takes care of it, who lives near it, and who is forced to live under or do without it" (16–17). Neoliberal-era Mexico City poems, like Espada's "Circle Your Name," frequently depict infrastructure in ways that do not require readers "to dig." Their forms of dialectical "play" follow tropes of above/below to critique "infrastructural privilege." This latter word appears conspicuously in Pacheco's "'H&C,'" which examines the linguistic and geographic contours of access to clean water. Whereas infrastructure and the ecological processes circulating through them are mostly marginal to urban literary studies of the Americas and often absent from urban literature, they are prominent in Mexico City poems.[10]

When paired with ecopoetics, metropoetics can more fully comprehend the ways in which texts map antagonistic interactions between processes of nature, infrastructural networks, economic flows, and cultural relations that collectively produce "the city." A flexible but rigorous sense of infrastructure-nature linkages lends critical weight to the examination of large-scale urbanism. After all, as Lefebvre points out, large cities "legitimize inequality" through spatialized segregation, and they "poison" and "devour" nature. For neoliberal capitalism these are not structural problems: large cities "grow richer" through these very processes (*Urban Revolution* 91–92). Yet as an ensemble of processes of nature that sustain Mexico City, "the environment" provides a theoretical-practical hedge against atomization, the dissolution of collective bonds, and spatialized inequality. "*The* city is able to exist," García Canclini concedes, only through a "shared concern about the environment" (*Consumers* 63). Paradoxically, then, the city's "broken" parts approach wholeness through "the pollution," in a collective recognition of the ecological aspects of urban space.[11] Together, metropoetics and ecopoetics reckon with these "strange intersections," to use Juan Felipe Herrera's phrase again. Whereas the former operates by conceptualizing fragmentation, ruin, and loss, the latter proceeds from a principle of holistic interconnection. Ecopoetry, Leonard M. Scigaj writes, preserves the referential base for language while also problematizing literary representation, and depicts nature "as a dynamic, interrelated series of cyclic feedback systems" (37, 78–79). As such, ecopoetics creates forms that attempt to repair what Foster, Clark, and York call "the ecological rift" between humans and nature. By pairing material fragmentation and conceptual wholeness, metropoetics and ecopoetics offer insight into the ways in which "the broken" access nature, resources, and infrastructure.

This critical approach disrupts false boundaries between urban space and its supposedly constitutive outside, as in the realm of nature, the country, and industrial agriculture, by exposing their interwoven constructions. Because "society has been completely urbanized" (Lefebvre, *Urban Revolution* 1), the city should be mapped through these permeable outsides, which function through urban flows and logic. Lefebvre's suggestive description of future urban development as a "process of implosion-explosion" eerily portrays Mexico City's. This process includes both "the tremendous concentration (of people, activities, wealth, goods, objects, instruments, means, and thought) of urban reality" as well as "the immense explosion, the projection of numerous, disjunct fragments (peripheries, suburbs, vacation homes, satellite towns) into space" (*Urban Revolution* 14). Vacation homes, oil and gas pipelines, and cornfields constitute the city as much as the Metro, slums, shopping malls, and museums. The city, García Canclini concurs, "is constituted not only by what takes place within its territory, but also by the way in which it is traversed by migrants and tourists, messages and goods" (*Consumers* 62). Precarious development of mountainsides, absorption of outlying villages and parks, dissolution of rural communities and ensuing migratory pressures, increasing yields achieved through "efficient" industrial agriculture, and intensified capital (financial and cultural) penetration have accompanied Mexico City's "implosion-explosion" and thus appear across many poems set in Mexico City.[12]

The following pages appraise how poetic figures of infrastructure offer insight into these processes. First, Pacheco's "Mercado libre" ["Free Market"] and "'H&C'" examine the production, delivery, and corporatization of food and water. Second, Bolaño's "Godzilla in Mexico" imagines urban domestic space as an affective topography of fear and uncertainty. This capacious view of infrastructure includes streets and apartments, the city's building blocks. The Latino writers who have guided *Broken Souths* thus far offer some figurative keywords for readings these texts. Cruz's Los Angeles and Mexico City are each comprised of "a wiring of freeways" (*Panoramas* 102). Espada's "city hidden from the city" (*Trouble Ball* 33) distills the infrastructural dialectic of visibility/invisibility. And Herrera's rural-urban "underground sea of petrochemical channels and sewers and the complex systems of hydroelectric power" that produces "boiling under [the] feet" of Mexico's poor and indigenous points up the relation of infrastructure to the alienated labor who produce it and are often excluded from its use (*Mayan Drifter* 22). The keywords "wiring," "hidden," "network," "underground," "channels," and "systems" map a dynamic, uneven poetics of infrastructure, from the most visible (water towers, overpasses) to the least (sewers, domestic spaces, the disposable poor). The chapter ends by positing that these "systems" are run by what Huerta calls the "Song of Money," a poem that finds a degree of pleasure in submitting to capital's influence. The existing "scholarly infrastructure" is, Yaeger writes, "inadequate for describing the pleasures and pounding of most urban lives, or the fact that many city dwellers survive despite all odds" (15). Together, this chapter's poems explore how *chilangos*, Mexico City residents, survive and find consolation and sometimes pleasure in what Huerta calls the "too large" city (187).

Pacheco's Ecopoetic Critique of Market-Based Access to Food and Water

In examining infrastructural dialectics of surface/depth and hypervisibility/invisibility, along with access/exclusion and appearance/reality, Pacheco's "Mercado libre" and "'H&C'" expose the injustices of market-based "freedom." Free-market infrastructure, they suggest, distributes necessities such as food and water unevenly if not nefariously. Although neither poem mentions Mexico City explicitly, each situates allusions and narrative traces within the city that appears across his collections as a monstrously expanding totality.[13] "Mercado libre" clearly defines its subject—the titular "free market"—but performs its critique indirectly by reproducing the figurative "pollution" created by the ideology of free trade and free-market fundamentalism. The poem's abrupt, false ending cedes the last word to multinational capital as the guiding infrastructural energy that continuously reproduces Mexico City in its own image. Its antipoetic, antipastoral setting on a factory farm links the city's means of reproduction to constitutive outsides and the production of nature to an urban, brand-driven subjugation to capital. This sounds grave, but "Mercado libre" makes these points with mirth, misdirection, and mock envy. Yet dispossession underlies the poem; it was published in 1996, two years after NAFTA condemned Mexico's small farmers to the "blank page" of agribusiness.

"Mercado libre" imagines the factory rooster mocking the "surly arrogance" of his human observers (*Tarde o temprano* 437–438).[14] In assuming the rooster copulates blissfully, they misapprehend their own role in reinforcing the reproduction of nature, with the consequence that they also misunderstand the limits of their own freedom. Although they envy "his unlimited diverse copulation" and his "iron fist that maintains the terror / of the fleeting chicken coop," the reality is decidedly different. Humans, the poem implies, confuse the mechanical process of reproduction with its prodigious results. For the rooster, our arrogance is believing in his power and freedom, our illusion in "believing he doesn't know the deal, unconscious / of his role as pawn in the sinister game of chess, / a simple gear in the infinite chain / that doles out eggs for breakfast // and Kentucky Fried Chicken."[15] Like many Pacheco poems, this one assumes the subject position of an animal (though not the voice, as some do). His figures of dogs, snails, turtles, bats, flies, ants, termites, rats, and other small, scorned, and defenseless creatures are partly figurative devices for modeling empathic responses to Mexico City's vulnerable poor. These allegories correlating animal to human suffering structure Pacheco's ecopoetics, in which humans are part of, rather than apart from and in control of, natural processes. Human survival and the contours of humanness are at stake in Pacheco's poems, where animals and nature serve as mirrors for human failings and suffering.[16]

"Mercado libre" furthers this project by reversing the human-animal epistemological hierarchy, implying that we too are "pawns" in the free market. This market, moreover, is not natural but a "sinister game of chess" that converts human (and human-nature) relations into rote mechanical operations and spatiotemporal relations into an "infinite[ly]" reproducing "chain" in an "infinite" city that wires freeways and consumers together to enrich corporations. As gears in commodity chains circulating "chicken" throughout the Americas, we are servants to, and protectors of, capitalist kings, the scores of Mexican billionaires created by NAFTA privatizations. Not only is our labor a commodity but more sadly, the rooster understands his place as alienated labor power. We lack consciousness; the rooster, an animal, does not, as the thinking usually goes. We are blinded by ideology, if not a religious faith in the "freedom" of markets. Whereas humans believe in this freedom, the rooster knows better. Neoliberals promote the free market as the best of all possible worlds, yet the henhouse produces nature through the lowest common denominator of corporate plunder symbolized by a debased brand.

Because the "free market" is frequently defended as the "natural" endpoint of human culture and material progress, the rooster's observers do not recognize the farm's reproduction of "nature" as grotesque instead of enviable. This particular "occupation and utilization of space," like other manufacturing processes, "depends upon an anthropocentric reconfiguration of natural processes and their products" (Dear and Flusty 60). The hyper-(re)production of chicken and eggs exposes the voyeuristic human gaze as mistaking productivity for pleasure, conscription for freedom, and "chains" and "gears" for food. In examining historical-geographical relations between nature, capital, and ideology, Smith explains that "nature, not human history, is made responsible" for capitalism's negative impacts and that "capitalism is treated not as historically contingent but as an inevitable and universal product of nature" (*Uneven Development* 16). "Mercado libre" suggests the absurdity of "nature"—the rooster—being "made responsible" for the ideology and outcomes of capitalist modes of production. But it does not stop there: it imagines the rooster, as a representative of "nature," rejecting this ascription. Seen this way, envying the rooster's assumed prowess and blissful naïveté misses the poem's sublimated truth: that we too are gears in "the infinite chain" of capitalism, by consuming and copulating. Not only is the rooster alienated from the products of his own labor, and the pleasure presumably derived from their production, we, supposedly detached observers, cannot see how the "free market" produces us. Rather than external observers, we are embedded in the process and internalized by the factory farm, which enters our bodies and reconstitutes us as consumers.

In this consumer context, "Kentucky Fried Chicken" is a provocative symbol of corporate power, acting as a final arbiter of human sustenance and announcing that the rooster, unlike his observers, knows for whom he works: capital. "Mercado libre" thus dilates the focus of Pacheco's "Now Everybody Knows Who They're Working For," which catalogues the multinationals enriched by our falsely individuated daily practices (*Don't Ask* 39). Most pertinent to the case at hand are the nearly one hundred KFCs in Mexico City. Although published before this rapid growth of KFCs, "Mercado Libre" "produce[s] yet other [new] reactions," as Docter writes of Pacheco's poems, "not because his words have changed, but because *we* [and the city] are different" (388). Now the allusion reinforces Mexico City's official motto, "Capital in Movement," which evokes a double entendre on "capital" that rejects the positive previous motto, "City of Hope," by replacing "hope" with "movement" and "City" with "Capital."[17] "Mercado libre" critiques the very notion of capital moving in and through Mexico City, from US corporate headquarters to industrial poultry farms to street corner franchises. As such, the factory farm's "fleeting henhouse" is a "transit station" "like the land on which it is located."[18] The henhouse is capitalized infrastructure; its value lies not in its occupants, products, or building, but in its ability to produce exchange-values. As in Cardenal's "Room 5600," the final product is immaterial: "Whether milk or poison [or chicken] / the product doesn't matter." As a "transit station" coordinating capital investments with consumers in the "free" market, the henhouse exists to be passed through, like a "non-place." (Similarly, KFC franchises in Mexico City and Iowa City are more or less indistinguishable—such standardization defines non-places.) In this formulation of the relation of production to "the land on which it is located," "the land" and "nature" are disposable, replaceable, mere "transit stations" for capital accumulation.

The attempt to dominate nature is fundamental to the development of capitalism in general and urban space in particular. Objectifying nature, as in the abstracted view of the rooster, ensures continued profit and growth symbolized by the rooster's machinelike copulation. As critical geographers argue, the conquest of geographical space *is* "progress" in the capitalist imaginary. This process relegates nature to an accumulation strategy, both as "a simple gear" *in* the machine and the product *of* the machine. While "Mercado libre" conceptualizes these market functions, it also refers to the act of making poems with "fleeting," contingent signifiers such as "Kentucky Fried Chicken." We might view this corporate logo and Pacheco's rendering of it in the terms of Cardenal's poem cited in the introduction to *Broken Souths*: "primitive and barbaric / but poetic." In enacting the geographic displacement of this corporate icon of the US South, Pacheco's poem suggests that "Kentucky Fried Chicken" is a floating signifier, a gear in the chain of capitalist symbols rewriting the topographies of "Broken Souths." Yet KFC does not belong to Appalachian Kentucky or to a nation-state. Its purview is a globe written over with portable corporate images in service of capitalism's reproduction, as putatively neutral observers (economists, NGOs, government officials) reinforce dependence on industrial agriculture. Neoliberal ideology's "exaltation of diversity," Hopenhayn writes, "leads to the exaltation of the market, considered as the only social institution that orders without coercion, guaranteeing a diversity of tastes, projects, languages, and strategies" (82). Pacheco uncovers this delusion: industrial food production relies on and creates coercion and limits diversity in the marketplace, partly because multinational capital tends to turn all chicken into "Kentucky Fried."

"'H&C'" depicts the influence of foreign capital in Mexico City by further disordering hegemonic signifiers for hemispheric and US souths. Shifting the locus from food production to water and sewerage dramatizes disorienting individual interactions with free-market languages, revealing the spatiotemporal and linguistic slippages underpinning uneven access to clean water and sanitary sewers. The paired letters "H" and "C" are familiar to English-speaking North Americans as *hot* and *cold* on water faucets, but to Spanish-speaking Mexicans they signify *helada* (cold) and *caliente* (hot). The ironic, confusing contingency of these translations between "H" and "C" is the poem's main conceit. "'H&C'" plays with these binaries by mapping infrastructural inequality across Canada, the United States, and Mexico—NAFTA's territory—with plainspoken but contradictory facts that disorder systems of privilege. It begins with a declaration: "In the old houses of this city the water faucets / have a different order." The equivocal deictic "this" establishes Mexico City as the text's location when the collection *Islas a la deriva* [In the Drift of the Islands] in which "'H&C'" appears is read as a topographical map rather than as a linear text (73–74).[19] Like many Pacheco collections, this one has discrete sections: "Prologue"; "Mexican Antiquities"; "Winter Scenes in Canada"; "Common Language"; and "Endangered Species (and Other Victims)."[20] The placement of "'H&C'" within "Habla común" ["Common Language"] raises two possibilities: that the "common" language of Spanish and English, the Latin alphabet, actually offers a contradictory and potentially harmful commonality; and that "H" ("habla") and "C" ("común") are unstable symbols that make reading properly in one language failing to in the other. This linguistic instability reflects the uneven geography of supply and access along with H_2O's variable forms: vapor, liquid, and solid.

Reading the collection as a map of spatial relations positions "'H&C'" between Canadian winter, with snow its particular form of water, and the threat of extinction. It is thus possible to deduce that the poem does not take place in Canada or in the United States, for the poem's unspecified "empire" lacks cities as old as Mexico City. The geographical rupture suggested by the section transition from ancient Mexico to contemporary Canada, moreover, both de-centers the United States and contextualizes it as the unnamed, because so "obvious" ("obvio"), in the language of "'H&C,'" "empire." Nor is the poem in "Mexican Antiquities." These coordinates place "this city" in contemporary Mexico. Mexico City, furthermore, has intractable problems with drought, flooding, infrastructure, supply, and sanitation and has "waged a constant, and never quite victorious, battle against the ancestral waters" since the Spanish drained the valley's lakes (Johns 43). Recent events reinforce these points: pumping stations built in the southwest part of the city in 1910 (Johns 47) reached crisis levels in April 2009 just before the H1N1 flu scare, when the water supply was shut off in several parts of the city. On this evidence, it is prudent to conclude that "'H&C'" is set in Mexico City, where water supply and geology, like H_2O, are unstable.[21]

"'H&C'" thus intimates that clean water, which makes life possible in Mexico City, also constitutes an ironic source of confusion and a symptom of uneven access to infrastructure. The conflation of *hot* with *helada* and *cold* with *caliente* points to something "more obvious" if unspoken and named only symbolically as "the empire": "That's not to speak of the most obvious thing: / How the empire exports to us a world / that we still don't know how to manage or understand."[22] In this reckoning, the "common language" is the US-controlled market that is neither free nor fair. Although the poem was originally published in 1976, it appears unchanged in *Tarde o temprano* (194–195), a rarity within Pacheco's poetics of continual revision, and a stark contrast to the poem "1968" discussed in chapter 1; it thus prefigures NAFTA's obfuscatory language of "efficiency gains" achieved through increased competition and open borders. NAFTA's "habla común" paradoxically unites Mexico, the United States, and Canada through miscommunication, patterned inequality, and an unbalanced system of "exports." These lines contain the poem's sole first-person verbs, and their plural forms suggest a collective condition that does not affect all *chilangos* directly (few live in old houses, though "old" is ambiguous), but they do imply that all live under the shadow of the "common language." In this way, the second stanza's question and epigrammatic answer about the implications of "H" and "C" — "What conclusions can be drawn from all of this? / Nothing is what it seems." — can be traced through the final poem of "Habla común," "El pozo" ["The Well"] (79), even as it reinforces the trope of illusory freedom in "Mercado libre."[23]

"El pozo" begins with an epigraph about the outdated Mexican practice of placing turtles in wells to filter impurities, a practice that led to greater contamination. The poem ends with the ominous phrase "emponzoñadas filtraciones" ["poisoned filtrations"] and the suggestion that where water and methods used to filter it through language are concerned, "nothing is what it seems." This constitutive disordering of binaries (filtered/poisoned, clean/dirty, hot/cold) indicates that what is held in common across the poem's and the collection's North-South geography is difference and therefore the act of translation itself. In the poem, "H" signifies both *helada* and *hot* but produces hot water, while "C" signifies and produces *cold* at the beginning but signifies *cold* and produces *caliente* at the end. What is seemingly shared, the alphabet, must also be translated, if not mistrusted, like NAFTA's shared "freedom." The last stanza begins with such a declaration of ongoing deferral: "Every act is a translation." This perpetual translation structures global capital's circulation across space and through time, often in search of novel financial instruments — new languages — to conjure fictional wealth. In "'H&C,'" *chilangos* are trapped in these similarly disordering cycles of "bicephalous progress." This illusory "progress" is "creator / and destructor at the same time," reproducing unequal social relations with profound effects on the use of, and access to, clean water.[24]

Joseph Schumpeter's notion of capitalism's "creative destruction," as "bicephalous" a concept as has ever been conceived, models destruction as a creative force that opens space for future capital accumulation. The letters "H" and "C" follow this logic by implicitly critiquing its dangerous looseness with language: if it looks like destruction, it is actually construction, and if it looks like cold, it is actually hot. In either case, the poem implies, someone somewhere suffers. This beguiling ideological-material matrix of "empire," "export[s]," "progress," and creative destruction, moreover, is "not easy to quit," a frustrating fact given that barriers to entry to the "free market" are so many and that one — polluted water — is sufficiently devastating. "'H&C'" examines these contradictions through a two-headed potential resolution, to follow the "bicephalous" figure: "privilege" and the "code." This ecopoetic figure joins a material/referential concern (water) with a textual one (a "code") by modeling a poetics of interpreting infrastructure through the lens of privilege. The poem refers to the statement "every act is a translation" as *the* "code": "without this code / one who reaches below *C* for cold water / will be scalded."[25] This code protects against injury, both by hot water and the symbolic "burning" by market forces, thus suggesting what happens figuratively when languages (*as* codes) get displaced: someone suffers. The "habla común" of the market is change, uncertainty, and loss—someone *will* lose when water is subject to its cycles and crises. As such, translation is essential for mitigating the negative impacts of markets on the poor.[26]

Unfortunately, knowing this code is a function of privilege. The penultimate stanza suggests this idea: "No one who already enjoys the privilege / (to have hot water is a privilege) / will have to dig wells, to draw / contaminated water from a stream."[27] First, the unnamed persons using "contaminated water" likely live in one of the city's peri-urban informal settlements, perhaps near sewer or industrial runoff, without access to purified water mains. Second, the parenthetical repetition of "privilege" insists that access to hot water is a privilege. Because "C," as in "caliente," yields *cold* and *hot* water in the poem, having access to running water at all is, relatively speaking, a privilege. When paired with "extraer" ("to draw") the poem's other marked repetition—first in "drawing" knowledge from the "different order" of water faucets, then in "drawing" polluted water from a stream—"privilege" can be viewed as a product of knowledge creation in and through language, and its lack can be mapped by the uneven development of capitalism from North to South and in complex patterns across Mexico City. Thus the poem's claim that "between object and word falls a shadow" implies that "the shadow" of suffering follows capital while dividing the source of life (water) from the language used to access it. This "shadow" is the material-ideological "contamination" or "pollution" that the "habla común" of NAFTA distributes unevenly across North America.[28]

The final lines of "'H&C'" put privilege and suffering into perspective for someone who turns to "H" (hot) looking for *helada* (cold): "The years will pass without warming / the flowing *H*."[29] This turn to the future tense in the final stanza does not prophecy; rather, "escaldará" and "pasarán" state facts. "C" will scald anyone who turns it looking for cold water when it produces *agua caliente*; "H" will not provide the relief of *agua helada* when it produces hot water. These facts also serve figurative ends: water, which sustains life, also endangers it. This depiction of unequal access to sanitary sewers and potable water pipelines suggests the abiding uncertainty of the relation between infrastructure and the poor. These lines also allude to the unwitting (or arrogant) English-speaking tourists fooled by familiar letters on faucets as well as the possibility that faucets used in Mexico are manufactured by (or to the specifications of) US corporations. Most disturbing are the contexts for these implications within the textual geography of *Islas a la deriva*. The Latin alphabet, the "habla común" ("H" and "C") joining Canada, the United States, and Mexico, excludes many indigenous languages. This exclusion registers in two ways. First, it alludes to the section "Mexican Antiquities," which focuses on pre-Hispanic and conquest subjects, beginning with "La llegada" ["The Arrival," originally titled "Descubrimiento," "The Discovery"] and ending with "Crónica" ["Chronicle"]. Second, "El pozo" makes water an explicit theme of transition into the final section, "Endangered Species (and Other Victims)." Just as "the empire" is "obvious[ly]" the United States, it should be equally obvious that these unnamed victims are the poor, indigenous, and those driven into deeper poverty by neoliberal reforms; by drinking contaminated water in order to survive they suffer from the very act of drawing from the source of life. "Nothing is what it seems" when surficial forms of appearance misrepresent hidden realities and when figurative "pollution" substitutes for the clarity and cleanliness it displaces.

"Mercado libre" and "'H&C'" simultaneously reify and blur boundaries between NAFTA nations and their languages, markets, and corporate icons. They subtly critique the unspoken, because so "obvious" and ubiquitous, triumph of market logic in governing inter-American relations and the hyper-urban infrastructure interweaving transnational rural, agricultural, and putatively "natural" spheres and processes. Problems of privatization, deregulation, and increasing alienation and confusion are, in this calculation, secondary to human survival. Pacheco's permeable interfaces between urban and rural spheres trouble the city-country binary fundamental to Latin American cultural histories while dramatizing the consequences of "complete" urbanization and the "contaminated streams" from which slum dwellers must "draw" both water and their knowledge of the world. In these ways, the conclusion central to Pacheco's conversational ecopoetics, "nothing is what it seems," grounds this literary mapping of infrastructure, market "code[s]," and "privilege." As Scigaj notes is common in ecopoetry, Pacheco understands that "language cannot capture essences in the referential world" so seeks instead to redefine dominant perceptions by "highlighting sedimented language" as "worn-out" (41). Similarly, "Mercado libre" lays bare Derksen's point that cultural products often "circulate globally as if they carry no ideology" (95–96) by connecting KFC to illusory freedom, prosperity, and abundance. This "as if" logic of "seeming" subverts that of market freedom, not by substituting its opposite (slavery for freedom, coercion for choice) but by showing how it constricts humanity.

Pacheco's poems ask how market-exclusive freedom diminishes humanity when it is defined solely by the capability and desire to reason and communicate in an instrumental, acquisitive "code" of "privilege." Brown's sense that neoliberal rationality implements "market values" across institutions and exercises control over individuals *"through* their freedom" (39–40, 44) puts Pacheco's dialectics of seeming and being in sharp relief. The rooster, his observers, and slum dwellers are controlled in inverse relationship to their understanding of the "codes" and "privileges" of market freedom. If the "code" is translation and the critique of "privilege" is the result, their counterpart is the perverse desire of neoliberal thinking: that food and water should not exist—not merely that they would be inaccessible—outside the capitalist marketplace, which provides for human needs efficiently and transparently through privately owned infrastructure. For Pacheco, this is a tragedy. His "Paseo de la Reforma" describes an ash tree in the Reforma median as "a monument / to the beauty of the earth." This durable monument carries no ideology; it allows us to breathe. Yet Reforma is so choked with exhaust the city becomes an "ignoble and lethal / penitentiary" (*Tarde o temprano* 293–294).[30] "Beauty," he does not need to say, is determined by the "Mercado libre," which fails to provide basic necessities, and which circulates "the pollution" through its crumbling material and ideological infrastructures.

These Pacheco poems ultimately remap NAFTA-era global and US souths. The letters "H" and "C," after all, conjure intransigent binaries meant to devalue the South vis-à-vis the North, both within the United States and between the United States and Mexico and the rest of Latin America, as global souths. In this schema the South is "H" (*hot,* angry, passionate, emotional), whereas the North is "C" (*cold,* dispassionate, rational). In Spanish, well . . . The poem mocks the absolute geographies of these binaries, showing how unreliably even simple linguistic and market theories ("codes") map to reality. The alphabet itself is uncertain when borders are crossed and historical-geographical contexts shift, even under supposed market unification. In historicizing the US South in inter-American contexts, Jon Smith and Deborah Cohn conclude that Jefferson's 1785 list of differences between North and South shows that "the whole enterprise" is "arbitrary" (9, 11). Mignolo goes further with Sarmiento's "nature" (South) versus "civilization" (North) paradigm. "Once the terms are reconceived as dialogical instead of based on a logic of contradictory terms," Mignolo writes, the civilizers become the barbarians (xviii).[31] Together, these historical geographies of southern displacement, reproducible "nature," and inequitable infrastructure de-center exclusive claims to the "southernness" of the US South, linking it to the "Broken Souths" of the Caribbean and Latin America. From Louisiana to West Virginia, from Bonita and Montezuma to Alma and Bolivar, there are over one hundred Spanish-language place names in the US South and Appalachia. There is approximately the same number of KFCs in Mexico City. In Pacheco's words, "what conclusions can be drawn from" these convergent numbers? That corporate images of the US South reproduce "Broken Souths" in Latin America; that "strange intersections" define inter-American relations through disconnection; and that otherwise to NAFTA's "order" are urgently needed.

Bolaño on Uncertain Shelter and the Contours of Humanness

Because the "majority of the population spend their 'free' time in the seclusion of their home life" (García Canclini, *Consumers* 52), shelter is a main piece of the "disassembled jigsaw puzzle" that is Mexico City's infrastructure. As one might expect, poetic images of this "seclusion" foreground eerie isolation and paradoxical connection. In "How to Look at Mexican Highways" (*Talk Shows* 9–10), for instance, the Latina poet Mónica de la Torre asks us to measure Mexico City by "the things that you don't see when you're indoors," from "water towers" to "cables bringing electricity to light bulbs and refrigerators," the infrastructure joining domestic spaces together. Outside, on polluted overpasses and bridges, her narrator-observer is "surrounded by monads going somewhere." This monotonal, polysyllabic phrase reflects constant movement without progress and thus the sensation that "somewhere" is actually nowhere, an anonymous, isolated shelter. While the architects of post-1973 Chile promoted *homo economicus*—the normative neoliberal "monad"—to destroy labor power and to produce "order," in Mexico City this process began in 1968 as a defensive measure after the Tlatelolco massacre.[32] Vicky Unruh explains that the Mexico City playwright Sandra Berman introduces a play about "her generation" following the "'catastrophe of the 1968 utopia'" by describing a "struggle between individual isolation and the need to develop a social conscience" (145).

Another member of this "generation," the Mexico City poet Antonio Deltoro, imagines the apartment as a form divided between "individual isolation" and "social conscience." "Neighbors," which appears in *Reversible Monuments*, an anthology of Mexican poetry coedited by de la Torre, mixes whimsical play and high seriousness. With "one person's floor the reverse of another's ceiling," the poem sees anomie as paradoxical, given that others are feet away. It ends: "Apartments: like the sidewalks of a street, / parallel yet opposite, one in light, the other in shadow. / One night I suffered interminably / while on the floor below everything slept" (203). Shifting, dialogical oppositions make Deltoro's apartment peaceful (for those below) and nightmarish (for those above), but he also suggests that above/below and one side/the other shift with locational perspective. What remains constant is the unknown: the speculation, secrecy, and imagination defining relations between the megacity's de-familiarized "neighbors."

Bolaño, who emigrated to Mexico City in 1968 with his parents, often alludes to the defeat of his "generation" and its struggle between individualism and collectivism. Like Deltoro's apartment, Bolaño's Mexico City shelters highlight this struggle through abiding uncertainty and unease. Urban apartments proliferate in Bolaño's poetry and prose, often as places of isolation, madness, interminable conversation, tireless writing and reading, drinking, violence, and, occasionally, happiness. These atmospheric settings pressure the imagination to produce positive visions of proximate others and critiques of hegemonic power. The most chilling apartment appears in *Nazi Literature in the Americas*, where "the Infamous Ramírez Hoffman," a skywriting Nazi poet and Pinochet henchman whose character inverts Zurita's emancipatory skywriting, exhibits his depraved photographs. For Bolaño and for readers, if not for Hoffman's horrified guests, the photographs are unspeakable, beyond representation. Bolaño does not describe the photos, only guest reactions and the growing dread (190–193).[33] Whereas this text depicts a human monster occupying the apartment and his works covering its walls, the poem "Godzilla in Mexico" (*Romantic Dogs* 65) makes the monster the city surrounding the apartment. This monster, too, is not directly represented; the film icon of urban destruction appears only in the title. The compromised mobility, environmental destruction, spatialized inequality, and imposed monadism of neoliberal-era Mexico City reach their poetic apotheosis in this nominative act of monstering.

"Godzilla in Mexico" models a poetics of what it means to be human in the face of monstrosity, "complete" urbanization, and literal and figurative "pollution." There's little greater affront to the apartment *as* shelter than the monster. One is small, the other is large, one an intimate, known refuge, the other an invading, incomprehensible grotesque. Yet Bolaño blurs the apartment's borders, making it difficult to determine where walls end and city begins. What is certain is that the theoretically isolated apartment remains permeable to the streets, with their pollution and, as in Espada's "Circle Your Name," spaces for resistant narratives and asymmetric solidarities.[34] In Bolaño's Chile texts, the source of violence is known but the response uncertain; in "Godzilla in Mexico," the inverse holds. It offers a disturbing domestic figuration of how to survive and narrate what Pacheco calls an "epic of devastation" (*City of Memory* 159). Whereas Pacheco's poems focus the neoliberal social order's epistemological and textual uncertainties, the first-person speaker of "Godzilla in Mexico" narrates through uncertainty, "pollution," and fear until the end, when he declares his humanity in defiance of attempts to diminish it.

This constitutive uncertainty can be read through Borges's reflections on his own poetics. Borgesian metaphors (Heraclitus's river), archetypes (labyrinths, dreams), and conceits (fate, chance) appear repeatedly in Bolaño's and Pacheco's texts, where they are implicitly praised and revised. At his publisher's request to explain his *ars poetica*, Borges rejects the possibility or desirability of aesthetic codes. Yet he deigns to describe "a few devices," including "to choose ordinary rather than surprising words," "to intrude slight uncertainties, since reality is precise and memory is not," and "to narrate events as if I did not entirely understand them" (*Selected Poems* 265). These infinitives delineate parameters for Bolaño's poetics and a hermeneutics for reading "Godzilla in Mexico's" uncertainties, imprecise memories, and the narrator's seeming lack of understanding of the events he describes for his son and for us. The poem's main suggestion, that Godzilla has visited Mexico City, is itself subject to doubt. Because "Godzilla" appears only in the title questions linger. Does "Godzilla" appear on television during an environmental disaster, when "the air carried poison through / the streets and open windows"? Is he a metaphor for another type of disaster or for "the pollution"? Are the poem's "bombs," "poison," "dizziness," and "nausea" produced by Godzilla or are they metonyms for an unnamed disaster?

The poem's lack of resolution on these questions constitutes its strength. Uncertainty and fear, with literary beauty composed in their midst, remain the enduring takeaway. The poem begins with the speaker imploring his son to "listen carefully" to his story: "Listen carefully, my son: bombs were falling / over Mexico City / but no one even noticed. / The air carried poison through / the streets and open windows." These tensions between presumably ear-shatteringly loud bombs, the father's hushed retelling of them, and every other resident's failure to hear or see them at all establish a touchstone Bolaño conceit. The speaker-poet is a detective who assembles truths from incomplete, confusing evidence by following trails that go cold or double back, as in a labyrinth. Yet these neoliberal-era labyrinths have no strings and the Minotaur ("Godzilla") is both invisible and ubiquitous. In this sense, "Godzilla" is the Mexico City version of the "imaginary being" haunting Bolaño's Chile, as discussed in chapter 3. The opening lines imply that unspeakable things have happened that were ignored, missed, or unseen; intensely private and isolating, the falling "bombs" nonetheless enter the apartment from "the streets." This beginning creates a permeable inside/outside interface through which "poison" enters the residence. The poem's "veneno" ("poison") differs from *contaminación* (pollution), but the toxic (though recently much improved) air quality of the city is often referred to using the former term. Here the type of poison may be ambiguous, but its effects ("dizziness and nausea") are not. This ambiguity leads to the following lines, where the speaker continues with his intimate direct address by reminding his son that he had "just finished eating" when the bombs fell and that he was "watching / cartoons" while the speaker read "in the bedroom next door."

Whereas domestic images conventionally order the confusing world outside, Bolaño's disorient time and space and thus the verb tenses that would otherwise locate actions in space-time. As the speaker reads in the bedroom, he "realized [they] were going to die." For Bolaño, reading is an essential, romantic, and even revolutionary practice. Here, however, the act is interrupted by a disturbingly calm realization. After "dragg[ing]" himself out of the bedroom and finding his son "on the floor" and "hug[ging]" him, the son "asked what was happening." Then the speaker interprets the event for his bewildered son, and we must also rely on this interpretation of an event we grasp even less than the child. In response to the boy's question, the speaker offers a negative assertion followed by a vague reassurance: "I didn't tell you we were on death's program / but instead that we were going on a journey, / one more, together, and that you shouldn't be afraid." This negative construction suggests they were on "death's program" and that "journey" is a protective euphemism for that very "program." At first glance, this certainty of death juxtaposed to the poem's abiding uncertainties opens interpretive tensions. In subsequent lines, however, the personified "la muerte," a Mexican archetype, "le[aves]," in the narrator's retelling, without "even / clos[ing] [their] eyes."

This relation between "Godzilla" and "la muerte" remains fuzzy; so too whether one is harbinger, image, metaphor, or incarnation of the other.

This is to say the child's confusion is reproduced and magnified in readers. That he needs an answer to the unanswerable is perhaps obvious, but what remains pivotal to readers is the question "what was happening"? What exactly constitutes the question becomes an overarching conceit, as the poem ends with the son's second and third questions and the father's cryptic final answer. This conclusion reinforces the Borgesian pairing of imprecise memory with precise but inaccessible reality that becomes bearable only with an apt combination of literary articulations. The end pinpoints a key dimension of the poetics of "Broken Souths"—the struggle to redefine humanity against *homo economicus*, in which every last atom, gene, and tissue surrenders to market rationality: "What are we?," the son "ask[s] a week or year later, / ants, bees, wrong numbers / in the big rotten soup of chance?" The father-narrator's response is strange: "We're human beings, my son, almost birds, / public heroes and secrets." The son's questions assume the existence of a collective, interpersonal identity. He does not ask, "What am I?" Instead he uses conspicuously plural nouns as if casting about for understanding. "Ants" and "bees" are often used, in the popular sense, as symbols for workers and the poor: ants build colonies and worker bees collectively serve a queen. Like the beetles/indigenous campesinos "the color of the earth" in Espada's "Sing Zapatista" who resist the boot's heel that stomps "from above," ants and bees are tiny, symbolically marginal and often despised creatures who dwell close to the ground. This figurative, atmospheric tension pits powerful political and economic forces that descend "from above," like falling bombs and Godzilla's limbs, against those from below. This signature vision of the relation between abstract, hegemonic ideology backed by state power and Mexico City's mostly powerless individuals struggling to create collective solidarities makes "Godzilla" a singular, unspeakable, and monstrous power that crushes and swats collectives of ants and bees from above. As an answer to "what are we," "wrong numbers" suggests the ruthless, quantitative assessment of human worth by means of a person's wealth. Pacheco's linking of animal to human suffering is especially pertinent here—the child in "Godzilla in Mexico" is "on death's program" because he is one of innumerable "victims whose only crime is being born" (*City of Memory* 77).

The declaration "We're human beings" tests boundaries dividing human from animal and "public" from private, as symbolized in "secrets." It implies that "human beings" are not ants, bees, or "wrong numbers" but that they are "almost birds." This strange qualification leads to the odder pairing of "public heroes and secrets." Its seeming incompatibility gestures toward the disordering of "public" and "private" in neoliberalism, with the privatization of public and state lands, resources, and industries and the trend toward the privatization of the commons, such as air, water, and plant life, along with the commodification of carbon pollution and genetic material. With the exception of security and defense (largely to protect private property, and often publicly funded to enrich private entities), neoliberal ideology dispenses with the "public" sphere to privatize nearly everything. If father and son are "public heroes" for hearing and seeing what no one else noticed—wide-scale urban devastation—they are also "secrets," their knowledge essentially private, possessed by atomized individuals. Cloistered in their apartment, unable to share their understanding with others, "social conscience" becomes impossible. This isolation, it is important to recall, follows "bombs falling / over" Mexico City. Global capital interests, which descend from above in the form of free-trade agreements, privatization schemes, and IMF/World Bank structural adjustments, are orchestrated to cause such disorder and confusion on the ground. As Klein details, neoliberal "shock treatments" have been deployed to disorient populations—to create "pollution" of thought. Once confused and desperate, Klein argues, they are less likely to resist the gutting of public services and in any case ill equipped to do so. In "disaster capitalism," "natural" and thoroughly unnatural (coups, wars, recessions) disasters serve as the stage, means, and legitimacy for implementing radical free-market policies.

"Godzilla in Mexico" draws an implicit through-line from the fear of nuclear annihilation during the Cold War to the abiding fear of instability in the neoliberal era. Yet if the former follows the logic of unintended consequences, the latter proceeds from a murkier equation. Whether neoliberals merely take advantage of such "disasters" or purposely create them, or some combination thereof, remains an open question. On this front, the poem converts Godzilla from an iconic, monstrous image of nuclear fallout to a flexible symbol of the (un)intended consequences of ambition for power and the accompanying disorienting fear that ensures the consent and subjugation of human beings *as* "ants," "bees," and "wrong numbers." These are yet more poetic figures of disposable subjects under neoliberal social-economic arrangements, like Espada's "all the others" and Kilwein Guevara's "So-and-so" and garbage pickers. In an era in which "history" and "ideology" are dead, with capitalism triumphant over all other -isms, and technology ascends as a putative force for individual affirmation, satisfaction, and happiness, Godzilla is the monster no one notices. He *is* crisis in an age in which crisis is the norm, the quotidian. What then of the odd qualification "almost birds" that seems to glimpse a pushback against crisis? It pairs a human limitation (the inability to fly) with the possibility of freedom from groundedness, which retains a positive, even emancipatory, register elsewhere in *Broken Souths*. It also suggests a revision of Marx's conception of "the free and rightless" worker. In his translation of *Capital*, Ben Fowkes notes that the original German, *vogelfrei*, literally means "as free as a bird." He glosses this type of freedom as "free but outside the human community and therefore entirely unprotected and without legal rights" (896). This "freedom" actually constrains and dehumanizes workers while preventing them from joining with others to better their lot. In this reckoning, Bolaño's "almost birds" diminishes the registers of "freedom"—we are no longer *even* birds. His speaker implies that for most people in the current era to be human is to lack even the most basic of securities. It is to be afraid, isolated, figuratively trapped in an apartment without recourse to a community of others with shared experiences.

This negative valence of groundedness challenges the place-based poetics of "Broken Souths." Bolaño's Mexico City poetics offers instead a differential resistance to neoliberal norms. In linking revolutionary possibility ("public heroes") to individuated literary interiority ("secrets"), the poem combines the "proper name" and the "common noun," as Badiou and Derrida understand them, and as I examined them in chapter 1, into the strangely banal but defiantly resistant, noticeably collective, and empowering "human beings." The poem thus eerily renders urban upheavals by suggesting how the most terrifyingly real monsters, like economic crashes, cannot be seen or heard. They are, nonetheless, real imaginary forms, like derivatives and credit-default swaps. In Marx's terms, they are "immaterial but objective" forms that conceal relationships between people ("human beings") as those between things. In "Godzilla in Mexico," these relations are also "immaterial," but something disastrous has undoubtedly happened. The task, then, is to name it, survive it, and attempt to exceed its limitations, even if "almost."

This reading of the urban shelter as a component of a poetics of infrastructure problematizes Bachelard's phenomenology of the intimate spaces of dwellings, *The Poetics of Space*. Readers of this text can likely deduce how my reading of the Mexico City apartment as a symbolic space within the neoliberal architecture of above/below reframes Bachelard's poetics of cellar and garret and the house as a space that nurtures, comforts, and encourages daydreaming. Bachelard argues that two essential features, "verticality" and "centrality," produce the "body of images" that lend to dwellings "proofs or illusions of stability" (17). Yet in the context of the large city—Bachelard has Paris in mind; Mexico City intensifies these effects—where residents live in "superimposed boxes" (26), "*Home has become mere horizontality*" (27). When this notion of horizontality is applied to "Godzilla in Mexico," the poem's characters can be seen as belonging neither above nor below. They are detached from, dependent upon, and subject to power from above and alienated from the natural processes and potential social movements that emerge from below. The apartment, in this reading, reproduces de la Torre's monads and enacts the immobilizing underside of Derksen's "super individualization" (66), which is an aggregation of neoliberal processes that convert public, collective, and social rights and responsibilities into individualized rewards and burdens.

In these theoretical contexts, "Godzilla in Mexico" reimagines conceptions of the relation between nature and the city. "Where houses are no longer set in natural surroundings," Bachelard writes, "the relationship between house and space becomes an artificial one" (27). This delimited notion of nature demarcates urban space from ecological, geological, and climatological processes and urban infrastructure from what it carries: water, energy, waste, transportation vehicles, and persons. When "nature" is understood more capaciously as a set of processes circulating in and through urban spaces this separation can be seen for what it is: an enduring ideological construct held across the political spectrum that serves capital and produces the "human rootlessness" Cruz laments in chapter 5. In the city, Bachelard concludes, "houses are no longer aware of the storms of the outside universe," and because they are "set close one up against the other, we are less afraid" (27). Bolaño's poem has it otherwise. As "storms of the outside universe," economic and environmental crises enter "through / the streets and open windows" while also descending like bombs "falling" from above. These "storms" become constitutive parts of the apartment; rather than engendering less fear, an *apart*-ment generates uncertainty and isolation, dividing potential solidarities through the affective conversion into "disassembled jigsaw puzzle[s]."

Critics from multiple disciplines argue that affect and emotion, in this case fear, are part of neoliberal capitalism's infrastructure. For Klein, fear lays the groundwork for radical economic policies and a form of sanctioned class war. And for Derksen, the post–September 11, 2001, discourse of "the end of 'ever feeling secure again,'" which echoes that of the Cold War, joins the other "ends" supposedly ushered in by neoliberalism, including the welfare state (58). The translation of "Godzilla en México" that appeared in the November 5, 2007, issue of the *Nation* during the national conversation about Iraq, torture, and the War on Terror reinforces this reading. Finally, Brian Massumi examines the verifiable fact that unquantifiable emotions move and shape financial markets. "The ability of affect to produce an economic effect more swiftly and surely than economics itself," he writes, "means that affect is a real condition, an intrinsic variable of the late capitalist system, as infrastructural as a factory" (45). Lest we forget, the Consumer Confidence Index is a leading indicator of the US economy's "health."

Bolaño's poem implicitly critiques how this material-affective infrastructure entangles urban habitats into its logic. Yet it also celebrates, if with measured calm, the survivors of its venomous pollution that descends from above ("like bombs") and below ("from the streets"). In this sense, Bolaño's apartment provides shelter, as father and son seem to endure to narrate an uncertain perspective. "For the sake of those displaced from country to city, or from place to place in the same city," Yaeger writes, "we must recognize that for all theory's talk of urban individualism, alienation, and economic flows, the city is above all a place that gives shelter. It must be nurturing for its inhabitants to survive" (18). This idea of nurturance raises two questions by way of conclusion. Given the conviviality of hyperurban living underscoring the "wage puzzle," as economists call their inability to grasp how millions survive on incomes inadequate to purchase the means of subsistence, how can we account for the city's "pleasures" as well as "pounding"? And what keeps stressed infrastructure working, at least for some?

Huerta's "Song of Money" (*Before Saying Any of the Great Words* 187) focuses both queries with simultaneous attachment and revulsion.[35] As the poet walks the city besieged by a ubiquitous "song" he resists but ultimately sings, he experiences awe and something akin to joy. This "song of money" echoes through streets, homes, banks, cars, subways, pipes, conduit, museums, and parks, the lone guarantor of infrastructure and everyday life. "Song of Money" is an ironic, politically equivocal, and individuated counterpart to the hemispheric structural critique of neoliberal logic in "Room 5600." The poem's eight unpunctuated, first-person tercets chronicle the poet's navigation of the "too large" city. His exasperation at his inability to navigate not the city per se but its near-absolute financialization conjures the defining feature of neoliberal restructuring, in micro and macro ways. Individual consumer debt has soared in recent decades, and huge corporations—General Electric, for one—have shifted profit making from production to complex investment services that entangle the construction and maintenance of infrastructure with high-risk financial market machinations. Huerta narrates from a pedestrian's perspective, ruing "I have to go in person to the banks and offices" "to pay one thing and another," including "taxes / and debts." The former is intended, at least in part, for infrastructure, and the latter is likely attached to a residence. The underlying warrant is clear. Just when one is told to rely exclusively on oneself—as in Agüeros's laborer as "his own horse"—the "too large" city has become less accessible to the individual scale and financial burdens have increased. Simultaneously, the transactions one has to complete to survive (let alone to compete) have grown; "one thing and another" now includes the "cable television" that increases Carlos Slim's telecommunications empire. The prepositional phrase concluding "the city was always too large for me" laments the individual's inability to reproduce his own life legally amid growing debts and shrinking means. An unspoken undercurrent in the poem is this pressure on individuals to enter the vast informal sector in order to secure "one thing and another."

As the poem's unpunctuated sentences, phrases, and lines run into each other, the speaker's wonderment at the imaginary properties of the money form rise to the fore. With the lines calling money "the most bloodthirsty abstraction / the most powerful weapon the conclusive argument," Marx's notion of value and money as "immaterial but objective" forms begins to orchestrate the "song." The "obsessive" attraction to money is, as the poem's repeated adjective describes it, defined as a social good in neoliberal thought. For Huerta, however, when this particular "abstraction" guides and governs everyday practices, it converts "happiness" into the obsession for money, which subsequently produces "a state so similar [to happiness] it's hard to tell the difference." The poem ends with levity, even a nearly joyous submission, as the speaker-poet admits that he writes under the neoliberal sign, which elevates money to the final arbiter of literary value: "I write poems so that among other reasons I don't have to / sing songs to money but as you all can see up there at the top / it says Song of Money it was bound to happen sooner or later." These lines depict the inevitability of subsumption under capitalist values, especially for poets. "If [he] were a millionaire," as he says earlier, he could hire a "courier" to complete his daily tasks, but one cannot outsource the writing of poems. The poem implores us to conclude that writers are never independent, art for art's sake is impossible, and "money" is the era's muse.

Literary subjectivity is mediated through this muse, as the poet sings to an abstraction, obsession, and god governing from above, "there at the top" of the page. Poets and critics now rarely speak of the muse, with the exception of Bolaño's "Muse," the unselfconscious final poem in *The Romantic Dogs* (135). Whereas muses are sources of inspiration more than exasperation, prime movers more than last resorts, and kick-starters more than finishers, "money" has both the first and last word under neoliberal rationality. Following its "song" leads to the border, where *Broken Souths* began with Herrera's and Wideload's lessons. The coda thus turns to Juárez, where the globalizing logic of neoliberalism finds an ideal form, the *maquiladora*, and where Latina/o poets search for languages to understand the paired violence of femicide and free trade.

"Too much of it"

Marjorie Agosín's and Valerie Martínez's Representations of Femicide in the *Maquila* Zone

Every advance of the productive forces is a victory for both civilisation and barbarism. If it brings in its wake new possibilities of emancipation, it also arrives coated in blood.
> —Terry Eagleton, *Why Marx Was Right* (44–45)

These crimes [. . .] did not occur where capitalism is lacking, *rather where* there is too much of it.
> —Eduardo Galeano, "To Be Like Them" (128)

Let us turn the map until we see clearly:
The border is what joins us,
Not what separates us.
> —Alberto Ríos, from "Border Lines"

Ciudad Juárez, the fourth largest city in Mexico, and El Paso, on the other side of the Rio Grande, dramatize North/South relations more acutely than any other urban agglomeration, border zone, or convergence of multinational capital formations in the hemisphere. As a stunning case of neoliberalism's uneven geographic development and production of space through violent enclosures, Juárez and El Paso meet under the authority of the "Song of Money," a ubiquitous muse. Nowhere is the border more "coated in blood." Juárez's abject violence does "not occur where capitalism is *lacking*" but "where *there is too much of it.*" At the scale of production of Juárez's three-hundred-plus *maquiladoras*, the tax-free assembly factories of multinational corporations, Eduardo Galeano's claim questioning the civilizing capacity of capitalism has particular resonance. In addition to producing televisions and other consumer items, they produce "geographies of danger" that circulate capital and crime and restrict the mobility and power of labor, further augmenting North-South inequalities.[1]

Alberto Ríos's "Border Lines" is an archetypal Chicano illustration of the border as an interface that "joins" rather than "separates" Juárez and El Paso and Mexico and the United States. His active, collective verb, "turn," a cartographic version of "to break," suggests that "joining" conceptually repairs "broken" subjectivities and fragmentations of class, ethnicity, and nation wrought by transnational free-trade agreements and national-level neoliberal reforms and their unintended consequences, including organized crime and "traffics," Ileana Rodríguez's umbrella term for the trade of drugs, arms, and bodies. Ríos's poem exemplifies how location often determines writing about the border. Using the insights of Debra Castillo and María Socorro Tabuenca Córdoba to critique cultural production about femicide, Steven S. Volk and Marian E. Schlotterbeck put this dynamic simply. Whereas Chicano cultural texts often use the border to emphasize commonalities between Mexicans and Chicanos, Mexican literary texts generally foreground the differences (124).[2] Like the directive of hemispheric American studies dramatized in Cardenal's "Room 5600," connection and division underscore literary conceptions of the border at Juárez/ El Paso. In Ríos's poem, connection predominates, as in the humanistic, aspirational figure of "turning." "We seem to live in a world of maps," he writes. "But in truth we live in a world made / Not of paper and ink but of people." This echo of the character Wideload's command to mind the "living, breathing, dreaming men, women and children" "under all this talk of Money and Markets" (77) critiques the money form, the measure of universal value printed on "paper and ink." But it also connotes the tools, appearance, and material of literature. As such, Ríos's lines can also be read as implications that much writing in "paper and ink" fails to mind the dreamers in Herrera's "busted makeshift hotel[s]" along the border.

As "the guiding metaphor of Latino Studies," as Juan Flores posited in 2000 (212), the primary role of the border has been paid forward indefinitely with little scholarly dispute. Yet has "the guiding metaphor" shifted, multiplied, or dispersed, as Herrera suggests at the conclusion of chapter 2? Has it been displaced by individual psychological internalization, in the manner envisioned by Verdecchia? What's at stake in maintaining *the* border as *the* metaphor of Latino studies? Any Latina/o imaginary requires border figures, including possibilities for their transgression and creative reinscription, but such questions are intellectually and politically pertinent. For its part, *Broken Souths* shifts the focus from *the* border to multiple, variegated souths as spaces for critique, insight, and resistance, and as place-based interfaces from which to imagine "otherwises" to the neoliberal order. By doing so, it has crossed the United States–Mexico border backward, in the manner of Benjamin's "Angel of History" and the character Verdecchia, mapping a literary cartography of the neoliberal era on the common ground of critique in Latino and Latin American poetries. This approach foregrounds the neoliberal project's impacts on Latino literary subjectivity, especially in relation to Latin American historical geographies, while multiplying and expanding border constructs.

The institutionalization of *the* border should give scholars cause for reflection as well as the impetus to apply theoretical constructs to particular border locations. In this sense, Juárez/El Paso animates contradictions of connection and division and "breaking" points between North and South, the United States and Mexico, rich and poor, and capital and labor in disturbing ways. Volk and Schlotterbeck follow this strategy in arguing that critical responses to femicide must "unpack the explicit geography of this particular 'transnational' setting" (122–123). Latino tendencies to "join" rather than to "separate," as in Ríos's poem, also require "unpacking." What truths do "joining" Juárez and El Paso foreclose and expose? One of Blanchot's fragments meditating on disaster has an answer: "In common we have: burdens. Insupportable, immeasurable, unsharable burdens." Defined by "disproportion," a lack of "mutual exchange," and "the nonreciprocal" (87), these burdens symbolize the failure of "paper and ink" to overcome divisions and the startling asymmetries that "join" Juárez and El Paso.

Blanchot's terms pinpoint the neoliberal social compact as inherently unequal. Nowhere are these outcomes clearer than in the *maquila* zone, where free trade was purported to follow the logic of equal exchange and to produce greater freedom and fairness. And yet "everything at the border is lopsided," as Ileana Rodríguez summarizes it (154). The most dramatic instance: whereas Juárez has the world's highest murder rate, El Paso is the safest city in the United States.[3] This inverse relation is no coincidence; it recalls Rukeyser's exasperated "for God's sake / they are connected / underneath" cited in chapter 5 and Pacheco's "'H&C,'" where the free market's "habla común" paradoxically "joins" the NAFTA nations via mistranslation. If troubling binaries is de rigueur in cultural studies, the Juárez/El Paso divide suggests their retrenchment and augmentation. A smaller, borderless world, as in the IBM ad in Verdecchia's *Fronteras Americanas*, largely exists only for corporations and the super-rich. Between Juárez and El Paso a private bridge allows capital to travel quickly and safely, ensuring that component parts and finished products reach their southern and northern destinations. If Juárez is the "laboratory of our future," as the Juárez chronicler Charles Bowden declares, what hypothesis is it testing? How might its evidence be measured?

In these ways, it is worth considering the Juárez/El Paso relation as a celebratory conquest for capital and an opportunity for greater accumulation rather than a crisis of legitimacy or barrier to growth. Why does such unevenly distributed prosperity, security, and mobility where "the advance of the productive forces," in the form of *maquilas,* has been most pronounced fail to create a legitimacy crisis? Whereas it is no longer true that "serious social problems in Mexico remain unattended because they have become part of the 'authentic' Mexicanness the tourist pays to see" (Cooper Alarcón xix), the security and surveillance industries, and a desperate labor force, do presage big profits. The tentative evidence is in: an August 2011 National Public Radio report describes the "booming" *maquilas* after a brief downturn following the 2008 global financial crisis. Juárez, the report concedes without irony, "might not seem like an ideal business environment, but foreign companies are investing heavily," as "cheap labor and proximity to the huge U.S. market are outweighing concerns about security." In a sign of fealty to capital over workers, the report declares "foreign factories unscathed by violence," and concludes, "the city's murder rate rivals that of a war zone, yet its factories are exporting products at a record level" (Beaubien). Because wars often increase industrial production, substituting "so" for "yet" makes for a more accurate sentence. If "the ideological monopoly of neoliberalism has without doubt been fractured" in Latin America (Dello Buono and Bell Lara 4), such evidence combines with imposed austerity programs in Europe and Tea Party–led voluntary austerity in the United States, to suggest that neoliberalism remains alive, if not fully well, and only for the unscathed few. Neoliberal ideals and policies, and their promoters, have retrenched in the face of massive evidence against them.

These points bring us to the ideological legitimations securing the reign of free-market fundamentalism. In addition to what Giroux calls the "corporate public pedagogy" dramatized in "Room 5600," the idea that inequality, plunder, and astronomic individual wealth promote the common good is also legitimized from below. In analyzing the post-1968 capitalist system, Luc Boltanski and Eve Chiapello explain that "*the ideology that justifies engagement in capitalism,*" which they call "the spirit of capitalism" and which must "coincide with people's moral experience of daily life and suggest models of action they can grasp," contrasts "professorial capitalism, which trots out neo-liberal dogma from on high" (8, 14). In Juárez, the "moral experience of daily life" and feasible "models of action" have been obliterated *by* capitalism, in part by the unintended consequences of free trade. Under these conditions, Ileana Rodríguez argues that *maquilas* are "stronger than the local state or national government." Their form of governmentality, she suggests, "represent[s] real governance" in "occup[ying] territory" and "appropriat[ing] space" for their exclusive benefit (168). Is it not appropriate then to consider the nonreciprocal, disproportionate quality fundamental to Blanchot's notion of the disaster as "the spirit" of neoliberalism, with its "model of action" based on conquest, occupation, and appropriation? As a symbol of neoliberalization and Juárez's abjection, Rodríguez concludes, the *maquila* "creates a reverse of the common good for the well-being of capital" (167). This is precisely the neoliberal project: "the common good" is measured solely by "the well-being of capital." Open borders for capital means open borders for illegal traffics, just as disavowing "the common good" means normalizing plunder by the few.[4]

In his September 21, 2010, speech at the National Autonomous University of Mexico (UNAM) in Mexico City, Noam Chomsky had these dynamics in mind when asserting that NAFTA has been more harmful to the people of Mexico than was the conquest.[5] As a conquest, the neoliberal project finds one of its most potent material symbols in the *maquila*. Mexico's National Border Program (PRONAF) and Border Industrialization Program (BIP) facilitated the opening of *maquilas* in 1965, picking up where their forerunner, the Bracero Program, left off. The *maquilas* highlight several decades-long transitions in terms of labor: from rural to urban, agriculture to assembly plants, locations within the US to the border, temporary to permanent exploitation, and male to female. Most significantly, although the percentage of female workers has recently decreased, the *maquila* symbolizes the feminization of the global workforce. As of 2006, Juárez *maquilas*, including corporate giants Nike, RCA, Delphi, and GM, employed about 220,000 workers, 60 percent of them female (Gaspar de Alba, "Poor Brown Female" 64). In Terry Eagleton's terms, the *maquilas* represent "new possibilities of emancipation" for Mexican women that have nonetheless had violent repercussions. Volk and Schlotterbeck argue that masculinist literary, political, and popular discourses see female incorporation into the wage labor force as creating disorder that must be fixed by restoring patriarchal order (122). If the *maquila* is "the most organized form of labor devised by high capitalism" (Rodríguez, *Liberalism* 161) and if it represents an "advance of the productive forces" in efficiency and specialization, it is also "coated in [female] blood." Although not all femicide victims were *maquilas* workers, most scholars link the crimes to the industry, at least indirectly. Although reliable statistics are hard to come by, estimates put the number of femicide victims since 1994 at around eight hundred, an astounding number that nonetheless pales in comparison to the 3,495 total murders between January 1994 and mid-2008 and the 4,747 homicides committed in the state of Chihuahua (where Juárez is located) in 2010 alone.[6] Menstruation checks by *maquila* management viscerally reinforce Eagleton's image and neoliberalism's globalizing logic: private bridges for capital, insecurity for labor, and bloodshed to lubricate the relation.

In Eagleton's dialectical frame, a sign of "civilization," the "paper and ink" of literature, has emerged against this "barbarism." To conclude this study of Latina/o poetics, I briefly explore how two book-length poems search for poetic registers to understand this frequently opaque and contradictory triangular relationship. *Secrets in the Sand: The Young Women of Juárez*, by Marjorie Agosín, a Latina-Chilean, and *Each and Her*, by the Chicana Valerie Martínez,[7] serve as excellent final examples of the ways in which Latina/o poets and their Latin American counterparts examine "the tension between the theory of neoliberalism" (free trade liberates all) and "the actual pragmatics of neoliberalization" (the use of violence and repression to consolidate wealth and power) (Harvey, *Brief History* 21). This dynamic compels Agosín's and Martínez's searches for modes to depict the complex global dimensions of Juárez's violence and the devastating plainness of brutalized female bodies. These searches enfold questions of (in)visibility, the public role of poets in writing against injustice, and the desire to do socially significant work through the literary—in short, the challenges of writing the disaster. The Chicana writer Alicia Gaspar de Alba's tacit apologia about her widely discussed fictional account subtly engages these questions: "Just because I published a novel called *Desert Blood: The Juárez Murders* does not mean the Juárez murders are fiction" ("*Feminicidio*" 1). The desire not to trivialize, mislead, or conflate with mere "fiction," and the corollary desire for literature to hew closely to reality in order to create awareness, focus outrage, and spur activism defines femicide texts. This is true for Agosín's and Martínez's poetry as well as for novels, with a key difference: each of their books eschews narrative arcs, problematizes narrative tropes, and rejects the desire to explicate events that are in a very real and visceral sense untellable.

Broken Souths has examined how poets contest systematic violence and oppression, from Espada's "empty mouths" to Villatoro's "squirrel's blood," but the femicide in Juárez presents particular difficulties for figurative languages. It is telling, for instance, that Bolaño's magnum opus, the epic *2666*, spends nearly three hundred pages tediously documenting the gruesome crime scenes in Juárez, known in the novel as Santa Teresa, forcing readers to endure rote, repetitive abjection *as* literature (353–633). The struggle to speak clearly and creatively about abject violence may not be new, but the magnitude, barbarism, and constitutive silences of femicide may be. A brief, digressive discussion of the relations between poetry and politics contextualizes this idea.

In a May 25, 1994, letter, Espada takes the poet Adrian C. Louis's "$25 bet" that his collection *City of Coughing and Dead Radiators* would win a major award. When Espada is proven right, he offers insight into the inverse relationship between a place-based poetics that emerges from spaces of dispossession and mainstream prestige. "As far as awards are concerned," Espada writes, "the Poetry Gods have dropped their pants and farted loudly." "The alternative," he concludes, "is to trade silence for acceptance. If we don't talk too much about El Barrio or Pine Ridge, they agree to like us in Harvard Square" ("Correspondence: Louis"). So long as Latino and Indian poets do not write "too much" about Pine Ridge (the Lakota Sioux reservation, the US's poorest, where Louis lived at the time) or El Barrio (the historically Puerto Rican neighborhood in New York City), Espada's thinking goes, "the Poetry Gods" will reward them.[8] This otherwise apt equation of "silence" and "acceptance" comes under scrutiny in reading the literature on femicide. Public, scholarly, and literary discourses on femicide center on the idea of "silence," in regard to both Mexican authorities' attempts to silence victims' families and their advocates and the resistance to silence within communities of survivors. But this idea misleads as a critical marker of the creative literature. There has been anything but silence in Latina/o and Mexican literatures on femicide. Ileana Rodríguez's comment on "the massive production of literature on the subject" (175) recalls Carlos Monsiváis's "hundreds of miles" of books on Tlatelolco and 1968.[9] Contra Espada, are there implicit rewards for rejecting "silence"? Does writing about femicide increase visibility, if not in the mainstream than within Latino literary studies? Can writers opportunistically confront injustice? Should literary production match the production of bodies? Is femicide literature a niche market? Is the literary "marketplace" oversaturated with it? Borrowing Galeano, is there "too much of it"? The answer must be resolute: we must continue to write the disaster with the knowledge that even "too much" will be insufficient for bringing back the dead. This challenge ultimately turns on the here/there binary implicit in Espada's terms. In the United States, the hegemonic mainstream invitation to confront suffering includes Asian sweatshops, African orphans, even femicide in Juárez, because each is a *there*, but it forecloses discussion of what happens *here* in the United States for ideological reasons. "What does it mean to be an 'author' in a distinctly transamerican sense?" Kirsten Silva Gruesz asks (*Ambassadors* 13). To write the femicide, it means depicting *here* and *there* as inextricable, intimately connected geographies, showing how what happens in El Barrio, for instance, is both connected to and different from what happens in Juárez.

In Agosín's and Martínez's books, this task means entangling innovative transnational poetic forms with the confounding political-economic realities of the events in Juárez. I see this inter-American interlacing of aesthetics with the immediacy of events as continuous with the origins and development of the field of Latino poetry, from the late 1960s to the present. In introducing *The Wind Shifts: New Latino Poetry*, Aragón reviews the canon of Latino poetry as it has been constituted by previous anthologies and, implicitly, by the Nuyorican and Chicano movements in the late 1960s. To do so, he explains that much Latino poetry is now "equally, if not more, informed by an exploration of language and aesthetics" than by "overtly political" issues, the femicide in the case of this coda.[10] This division has legitimacy. However, as William Rowe says of the avant-garde/political binary common in Latin American poetry studies, it deemphasizes how one always embeds the other (1), recalling Espada's "artistry of dissent," Appalachian Latino rejections of either-or binaries, and the critique of "post-" constructs in *Broken Souths*. Aragón rightly argues that the "subject matter and aesthetics" of Latino poetry have dramatically "widened," as chapter 4 and the ecopoetic readings in *Broken Souths* have shown. In this more expansive contemporary frame, many Chicano movement political poems, Aragón reasonably concludes, do not stand up as "good" poems by aesthetic metrics (1, 3, 10). Herrera would no doubt agree with this conclusion, so long as the energizing spirit of the late 1960s could be preserved in some form. But does dividing explorations of "language and aesthetics" from those of politics and society risk isolating poetic forms from their informing cultural contexts? Does it reinforce a hierarchy between political and language-oriented poetry that shifts, like Bolaño's statues of Neruda and Parra in chapter 3, depending on where you are standing?

These questions are particularly pertinent to poems about femicide, of which Aragón's anthology includes several. The violence in Juárez, he writes, is "on the minds of many Latino/a artists." Yet one must comb the superb anthology carefully to find poems addressing the femicide. Though Sheryl Luna's "Two Girls from Juárez" and "Poesía de Maquiladora" and Emmy Pérez's "Irrigation," "Ars Poetica," and "History of Silence" have much to recommend them, Aragón directs us to their experimental qualities. He explains that Latina/o poets increasingly "deploy a poetics that takes some of its cues from the more experimental tendencies in [US] American poetry" (4), pointing out Language poetry and "the experimental styles in the [US] American literary avant-garde" (9). These influences mark the anthology's poems *about* the femicide in Juárez, which they take on indirectly and in glances: in fact, some readers might not recognize that the poems address the femicide without Aragón's advance notice. As we will see shortly, a major strength of Agosín's and Martínez's book-length poems is that their innovative, unpredictable tropes and forms facilitate a more lucid access to the political, economic, and historical-geographical dimensions of the femicide.

Apart from the potential barriers to recognizing the political contents of experimental forms, recent Latino reinscriptions of innovative North American poetic traditions pair with Latino interpretations of Latin American practices to facilitate a view of Latino poetry as the inchoate vanguard poetry of the Americas. In this sense, subtending Aragón's notion of a "widening" aesthetic range is the idea that both the ontology and teleology of Latino poetry *as* a field are necessarily innovative and expansive. After all, as Aragón's introduction suggests, "the legacy" (10) of Latino poetry is experimental in the fundamental sense of the word: by testing generic, linguistic, and aesthetic margins, intersections, and disconnections between languages, discourses, systems of knowledge, and ways of producing meaning from multiple sources, Latino poets have always been interested in pushing poetry's boundaries and in finding new expressive forms and revising old ones. From Agosín to Jack Agüeros to Francisco X. Alarcón to Miguel Algarín to Alurista to Anzaldúa to Aragón himself—and these are surnames only from the first letter of the alphabet—Latino poetry has long been defined by formal diversity, accessible experimentalism, and an emergence from, engagement with, and bridging of transnational material conditions of oppression, injustice, upheaval, and compromised mobility. In coming decades some poems about femicide also will not stand up as "good" poetry. But is this measure appropriate? What if we turn it around? Decades from now will much of the Language poetry hold up as "good" poetry? Will much of *any* poetry? What if *urgency*, as in Bolaño's take on Nicanor Parra in chapter 3, and *lucidity*, as in poetry "that can be understood," as Cardenal describes the goal of his writing (*Pluriverse* xi), together constituted an alternative metrics?

In these contexts, the dimensions of "acceptance" (by whom?) and "silence" (to serve whom?) come to the fore. "Because any avant-garde conversation operates on a binary," generally between the putatively "new" and an implicitly retrograde, conventional "old," as the Chicano poet J. Michael Martinez and Jordan Windholz argue, "one must always ask how a work is avant-garde in relation to whom, to what, or to when" (84). Failing to establish these contextual relations further obscures the forces of ideology and marginalizes already marginal minority writers, who become confined to a putatively conventional identity-based poetics. To avoid this type of "political hijacking on the avant-garde's part" (81), it might alternately be useful to reframe the approach. By reading Latino poetry as a collection of diachronic expressive practices that, in relationship to North and Latin American poetry, has always been in the vanguard, a set of "new" in-formation languages neither here nor there, English nor Spanish, Latino poetry maintains both a sense of autonomous development and thoroughly interwoven relations with various poetic practices in the North and in the South. Agosín's and, especially, Valerie Martínez's femicide poems merge politics and aesthetics to reorient our gaze on extreme violence, but they also reorient our understanding of the ways in which Latina/o poets push into new expressive territory by borrowing from various traditions and by confronting the most dire of events, whether on a vast or an intimate scale. They display an innovative Latino poetics that avoids the avant-garde's frequently obscure, cloistered hostility to political margins and allegiance to literary-textual ones, while finding innovative ground to address the disproportionate burdens of the disaster.

I want to posit here that Agosín's and Martínez's book-length femicide poems can be read as urgent, lucid, and cutting-edge texts in the ways in which they "explicitly reinstate the dignity of the murdered," Ileana Rodríguez's description of the goal of femicide writing (180). Agosín's and Martínez's texts are "experimental," in the basic sense, testing modes of expression against their material contexts, and specifically in terms of North American poetry. In the former sense, figures of silence create experimental forms in each book, illuminating the challenges of representing and exceeding the violence of femicide. Agosín has been exploring how to write the disaster for decades, from her native Chile to Argentina's "dirty war." Her *These Are Not Sweet Girls: Poetry by Latin American Women* introduces North American readers to Latin American literary-historical geographies through the eyes of its female poets.[11] Agosín introduces this outstanding anthology with a dialectic of speech and silence: "throughout history," she writes, "women have been closer to words than to silence," although "they have often been barred from speaking" (21). In reflecting on *Circles of Madness: Mothers of the Plaza de Mayo*, her collection about Argentina's mothers of the disappeared, she offers prescient wisdom on writing about femicide, which emerges from a similar dialectic. After questioning the process of literary representation guiding the project, she concludes that "representing with an aesthetic symbolic discourse the horror of the political discourse" is "impossib[le]." This claim may echo Blanchot, but disavowing aesthetics in favor of "literature" rejects his measured theoretical meditations on the impossibility of writing. In the contexts of disaster, Agosín admits, "aesthetics no longer held center stage for me and it became more vital to simply make literature" ("How to Speak" 217, 219). This enigmatic statement delinks calm contemplation from literary-political praxis, implying that aesthetic experiment, meditation, and time itself are luxuries of detachment, absolute spaces of "not here," as in Espada's Chile poems. On the ground that Agosín identifies, literature is urgent, immediate, and raw, and it must be made quickly in response to events.[12]

In this way, Agosín sees poetry that focuses on aesthetics as entering a territory of silence, with carefully constructed language emerging from contemplation and text and reader meeting in solitude. This is, in part, what Pacheco has in mind in "In Defense of Anonymity" when he calls poetry "a form of love that only exists in silence, / in a secret place between two people, / almost always between two strangers" (*Selected Poems* 179). It is therefore critical to differentiate among silence as a trope/figure (as in Pacheco), aesthetic technique (i.e., a poem's white space), and external imposition (i.e., an oppressive state, the "blank page," the disaster). While the first guides Agosín's text and the second Martínez's, each attempts to create spaces for encountering and challenging the third. For Agosín, a writer must "respect the cadences and the zones of silence" that emerge from disaster, the third form of silence, and admit that she must write about "individual[s] who did not want to be history, but nevertheless [were] history" ("How to Speak" 220). Figures of silence structure *Secrets in the Sand*, from the title, to the first page's "empty echoes," "emptiness," "absence," "perfidious silence," and the limited epistemology of witness in "All we know about them / Is their death" (25), to "the sovereignty of absence" ruling victims' families (105). These tropes converge on an image of mothers whose daughters' remains "have not been found," who have been left with "the pages of an / Always empty diary / Like the spaces on a blank page / Or a life pierced by silence" (91). In Agosín's poem, this "blank page" has an affective character that Pacheco's "1968" lacks. Against the "[a]lways empty diary" paradoxically filled with dissolution, emptiness, and silence, Agosín's text is highly discursive and oneiric.[13]

To confront the disastrous form of silence, Agosín delivers these discursive, dreamlike, and often prophetic forms through intermittent Nerudian representational conceits. First-person declarations in a lyric voice—"I will tell you about them" (49) and "I pass judgment on the priests / And heads of companies" (71)—echo Neruda's *Canto general*, while the city itself takes on the character of a murdered woman. The "gagged city" (35) is an embodied, aggregate version of the silenced femicide victim, but in this case greed and inequality are structural culprits ensuring the retrenchment of North/South divisions (75, 77). Such figures of North/South inequality in Agosín and Martínez contextualize femicide as a transnational phenomena connected to the broader violence, if obliquely and opaquely. Unlike prototypical Latino depictions of the border, as Castillo and Tabuenca Córdoba identify them, Agosín sees only division, in which "a knife parts [victims] in two / North and South" (63). Agosín's metaphors of silence, tropes of inevitably compromised and partial witness, direct "judgments," and exilic renderings of North/South divisions confront the abject violence of femicide and restore a measure of dignity to the women of Juárez, who will nevertheless continue to dwell in "the sovereignty of absence."

Whereas Agosín prefers oneiric, disjunctive, and prophetic representational figures, Martínez confronts the disaster of silence with figures of movement and exchange created through experimental forms of intertextuality. *Each and Her* is comprised of seventy-two numbered one-page poems, with the exception of #61, a three-page list of victims with the first name "María." The list is just one of the text's many types of textuality, including lots of white space and one poem (#63) that is simply a blank page we might imagine as a page in Agosín's "empty diary." The list of victims pressures readers to pronounce each name carefully in an act of patience and humility rather than to skim for the gist of things. The sixty-four "Marías" thus enact Derrida's defense of proper names, which must not be mistaken for symbols or figures but understood *as* human beings. Together the list of names and the blank page find basic, elegant forms for attesting to Blanchot's "immeasurable, unsharable burdens" that define femicide as a disaster, precisely by obliterating its previous definitions. Additionally, Martínez cites wage and labor statistics and uses quotes, images, and definitions from a range of texts, both ancient and contemporary, and across the spectrum of high and low culture, from literature to business documents and advertisements. Among the text's texts are Agosín's *Secrets in the Sand* (38); Rudolfo Anaya's *Bless Me, Última* (64); and Univision host Teresa Rodríguez's *The Daughters of Juarez* (26, 49). References to the poet Adrienne Rich (epigraph), Diego Rivera (7), John Keats (8), and Aztec myth (65) entwine with those to websites, Christian theological texts, government documents, feminist theory, scholarly studies, conversations, and fragmented personal memories of Martínez's childhood and her relationship with her troubled sister. Together they make *Each and Her* a textual pastiche, a collage that Martínez gathers, compiles, and assembles from disparate parts, much like a *maquila* worker does on the assembly line. In this case, the end result is also a finished product to be purchased in the United States, but it is a highly fragmented, difficult book rather than a user-friendly television.

This idea stresses the book's use-value as a document produced from dispersed, broken, and often inaccessible given materials that are nearly useless on their own. One of its first images is of Juárez's women, many of whom migrated from southern Mexican states and many of whom work at *maquilas*, as "rivers of dots / on a migratory map" (3). As in Agosín, Martínez's text claims *not* to know them, as we are forced into "knowing them / only like this" (59). Although Martínez's deictic "this" remains unidentified in the book, its contexts imply that "like this" connotes as dead bodies and disembodied names. Further, "dots" depict migration much differently than Cruz's celebratory ecopoetics. Hers is the one-dimensional textuality and programmed movement of binary code, a literary pointillism in which single dots are infinitesimal, unimportant, in which they are whole (*as* dots) and comprehensible only when mapped together as an aggregation of countless dots. Such interpersonal forms of collectivity and movement guide the text, and roads, cars, trains, and buses underpin its poetics. As vectors of capital's production of space in Juárez, and for remapping the city as a place, buses, in particular, offer spaces for imagining a collective "break" from neoliberalism's atomized dots, abject violence, and bodily insecurity.

Each and Her thus picks up on the centrality of buses to the "geographies of danger" navigated by *maquila* workers. In Juárez, buses are a sign and symptom of the abuse of labor, uneven geographic development, unequal access to infrastructure, and the power of capital to produce space. The two main industrial parks with *maquilas* are located south and east of the city center, while most of the isolated *colonias* (informal neighborhoods, often slums without access to public infrastructure) are southwest of the city (Volk and Schlotterbeck 129). The foot routes to street pickups that wind through abandoned lots and the long, twisting bus routes across the city *maquila* workers take late at night and early in the morning sharply contrast capital's private bridge. "Safety," Gaspar de Alba writes, "is a commodity the workers cannot afford" ("Poor Brown Female" 65). It is critical to expand this notion of buses as key sites of insecurity, as Monsiváis does in his ironic claim that women can only protect themselves in Juárez by living "without bodies."[14] Most victims, after all, disappeared between 3:00 and 5:00 p.m., "within a radius of four kilometers of the *maquilas*" (Rodríguez, *Liberalism* 166). How does a poet account for this totalizing spatiotemporality of fear and insecurity, alongside the paradoxical empowerment of women's incorporation into the wage labor force?

Two ways stand out in *Each and Her*. One emerges from a figure of the bus, which stands in contrast to the *maquila*, the other from the paratext, which is posed against a place-based poetics. Martínez's three-line depiction of *maquilas*—"the assembly line // call it a revolution / in commodity forms"—comprises her #10 poem, her economic conclusion echoing Agosín's translator Celeste Kostopulos-Cooperman, who calls *maquilas* a "cultural revolution" (14). Against this cultural-economic capitalist revolution, Martínez uses the bus to model radical forms of collective subjectivity emerging from the commodification of female bodies. In particular, she constitutes struggle, security, and mobility interpersonally in a way that recalls Herrera's "interwoven" marchers: "*after the late shift / on the maqui bus // we stitch ourselves // one to another*" (37). Yet *Each and Her* also challenges the premise of *Broken Souths* that Latino poetics defends place against the neoliberal counter-revolution. The Rich epigraph—"Nothing less than the most radical imagination / will carry us beyond this place"— stakes claims against "this place" by calling for a "beyond," an otherwise to neoliberal exploitations. In this light, workers "stitch[ing]" themselves together militates against the neoliberal crackdown on organized labor in order to separate laborers from each other *as* discrete commodities and to ensure that they remain isolated individuals. Measured by Rich's claim calling for a radical imagination to transport us ("carry us") to an elsewhere, most femicide texts fall short of the radical anticapitalist imaginary necessary to break the power of *maquilas* over workers and men over women. As such, the infinitive "to remake the world" concludes Martínez's book (74). This form of "to break" suggests the need for alternative myths and tables of values, not by creating a blank page akin to those across the political spectrum in late 1960s models but *in* and *through* extant texts, some of which are merely dots to be stitched together into letters, words, and sentences. As in Pacheco's ecopoetics, *Each and Her* ends with the suggestion that all writing is rewriting and that all making is remaking.

The reviews on the back covers of Agosín's and Martínez's books offer convergent final insights on the pressures facing those who write about Juárez and femicide, especially in regard to the dearth of a radical imagination. Agosín's book features the preeminent Latina writer Julia Alvarez and the Chicano poet Tino Villanueva. Alvarez's statement includes these assessments of *Secrets in the Sand*: it "gather[s] women together to give testimony," "create[s] an empowering circle of sister voices," "challenges us all," "respond[s] with outrage and action," and "gives voice to the voiceless," a key Nerudian conceit. Villanueva's blurb emphasizes how Agosín's "intelligent humanity" "grants" the victims "dignity, and keeps their memory alive." *Each and Her* has blurbs from the poets Joy Harjo, Kilwein Guevara, and Aragón. Harjo's includes the statements "they [the victims] are us," "no more silence," and "pathway for justice." Kilwein Guevara writes that "every one of us is implicated." Aragón calls the text "both public and private." All told, these inclusive tropes promoting human rights discourses reflect the liberal consensus about dignity and silence, and they reinforce the main conceits of witness, testimonial, and representational literary modes. These important ideals and discourses nonetheless fail to confront overarching structural contexts, as Rich's epigraph suggests, and as both book-length searches for forms to write the disaster demonstrate. There is little trace of a "radical imagination" in these reviews and nothing about work or class.

As a conclusion to *Broken Souths: Latina/o Poetic Responses to Neoliberalism and Globalization*, my contrarian stance in reading these cover reviews stresses the penetrating, vanguard class perspective of *Each and Her*. In asking how Latina/o texts might represent working-class women, and dead ones at that, Martínez's book accentuates what the literary critic Peter Hitchcock calls "answerability." "A worker," he writes, "knows that capitalism has a lot to answer for, but there is no obvious space or place to seek redress from it since capitalism's own survival is guaranteed by" a totalizing, "amorphous" ideology. Because this ideology depicts "the extraction of surplus value from labor" as "akin to the eighth day of creation," articulations of answerability must be "insistently active" in foregrounding "ethical responsibility." "The working class must be theorized," Hitchcock concludes, "and this task is still before us" (27, 30). While not all of the femicide victims have been *maquila* workers, in this frame femicide texts might orient their challenges at the direct abuses and unintended consequences of the capitalist production of space, especially where "there is too much of it." This ethical act of theorization embeds "answerability" into texts to call to account the neoliberal state's service to surplus value and the "Song of Money." Theorizing a *maquila* class in a Latina/o poetics exposes the horrors of capitalism and its handmaiden, femicide.

Appropriately, then, Martínez ends *Each and Her* with the infinitive, "—to remake the world," as its one-line final poem. This ending tacitly and reflexively admits that all of the white space and silence that precede it comprise a halting start to doing so. In my estimation, however, this un-speaking silence starkly illuminates the loss of these named and unnamed women by refusing to speculate in appropriative ways or to narrate their unknown lives, and it reflects the frustration of the investigative response to the crimes by finding a lack of satisfying theories and clues. Whereas the final line does not make an outright call for revolution, it does call for what Hitchcock calls an "insistently active" ethical responsibility, and for creating a "radical imagination" of the kind in Espada's "Imagine the Angels of Bread," where border crossers "are greeted with trumpets and drums." Most broadly, the last poem bookends the text's "answerability" with an overarching theorization: if theory's tasks are to see the world more clearly and to imagine it differently, *Each and Her* theorizes with an ex-tended metaphor of rose cultivation. Threaded intermittently throughout the text, references to horticultural and market-based practices of planting, pruning, eliminating pests, and caring for roses offer figurative glimpses of the ways in which Juárez's working-class women, often unable to speak for themselves, are exploited, displayed, and discarded. The women are not compared to roses, nor are the roses trite symbols for women; rather, the detached scientific language of cultivating roses for their use- and exchange-value dovetails with the "rivers of dots" and "revolution / in commodity forms" in the *maquilas*. This nimble juxtaposition of cultural-economic forms of exploitation and control constitutes a poetics that theo-rizes a metanarrative of the femicide, if not its narrow, punishable causes or perpetrators. Overall, the poetics of *Each and Her* offers a keen, oblique warning about any putatively rational, civilized, and beneficent language concerned with the cultivation of beauty and order and the protection of the vulnerable from harm. This poetics constitutes the ground for charting a radically innovative Latina/o poetics at the intersections of neoliberal-era disasters and emancipatory otherwises.

I want to conclude on the border with a few words about "The An-gels of Juárez, Mexico," a poem by Ray Gonzalez, the prolific Latino poet and editor and an El Paso native (*Consideration of the Guitar* 106–107).

The poem suggestively delineates the North/South contours of the pressing need for new languages "to remake the world" with a different sort of reversal than in "Imagine the Angels of Bread." Whereas Espada's angels span the hemisphere's nations, reality and possibility, oppression and liberation, Gonzalez's angels "look over the *colonias*" and "hover over the Rio Grande," protecting Juárez's workers and Mexico's border crossers. But they never enter El Paso, which is an empty void rather than the proverbial land of opportunity. The poem ends with the claim that the "waiting streets of El Paso [will] never [be] / mistaken for the place of angels." Gonzalez's Juárez angels have an epistemological orientation that struggles to cross the border: they may not have access to the United States, but they "know about revolution and dying." Does the possibility of revolution, like the most intensified forms of exploitation, remain in the South? If so, it is separated by mere feet and not from a lack of desire, or need, to carry it north. This division in Gonzalez's poem can be read in a number of ways, including in contrast to the act of "joining" in Ríos's "Border Lines." As this study's final example of Latino poetics in the neoliberal era, one interpretation gains purchase. North by South readings require mapping connection and division as any radical imagination's response to neoliberalism's goal of unifying the globe under the control of capital while dividing any resistance to it. Latina/o poets excel precisely at envisioning and contesting this paradoxical double movement.

Notes

Introduction

1. For background on the terms "Latino," "Hispanic," and "Latin American," see Oboler; Aparicio ("[Re]constructing Latinidad" 39–43); Flores (7–8, 192–195); Flores and Yúdice (80 n. 1, 2); Gruesz (*Ambassadors* 213 n. 3); Mignolo (163 n. 3); Pérez-Torres ("Ethnicity" 538–541); and Verdecchia (26–27, 79 n. 3). Although "Latino" contrasts to "Hispanic," a census term with "assimilationist rather than pluralist connotations," it is also a "fictive construct" (Gruesz, *Ambassadors* 213 n. 3, xi). I use "Latina/o" and "Latino" interchangeably, the latter for simplicity, in reference to persons of Latin American descent living in the United States.

2. "The idea of 'Latin' America is being detached from fixed territorial contours," Mignolo writes, obviating "distinction[s] between an Anglo North and a Latin South" (134). Taylor notes the "interconnections of populations in the Americas, where the Third World is in the First World and the other way around" (1427). De la Campa similarly cautions against the myth of the "North/South divide" ("Latin, Latino, American" 374). Although these are legitimate admonitions for avoiding oversimplifications, *Broken Souths* shows that some North/South divisions have also retrenched under neoliberalism. "Latin America," like "Latino" and "America," is an invention. It came into usage in the late nineteenth century.

3. See Fukuyama's *End of History* and Mills's "Letter to the New Left" for background on these contexts and constructs.

4. For more on *Fronteras Americanas*, see Worthen and Adams (ch. 6).

5. Margaret Thatcher is credited with "there is no alternative." See Harlow on "elsewhere." I prefer "otherwise" because it encompasses space and time rather than primarily space.

6. In Argentina, those tortured for resisting neoliberal restructuring during the "Dirty Wars" in the 1970s and 1980s were called *quebrados* (broken ones). See Klein (138).

7. The relationship between postmodernist cultural modes and neoliberal ideological tenets can be sketched as follows: the former's multiplicity, indeterminacy, dispersal, ludic energies, critique of metanarratives and modernist projects for collective emancipation, and celebrations of diversity, fragmentation, popular culture, the individual, and mobility serve the latter's promotion of the individual and market-based organization of society. De la Campa writes that postmodernism and neoliberalism have

"a logic that fuses marketing, culture, and politics into a performative doctrine not far from a new metanarrative" (*Latin Americanism* 150). See Hopenhayn on postmodernism and neoliberalism in Latin America (77–93). I use "postmodern" to clarify literary-historical contexts, but the term often fails to illuminate Latino literary practices.

8. Smith and Cohn follow similar logic in choosing "New World Studies" as a field signifier.

9. "Neoliberalism" refers to the recuperation and dramatic extension of the principles of classical political economy as delineated by Adam Smith. Because economic liberalism differs from political liberalism, delinking capitalism and democracy is essential. See McChesney's summary of neoliberal logic and consequences. "Neoliberalism," de la Campa writes, is "not commonly used by cultural critics in the United States to describe the reigning political philosophy of globalization" (*Latin Americanism* 150–151). *Broken Souths* names neoliberalism specifically, and capitalism broadly, because each is effaced in discussions of "globalization" and the "free market." Even "capitalism," Boltanski and Chiapello note, has largely disappeared from post-1968 discourses, while Foster, Clark, and York outline the consequences of substituting "free market" for "capitalism" (30–31). This is due in part to terminology. "In most of the world," Klein writes, this "orthodoxy is known as 'neoliberalism,' but it is often called 'free trade' or simply 'globalization'" (17). Derksen clarifies the terms by saying that "the cultural logic of globalization" is "the imposition of neoliberalism's ideology of economic growth as progress" (17–18, 10). Eagleton simply calls it "the new capitalism" (5), describing the "shift" and "vital changes" in the capitalist system beginning in the early 1970s as intensifying capitalist exploitation (3–11). Comaroff and Comaroff call it "millennial capitalism" to capture its eschatological qualities. Finally, neoliberalism is often called "American-style" capitalism.

10. In 1947, Friedman, Friedrich Hayek, Ludvig von Mises, and others founded the Mont Pelerin Society, where neoliberalism was born. See Harvey's *Brief History of Neoliberalism* (19–22) and Friedman's *Capitalism and Freedom*. The Latino writer Francisco Goldman's *Long Night of White Chickens* alludes to Friedman's status in Latin America: "one exclusive rich kids' private university" in Guatemala City was "run like a temple to the worship of Milton Friedman" (123). See Carvalho's *Puerto Rico Is in the Heart* for an alternate genealogy of neoliberalism (5–16).

11. Flores calls the "in-between" "the space of the 'break' itself" in reference to the historical "break" constituted by Puerto Rican migration to New York in the mid-twentieth century (55–56). See also two canonical critical texts, Pérez Firmat's *Life on the Hyphen* and Stavans's *Hispanic Condition* (ch. 1, "Life in the Hyphen").

12. "The market-as-metaphor dominates conversation" in higher education (Judt 117). On neoliberal educational logic, see Carvalho and Downing and Fish.

13. See de la Campa's *Latin Americanism* on "the[se] processes of scholarly legitimation" (2–3). My approach is what Yarbro-Bejarano calls an "entry point" into Chicano/Latino studies (405). A drawback of New York as a locus of Latino poetry is its remove from Chicano literary formations. Robert Courtney Smith writes that Mexican New Yorkers reject "the label *Chicano* as a more politicized identity from California" (269). See Muñoz on the term "Chicano" in political-historical contexts (17, 19, 22, 26) and Dávila on Mexicans in New York (ch. 5).

14. For example, see Bruce-Novoa's *Chicano Poetry*; Limón's *Mexican Ballads, Chicano Poems*; and Pérez-Torres's *Movements in Chicano Poetry*.

15. On "space-time," see Dirlik, Massey, and Harvey (*Spaces of Global Capitalism* 122–123).

16. "Part of Latin American postmodernism," Kuhnheim writes, "entails this creation of diverse 'loci of enunciation,' Mignolo's term for these new speaking locations" (7). Whereas Kuhnheim and Mignolo see "speaking locations" primarily as subject positions, *Broken Souths* takes the notion of "locations" in a literal geographic sense as well as in a theoretical sense.

17. See Concannon, Lomelí, and Priewe on the ways in which transnational methodologies both reinforce and challenge precepts about mobility.

18. Gruesz writes, "Scholars are accustomed to think of lyric as at best opaque about, and at worst completely detached from, its informing contexts of collective identity and power" (*Ambassadors* 21).

19. Along with Dean (33–34), Boltanski and Chiapello see 1968 as the pivotal year in capitalism's restructuring along neoliberal lines.

20. My translation. Whereas Wimmer uses "books" in her translation of this passage (*Between Parentheses* 42), I translate "biblioteca" literally to maintain the specificity of the metaphor as a collection of texts.

21. See Adamson and Slovic on ethnicity and ecocriticism and María Meléndez's excellent ecopoetic collection *How Long She'll Last in This World*.

22. *Broken Souths* also fills a need for scholarship on poetry in Latino and hemispheric American studies. Recent volumes of Latino studies (Concannon, Lomelí, and Priewe; Dalleo and Machado Sáez; Flores and Rosaldo; and Sandín and Perez), and hemispheric studies (Levander and Levine; Shukla and Tinsman; and Smith and Cohn) give relatively little attention to poetry.

23. Hereafter I cite Cohen's translation of "Room 5600" in *Pluriverse* (184–188) rather than the version in *Cosmic Canticle* (213–217).

24. The Rockefellers are prominent in Harvey's history of 1973–82, a period of neoliberal history in which capitalists consolidated their power (*Enigma of Capital* 130–131).

25. For hemispheric paradigms, see Taylor; Levander and Levine; Marissa López; and Read.

26. See Friedman's *The World Is Flat*. The flattening of class and power relations, along with the uneven access to resources, is also common in postmodern theories emphasizing networks and flows. Castells's "space of flows" is emblematic (*Rise of the Network Society* 407–459).

27. Gibbons examines the techniques of what Cardenal calls *exteriorismo*. The political poet Mark Nowak counts Cardenal's documentary *exteriorismo* among his greatest influences. No poet in the United States has thought more carefully and creatively about how to respond to neoliberalism than Nowak. In "Notes Toward an Anti-Capitalist Poetics II," he calls neoliberalism's totalizing market-based vision of "freedom" "the hegemonic new poetics each of us faces each and every day, whether we acknowledge it or not, when we begin to put words on the page" (335).

28. My definition of rational choice is derived from Beverley's "Dos caminos."

29. Contrasting the capitalist production of nature, Cardenal's Sandinista poems depict an idealized socialist production of nature in the image of revolution, restoring ecological processes to health. See "New Ecology" (*Pluriverse* 176–177).

30. See Harvey on New York's neoliberal turn (*Enigma of Capital* 172; *Brief History* 44–48). In the late 1970s and 1980s, the city "turned to the production of debt and fictitious capital" and "the world of real estate, finance, and business services" (*Condition of Postmodernity* 331). Reliance on speculative, fictitious capital to create wealth dominates the current era.

Chapter 1

1. See Espada's essay "The Lover of a Subversive Is Also a Subversive" on the indigenous Taíno source of this image (17).

2. Critics frequently compare neoliberalism to the conquest. Klein describes neoliberalism as "the second colonial pillage" in Latin America, when wealth was "stripped from the state" (308). Grandin calls neoliberalism the "third conquest" of Latin America (160). "The sale of state enterprises was one of the largest transfers of wealth in world history," he writes. Between 1985 and 1992, over two thousand government industries were sold off ("privatized") at fire-sale prices to multinationals and Latin American "superbillionaires" (187–188). The neoliberal ascendancy in Mexico used what Eagleton calls "a form of daylight robbery politely known as privatization" (14), falsely justified by Mexico's monetary crisis. Klein quotes a former IMF economist on this period. "From 1983 onward," their "mission" was "to have the south 'privatised' or die" (205). In writing about the 2008 global financial crisis, Badiou also links finance capital to the conquest (96).

3. For example, see the biography on Espada's website, http://martinespada.net/.

4. On fraught historical relations between Chicanos and Mexicans, see Gaspar de Alba's "Poor Brown Female" (91–92 n. 9); Coco Fusco and Gómez-Peña ("Nationalism and Latinos" 162–168); and Burciaga (45–55). The divide has also been between Latinos and "immigrant groups of Latin Americans who see themselves strictly as exiles and foreign nationals" (de la Campa, "Latinos and the Crossover Aesthetic" xiv). See Aparicio's "Reading the 'Latino' in Latino Studies" on intergroup relations.

5. De la Campa links postmodernism's "celebrated sense of liminality" to "the free-floating expansionism of globalization" and notes capitalism's "shifts from postmodernist dispersion toward neoliberal enclosure" (*Latin Americanism* 151, 168).

6. For background on these constructs of space, place, and nature, see Brady (7–12); Harvey's "Space as a Key Word" (*Spaces of Global Capitalism* 119–148); Lefebvre (*Production of Space* 31); Scigaj (chs. 1 and 2); Smith (*Uneven Development* 18–20); and Soja (79–80). See Igoe and Brockington on the neoliberal commodification of nature under the auspices of "conservation."

7. The term "place-maker" is from Basso's study of the Apache.

8. "It is a categorical error to view globalization as a causal force in relation to local development," Harvey writes. "The most avid globalizers will support local developments [. . .] antagonistic to globalization" when they create profits ("Art of Rent" 101).

9. In his legal scholarship on the Zapatistas, Pérez-Bustillo writes: "There is no way to disentangle the legal resolution of demands for indigenous human rights in Mexico from the transformation of generalized conditions of socio-economic and political

marginalization in which they are immersed." "'Neoliberal' economic policies," he concludes, worsened these historical conditions (176–177).

10. Rosenthal argues that the plaza is "a primary locus for the spectacle of class conflict" in Mexico (47). Also see Low's *On the Plaza*.

11. This figure also guides Neruda's *Canto General*.

12. See Castells on Zapatista communication strategies (*Power of Identity* 75–86).

13. Bell Lara and López refer to "the cumulative social impact resulting from the application of neoliberal policies" in Latin America as the "Harvest of Neoliberalism" (17).

14. Pacheco follows Borges in rejecting the trope of literary "property." See "Borges and I" (*Selected Poems* 93).

15. In an e-mail to the Cuban American poet Rafael Campo, Espada laments the preeminent "English-speaking lady" Ruth Lilly's recent gift of $100 million to the Poetry Foundation. "What if Ruth Lilly had given her hundred million dollars to a hundred publishers of poetry?" he asks. "One million dollars each to 50 journals and 50 small presses? How would that change the face of poetry in this country?" "The hundred million dollars," he concludes, "represents one elite spawning another elite. Even in the act of charity, the aristocracy thinks as an aristocracy: the concentration of enormous wealth in a few hands is good—as long as they're the right hands" ("Correspondence: Campo"). Here Espada identifies neoliberalism's core logic: to consolidate class power and wealth.

16. Espada's "The King of Books" (*Rebellion* 66–68) praises Pérez-Bustillo's work in El Salvador in the 1980s, while "Sleeping on the Bus" laments how collective memories of 1960s activism are lost in the atomizing "babble of headphones" (*Imagine the Angels* 77–78).

17. See Beverley (*Against Literature*), Gugelberger, Rabasa (*Without History*), and Espada's "The Poet-Lawyer" and "A Branch on the Tree of Whitman" (both in *Lover of a Subversive*) and "Poetics of Advocacy."

18. This "because" device structures Espada's "The Meaning of the Shovel," set in Managua following the Sandinista victory (*Imagine the Angels* 53–54).

19. Herrera's *Thunderweavers/Tejedoras de rayos* addresses Acteal at length.

20. Espada calls his poem "inadequate" to protect "the fragility of Camilo's life" but suggests that the list is "the locus of power for the subversive, a prized representation of courage and integrity" ("Poetics of Advocacy" 130).

21. "Fingering" was Pinochet's modus operandi. See Constable and Valenzuela (146), Klein (93), and Espada's "Something Escapes the Bonfire" (*Republic* 8–11).

22. Bañuelos's "Huelga de hambre" [Hunger Strike] (24–26) inversely depicts the screams of political prisoners attacking doors, monuments, and walls of government buildings in Mexico City.

23. The statue has since been moved to Plaza Manuel Tolsá on Calle de Tacuba in the *centro*.

24. Monsiváis describes the metro similarly: "The metro's perpetual novelty consists in squeezing the entire country into one square meter" ("Metro" 144–145).

25. Other Mexico City poems featuring buses include Bañuelos's "Circuito Iztapalapa-Bondojito" (38); the untitled first poem in Bolaño's *Fragmentos* (9–13); and Óscar Oliva's "At the Wheel of a Car."

26. "La multitud inerme en Tlatelolco"; "Es terrible describir a un movimiento por sus víctimas, pero estas víctimas lo fueron por considerar posible la creación de alternativas." All Monsiváis translations are mine.

27. "Se producen libros sobre el 68 que alcanzan a cientos de miles"; "la poesía desempeña un papel central." For example, see Elsa Cross's poem "The Lovers of Tlatelolco." For context and criticism, see Carey; Carpenter; Messinger Cypess; Poniatowska; Sorensen; and Young.

28. Friis writes: "The two major aspects of Pacheco's work that have caught critics' eyes are the temporal and the intertextual" (16). My "Of the Smog" provides an alternative assessment.

29. See Harvey on modernism's creative destruction (*Condition of Postmodernity* 16–18).

30. "The theoretical utopianism of neoliberal argument," Harvey writes, has "worked as a system of justification and legitimation." He concludes: "When neoliberal principles clash with the need to restore or sustain elite power, then the principles are either abandoned or become so twisted as to be unrecognizable" (*Brief History* 19).

31. "The view that the pursuit of individual interests serves the general interest," Boltanski and Chiapello write, "has been the object of an enormous, incessant labour, which has been taken up and extended throughout the history of classical economics" (12).

32. For example, see "What country is this?" (*Selected Poems* 187–193). The "blank page" has a positive slant in Mexican poetics in *ninguneo*, the parodic act of turning a "somebody" into a "nobody." See Friis for background (176–178, 188) and on Pacheco's negotiation of literary influences.

Chapter 2

1. In contrast, critics such as Carvalho, Cepeda, and Fink emphasize resistance in Espada's poetry.

2. Alexander's *New Jim Crow* is the most trenchant, carefully argued critique of how a "post-racial" ideology conceals the systemic dispossession of African Americans through mass incarceration.

3. The MLA's "Statement on Tucson Mexican American Studies Program" opposes the state's ruling by appealing, in part, to the language of individualism.

4. The foundational Chicano movement poet Alurista's influence is apparent in this section of early poems. "Crescent Moon on a Cat's Collar" (*Half of the World* 45–46) is dedicated to him.

5. "One Year Before the Zapatista Rebellion" first appeared in slightly different form as "The Third Conversation" in *Mayan Drifter*. The version in *187 Reasons Mexicanos Can't Cross the Border* benefits from an additional decade of reflection. I toggle between the essay in *187 Reasons* and the full text of *Mayan Drifter*. "Maga" is Herrera's wife, the artist Margarita Luna Robles.

6. See the film *A Day Without a Mexican* and Herrera-Sobek on the film and the march. The 400,000 figure comes from Gorman, Miller, and Landsberg. H.R. 4437 was known as "The Border Protection, Anti-Terrorism, and Illegal Immigration Control Act"; it passed the House but failed in the Senate. Herrera's poem is dedicated

to Anthony Soltero, the fourteen year old who committed suicide after being told he would be jailed for organizing a school walkout to protest the bill.

7. "Zapata" retains its symbolism (Rabasa, *Without History* 104, 109–110). Herrera observes Zapata signs and posters carried by Chicanos in 1970, Indians in Chiapas in 1993 (*Mayan Drifter* 248), and in the 2006 march. See also Espada's essay collection, *Zapata's Disciple*.

Chapter 3

1. The UN ranks Chile 116 out of 123 nations measured in income equality. "If that track record qualifies Chile as a miracle for Chicago school economists," Klein concludes, the neoliberal project "was meant to do exactly what it did—hoover wealth up to the top and shock much of the middle class out of existence" (105). Also see Constable and Valenzuela (245); Valdés on Chile "as a permanent laboratory" for free-market fundamentalism (1); and Grandin on Chile as "empire's workshop." See Stephens's "How Milton Friedman Saved Chile" for the triumphalist view.

2. The neoliberal state oscillates between "roll-back" and "roll-out" forms. The first proceeds through deregulation, privatization, and the cessation of social safety nets. The second "rolls-out" "reregulation" that aims to restore (or create) capitalist class power. See Derksen (20–21) and Harvey (*Brief History* 64–86). In Chile, neoliberals proposed a "modern," "competitive," and "acquisitive" individual as the prototype for a "'nation of owners'" (Valdés 6). This construct prefigures George W. Bush's "ownership society."

3. Gruesz's *Ambassadors of Culture* examines how print cultures, poetry especially, shaped proto-Latino literary formations in the late nineteenth century.

4. The image also recalls Hobbes's figure of the state as a "Leviathan." See Hart and Hansen on this metaphor of the "monstrous artificial man" in relation to the contemporary state (492).

5. *Nazi Literature in the Americas* is Bolaño's encyclopedic version of Borges's "Book of Imaginary Beings."

6. Harvey writes: "The genius of capitalism [is] that it relies upon the instincts, enterprise and sometimes crazy ideas (the 'animal spirits' invoked by both Marx and Keynes) of individual entrepreneurs" (*Enigma of Capital* 160). See *Capital* on "animal spirits" (443–444, 447, 460).

7. On neoliberalism as a revolution, see Constable and Valenzuela (39, 80, 187); Valdés (10, 13, 36, 48, 51, 56, 100); Munck (65); and Duménil and Lévy.

8. See Bolaño's "hallway" ["pasillo"] (*Romantic Dogs* 129; *Between Parentheses* 75) and "island" figures (Dés 145; *Between Parentheses* 85). He describes Chilean poetry as a "dog" with syntax similar to his take on September 11 (*Between Parentheses* 95).

9. Parra's "Apropos of Nothing" stars an anthropomorphized "poetry": "poetry is tailing you / and me too / it's after all of us" (*Antipoems* 21). See Grossman's succinct overview of Parra's "antipoetry."

10. Bolaño first gained notoriety in Mexico City when he and his teenage friends (the self-proclaimed *infrarealistas*) shouted their own poems from the audience during public readings.

11. Bolaño concludes the "self-portrait" [*autorretrato*] prefacing *Between Parentheses* similarly: "I'm much happier reading than writing" (16).

12. In saying that he left Mexico for Chile in 1973 "a hacer la revolución y decidí ir solo" (Dés 143), Bolaño pairs collective revolution and individual autonomy. His imprisonment appears in the second sentence of his "self-portrait" (*Between Parentheses* 15), suggesting its importance to his self-fashioning.

13. This is certainly true of *The Savage Detectives*, a novel composed in this spirit and tradition, but Bolaño's poetry is much grittier and difficult to package in the United States.

14. A similar movement north structures the poem "The Donkey" (*Romantic Dogs* 121–127).

15. Borges writes that "intellectual poetry" "is almost an oxymoron." Whereas the intellect, *as* "wakefulness," "thinks by means of abstractions," poetry, *as* "dream," thinks "by means of images, myths, or fables." Intellectual poetry, he concludes, "should pleasingly interweave these two processes" (*Selected Poems* 422). In Bolaño, the "dream" fails without this interweaving.

16. Bolaño was often antagonistic to Chile ("los chilenos son terribles") and almost unequivocally earnest about his love for Mexico (Dés 145–146, 153). However, his frequent turns to Chile as an idea and as subject matter suggest greater ambivalence.

17. Images of the coup structure "The Firing Squad Is Singing in Chile" (*Trumpets* 46–48) and "The Good Liar Meets His Executioners" (*Imagine the Angels* 82–85). "The Fugitive Poets of Fenway Park" (*Imagine the Angels* 79–81) is about Neruda; see Longo ("Post Wonder Bread") on this poem. *The Republic of Poetry* was one of three finalists for the Pulitzer Prize.

18. Bolaño also admired Cardenal. "In 1973," he wrote, "any twenty-year-old who wanted to be a poet read Ernesto Cardenal" (*Between Parentheses* 181).

19. On Zurita and Neruda, see Kuhnheim (80). Also see Rowe (281–326). Bolaño writes that Zurita "stands out among his generation" but dislikes "his eschatology and messianism" (*Between Parentheses* 96).

20. Recurrent images of vision in "Not Here" allude to Zurita's attempted self-blinding. On Zurita's torture, see *Purgatory* and Kuhnheim (72–74).

21. After September 11, 2001, Derksen similarly notes, "poetry was being shaped in the same manner as a [US] citizen": inward looking, private, and isolated (66).

22. Pérez-Torres likewise interprets the disembodied power of the Texas Rangers in Jimmy Santiago Baca's "*Mi Tío Baca el Poeta de Socorro*" (*Black Mesa* 73–75) (*Movements* 81).

23. Zurita and Eltit were once married, and he dedicates *Purgatory* to her (5).

24. See Allende's "Last Words Transmitted."

25. Dorfman's poem "Cost of Living" (*Last Waltz* 33–34) addresses the assassination and is dedicated to Letelier's widow.

26. These lines echo William Carlos Williams on "get[ting] the news from poems" (318).

Chapter 4

1. For instance, the film *María Full of Grace* depicts a drug mule's trip to Queens.

2. The Mexican philosopher O'Gorman's *Invention of America* developed the idea of "invention."

3. Some writers conclude that Appalachia is "a territory only of the mind" (Williams 9). For example, see Batteau.

4. Two stereotypes emerged in the 1960s: the mountaineer ("noble," "independent") and hillbilly ("amusing," "threatening," "devian[t]," "aberra[nt]") (Williams 17).

5. See Harvey (*Brief History* 27–28) and Grandin (51) on the roots of "the new imperialism" in Nicaragua in the 1930s and again in the 1980s and Harvey on "accumulation by dispossession" (*Spaces of Global Capitalism* 41–50; *New Imperialism* ch. 4).

6. The Alliance for Appalachia first used the phrase in the 1970s.

7. I follow the ARC and Williams (12–13) in including western Pennsylvania and northern Alabama in Appalachia proper. In Dalton, Georgia, "the carpet capital of the world," the labor force is now 40 percent Latino, and Mexican immigrants have "transformed Dalton's social and spatial boundaries" (Zúñiga and Hernández-León, "Dalton Story" 34, 42).

8. Villatoro's name combines the earliest Scots-Irish and the latest Latino arrivals. Villatoro was Mark McPeek growing up in Tennessee but Marcos McPeek when visiting Salvadoran family in California. He began using both in Guatemala in the 1980s: "Since then it's been Marcos McPeek Villatoro, an obvious adherence to the Latino roots without forgetting the Appalachian" (Minick 211).

9. *Autobiography* was nominated for the Pulitzer and the National Book Critics Circle Award.

10. His poems frequently allude to Colombian history. Three additional examples are "The Easter Revolt Painted on a Tablespoon" (*Poems* 55), "El 9 de abril" (*Autobiography* 15), which examines 1948's infamous "Bogotazo," and "Hector the Colombian Who Butchered the Hair of Juan Ramón" (*Poema* 51–52).

11. Stavans calls magic realism "eminently marketable" in the United States (14–15). See Faris and Zamora, who reprint Franz Roh's and Alejo Carpentier's original formulations of "magical realism" and "the marvelous real," respectively.

12. Also see Kilwein Guevara's "The Yellow Borges: An Answer to a Question" (*Poems* 42).

13. For instance, see the Cuban American poet Virgil Suárez's reinscription of archetypal figures of marginality in Latin American and Caribbean studies. The Prospero/Caliban pairing appears in "*La tempestad de las palabras blancas*" and in "Prospero in Havana" (83, 86).

14. Baca's "El Pablo" is another Latino portrait of a janitor (*Martín & Meditations* 72–73).

15. Other recent collections I would put in this category include Eduardo C. Corral's *Slow Lightning*, which won the Yale Series of Younger Poets award in 2011; J. Michael Martinez's *Heredities*, which won the Walt Whitman award in 2009; Valerie Martínez's *Each and Her*; and Urayoán Noel's *Hi-Density Politics*. These collections differ dramatically in their poetics.

16. Publications include a novel of El Salvador (*A Fire in the Earth*); a memoir of his time in Guatemala (*Walking to La Milpa*); and three crime novels. Villatoro worked as an activist in Nicaragua during the Contra-Sandinista war and has received awards for his National Public Radio commentaries.

17. These quotes are drawn from Minick; Villatoro's website, http://www.marcos villatoro.net/; his "In Search of Literary *Cojones*" (171); and the contributors' notes in Longo's *Pablo Neruda and the U.S. Culture Industry* (225).

18. Francisco X. Alarcón is one of the leading poets in this category. His selected poems, the bilingual collection *From the Other Side of Night*, features translations by Francisco Aragón. See also Ana Castillo's *My Father Was a Toltec*, Huerta's *Some Clarifications*, and Pérez Firmat's *Bilingual Blues*.

19. For further discussion of the cover, see my *American Political Poetry* (123–124, 147–148).

20. Whereas Espada and Villatoro reference Latin American historical and literary geographies, Aragón's text is set in Spain (although he too refers to Latin American icons such as Darío), where he creates bridges between Latino and peninsular Spanish dialects. Aragón also echoes Pacheco's language of "approximations" and "versions" rather than "translations."

21. See the cover jackets of *Alabanza* and *The Republic of Poetry*.

22. I prefer the term *autorretrato* (self-portrait) to *testimonio* here because it emphasizes artifice in depicting individual experience. See Gugelberger on testimonial discourse.

23. See Preston for background on H.B. 56.

24. The four groups are institutionalized in the first *Norton Anthology of Latino Literature*, edited by Stavans. Of 126 writers included in the post-1946 period, the vast majority is from these groups, with the outliers exiles such as Dorfman, Isabel Allende (Chile), and Daniel Alarcón (Peru). In "What Was Latino Literature?" Gruesz critiques the anthology's (mis)constructions of Latino literary history, periodization, and canon formation.

25. The Affrilachian Poets were founded by Frank X Walker to bring visibility to African American cultures in Appalachia. See his collection *Affrilachia*.

26. On formal Latino poetry, see Aragón (Introduction). For two examples, see Kilwein Guevara's villanelle "Ohiopyle Unrhymed" (*Poems* 48) and Villatoro's sestina "On Tuesday, When the Homeless Disappeared" (*On Tuesday* 7–8).

Chapter 5

1. *L'il Abner* ran from 1934 to 1977. See Flores (224–225) and LULAC's Regla Gonzalez on Feder.

2. Flores notes that Puerto Ricans are often "the 'exception'" to assimilation discourses (8).

3. "Cultural nationalism, involving the preeminence of culture to the maintenance of Puerto Rican identity," Dávila writes, "continues to be a binding force uniting Puerto Ricans from the island and the U.S." (80–81).

4. It is partly for this reason that Espada embraces "Nuyorican" hesitantly, distancing himself from the performative aspects of Nuyorican poetry while maintaining the identity as a point of pride and struggle. See *Lover of a Subversive* (75) and Pérez-Erdelyi (84–85). Salgado writes that Espada "avoids compulsive 'Spanglish' wordplay" (205), a cranky view of Nuyorican and Chicano poetics that dismisses the elegant, groundbreaking dimensions of word play. *Broken Souths* largely brackets discussion of the performative aspects of Latino poetics. See *Aloud: Voices from the Nuyorican Poets*

Café, the anthology edited by Miguel Algarín and Bob Holman, published in 1994, before the shift I have identified here. Also see Noel's creative and critical work for in-depth examinations of performativity in Latino poetry.

5. Although he published his first book in 1991, at fifty-seven, Agüeros had long been a public figure, including as executive director of El Museo del Barrio (1977–1986). He was recently diagnosed with Alzheimer's disease. See Espada's essay "Blessed Be the Truth-Tellers" (*Lover of a Subversive* 32–49) and the eponymous poem (*Trouble Ball* 18–19).

6. Espada's "Jim Crow" figure joins African American, Latino, and Latin American historical geographies. Cruz's "The Lower East Side of Manhattan" begins with a similar allusion to "Ricans and Afros" (*Panoramas* 28). See Dávila on the "emergent category" "Black Latino" (77) and John Murillo's collection *Up Jump the Boogie*, which melds African American and Chicano poetic traditions. The "Mexican" restaurant is a service industry iteration of what Dávila calls "marketable ethnicity" (10–11), whereby diluted forms of ethnic difference are used to market real estate as authentically multicultural.

7. For more on the here/there relationship see Márquez (Introduction xxxvi) and Edrik López (211). "The Latin Deli" reinforces the claim that "geographic separation and distance, rather than deadening all sense of community and cultural origins, may have the contrary effect of heightening the collective awareness of belonging," as Flores writes (52).

8. See Munck on consumption in neoliberalism (65–66).

9. See Dalleo and Machado Sáez on this aspect of Stavans's thought (5–7, 108–110). It is interesting to note that Stavans solicited Espada's papers for the archive at Amherst College.

10. Scholarship on Cruz focuses on his poetry. See Aparicio ("*Salsa, Maracas,* and *Baile*"); Esterrich; Gruesz ("Walt Whitman"); Noel ("Bodies That Antimatter"); and my "Post-1952 Puerto Rican Poetry" and "Spaces for Congregation."

11. Cruz's essay also provides an index to a shifting terminology: Cruz's "Hispanic" here is exclusively "Latino" in *Panoramas*, six years later. Its inclusion in the *Norton Anthology of Postmodern American Poetry* often seems to burden the essay with being *the* Latino perspective on postmodernist poetics. Like Martí's *crónicas*, Cruz's essays triangulate New York, the Caribbean, and Latin America but largely eschew Martí's direct political engagement.

12. Noel remarks similarly about "Seeds," a section of poems about artists in Cruz's *Maraca*: "What all these figures share is a genius fueled by displacement and a willingness to engage with and respond to the dislocations of the self in the world" (859).

13. For example, see "Mountain Building" (*Maraca* 121–122).

14. Baldrich and Quintero-Rivera historicize the tabaqueros' tradition of dissent, emergence from artisan guilds, and transition to a broader working-class consciousness.

15. See Aparicio ("*Salsa, Maracas,* and *Baile*") on musical forms in Cruz's poetry.

16. See Márquez on this paradoxical crisscrossing ("Sojourners" 105–106) and Flores on migration and class (178–179).

17. Also of interest here is Cruz's poem "An Essay on William Carlos Williams" (*Red Beans* 52).

18. Caplan does not attend to Campo's Cuban/Latino identity, as if to imply that the sonnet may be queered but not Latino. He also uses Borges to reframe polarized

debates on conventional and experimental forms, pointing out that the "exemplar of postmodernity" wrote sonnets, prose poems, and free verse. Caplan's conclusion — "contemporary poetry demands the catholicity that Borges advocates" (5–6) — is useful for mapping Latino poetry's plural forms, but his "postmodernist" Borges erases Argentine and Latin American contexts. See de la Campa on this type of erasure (*Latin Americanism* 34).

19. Espada continues, "The physical landscape resembles the literary landscape: there is not a single statue of a Puerto Rican in the city of New York" (46). See Flores for more on the issue of cultural capital (178–180, 184).

20. The name "Plaza" ultimately redirects the iconic Latin American public space from civic participation to consumption, a shift also apparent in "plaza" as a term for drug turf. See my "Spaces for Congregation," Ortiz-Negrón's qualified defense of consumption at Plaza Las Américas, and Kuhnheim on the mall in Latin American cultural studies (73).

21. Cofer's "Idea of Islands" provides an alternate perspective.

22. For other mappings of Puerto Rican poetry, see López Adorno's "Making the Decolonized Visible" and Márquez's centuries-spanning anthology *Puerto Rican Poetry*. Also see Noel's *Kool Logic* and *Hi-Density Politics* and Girmay's *Kingdom Animalia*.

Chapter 6

1. Mexico City's population growth has slowed in recent years. See Davis's *Planet of Slums* on this "polarization reversal" (2 n. 6), neoliberal-era urbanization, and rural-to-urban migration (1–11).

2. For more localized Latino views, see Gary Soto's "*Chisme* at Rivera's Studio" (152–153) and Kilwein Guevara's "Make-up" (*Poems* 43), set respectively in San Ángel and Coyoacán, two wealthy colonial neighborhoods in the south of the city.

3. García Canclini sardonically calls Los Angeles "the third-largest Mexican city" ("From National Capital" 211–212).

4. Mexico City's air was the world's worst in the 1980s; it has improved greatly since. See Cave for details ("Lush Walls"). See Cooper Alarcón on Chicano, Anglo-American, and touristic literary constructions of Mexico and Weinberger on US writers in Mexico.

5. Nezahualcoyotl, Chalco, Iztapalapa, and Chimalhuacan together comprise a slum of four million residents (Davis, *Planet of Slums* 28).

6. Mexico City has been declared a "'city of refuge' for persecuted writers" (García Canclini, "From National Capital" 212). Bolaño's poem "Visit to the Convalescent" (*Romantic Dogs* 57–63) praises this quality.

7. The city is officially México, DF. The Federal District comprises the city's core. The larger city, the Área Metropolitana, encompasses hundreds of square miles of old villages and new suburbs. The wider area is commonly referred to as "DF." My "Mexico City" refers to the expansive whole. See Guillermo Samperio's brilliant prose poem "DFS."

8. On the Latin American city as a text, see Read's "Obverse Colonization" and Holmes's introduction to *City Fictions* (13–32), which examines "ruptures" in urban

texts. Aguilar describes Mexico City's "urban peripher[ies]" as "polycentric islands" and "expanded fringes" that comprise a "new form of city expansion" "incorporat[ing] small towns and rural peripheries into a wider and more complex metropolitan system" (133–134). Given this disconnection and isolation, García Canclini wonders whether "we will be able to narrate the city again" and concludes "that the city today cannot be narrated, described, or explained as it might have been at the beginning of the century" (*Consumers* 85, 81). Yet the massive and complex must be imagined. Heise argues that a global environmental imaginary confronts problems on their proper scales; the same is true for the megacity, understood in diachronic, multivalent relation to its parts. García Canclini also brackets the dispossessions of the early twentieth century, when poor and indigenous people were removed from the center and placed into slums to build the new art deco *colonias*. By 1910, the city "had acquired the principal geographic feature that defines it to this day—a division into a rich west and a poor east" (Johns 4–5). This spatialization has been complicated by the integration of outlying villages (i.e., Coyoacán and Tlalpan) and the growth of slums, informal settlements, and *fraccionamientos* (tract housing developments).

9. See, for example, Josué Ramírez's long poem "Tepozán" (in *Los párpados narcóticos*), which ranges from Chapultepec Park to Ciudad Universitaria, the sprawling campus of the National Autonomous University of Mexico (UNAM).

10. Yaeger also emphasizes the presence of ruins in the urban imaginary. Ruins define Pacheco's poetry. See Lazzara and Unruh; Messinger Cypess; and Herrera's poem "Will You Visit the Rubble Museum" (*Half of the World* 268).

11. García Canclini adds that a collective sense of *the* city as a whole emerged after the 1985 earthquake (*Consumers* 56, 58, 63). Pacheco's elegy for the victims, *I Watch the Earth*, links the conquest (and the draining of the city's lakes) to neoliberal restructuring via the concept of debt: "We dried up all the city's water, destroyed / the fields and trees *with usury*" (*City of Memory* 123). Pacheco believes we have taken out loans on nature—our primary means of sustenance—that we can never repay.

12. More than 50 percent of the Mexico City population was born elsewhere in Mexico, and 20 percent "regularly leave" on weekends (García Canclini, *Consumers* 68, 52). These facts further erode the city-country divide prominent to literary-historical representations. Angel Rama writes that Latin American cultural production was shaped post-conquest by Spain's opposition to "all local expressions of particularity, imagination, or invention," many of which were rural (10).

13. Phrases like "esta inmensa zona de desastre que es México" [this immense disaster zone that is Mexico City] (*Tarde o temprano* 299) are common in Pacheco. Also see "Bend in the Ajusco Mountain" (*City of Memory* 45) and my "Of the Smog." In this section, I develop an infrastructural dimension of Pacheco's "environmentalist consciousness" (Doudoroff 268), "ecoliterature" and "environmental dystopia" (DeGrave 89, 94), and ethical-environmental commitment ["poética de compromiso ético-ambientalista"] (Graniela 73–74). Graniela writes that his poems reject nature as a contemplative device (77). In Pacheco's poetry nature is an "active agent" with its "own voice and ethical position," as Scigaj says of ecopoetics (10).

14. "Hirsuta arrogancia." With no extant English translation available, all translations of "Mercado libre" are mine.

15. "Su ilimitada cópula diversa"; "mano de hierro con que mantiene el terror / en el fugaz gallinero"; "creer que él no lo sabe, no está consciente / de su lugar de peón en

el siniestro ajedrez, / simple engranaje en la cadena infinita / que proporciona huevos para el desayuno // y Kentucky Fried Chicken."

16. *An Ark for the Next Millennium* collects Pacheco's animal poems. Graniela claims that they elevate the animal world over human culture (75), which minimizes their allegorical dimensions. Two of his finest animal poems, "Sea Snail" and "A Dog's Life," appear in the later *City of Memory* (3, 25).

17. See http://www.kfc.com.mx/ and http://www.df.gob.mx/index.jsp.

18. "Fugaz gallinero"; "estación de paso"; "como la tierra misma en que se encuentra alojado."

19. "En las casas antiguas de esta ciudad las llaves del agua / tienen un orden diferente." With no extant English translation available, all translations of "'H&C'" are mine. Unless specified otherwise, in Pacheco's poetry "this city" is Mexico City.

20. "Prólogo"; "Antigüedades Mexicanas"; "Escenas del invierno en Canadá"; "Habla común"; "Especies en peligro (y otras víctimas)."

21. On recent water problems, see Romero and Enciso. For historical contexts, see Miller (18–23, 70–76).

22. "Para no hablar de lo más obvio: / Cómo el imperio nos exporta un mundo / que aún no sabemos manejar ni entender."

23. "Qué conclusiones extraer de todo esto? / Nada es lo que parece."

24. "Todo acto es traducción"; "progreso bicéfalo"; "creador / y destructor al mismo tiempo."

25. "No es fácil renunciar"; "privilegio"; "código"; "sin este código / se escaldará quien busque / bajo C el agua fría."

26. Dean critiques "the neoliberal fantasy" that everyone "wins" with free trade (49–74).

27. "Nadie que ya disfrute el privilegio / (tener agua caliente es privilegio) / se pondrá a cavar pozos, a extraer / aguas contaminadas de un arroyo."

28. "Entre objeto y palabra cae la sombra."

29. "Los años pasarán sin que se entibie / la que mana de *H*."

30. "Monumento / a la belleza del mundo"; "nos dejó respirar"; "la innoble y letal colonia / penitenciaria." My translations.

31. Pacheco's "Ciudades," part of a series of epigrams titled "Sentido contrario" [Contrary Sense], sees cities as spaces of destruction that paradoxically make "civilization" (*Tarde o temprano* 221).

32. See Constable and Valenzuela on the Chilean case (148–149, 238).

33. Bolaño's novel *Distant Star* revisits Hoffman, known alternately as Carlos Weider and Alberto Ruiz-Tagle.

34. Streets are touchstones in countless Mexico City poems. Two representative ones are Roberto Arizmendi's "Las calles de la ciudad" and Huerta's "Calle de Amsterdam."

35. Son of the iconic poet Efraín Huerta, Huerta is usually read as a Mexican Neobaroque poet (along with Coral Bracho and others) and through North American Language poetry. See Haladyna and Kuhnheim, who cleverly position the Neobaroque against neoliberal instrumentality (115–144). Unlike many of his other poems, the direct, accessible narrative of "Song of Money" is ill-fitting within these theoretical readings.

Coda

1. "Geographies of danger" is the term of Sergio González, one of the foremost authorities on the femicide (Rodríguez, *Liberalism* 178).

2. See Volk and Schlotterbeck's useful list of border studies texts (148 n. 11).

3. See Cave's report on this inverse relation ("Bridging a Gap").

4. A "side effect" of *maquila* governmentality, Ileana Rodríguez writes, is "the destruction of bodies, be it in the form of lowering costs of production or in the direct killing of women" (195).

5. On Chomsky's speech, see Cristina Rodríguez. Also see Chomsky's "Notes on NAFTA."

6. For statistics, see Bowden (*Murder City* 166); "Durante 2010"; and Volk and Schlotterbeck (147–148 n. 2). On femicide in relation to the broader violence, see Gaspar de Alba ("*Feminicidio*" 1, 19 n. 1; "Poor Brown Female" 85) and Volk and Schlotterbeck (131).

7. *Each and Her* was nominated for the Pulitzer Prize and National Book Award.

8. See Louis's superb collection about Pine Ridge, *Ceremonies of the Damned*.

9. A useful appendix of books, films, and songs about the femicide appears in Gaspar de Alba's *Making a Killing* (298–300). Also see Fregoso and Bejarano, who expand the lens on femicide throughout the Americas, and Herrera on El Paso/Juárez ("Vulture Road") and the femicide ("Señorita X: Song for the Yellow-Robed Girl from Juárez"), both in *187 Reasons* (71, 76).

10. See the anthologies *El Coro* (ed. Espada); *Paper Dance* (ed. Cruz, Quintana, and Suárez); and *After Aztlán* and *Touching the Fire* (both ed. Gonzalez). Aragón's introduction deftly negotiates the canon of Latino poetry as it has been established by these anthologies.

11. Agosín calls herself a Latin American of the "generation of 'disenchantment,'" which includes those born between 1945 and 1955, like Bolaño and Zurita ("How to Speak" 214).

12. Agosín alternately describes witness as her "vocation" and "obsession" ("How to Speak" 219–220).

13. Like *Circles of Madness*, mothers haunt *Secrets in the Sand*, ending as a "mother wails" (129).

14. See Ileana Rodríguez on Monsiváis (177). One of many theories about the femicide's perpetrators centers on bus drivers.

Bibliography

Adams, Rachel. *Continental Divides: Remapping the Cultures of North America*. Chicago: U of Chicago P, 2009.

Adamson, Joni, and Scott Slovic, eds. *Ethnicity and Ecocriticism*. Spec. issue of *MELUS* 34.2 (2009).

Adorno, Theodor. *Minima Moralia: Reflections on a Damaged Life*. Trans. E. F. N. Jephcott. New York: Verso, 2006.

——. *Notes to Literature*. Vol. 1. Trans. Shierry Weber Nicholsen. New York: Columbia UP, 1991.

Agosín, Marjorie. *Circles of Madness: Mothers of the Plaza de Mayo* [*Círculos de locura: Madres de la Plaza de Mayo*]. Trans. Celeste Kostopulos-Cooperman. Fredonia: White Pine P, 1992.

——. "How to Speak with the Dead? A Poet's Notebook." *Human Rights Quarterly* 16.1 (1994): 214–223.

——. Introduction. Agosín 21–31.

——. *Secrets in the Sand: The Young Women of Juárez*. Trans. Celeste Kostopulos-Cooperman. Buffalo: White Pine P, 2006.

——, ed. *These Are Not Sweet Girls: Poetry By Latin American Women*. Trans. Chris Allen et al. Fredonia: White Pine P, 1994.

Agüeros, Jack. *Sonnets from the Puerto Rican*. Brooklyn: Hanging Loose P, 1996.

Aguilar, Adrian Guillermo. "Peri-Urbanization, Illegal Settlements and Environmental Impact in Mexico City." *Cities* 25.3 (2008): 133–145.

Aguilera, Pilar, and Ricardo Fredes, eds. *Chile: The Other September 11*. New York: Ocean P, 2006.

Alarcón, Francisco X. *From the Other Side of Night/Del otro lado de la noche: New and Selected Poems*. Trans. Francisco Aragón. Tucson: U of Arizona P, 2002.

Alexander, Michelle. *The New Jim Crow: Mass Incarceration in the Age of Colorblindness*. Rev. ed. New York: New P, 2012.

Algarín, Miguel, and Bob Holman, eds. *Aloud: Voices from the Nuyorican Poets Cafe*. New York: Holt, 1994.

Allende, Salvador. "Last Words Transmitted by Radio Magallanes, September 11, 1973." Aguilera and Fredes 8–11.

Anaya, Rudolfo. *Bless Me, Última*. New York: Warner Books, 1972.

Anderson, Benedict. *Imagined Communities: Reflections on the Origin and Spread of Nationalism*. 1983. New York: Verso, 2006.

249

Anglin, Mary K. "Lessons from Appalachia in the 20th Century: Poverty, Power, and the 'Grassroots.'" *American Anthropologist* 104.2 (2002): 565–582.

Anzaldúa, Gloria. *Borderlands/La Frontera: The New Mestiza.* 1987. 3rd ed. San Francisco: Aunt Lute Books, 2007.

Aparicio, Frances. "Reading the 'Latino' in Latino Studies: Toward Reimagining Our Academic Location." *Discourse: Studies in Media and Culture* 21.3 (1999): 3–18.

———. "(Re)constructing Latinidad: The Challenge of Latina/o Studies." Flores and Rosaldo 39–48.

———. "*Salsa, Maracas,* and *Baile*: Latin Popular Music in the Poetry of Victor Hernández Cruz." *MELUS* 16.1 (1989–1990): 43–58.

Aparicio, Frances R., and Susana Chávez-Silverman. *Tropicalizations: Transcultural Representations of Latinidad.* Hanover: Dartmouth UP, 1997.

Apter, Maxwell Simon. "The Winter of Our Discontent." *Virginia Quarterly Review* 85.4 (2009): 11–12.

Aragón, Francisco. Introduction. Aragón 1–10.

———. *Puerta del Sol.* Tempe: Bilingual P, 2005.

———, ed. *The Wind Shifts: New Latino Poetry.* Tucson: U of Arizona P, 2007.

Arias, Santa. "Inside the Worlds of Latino Traveling Cultures: Martín Espada's Poetry of Rebellion." *Bilingual Review* 21.3 (1996): 231–240.

Arizmendi, Roberto. "Las calles de la ciudad." Carreto 184–186.

Augé, Marc. *Non-Places: Introduction to an Anthropology of Supermodernity.* 1992. Trans. John Howe. New York: Verso, 1995.

Baca, Jimmy Santiago. *Black Mesa Poems.* New York: New Directions, 1989.

———. *Martín & Meditations on the South Valley.* New York: New Directions, 1987.

Bachelard, Gaston. *The Poetics of Space.* 1958. Trans. Maria Jolas. Boston: Beacon P, 1994.

Badiou, Alain. *The Communist Hypothesis.* 2008. Trans. David Macey and Steve Corcoran. Brooklyn: Verso, 2010.

Baldrich, Juan José. "From Handcrafted Tobacco Rolls to Machine-Made Cigarettes: The Transformation and Americanization of Puerto Rican Tobacco, 1847–1903." *CENTRO Journal* 17.2 (2005): 144–169.

Bañuelos, Juan. *Donde muere la lluvia: Antología poética.* Ed. Marco Antonio Campos. Guadalajara: Editorial Luvina, 1992.

Barcus, Holly R. "The Emergence of New Hispanic Settlement Patterns in Appalachia." *Professional Geographer* 59.3 (2007): 298–315.

Basso, Keith. *Wisdom Sits in Places: Landscape and Language Among the Western Apache.* Albuquerque: U of New Mexico P, 1996.

Batteau, Allen W. *The Invention of Appalachia.* Tucson: U of Arizona P, 1990.

Beaubien, Jason. "Business Booms on Mexican Border Despite Violence." *Morning Edition.* National Public Radio, 4 Aug. 2011. Web, 5 Aug. 2011.

Bell Lara, José, and Delia Luisa López. "The Harvest of Neoliberalism in Latin America." Dello Buono and Bell Lara 17–35.

Benjamin, Walter. *Illuminations.* 1955. Trans. Harry Zohn. New York: Schocken Books, 1969.

Berger, John. *The Shape of a Pocket.* New York: Vintage, 2001.

Berry, Wendell. *The Unsettling of America: Culture and Agriculture.* San Francisco: Sierra Club Books, 1996.

Beverley, John. *Against Literature*. Minneapolis: U of Minnesota P, 1993.

——. "Dos caminos para los estudios culturales centroamericanos (y algunas notas sobre el latinoamericanismo) después de '9/11.'" *Istmo: Revista Virtual de Estudios Literarios y Culturales Centroamericanos* 8 (2004): n. pag. Web, 29 Sept. 2010.

Blanchot, Maurice. *The Writing of the Disaster*. 1980. Trans. Ann Smock. Lincoln: U of Nebraska P, 1995.

Blanco, José Joaquín. "Tacubaya, 1978." Gallo 198–201.

Bolaño, Roberto. *2666*. Trans. Natasha Wimmer. New York: Farrar, Straus and Giroux, 2008.

——. *Amulet*. 1999. Trans. Chris Andrews. New York: New Directions, 2006.

——. *Between Parentheses: Essays, Articles, and Speeches, 1998–2003*. Ed. Ignacio Echevarría. Trans. Natasha Wimmer. New York: New Directions, 2011.

——. *By Night in Chile*. 2000. Trans. Chris Andrews. New York: New Directions, 2003.

——. *Distant Star*. 1996. Trans. Chris Andrews. New York: New Directions, 2004.

——. *Entre paréntesis: Ensayos, artículos y discursos (1998–2003)*. Ed. Ignacio Echevarría. Barcelona: Editorial Anagrama, 2004.

——. *Fragmentos de la universidad desconocida*. Toledo: Ayuntamiento de Talavera de la Reina, 1993.

——. "Godzilla in Mexico." Trans. Laura Healy. *Nation* 5 Nov. 2007, 42.

——. *Nazi Literature in the Americas*. 1996. Trans. Chris Andrews. New York: New Directions, 2008.

——. *The Romantic Dogs: Poems 1980–1998*. 2006. Trans. Laura Healy. New York: New Directions, 2008.

——. *The Savage Detectives*. 1998. Trans. Natasha Wimmer. New York: Picador, 2007.

——. *Tres*. 2000. Trans. Laura Healy. New York: New Directions, 2011.

Boltanski, Luc, and Eve Chiapello. *The New Spirit of Capitalism*. 1999. Trans. Gregory Elliott. New York: Verso, 2005.

Borges, Jorge Luis. *The Book of Imaginary Beings*. 1967. With Margarita Guerrero. Trans. Andrew Hurley. New York: Penguin, 2005.

——. *Selected Poems*. Trans. Willis Barnstone et al. Ed. Alexander Coleman. New York: Penguin, 1999.

Boullosa, Carmen. "Roberto Bolaño, Interview." *BOMB Magazine* 78 (2002): n. pag. Web, 1 Apr. 2010.

Bowden, Charles. *Juárez: The Laboratory of Our Future*. New York: Aperture, 1998.

——. *Murder City: Ciudad Juárez and the Global Economy's New Killing Fields*. New York: Nation Books, 2010.

Brady, Mary Pat. *Extinct Lands, Temporal Geographies: Chicana Literature and the Urgency of Space*. Durham: Duke UP, 2002.

Brown, Wendy. "Neoliberalism and the End of Liberal Democracy." *Edgework: Critical Essays on Knowledge and Politics*. Princeton: Princeton UP, 2005. 37–59.

Bruce-Novoa, Juan. *Chicano Poetry: A Response to Chaos*. Austin: U of Texas P, 1982.

Bryson, J. Scott. *The West Side of Any Mountain: Place, Space, and Ecopoetry*. Iowa City: U of Iowa P, 2005.

Burciaga, José Antonio. *Drink Cultura: Chicanismo*. Santa Barbara: Joshua Odell, 1993.

Burt, Stephen. "Punk Half Panther." Book review. *New York Times* 10 Aug. 2008. Web, 31 Aug. 2011.

Caballero, Juan Manuel López. *Alvaro Uribe: El Caballo de Troya del neoliberalismo.* Bogotá: Editorial Oveja Negra, 2009.

Campo, Rafael. *What the Body Told.* Durham: Duke UP, 1996.

Caplan, David. *Questions of Possibility: Contemporary Poetry and Poetic Form.* New York: Oxford UP, 2005.

Cardenal, Ernesto. *Cosmic Canticle.* 1989. Trans. John Lyons. Willimantic: Curbstone P, 1993.

——. *Pluriverse: New and Selected Poems.* Trans. Jonathan Cohen et al. Ed. Jonathan Cohen. New York: New Directions, 2009.

Carey, Elaine. *Plaza of Sacrifices: Gender, Power, and Terror in 1968 Mexico.* Albuquerque: U of New Mexico P, 2005.

Carpenter, Victoria. "The Echo of Tlatelolco in Contemporary Mexican Protest Poetry." *Bulletin of Latin American Research* 24.4 (2005): 496–512.

Carreto, Hector, ed. *La región menos transparente: Antología poética de la Ciudad de México.* Mexico City: Editorial Colibrí, 2003.

Carvalho, Edward J. *Puerto Rico Is in the Heart: Emigration, Labor, and Politics in the Life and Work of Frank Espada.* New York: Palgrave, 2013.

Carvalho, Edward J., and David B. Downing, eds. *Academic Freedom in the Post-9/11 Era.* New York: Palgrave, 2010.

Castells, Manuel. *The Power of Identity.* Vol. 2 of *The Information Age: Economy, Society and Culture.* Malden: Blackwell, 2004.

——. *The Rise of the Network Society.* Vol. 1 of *The Information Age: Economy, Society and Culture.* Malden: Blackwell, 2000.

Castillo, Ana. *My Father Was a Toltec and Selected Poems, 1973–1988.* New York: Anchor Books, 2004.

Castillo, Debra, and María Socorro Tabuenca Córdoba. *Border Women: Writing from La Frontera.* Minneapolis: U of Minnesota P, 2002.

Cave, Damien. "Bridging a Gap Between Fear and Peace." *New York Times* 14 Feb. 2011. Web, 16 Feb. 2011.

——. "Lush Walls Rise to Fight a Blanket of Pollution." *New York Times* 9 Apr. 2012. Web, 15 Aug. 2012.

Cepeda, María Elena. "El 'Beloved Spic' que no habla *English Only*: Oposición y resistencia en la poesía de Martín Espada." *Revista Canadiense de Estudios Hispánicos* 24.3 (2000): 517–529.

Chasteen, John Charles. Introduction. *The Lettered City.* By Angel Rama. Trans. John Charles Chasteen. Durham: Duke UP, 1996. vii–xiv.

Chavez, Leo R. *The Latino Threat: Constructing Immigrants, Citizens, and the Nation.* Stanford: Stanford UP, 2008.

Chomsky, Noam. "Notes on NAFTA: The Masters of Mankind." *Juárez: The Laboratory of Our Future.* By Charles Bowden. New York: Aperture, 1998. 13–20.

——. *Profit Over People: Neoliberalism and Global Order.* New York: Seven Stories P, 1999.

Clarke, Simon. "The Neoliberal Theory of Society." Saad-Filho and Johnston 50–59.

Clover, Joshua. "Autumn of the System: Poetry and Financial Capital." *JNT: Journal of Narrative Theory* 41.1 (2011): 34–52.

Cofer, Judith Ortiz. "The Idea of Islands." Márquez, *Puerto Rican Poetry* 449.

——. *The Latin Deli: Prose and Poetry.* New York: Norton, 1993.

Comaroff, Jean, and John L. Comaroff. "Millennial Capitalism: First Thoughts on a Second Coming." *Public Culture* 12.2 (2000): 293–343.

Concannon, Kevin, Francisco A. Lomelí, and Marc Priewe, eds. *Imagined Transnationalism: U.S. Latino/a Literature, Culture, and Identity.* New York: Palgrave, 2009.

———. Introduction. Concannon, Lomelí, and Priewe 1–12.

Constable, Pamela, and Arturo Valenzuela. *A Nation of Enemies: Chile under Pinochet.* New York: Norton, 1991.

Cooper Alarcón, Daniel. *The Aztec Palimpsest: Mexico in the Modern Imagination.* Tucson: U of Arizona P, 1997.

Corral, Eduardo C. *Slow Lightning.* New Haven: Yale UP, 2012.

Cross, Elsa. "The Lovers of Tlatelolco." Trans. Sheena Sood. *Connecting Lines: New Poetry from Mexico.* Ed. Luis Cortés Bargalló and Forrest Gander. Louisville: Sarabande Books, 2006. 7–9.

Cruz, Victor Hernández. *Maraca: New and Selected Poems, 1965–2000.* Minneapolis: Coffee House P, 2001.

———. *Panoramas.* Minneapolis: Coffee House P, 1997.

———. *Red Beans.* Minneapolis: Coffee House P, 1991.

Cruz, Victor Hernández, Leroy V. Quintana, and Virgil Suárez, eds. *Paper Dance: 55 Latino Poets.* New York: Persea Books, 1995.

Culler, Jonathan. "Why Lyric?" *PMLA* 123.1 (2008): 201–206.

Dalleo, Raphael, and Elena Machado Sáez. *The Latino/a Canon and the Emergence of Post-Sixties Literature.* New York: Palgrave, 2008.

Damon, Maria. "Avant-Garde or Borderguard: (Latino) Identity in Poetry." *American Literary History* 10.3 (1998): 478–496.

Darío, Rubén. *Stories and Poems/Cuentos y poesías: A Dual-Language Book.* Trans. and ed. Stanley Appelbaum. Mineola: Dover Publications, 2002.

Dávila, Arlene. *Barrio Dreams: Puerto Ricans, Latinos, and the Neoliberal City.* Berkeley: U of California P, 2004.

Davis, Diane E. *Urban Leviathan: Mexico City in the Twentieth Century.* Philadelphia: Temple UP, 1994.

Davis, Mike. *Magical Urbanism: Latinos Reinvent the U.S. City.* New York: Verso, 2000.

———. *Planet of Slums.* New York: Verso, 2006.

A Day Without a Mexican. Dir. Sergio Arau. Altavista Films/Televisa Cine, 2004. Film.

De Certeau, Michel. *The Practice of Everyday Life.* 1980. Trans. Steven Rendall. Berkeley: U of California P, 1988.

De la Campa, Román. "Foreword: Latinos and the Crossover Aesthetic." *Magical Urbanism.* By Mike Davis. New York: Verso, 2000. xi–xviii.

———. *Latin Americanism.* Minneapolis: U of Minnesota P, 1999.

———. "Latin, Latino, American: Split States and Global Imaginaries." *Comparative Literature* 53.4 (2001): 373–388.

———. "Latinas/os and Latin America: Topics, Destinies, Disciplines." Flores and Rosaldo 461–468.

De la Torre, Mónica. *Talk Shows.* Chicago: Switchback Books, 2006.

De la Torre, Mónica, and Michael Wiegers, eds. *Reversible Monuments: Contemporary Mexican Poetry.* Trans. Esther Allen et al. Port Townsend: Copper Canyon P, 2002.

Dean, Jodi. *Democracy and Other Neoliberal Fantasies: Communicative Capitalism and Left Politics.* Durham: Duke UP, 2009.

Dear, Michael, and Steven Flusty. "Postmodern Urbanism." *Annals of the Association of American Geographers* 88.1 (1998): 50–72.

DeGrave, Analisa. "Ecoliterature and Dystopia: Gardens and Topos in Modern Latin American Poetry." *Confluencia* 22.2 (2007): 89–104.

Dello Buono, Richard A., and José Bell Lara, eds. *Imperialism, Neoliberalism, and Social Struggles in Latin America.* Chicago: Haymarket, 2006.

——. "Neoliberalism and Resistance in Latin America." Dello Buono and Bell Lara 1–13.

Deltoro, Antonio. "Neighbors." Trans. Christian Viveros-Fauné. De la Torre and Wiegers 201–203.

Derksen, Jeff. *Annihilated Time: Poetry and Other Politics.* Vancouver: Talonbooks, 2009.

Derrida, Jacques. *Specters of Marx: The State of the Debt, the Work of Mourning and the New International.* Trans. Peggy Kamuf. New York: Routledge, 1994.

Dés, Mihály. "Entrevista a Roberto Bolaño." González Férriz 137–153.

Díaz-Quiñones, Arcadio. *La memoria rota: Ensayos sobre cultura y política.* Río Piedras: Ediciones Huracán, 1993.

Dirlik, Arif. "Place-Based Imagination: Globalism and the Politics of Place." *Places and Politics in an Age of Globalization.* Ed. Roxann Prazniak and Arif Dirlik. New York: Rowman and Littlefield, 2001. 15–51.

"Dismissed Official in Antipoverty Unit Continues His Fast." *New York Times* 30 June 1968. 55.

Docter, Mary. "José Emilio Pacheco: A Poetics of Reciprocity." *Hispanic Review* 70.3 (2002): 373–392.

Dorfman, Ariel. *Heading South, Looking North: A Bilingual Journey.* New York: Penguin, 1998.

——. "The Last September 11." Aguilera and Fredes 1–5.

——. *Last Waltz in Santiago and Other Poems of Exile and Disappearance.* Trans. Edith Grossman. New York: Viking, 1988.

Doudoroff, Michael J. "José Emilio Pacheco: An Overview of the Poetry, 1963–86." *Hispania* 72.2 (1989): 264–276.

Dowdy, Michael. *American Political Poetry into the Twenty-First Century.* New York: Palgrave, 2007.

——. "'Andando entre dos mundos': Towards an Appalachian Latino Literature." *Appalachian Journal* 39.3–4 (2012): 270–288.

——. "'A mountain / in my pocket': The Affective Spatial Imagination in Post-1952 Puerto Rican Poetry." *MELUS* 35.2 (2010): 41–67.

——. "'Of the smog': José Emilio Pacheco's Concussive Poetics of Mexico City." *Hispanic Review* 79.2 (2011): 291–316.

——. "Spaces for Congregation and Creative Play: Martín Espada's and Victor Hernández Cruz's Poetic Plazas." *College Literature* 37.2 (2010): 1–23.

Duany, Jorge. "Nation and Migration: Rethinking Puerto Rican Identity in a Transnational Context." Negrón-Muntaner 51–63.

Duménil, Gérard, and Dominique Lévy. "The Neoliberal (Counter-)Revolution." Saad-Filho and Johnston 9–19.

"Durante 2010 hubo 24 mil 374 homicidios en México: Inegi." *La Jornada* 28 July 2011. Web, 28 July 2011.

Eagleton, Terry. *Why Marx Was Right*. New Haven: Yale UP, 2011.

Eller, Ronald D. *Uneven Ground: Appalachia since 1945*. Lexington: UP of Kentucky, 2008.

Eltit, Diamela. "Public Domain." *PMLA* 124.5 (2009): 1800–1805.

Espada, Martín. *Alabanza: New and Selected Poems 1982–2002*. New York: Norton, 2003.

———. "Alabanza: New and Selected Poems, 1982–2002—New York Times Book Review and Letters 2003." N. pag. Box 2, Folder 48, Martín Espada Papers, Amherst College Archives and Special Collections, Amherst College Library.

———. "Bankruptcy and Foreclosure 1993." N. pag. Box 11, Folder 22, Martín Espada Papers.

———. "Cardenal, Ernesto—Introductions of at Smith and Hartford 1998–2002." N. pag. Box 9, Folder 20, Martín Espada Papers.

———. *City of Coughing and Dead Radiators*. New York: Norton, 1993.

———, ed. *El Coro: A Chorus of Latino and Latina Poets*. Amherst: U of Massachusetts P, 1997.

———. "Correspondence: Campo, Rafael 2002–2003." N. pag. Box 5, Folder 11, Martín Espada Papers.

———. "Correspondence: Louis, Adrian 1993–1996." N. pag. Box 5, Folder 39, Martín Espada Papers.

———. *Imagine the Angels of Bread*. New York: Norton, 1996.

———. *The Immigrant Iceboy's Bolero*. 1982. In *Trumpets from the Island of Their Eviction*. By Martín Espada. Tempe: Bilingual P, 1994. 69–100.

———. *The Lover of a Subversive Is Also a Subversive: Essays and Commentaries*. Ann Arbor: U of Michigan P, 2010.

———. *A Mayan Astronomer in Hell's Kitchen*. New York: Norton, 2000.

———. "Mexico—Mexico City and Guadalajara 2001." N. pag. Box 4, Folder 54, Martín Espada Papers.

———. "Mexico—'Sing Zapatista' (Poem) 2001–2002." N. pag. Box 4, Folder 55, Martín Espada Papers.

———. "The Poetics of Advocacy: Three Poems." *Hopscotch* 2.4 (2001): 128–133.

———, ed. *Poetry Like Bread: Poets of the Political Imagination from Curbstone Press*. 1994. Willimantic: Curbstone P, 2000.

———. *Rebellion Is the Circle of a Lover's Hands/Rebelión es el giro de manos del amante*. Trans. Camilo Pérez-Bustillo and Martín Espada. Willimantic: Curbstone P, 1990.

———. *The Republic of Poetry*. New York: Norton, 2006.

———. "'Taking Back the Street Corner': Interview with Martín Espada." Interview by Edward J. Carvalho. *Works and Days* 51/52, 53/54, vols. 26 and 27 (2008–2009): 539–550.

———. *The Trouble Ball*. New York: Norton, 2011.

———. *Trumpets from the Islands of Their Eviction*. 1987. Tempe: Bilingual P, 1994.

———. *Zapata's Disciple: Essays*. Cambridge: South End P, 1998.

Esterrich, Carmelo. "Home and the Ruins of Language: Victor Hernández Cruz and Miguel Algarín's Nuyorican Poetry." *MELUS* 23.3 (1998): 43–56.

Faris, Wendy B., and Lois Parkinson Zamora, eds. *Magical Realism: Theory, History, Community*. Durham: Duke UP, 1995.

Feder, Don. "No Statehood for Caribbean Dogpatch." *Boston Herald* 30 Nov. 1998. 27.

Fink, Thomas. "Visibility and History in the Poetry of Martín Espada." *Americas Review* 25 (1999): 202–221.

Finnegan, William. "Silver or Lead: A Drug Cartel's Reign of Terror." *New Yorker* 31 May 2010. 38–51.

Fish, Stanley. "The Value of Higher Education Made Literal." *New York Times* 13 Dec. 2010. Web, 13 Dec. 2010.

Flores, Juan. *From Bomba to Hip-Hop: Puerto Rican Culture and Latino Identity.* New York: Columbia UP, 2000.

Flores, Juan, and George Yúdice. "Living Borders/Buscando America: Languages of Latino Self-Formation." *Social Text* 24 (1990): 57–84.

Flores, Juan, and Renato Rosaldo, eds. *A Companion to Latina/o Studies.* Malden: Blackwell, 2007.

Flores, Lauro. "Auto/referencialidad y subversion: Observaciones (con)textuales sobre la poesía de Juan Felipe Herrera." *Crítica* 2.2 (1990): 172–181.

Foster, John Bellamy, Brett Clark, and Richard York. *The Ecological Rift: Capitalism's War on the Earth.* New York: Monthly Review P, 2010.

Fregoso, Rosa-Linda, and Cynthia Bejarano, eds. *Terrorizing Women: Feminicide in the Americas.* Durham: Duke UP, 2010.

Friedman, Milton. *Capitalism and Freedom.* 1962. Chicago: U of Chicago P, 2002.

Friedman, Thomas L. *The World Is Flat: A Brief History of the Twenty-First Century.* New York: Farrar, Straus and Giroux, 2005.

Friis, Ronald J. *José Emilio Pacheco and the Poets of the Shadows.* Lewisburg: Bucknell UP, 2001.

Fuentes, Carlos. *Where the Air Is Clear.* 1958. Trans. Sam Hileman. Chicago: Dalkey Archive P, 2004.

Fukuyama, Francis. *The End of History and the Last Man.* New York: Avon Books, 1992.

Fusco, Coco, and Guillermo Gómez-Peña. "Bilingualism, Biculturalism, and Borders." *English Is Broken Here: Notes on Cultural Fusion in the Americas.* New York: New P, 1995. 147–158.

———. "Nationalism and Latinos, North and South: A Dialogue." *English Is Broken Here: Notes on Cultural Fusion in the Americas.* New York: New P, 1995. 159–168.

Galeano, Eduardo. "To Be Like Them." *Juárez: The Laboratory of Our Future.* By Charles Bowden. New York: Aperture, 1998. 121–129.

Gallo, Rubén, ed. *The Mexico City Reader.* Trans. Lorna Scott Fox and Rubén Gallo. Madison: U of Wisconsin P, 2004.

Gander, Forrest. "Un Lio Bestial." *Nation* 31 Mar. 2008: 39–42.

García Canclini, Néstor. "A City That Improvises Its Globalization." Sommer 82–90.

———. *Consumers and Citizens: Globalization and Multicultural Conflicts.* 1995. Trans. George Yúdice. Minneapolis: U of Minnesota P, 2001.

———. "From National Capital to Global Capital: Urban Change in Mexico City." Trans. Paul Liffman. *Public Culture* 12.1 (2000): 207–213.

Gaspar de Alba, Alicia. *Desert Blood: The Juárez Murders.* Houston: Arte Público P, 2005.

———. "*Feminicidio*: The 'Black Legend' of the Border." Gaspar de Alba 1–21.

———, ed. *Making a Killing: Femicide, Free Trade, and La Frontera.* With Georgina Guzmán. Austin: U of Texas P, 2010.

———. "Poor Brown Female: The Miller's Compensation for 'Free' Trade." Gaspar de Alba 63–93.

Gibbons, Reginald. "Political Poetry and the Example of Ernesto Cardenal." *Critical Inquiry* 13.3 (1987): 648–671.

Girmay, Aracelis. *Kingdom Animalia*. Rochester: BOA Editions, 2011.

Giroux, Henry A. *Against the Terror of Neoliberalism: Politics Beyond the Age of Greed*. Boulder: Paradigm, 2008.

Goldman, Francisco. *The Long Night of White Chickens*. New York: Grove P, 1992.

Gonzalez, Ray, ed. *After Aztlán: Latino Poetry of the Nineties*. Boston: David R. Godine, 1992.

——. *Consideration of the Guitar: New and Selected Poems 1986–2005*. Rochester: BOA Editions, 2005.

——, ed. *Touching the Fire: Fifteen Poets of Today's Latino Renaissance*. New York: Doubleday, 1998.

Gonzalez, Regla. "Statement by Regla Gonzalez on Don Feder Article." *League of United Latin American Citizens*. LULAC, n.d. Web, 16 Aug. 2012.

González Férriz, Ramón, ed. *Jornadas homenaje Roberto Bolaño (1953–2003): Simposio internacional*. Barcelona: ICCI Casa Amèrica a Catalunya, 2005.

Gorman, Anna, Marjorie Miller, and Mitchell Landsberg. "Marchers fill L.A.'s streets." *Los Angeles Times* 2 May 2006. Web, 24 Aug. 2012.

Grandin, Greg. *Empire's Workshop: Latin America, the United States, and the Rise of the New Imperialism*. New York: Metropolitan, 2006.

Graniela, Magda. "José Emilio Pacheco: Una poética de ética ambientalista." *Atenea* 19.1–2 (1999): 69–78.

Gras, Dunia. "Roberto Bolaño y la obra total." González Férriz 51–73.

Grescoe, Taras. *Straphanger: Saving Our Cities and Ourselves from the Automobile*. New York: Times Books, 2012.

Grossman, Edith. *The Antipoetry of Nicanor Parra*. New York: New York UP, 1975.

Gruesz, Kirsten Silva. *Ambassadors of Culture: The Transamerican Origins of Latino Writing*. Princeton: Princeton UP, 2002.

——. "Walt Whitman, Latino Poet." *Walt Whitman, Where the Future Becomes Present*. Ed. David Haven Blake and Michael Robertson. Iowa City: U of Iowa P, 2008. 151–176.

——. "What Was Latino Literature?" *PMLA* 127.2 (2012): 335–341.

Gugelberger, Georg M. "Institutionalization of Transgression: Testimonial Discourse and Beyond." *The Real Thing: Testimonial Discourse and Latin America*. Ed. Georg M. Gugelberger. Durham: Duke UP, 1996. 1–19.

Haladyna, Ronald. *La contextualización de la poesía postmoderna mexicana: Pedro Salvador Ale, David Huerta y Coral Bracho*. Mexico City: Universidad Autónoma del Estado de México, 1999.

Hames-García, Michael. "Dr. Gonzo's Carnival: The Testimonial Satires of Oscar Zeta Acosta." *American Literature* 72.3 (2000): 463–493.

Harlow, Barbara. *Resistance Literature*. New York: Routledge, 1987.

Hart, Matthew, and Jim Hansen. Introduction. *Contemporary Literature and the State*. Ed. Matthew Hart and Jim Hansen. Spec. issue of *Contemporary Literature* 49.4 (2008): 491–513.

Harvey, David. "The Art of Rent: Globalization, Monopoly and the Commodification of Culture." *Socialist Register* (2002): 93–110.

——. *A Brief History of Neoliberalism*. New York: Oxford UP, 2005.

——. *The Condition of Postmodernity*. Cambridge: Blackwell, 1989.

——. *The Enigma of Capital and the Crises of Capitalism*. New York: Oxford UP, 2010.

——. *The New Imperialism*. New York: Oxford UP, 2003.

——. *Spaces of Global Capitalism*. New York: Verso, 2006.

——. *Spaces of Hope*. Berkeley: U of California P, 2000.

Hayden, Tom. "In Chiapas." Hayden 76–98.

——, ed. *The Zapatista Reader*. New York: Nation Books, 2002.

Hayden, Wilburn. "Appalachian Diversity: African-American, Hispanic/Latino, and Other Populations." *Journal of Appalachian Studies* 10.3 (2004): 293–306.

Hegel, Georg Wilhelm Friedrich. *The Philosophy of History*. 1822. Trans. J. Sibree. Kitchener: Batoche Books, 2001.

Heise, Ursula K. *Sense of Place and Sense of Planet: The Environmental Imagination of the Global*. New York: Oxford UP, 2008.

Hernández Navarro, Luis. "Mexico's Secret War." Hayden 61–68.

Herrera, Juan Felipe. *187 Reasons Mexicanos Can't Cross the Border: Undocuments 1971–2007*. San Francisco: City Lights, 2007.

——. "Foreword: The Sweet Vortex of Singers." Aragón xiii–xvii.

——. *Half of the World in Light: New and Selected Poems*. Tucson: U of Arizona P, 2008.

——. *Lotería Cards and Fortune Poems: A Book of Lives*. Linocuts by Artemio Rodríguez. San Francisco: City Lights, 1999.

——. *Mayan Drifter: Chicano Poet in the Lowlands of America*. Philadelphia: Temple UP, 1997.

——. *Night Train to Tuxtla*. Tucson: U of Arizona P, 1994.

——. *Notebooks of a Chile Verde Smuggler*. Tucson: U of Arizona P, 2002.

——. *Thunderweavers/Tejedoras de rayos*. Tucson: U of Arizona P, 2000.

Herrera-Sobek, María. "Transnational Migrations and Political Mobilizations: The Case of *A Day Without a Mexican*." Concannon, Lomelí, and Priewe 61–74.

Hitchcock, Peter. "They Must Be Represented? Problems in Theories of Working-Class Representation." *PMLA* 115.1 (2000): 20–32.

Holmes, Amanda. *City Fictions: Language, Body, and Spanish American Urban Space*. Lewisburg: Bucknell UP, 2007.

Hopenhayn, Martín. *No Apocalypse, No Integration: Modernism and Postmodernism in Latin America*. 1995. Trans. Cynthia Margarita Tompkins and Elizabeth Rosa Horan. Durham: Duke UP, 2001.

Huerta, David. *Before Saying Any of the Great Words: Selected Poems*. Trans. Mark Schafer. Port Townsend: Copper Canyon P, 2009.

——. "Calle de Amsterdam." Carreto 94.

Huerta, Javier O. *Some Clarifications y otros poemas*. Houston: Arte Público P, 2007.

Igoe, Jim, and Dan Brockington. "Neoliberal Conservation: A Brief Introduction." *Conservation and Society* 5.4 (2007): 432–449.

Jackson, Virginia. "Who Reads Poetry?" *PMLA* 123.1 (2008): 181–187.

Jameson, Fredric. *Postmodernism, or, the Cultural Logic of Late Capitalism*. Durham: Duke UP, 1991.

Johns, Michael. *The City of Mexico in the Age of Díaz*. Austin: U of Texas P, 1997.

Johnson, Mark. *The Meaning of the Body: Aesthetics of Human Understanding*. Chicago: U of Chicago P, 2007.

Judt, Tony. *Ill Fares the Land*. New York: Penguin, 2010.

Kaplan, Caren. *Questions of Travel: Postmodern Discourses of Displacement*. Durham: Duke UP, 1996.

Kerouac, Jack. *On the Road*. 1957. New York: Penguin, 1999.

Kilwein Guevara, Maurice. *Autobiography of So-and-so: Poems in Prose*. Kalamazoo: New Issues, 2001.

——. "Essay on MKG." Message to Michael Dowdy. 14 Apr. 2013. E-mail.

——. *Poema*. Tucson: U of Arizona P, 2009.

——. *Poems of the River Spirit*. Pittsburgh: U of Pittsburgh P, 1996.

——. *Postmortem*. Athens: U of Georgia P, 1994.

Klein, Naomi. *The Shock Doctrine: The Rise of Disaster Capitalism*. New York: Picador, 2007.

Kostopulos-Cooperman, Celeste. Preface. *Secrets in the Sand*. By Marjorie Agosín. Trans. Celeste Kostopulos-Cooperman. Buffalo: White Pine P, 2006. 13–21.

Kuhnheim, Jill S. *Spanish American Poetry at the End of the Twentieth Century: Textual Disruptions*. Austin: U of Texas P, 2004.

Larsen, Neil. *Reading North by South: On Latin American Literature, Culture, and Politics*. Minneapolis: U of Minnesota P, 1995.

Lazzara, Michael J., and Vicky Unruh, eds. *Telling Ruins in Latin America*. New York: Palgrave, 2009.

Lefebvre, Henri. *The Production of Space*. 1974. Trans. Donald Nicholson Smith. Malden: Blackwell, 1991.

——. *The Urban Revolution*. 1970. Trans. Robert Bononno. Minneapolis: U of Minnesota P, 2003.

Letelier, Orlando. "The 'Chicago Boys' in Chile: Economic 'Freedom's' Awful Toll." *Nation* 28 Aug. 1976: 137–142.

Levander, Caroline F., and Robert S. Levine, eds. *Hemispheric American Studies*. New Brunswick: Rutgers UP, 2008.

Levinson, Brett. "Dictatorship and Overexposure: Does Latin America Testify to More Than One Market?" *Discourse* 25 (2004): 98–118.

Libretti, Tim. "'A Broader and Wiser Revolution': Refiguring Chicano Nationalist Politics in Latin American Consciousness in Post-Movement Literature." Concannon, Lomelí, and Priewe 137–156.

Limón, Ada. *Lucky Wreck*. Pittsburgh: Autumn House P, 2006.

Limón, José E. *Mexican Ballads, Chicano Poems: History and Influence in Mexican-American Social Poetry*. Berkeley: U of California P, 1992.

Lomelí, Francisco A. "Foreword: Trajectory and Metamorphosis of a Chicano Poet Laureate." *Half of the World in Light*. By Juan Felipe Herrera. Tucson: U of Arizona P, 2008. xv–xxiv.

Longo, Teresa. Introduction. "Poetry Like Wonder Bread." Longo xv–xxvii.

——, ed. *Pablo Neruda and the U.S. Culture Industry*. New York: Routledge, 2002.

——. "A Poet's Place, 2004: From Machu Picchu to a Starbucks Parking Lot." *Crítica Hispánica* 28.1 (2006): 181–196. Web, http://tvlong.blogs.wm.edu/2008/12/15/poetry/. N. pag. 28 Sept. 2009.

——. "Post Wonder Bread: Pablo Neruda in Centerfield?" Longo 141–150.

López, Edrik. "Nuyorican Spaces: Mapping Identity in a Poetic Geography." *CENTRO Journal* 17.1 (2005): 203–219.

López, Marissa. *Chicano Nations: The Hemispheric Origins of Mexican American Literature.* New York: New York UP, 2011.

López Adorno, Pedro. "Making the Decolonized Visible: Puerto Rican Poetry of the Last Four Decades." *CENTRO Journal* 18.2 (2006): 4–23.

Louis, Adrian C. *Ceremonies of the Damned.* Reno: U of Nevada P, 1997.

Low, Setha M. *On the Plaza: The Politics of Public Space and Culture.* Austin: U of Texas P, 2000.

Luna, Sheryl. Poems. Aragón 162–170.

Marcos, Subcomandante. "The Word: The Writings of Insurgent Subcomandante Marcos and the EZLN." Hayden 205–315.

Maria Full of Grace/María eres de gracia. Dir. Joshua Marston. Fine Line Features, 2004. Film.

Márquez, Roberto. Introduction. Márquez, *Puerto Rican Poetry* xxv–xxxvii.

——, ed. *Latin American Revolutionary Poetry/Poesía revolucionaria latinoamericana.* New York: Monthly Review P, 1974.

——, ed. *Puerto Rican Poetry: A Selection from Aboriginal to Contemporary Times.* Amherst: U of Massachusetts P, 2007.

——. "Sojourners, Settlers, Castaways and Creators: A Recollection of Puerto Rico Past and Puerto Ricans Present." *Massachusetts Review* 36.1 (1995): 94–118.

Martinez, J. Michael. *Heredities.* Baton Rouge: Louisiana State UP, 2010.

Martinez, J. Michael, and Jordan Windholz. "A Poetics of Suspicion: Chicana/o Poetry and the New." *Puerto del Sol: A Journal of New Literature* 45.1 (2010): 75–84.

Martínez, Valerie. *Each and Her.* Tucson: U of Arizona P, 2010.

Marx, Karl. *Capital: Volume 1.* 1867. Trans. Ben Fowkes. New York: Penguin, 1990.

Massey, Doreen. *Space, Place, and Gender.* Minneapolis: U of Minnesota P, 1994.

Massumi, Brian. *Parables for the Virtual: Movement, Affect, Sensation.* Durham: Duke UP, 2002.

McChesney, Robert W. Introduction. *Profit Over People: Neoliberalism and Global Order.* By Noam Chomsky. New York: Seven Stories P, 1999. 7–16.

McClennen, Sophie A. "The Diasporic Subject in Ariel Dorfman's *Heading South, Looking North.*" *MELUS* 30.1 (2005): 169–188.

Meléndez, María. *How Long She'll Last in This World.* Tucson: U of Arizona P, 2006.

Messinger Cypess, Sandra. "Tlatelolco: From Ruins to Poetry." Lazzara and Unruh 163–174.

Mignolo, Walter D. *The Idea of Latin America.* Malden: Blackwell, 2005.

Miller, Shawn William. *An Environmental History of Latin America.* New York: Cambridge UP, 2007.

Mills, C. Wright. "Letter to the New Left." *New Left Review* 5 (1960). N. pag. *Marxists Internet Archive.* Web, 16 Apr. 2012.

Minick, Jim. "Latino Hillbilly: An Interview with Marcos McPeek Villatoro." *Appalachian Journal* 28.2 (2001): 204–220.

Mohl, Raymond A. "Globalization and Latin American Immigration in Alabama." Odem and Lacy 51–69.

Monsiváis, Carlos. *El 68: La tradición de la resistencia.* Mexico City: Ediciones Era, 2008.

——. "The Metro: A Voyage to the End of the Squeeze." Gallo 143–145.

Munck, Ronaldo. "Neoliberalism and Politics, and the Politics of Neoliberalism." Saad-Filho and Johnston 60–69.

Muñoz, Carlos, Jr. *Youth, Identity, Power: The Chicano Movement.* 1989. Rev. ed. New York: Verso, 2007.

Murillo, John. *Up Jump the Boogie.* New York: Cypher Books, 2010.

Nazario y Colón, Ricardo. *Of Jíbaros and Hillbillies.* Austin: Plain View P, 2010.

Negrón-Muntaner, Frances. Introduction. Negrón-Muntaner 1–17.

——, ed. *None of the Above: Puerto Ricans in the Global Era.* New York: Palgrave, 2007.

Neruda, Pablo. *Canto General.* 1950. Trans. Jack Schmitt. Berkeley: U of California P, 1991.

Noel, Urayoán. "Bodies That Antimatter: Locating U.S. Latino/a Poetry, 2000–2009." *Contemporary Literature* 52.4 (2011): 852–882.

——. *Hi-Density Politics.* Buffalo: BlazeVOX, 2010.

——. *Kool Logic/La Lógica Kool.* Tempe: Bilingual P, 2005.

Nowak, Mark. "Poetics Statement: Notes toward an Anti-Capitalist Poetics II." *American Poets in the 21st Century: The New Poetics.* Ed. Claudia Rankine and Lisa Sewell. Middletown: Wesleyan UP, 2007.

Oboler, Suzanne. *Ethnic Labels, Latino Lives: Identity and the Politics of (Re)Presentation in the United States.* Minneapolis: U of Minnesota P, 1995.

Odem, Mary E., and Elaine Lacy. Introduction. Odem and Lacy ix–xxvii.

——, eds. *Latino Immigrants and the Transformation of the U.S. South.* Athens: U of Georgia P, 2009.

O'Gorman, Edmundo. *The Invention of America: An Inquiry into the Historical Nature of the New World and the Meaning of Its History.* 1961. Westport: Greenwood P, 1972.

Oliva, Óscar. "At the Wheel of a Car, by the Pan-American Highway from Tuxtla to Mexico City." *The River Is Wide/El río es ancho: Twenty Mexican Poets, a Bilingual Anthology.* Ed. and trans. Marlon L. Fick. Albuquerque: U of New Mexico P, 2005. 285–295.

Oliver-Rotger, Maria Antònia. "Travel, Autoethnography, and Oppositional Consciousness in Juan Felipe Herrera's *Mayan Drifter.*" Concannon, Lomelí, and Priewe 171–200.

Ortiz-Negrón, Laura L. "Space out of Place: Consumer Culture in Puerto Rico." Negrón-Muntaner 39–50.

Pabón, Carlos. "The Political Status of Puerto Rico: A Nonsense Dilemma." Negrón-Muntaner 65–72.

Pacheco, José Emilio. *An Ark for the Next Millennium.* 1991. Trans. Margaret Sayers Peden. Austin: U of Texas P, 1993.

——. *City of Memory and Other Poems.* Trans. Cynthia Steele and David Lauer. San Francisco: City Lights, 1997.

——. *Don't Ask Me How the Time Goes By: Poems, 1964–1968.* 1969. Trans. Alastair Reid. New York: Columbia UP, 1978.

——. *Islas a la deriva.* 1976. Mexico City: Biblioteca Era, 2006.

——. *No me preguntes cómo pasa el tiempo.* Mexico City: Ediciones Era, 2010.

——. *Selected Poems.* Trans. Thomas Hoeksema et al. Ed. George McWhirter. New York: New Directions, 1987.

——. *Tarde o temprano [Poemas, 1958–2000].* Mexico City: Fondo de Cultura Económica, 2000.

Parra, Nicanor. *After-Dinner Declarations.* Trans. Dave Oliphant. New York: Host Publications, 2009.

——. *Antipoems: How to Look Better & Feel Great.* Trans. Liz Werner. New York: New Directions, 2004.

Pérez, Emmy. "Poems." Aragón 226–235.

Pérez-Bustillo, Camilo. "An Army of Ideas: Marginalisation, Indigenous Rights and Civil Society in Mexico since the Zapatista Rebellion." *Poverty and the Law.* Ed. Peter Robson and Asbjørn Kjønstad. Oxford: Hart, 2001. 175–188.

Pérez-Erdelyi, Mireya. Interview. "With Martín Espada." *Americas Review* 15.2 (1987): 77–85.

Pérez Firmat, Gustavo. *Bilingual Blues: Poems, 1981–1994.* Tempe: Bilingual P, 1995.

——, ed. *Do the Americas Have a Common Literature?* Durham: Duke UP, 1990.

——. "Introduction: Cheek to Cheek." Pérez Firmat 1–5.

——. *Life on the Hyphen: The Cuban-American Way.* Austin: U of Texas P, 1994.

Pérez-Torres, Rafael. "Ethnicity, Ethics, and Latino Aesthetics." *American Literary History* 12.3 (2000): 534–553.

——. *Movements in Chicano Poetry: Against Myths, Against Margins.* New York: Cambridge UP, 1995.

Pollack, Sarah. "Latin America Translated (Again): Roberto Bolaño's *The Savage Detectives* in the United States." *Comparative Literature* 61.3 (2009): 346–365.

Poniatowska, Elena. *Massacre in Mexico.* Trans. Helen R. Lane. Columbia: U of Missouri P, 1975.

Pratt, Mary Louise. *Imperial Eyes: Travel Writing and Transculturation.* New York: Routledge, 1992.

Preston, Julia. "In Alabama, a Harsh Bill for Residents Here Illegally." *New York Times* 4 June 2011. A10.

Quintero-Rivera, A. G. "Socialist and Cigarmaker: Artisans' Proletarianization in the Making of the Puerto Rican Working Class." *Latin American Perspectives* 10.2/3 (1983): 19–38.

Rabasa, José. "Of Zapatismo: Reflections on the Folkloric and the Impossible in a Subaltern Insurrection." *The Politics of Culture in the Shadow of Capital.* Ed. Lisa Lowe and David Lloyd. Durham: Duke UP, 1997. 399–431.

——. *Without History: Subaltern Studies, the Zapatista Insurgency, and the Specter of History.* Pittsburgh: U of Pittsburgh P, 2010.

Rama, Angel. *The Lettered City.* Trans. John Charles Chasteen. Durham: Duke UP, 1996.

Ramírez, Josué. *Los párpados narcóticos.* Mexico City: Fondo de Cultura Económica, 1999.

Read, Justin A. *Modern Poetics and Hemispheric American Cultural Studies.* New York: Palgrave, 2009.

——. "Obverse Colonization: São Paulo, Global Urbanization and the Poetics of the Latin American City." *Journal of Latin American Cultural Studies* 15.3 (2006): 281–300.

"Rejected in Tucson." Editorial. *New York Times* 21 Jan. 2012. Web, 21 Jan. 2012.

Ríos, Alberto. "Líneas fronterizas/Border Lines." *Virginia Quarterly Review* 83.2 (2007): 4–5.

Rivas, Marguerite Maria. "'Lengua, Cultura, Sangre': Song of the New Homeland." *Americas Review* 21.3–4 (1993): 150–162.

Rodriguez, Andres. "Contemporary Chicano Poetry: The Work of Michael Sierra, Juan Felipe Herrera and Luis J. Rodriguez." *Bilingual Review* 21.3 (1996): 203–218. *Academic Search Complete*. Web, N. pag. 10 Jan. 2012.

Rodríguez, Cristina. "Chomsky: TLC, más dañino que el colonialismo español." *La Jornada* 21 Sept. 2010. Web, 21 Sept. 2010.

Rodríguez, Ileana. *Liberalism at Its Limits: Crime and Terror in the Latin American Cultural Text*. Pittsburgh: U of Pittsburgh P, 2009.

Rodriguez, Teresa, Diana Montané, and Lisa Pulitzer. *The Daughters of Juarez: A True Story of Serial Murder South of the Border*. New York: Atria Books, 2007.

Romero, Gabriela, and Angélica Enciso. "Gobierno federal y GDF, en guerra de cifras por el agua." *La Jornada* 8 Apr. 2009. Web, 20 Apr. 2009.

Rosenthal, Anton. "Spectacle, Fear, and Protest: A Guide to the History of Urban Public Space in Latin America." *Social Science History* 24.1 (2000): 33–73.

Rowe, William. *Poets of Contemporary Latin America: History and the Inner Life*. New York: Oxford UP, 2000.

Rukeyser, Muriel. *The Collected Poems of Muriel Rukeyser*. New York: McGraw Hill, 1978.

Saad-Filho, Alfredo, and Deborah Johnston. Introduction. Saad-Filho and Johnston 1–6.

——, eds. *Neoliberalism: A Critical Reader*. London: Pluto P, 2005.

Saldaña-Portillo, María Josefina. "From the Borderlands to the Transnational? Critiquing Empire in the Twenty-First Century." Flores and Rosaldo 502–512.

Salgado, César A. "About Martín Espada." *Ploughshares* 31.1 (2005): 203–208.

Samperio, Guillermo. "DFS." Carreto 194.

Sandín, Lyn Di Iorio, and Richard Perez, eds. *Contemporary U.S. Latino/a Literary Criticism*. New York: Palgrave, 1997.

Sarlo, Beatriz. "Cultural Studies and Literary Criticism at the Cross-Roads of Value." *Contemporary Latin American Cultural Studies*. Ed. Stephen Hart and Richard Young. New York: Oxford UP, 2003. 24–36.

Sarmiento, Domingo Faustino. *Facundo: Civilization and Barbarism*. Trans. Kathleen Ross. Berkeley: U of California P, 2004.

Schumpeter, Joseph. *Capitalism, Socialism, and Democracy*. 1942. New York: Harper & Row, 1976.

Scigaj, Leonard M. *Sustainable Poetry: Four American Ecopoets*. Lexington: UP of Kentucky, 1999.

Sheridan, Guillermo. "Monuments." Gallo 149–151.

Shukla, Sandhya, and Heidi Tinsman, eds. *Imagining Our Americas: Toward a Transnational Frame*. Durham: Duke UP, 2007.

——. "Introduction: Across the Americas." Shukla and Tinsman 1–33.

Skinner, Jonathan. "Thoughts on Things: Poetics of the Third Landscape.")((Eco(lang) (uage (Reader)): The eco language reader*. Ed. Brenda Iijima. Brooklyn: Portable P/ Nightboat Books, 2010. 9–51.

Smith, Jon, and Deborah Cohn. "Introduction: Uncanny Hybridities." Smith and Cohn 1–19.

——, eds. *Look Away! The U.S. South in New World Studies*. Durham: Duke UP, 2004.

Smith, Neil. Foreword. *The Urban Revolution*. By Henri Lefebvre. Trans. Robert Bononno. Minneapolis: U of Minnesota P, 2003. vi–xxiii.

——. *Uneven Development: Nature, Capital, and the Production of Space*. 1984. Cambridge: Blackwell, 1990.

Smith, Robert Courtney. *Mexican New York: Transnational Lives of New Immigrants.* Berkeley: U of California P, 2006.

Smock, Ann. Translator's Remarks. *The Writing of the Disaster.* By Maurice Blanchot. Trans. Ann Smock. Lincoln: U of Nebraska P, 1995. vii–xiii.

Soja, Edward W. *Postmodern Geographies: The Reassertion of Space in Critical Social Theory.* New York: Verso, 1989.

Sommer, Doris, ed. *Cultural Agency in the Americas.* Durham: Duke UP, 2006.

Sorensen, Diana. "Tlatelolco 1968: Paz and Poniatowska on Law and Violence." *Mexican Studies/Estudios Mexicanos* 18.2 (2002): 297–321.

Soto, Gary. *New and Selected Poems.* San Francisco: Chronicle Books, 1995.

"Statement on Tucson Mexican American Studies Program." *Modern Language Association.* MLA n.d. Web, 16 Aug. 2012.

Stavans, Ilan. *The Hispanic Condition: Reflections on Culture and Identity in America.* New York: Harper Collins, 1995.

——, gen. ed. *The Norton Anthology of Latino Literature.* Ed. Edna Acosta-Belén, Harold Augenbraum, María Herrera-Sobek, Rolando Hinojosa, and Gustavo Pérez Firmat. New York: Norton, 2010.

Stephens, Bret. "How Milton Friedman Saved Chile." *Wall Street Journal* 1 Mar. 2010. Web, 11 Mar. 2010.

Suárez, Virgil. *90 Miles: Selected and New Poems.* Pittsburgh: U of Pittsburgh P, 2005.

Sugg, Katherine. "Literatures of the Americas, Latinidad, and the Re-Formation of Multi-Ethnic Literatures." *MELUS* 29.3/4 (2004): 227–242.

Taylor, Diana. "Remapping Genre through Performance: From 'American' to 'Hemispheric' Studies." *PMLA* 122.5 (2007): 1416–1430.

Terada, Rei. "After the Critique of Lyric." *PMLA* 123.1 (2008): 195–200.

Trillo, Mauricio Tenorio. "1910 Mexico City: Space and Nation in the City of the *Centenario.*" *Journal of Latin American Studies* 28 (1996): 75–104.

Unruh, Vicky. "'It's a Sin to Bring Down an Art Deco': Sabina Berman's Theater Among the Ruins." *PMLA* 122.1 (2007): 135–150.

Valdés, Juan Gabriel. *Pinochet's Economists: The Chicago School in Chile.* New York: Cambridge UP, 1995.

Verdecchia, Guillermo. *Fronteras Americanas/American Borders.* Vancouver: Talonbooks, 1997.

Villatoro, Marcos McPeek. *The Holy Spirit of My Uncle's Cojones.* Houston: Arte Público P, 1999.

——. "In Search of Literary *Cojones*: Pablo Neruda, U.S. Latino Poetry, and the U.S. Literary Canon: A *Testimonio.*" Longo 163–178.

——. *On Tuesday, When the Homeless Disappeared.* Tucson: U of Arizona P, 2004.

——. *They Say that I Am Two.* Houston: Arte Público P, 1997.

——. *Walking to La Milpa: Living in Guatemala with Armies, Demons, Abrazos, and Death.* Wakefield: Moyer Bell, 1996.

Villaveces-Izquierdo, Santiago. "The Crossroads of Faith: Heroism and Melancholia in the Colombian 'Violentologists' (1980–2000)." Sommer 305–325.

Villoro, Juan. "The Metro." Gallo 123–132.

Volk, Steven S., and Marian E. Schlotterbeck. "Gender, Order, and Femicide: Reading the Popular Culture of Murder in Ciudad Juárez." Gaspar de Alba 121–153.

Walker, Frank X. *Affrilachia.* Lexington: Old Cove P, 2000.

Weinberger, Eliot. Introduction. De la Torre and Wiegers 7–14.

Weintraub, Scott. "Messianism, Teleology, and Futural Justice in Raúl Zurita's *Antepa-raíso*." *CR: The New Centennial Review* 7.3 (2007): 213–238.

West, Don. *No Lonesome Road: Selected Prose and Poems*. Ed. Jeff Biggers and George Brosi. Urbana: U of Illinois P, 2004.

Williams, John Alexander. *Appalachia: A History*. Chapel Hill: U of North Carolina P, 2002.

Williams, William Carlos. *The Collected Poems of William Carlos Williams: Volume II, 1939–1962*. Ed. Christopher MacGowan. New York: New Directions, 2001.

Worthen, W. B. "Bordering Space." *Land/Scape/Theater*. Ed. Elinor Fuchs and Una Chaudhuri. Ann Arbor: U of Michigan P, 2002. 280–300.

Wypijewski, JoAnn. "Comic Relief, NEA Style." Hayden 68–72.

Yaeger, Patricia. "Introduction: Dreaming of Infrastructure." *PMLA* 122.1 (2007): 9–26.

Yarbro-Bejarano, Yvonne. "Reflections on Thirty Years of Critical Practice in Chicana/o Cultural Studies." Flores and Rosaldo 397–405.

Ybarra-Frausto, Tomás. "Post-Movimiento: The Contemporary (Re)Generation of Chicana(o) Art." Flores and Rosaldo 289–296.

Yeats, W. B. "Easter, 1916." *Yeats's Poetry, Drama, and Prose*. Ed. James Pethica. New York: Norton, 2000. 73–75.

Young, Dolly J. "Mexican Literary Reactions to Tlatelolco 1968." *Latin American Research Review* 20.2 (1985): 71–85.

Žižek, Slavoj. *First as Tragedy, Then as Farce*. New York: Verso, 2009.

Zúñiga, Víctor, and Rubén Hernández-León. "Appalachia Meets Aztlán: Mexican Immigration and Intergroup Relations in Dalton, Georgia." *New Destinations: Mexican Immigration in the United States*. Ed. Victor Zúñiga and Rubén Hernández-León. New York: Russell Sage, 2005. 187–219.

——. "The Dalton Story: Mexican Immigration and Social Transformation in the Carpet Capital of the World." Odem and Lacy 34–50.

Zurita, Raúl. *Anteparadise*. Trans. Jack Schmitt. Berkeley: U of California P, 1986.

——. *Purgatory*. 1979. Trans. Anna Deeny. Berkeley: U of California P, 2009.

Index

About the Author

Michael Dowdy is an assistant professor of English at Hunter College of the City University of New York, where he teaches twentieth-century North American and Latin American poetries, Latina/o literature, and multiethnic literatures of the United States. A former faculty fellow at the Center for Place, Culture, and Politics at the CUNY Graduate Center, he is the author of a critical study of contemporary poetry and hip hop music, *American Political Poetry into the 21st Century*, and *The Coriolis Effect*, a chapbook of poems.